RECEIVED

JUL 17 1991

Newark

FIRST FIDELITY BANK

HELMSLEY SPEAR, INC.

"Greater Newark's Enterprises"
by Paul Lavenhar
Published in cooperation with the
Greater Newark Chamber of Commerce
Windsor Publications, Inc.
Chatsworth, California

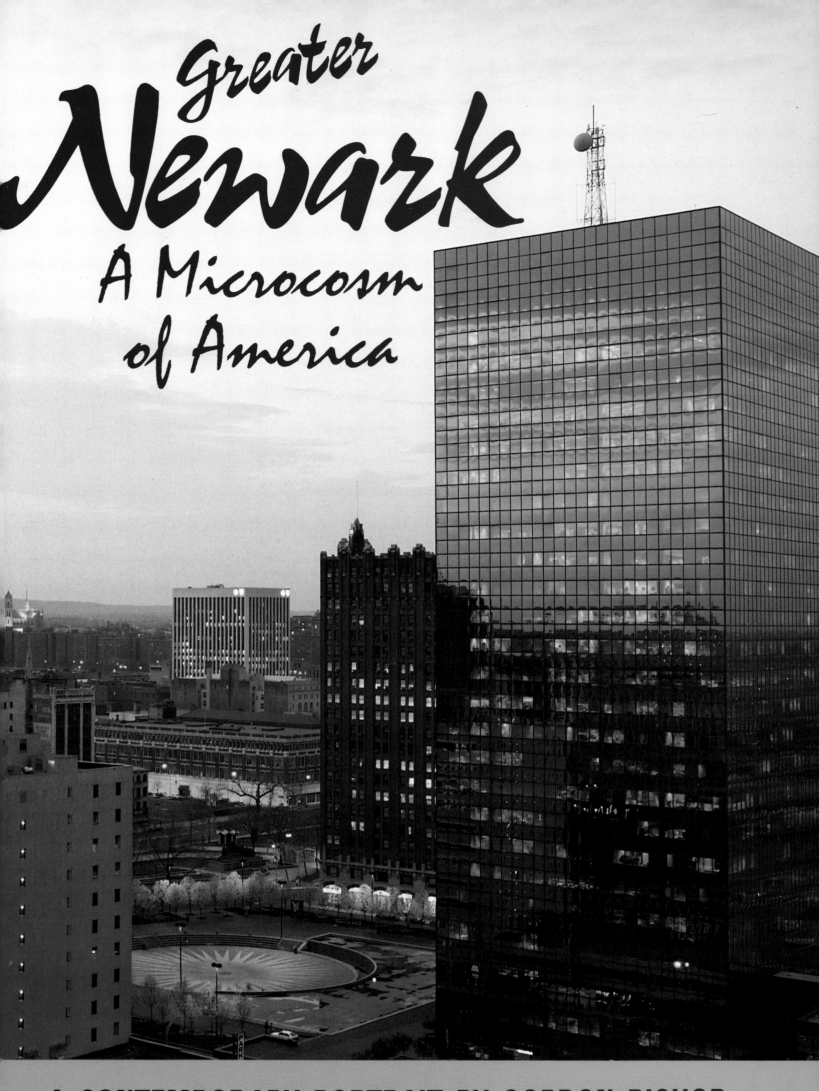

Greater Newark
A Microcosm of America

A CONTEMPORARY PORTRAIT BY GORDON BISHOP

Windsor Publications, Inc.—Book Division
Managing Editor: Karen Story
Design Director: Alexander D'Anca

Staff for *Greater Newark: A Microcosm of America*
Manuscript Editors: Lane A. Powell, Jeffrey Reeves
Photo Editor: Robin Mastrogeorge
Editor, Corporate Profiles: Judith L. Hunter
Production Editor, Corporate Profiles: Una FitzSimons
Proofreader: Liz Reuben
Customer Service Manager: Phyllis Feldman-Schroeder
Editorial Assistants: Kim Kievman, Michael Nugwynne, Michele Oakley, Kathy B. Peyser,
Susan Schlanger, Theresa J. Solis
Publisher's Representative, Corporate Biographies: Marcia Cohen, Steve Nafe, Rob Ottenheimer
Layout Artist, Corporate Biographies: Susan Wells
Production Assistant: Deena Tucker
Designer: Christina L. Rosepapa

Library of Congress Cataloging-in-Publication Data
Bishop Gordon, 1938-
Greater Newark, a microcosm of America : a contemporary portrait/
by Gordon B. Bishop.—1st ed.
p. cm.
Includes bibliographical references.
ISBN 0-89781-318-9
1. Newark (N.J)—Economic conditions.   2. Newark (N.J.)—Economic
conditions—Pictorial works.   I. Title.
HC108.N73B57   1989

330.9749' 32043—dc20

89-16694
CIP

Windsor Publications, Inc.
Elliot Martin, Chairman of the Board
James L. Fish III, Chief Operating Officer
Michele Sylvestro, Vice President/Sales-Marketing

*Previous page: Evening light softly falls over
Newark's city skyline. Photo by Michael Spozarsky*

*Facing page: Washington Park along Broad Street
provides a quiet oasis of greenery in the heart of
Newark's downtown district.
Photo by Michael Spozarsky*

Contents

*Newark's rich cultural heritage and cosmopolitan
flavor are rooted in a diverse ethnic background and
colorful local history.*

*Newark's strategic location astride the most important
transportation corridor in the East, serving more than
50 million people, has richly enhanced its diversity
and vitality over the last three centuries.*

*No city in America of comparable size can match
the number of Newark's resplendent green acres
and historic sites utilized as parks and public
recreation areas.*

*As the third-oldest major city in America, Newark
today stands as a unique living testament to more
than three centuries of American history.*

*The residents of Greater Newark are served by several
of the nation's finest medical and health care facilities.*

*Numerous and varied demands on Newark's educational
system are answered by a broad spectrum of opportunities
and alternatives.*

To Monsignor Paul F. Bradley,
A gifted spirtual leader and genuine patriot.

Photo by Barry M. Winiker

ACKNOWLEDGMENTS

The author is indebted to those who believe in Newark,
who assisted in the research and preparation of this book,
both materially and spiritually, especially:

Jeanne Reed, George and Elaine Homcy, Dave and Jan
Keetly, Charles Cummings, Simone Galik, Bob Blackwell,
Sharpe James, Richard Schoon, Robert Van Fossen, Robert
Winters, Robert Ferguson, Anton Campanella, Barbara
Kukla, Liz Del Tufo, Paul Boykas, Saul Fenster, William
Tremayne, Everett Shaw, Saul Taffet, Pam Goldstein, Doug
Eldridge, E. James Ferland, Vic De Luca, Richard Pereira,
Richard Cammarieri, Billy Marks, Msgr. Paul Bradley,
Elia Kazan

. . . and the countless others who contributed to
this project.

A sense of history, culture, and business blend together to make Newark a unique city of developing prosperity and opportunity. Photo by Rich Zila

Introduction

The impact of Newark on the American scene can be traced to its origins in 1666 as a Puritan settlement, an idyllic "Garden of Eden" that evolved into the nation's third-oldest major city and became the crossroads of the American Revolution and the manufacturing hub of the Industrial Revolution.

A compact city centered along the most important transportation corridor in the East—serving more than 50 million people—Newark and its environs remain a thriving melting pot, a unique home and workplace for more than 50 nationalities ranging from American Indian and African-American to Asian Indians and Europeans.

Newark is where Thomas Edison established his first factory; where the nation's first and second "county parks" were fashioned from the wet earth; where one of the country's great concert halls was built in the 1920s; where the world's largest insurance company was started; and where Princeton University graduated its first class.

Newark is home to one of the most treasured museums and public libraries in the United States, and to a rare combination of five colleges and universities.

Newark is the licensed franchise for WNET/THIRTEEN, the flagship station of the national Public Broadcasting System, and WBGO, the most listened-to public radio station in the country.

Newark is where you can find the busiest deepwater ports, the world's containerized shipping capital, one of the largest international airports, and an unparalleled network of railroads and highways. More than 30 million passengers a year make their way through Newark International Airport, while 80,000 riders a day can be counted at Newark's Penn Station.

Newark is the Gateway to New Jersey—the financial, commercial, and transportation nucleus of the Garden State, and is the base of operations for Public Service Electric & Gas Company, the nation's third-largest combined utility.

Newark is the proud caretaker of a 35,000-acre oasis in the thick of Urban America—the Pequannock Watershed that stands as "the last frontier" in New Jersey, the most densely developed and populated state in the nation.

Newark is a city of contrasting and changing neighborhoods, from the gritty Ironbound to Victorian Forest Hill, from fashionable Weequahic and Vailsburg to suburban Roseville and the brownstones of Lincoln Park. Add to these diverse locations such special new addresses as Society Hill, Tiffany Condos, Renaissance Towers, and University Heights and what you have is a way of life for everyone in New Jersey's premier city.

Newark boasts an international menu featuring the Mediterranean Manor and Jai Alai, Don Pepe's and Don's 21, the Portuguese Pavilion and the Santa Maria Restaurant.

Newark is an all-American ethnic city, with the Leaguers, the NAACP, La Casa de Don Pedro, B'nai Brith, Independent Irish Societies, Ukrainian Chornomorska Sitch, the Haitian/American Foundation, the Brazilian Center, Luso Americano, United Afro American, Newark Cubanos, and many more individual identities intermingling throughout Greater Newark.

Newark is a town with a 30-cent subway ride and a prominent landmark that's been a geographic constant for four centuries—Broad and Market streets, once the busiest intersection in the New World.

Newark is an incredible critical mass—a kind of socioeconomic fusion reaction igniting and attracting one exciting, productive, and creative activity after another—the New Jersey Symphony Orchestra, the New Jersey State Opera, the Garden State Ballet, the Literary Hall of Fame, the Institute of Jazz, the Black Film Festival, the New Jersey Historical Society, the New Jersey Television and Motion Picture Commission, the Ironbound Theatre, and the Theatre of Universal Images, to name a few.

Newark also has its ever-lengthening list of locals who "made it"—including such luminaries as Sarah Vaughan, Melba Moore, and Connie Francis; the Ritz Brothers, Jerry Lewis, and Eva Maria Saint; Stephen Crane, Philip Roth, and Russell Baker; Jerome Kern, Aaron Burr, and New York City Mayor Ed Koch; plus scores of other distinguished citizens in just about every walk of life.

Newark is precious antiquity and the unchart-

ered, limitless future, a city melding the past with the present and building a lasting foundation for its 325,000 residents and two million commuting workers.

On a brightening horizon are the world's tallest skyscraper, the New Jersey Center for the Performing Arts, a global computer clearinghouse, and monorails and people-movers among many architectural marvels materializing on the imaginative drawing boards of the city's leading thinkers.

Ranked 18th among American cities for its business climate, Newark is also among the top 100 most desirable places to live in the United States, placing 68th, 14 ahead of New York City.

Newark Mayor Sharpe James thinks of his community as a place where people come first. "It all begins with people . . . people born in Newark, people living in Newark, people working in Newark, people raising children in Newark, people attending school in Newark, people with the greatest stake in Newark."

Newark has come full circle since Puritan founder Captain Robert Treat laid out his "ideal village" on fertile land occupied by the Lenni Lenape Indians long before there was a United States of America. As Newark enters the twenty-first century, it is prepared to meet a future in which sixteenth-century Puritan values and African-American culture are still very much alive, harmoniously integrated with contemporary arts and a hi-tech economy flourishing with new ideas and innovations.

Newark—a continuing microcosm of America—is the manifest product of passion, faith, and hope, a city whose visionary ark is constantly being re-new-ed . . . a *new* and better *ark* for each generation.

Right: The new Gateway struc-ture is an outstanding achieve-ment of modern architecture. Photo by Elizabeth Bishop

Facing page: Newark's most precious resource is its people. Photo by Rich Zila

NO TURNS

Broad Street is alive with nighttime activity. Photo by Rich Zila

A Microcosm of America

This exceptional 1890 view of Broad Street in Newark shows the City Hall on the left and the Romanesque-style building of the Prudential Insurance Company visible down the street. Horse-drawn streetcars were still in use at that time. Courtesy, The Newark Public Library

A Historical Perspective

IN THE BEGINNING . . .

The Lenni-Lenape Indians occupied the moist, fertile land along a gently flowing river that wound down into a calm bay and the great ocean beyond. They called themselves Lenni-Lenape, the "original people," to distinguish themselves from other tribes in the area, such as the Hackensack and Acquackanonk. The Lenape were hunters and fishermen who lived off the bountiful natural resources of this hilly, low-lying tidal region below the distant mountains.

This Algonquin tribe seldom used wigwams, and by the time European settlers first observed the coastal natives in the early 1600s, the Lenape were living in sturdy community shelters that could accommodate large numbers. Their tribal life revolved around the clean, plentiful waters which they plied with their bark canoes, and within the protective and secluded meadowlands and woodlands teeming with wildlife. They ranged as far as the Delaware River and were alternately referred to as the Delaware Indians.

The same pristine river that lured the Lenape long before recorded history in the Old World also attracted America's original settlers, the Puritans, who had broken away from the Church of England in the sixteenth century. The Puritans settled in Massachusetts and Connecticut, the most famous landing being at Plymouth Rock in December 1620.

By 1662, Massachusetts had made it easier for the "unregenerate majority" to become church members, weakening the strong Puritan ethic. As a result, in May 1666, 30 Puritan families led by Captain Robert Treat of Milford, Connecticut, set out to find an isolated paradise to escape the "worldliness" of the colony, whose strict religious beliefs had been compromised and diluted.

Treat, whose father was an early settler of Wethersfield, Connecticut, had become a prominent citizen of Milford. Born in 1622, he settled in Milford in 1639. A surveyor and magistrate, Treat also served in the Colonial Assembly and on the Governor's Council.

Treat and his small band of followers—from Milford, Branford, Guilford, and New Haven—set sail on a spring day in 1666, searching for their perfect religious sanctuary. Their little wooden vessels sailed through Long Island Sound and into a bay at the mouth of the river where the Lenape made their camps. The Acquackanonk Indians, whose home was north of the Lenape in what today is Passaic and Clifton, gave the river its name, "Pesayk," which meant peaceful.

As the Puritans ventured into the bay they saw huge piles of oyster and clam shells on the banks where the Indians camped. For as far as the eye could see were wet, rippling meadows—a marshland environment similar to the one the Connecticut pilgrims had left. It looked like a place with plenty of available food where a settlement could survive the harsh winters. This quiet, secluded land along the river would be their new home. Robert Treat chose a spot where there were no Indian camps in sight to come ashore, and Elizabeth Swaine, daughter of a lieutenant, is believed to be the first settler to set foot on the banks of the Passaic River on May 17, 1666.

Although May 17 is the date that tradition has handed down as the beginning of Newark's recorded history, the first entry in the new settlement's minutes was made by Treat on May 21. The minutes refer to the Puritans' waterfront community as "Our town on Passaick River."

Originally called Milford, where the first group of settlers came from, Newark owes its name to the leader of the Puritan settlers from Branford, the Reverend Abraham Pierson. Pierson had been ordained a deacon in 1632 in the Collegiate Church

Robert Treat left his Connecticut home to establish the country's last Puritan settlement at Newark in 1666. Courtesy, The Newark Public Library

at Southwell, England, seven miles from Newark, site of the legendary castle by the River Trent.

Following the lead of Newark, New Jersey, there are, by the latest count, at least 22 Newarks in the United States and one in Australia. There are Newarks in Arkansas, California, Delaware, Illinois, Indiana, Maryland, Michigan, Missouri, Nebraska, New York, Ohio, South Dakota, Tennessee, Texas, Vermont, and West Virginia.

But America's first Newark went on to become the nation's third-oldest major city, after Boston and New York.

The first task for Robert Treat and his pioneering families was to fashion a community reflecting their own ideals. It began with the "cross" roads, the heart of the new settlement that became the famed Four Corners—Broad and Market streets, one of three busiest intersections in the United States by the 1950s.

The first roads were merely rudimentary improvements of the narrow Indian paths spoking out to other native villages nearby in places that would become the cities of Passaic, Paterson, and the closer suburbs of the Oranges, Montclair, and Springfield.

The main road, Broad Street, was laid out eight rods wide, or 132 feet. The other roads were half that width.

The founders set aside the crossroads for their meeting place. The first church, known as the "Meeting House," was built on Broad Street, at the intersection, in May 1668. The building served as both church and government headquarters—and as a "block house" against Indian attacks, although none were ever recorded.

The Lenape agreed to "sell" their land to the Puritans "for the consideration of fifty double-hands of powder, one hundred barrs of lead, twenty Axes, twenty Coates, ten Guns, twenty pistolls, ten kettles, ten Swords, four Blankets, four barrells of beere, ten paire of breeches, fifty knives, twenty howes, eight hundred and fifty fathem of wampen, two Ankors of Licquers or something Equivolent, and three troopers Coates," according to the bill of sale, executed in July 1667. The sale was recorded in the *East Jersey Records*, Book 1, folio 9.

The sale transferred the area along the "great

River Pesayak" to the "foot of the great mountaine called Watchung," and today includes Newark, Belleville, Bloomfield, Caldwell, Glen Ridge, Irvington, Maplewood, Montclair, Nutley, Orange, East Orange, South Orange, and Springfield.

For a few pennies an acre, the Puritans had purchased their remote Garden of Eden, an area embracing 62 square miles. New Jersey came to be known as the Garden State, although it has become the most densely developed and populated state in the nation. Newark today is by the far the smallest in size (23.5 square miles) of America's 50 most populous cities and second only to New York City as the most densely populated.

The urbanization of New Jersey began in Newark more than a century after the Puritans arrived there. It started humbly enough, however, by subdividing the land into lots. Robert Treat was given eight acres for his new home, and each of the other settlers were granted six acres, drawn by lot.

Through hard work and cooperation, the Puritans went about ditching and draining the lands in "the Neck," known today as the Ironbound section (iron because the area was later bounded by iron rails when steam was harnessed for locomotives). Each family received a parcel of land for the raising of salt hay. Each spring they burned away the marsh grass and swamp cedars to clear land for homes and shops.

The birthplace of Newark's industry can be traced to 1671, when Robert Treat built a gristmill on Mill Brook, or First River. Free-flowing, pure water would be the source of Newark's industrial-commercial success from its inception. By the twentieth century, however, the impact of a soaring population and uncontrolled industrial pollution transformed an inspiring fishing/farming paradise into a crowded, filthy environment, leaving the Passaic River and Newark Bay an open cesspool that is just beginning to be cleaned up, a process expected to take at least 50 years.

By "reclaiming" the wetlands and meadows for a growing economy, including the sprawling site of Newark International Airport built on a filled-in swamp, most of the city's early waterways have disappeared.

The early gristmills generated another industry: quarrying stones to grind the grain and corn. The

The picturesque Old Point House was built in the 1750s in the Woodside area of Newark along the Passaic River. It has served an interesting variety of purposes over the years, from a residence and a tavern through the early 1800s to a print and dye silk factory and a fireworks factory in the mid-1800s. Courtesy, The Newark Public Library

power for the waterwheels turning the giant grinding stones was free. As long as there was a constantly replenishing supply of fresh water, Newark could continue to expand and prosper.

The Puritans were aware of their natural gifts and what measures had to be taken to protect them. In the town proper, trees provided shade and beauty. On February 6, 1676, authorities set a penalty of 2 shillings for anyone caught cutting down a tree designated for the purpose of

shade. That decree established what was probably the first Shade Tree Commission in the New World.

By 1682, the population of the Newark settlement had reached 500. More buildings had to be provided for the farmers and craftsmen in this thriving new village between New York and Philadelphia. The first sawmill was erected in 1695 to keep up with the demand for lumber and other building materials.

A little swamp at the Four Corners became the focal point of Newark's first important industry—leather. As a neglected, untapped resource, it could not have been in a better place at a more propitious time. It was there that Azariah Crane set up his tan yard in 1698, eventually making Newark the shoemaking capital of the colonies. Crane had no difficulty getting hides for tanning. The farmers furnished the hides from their cows, pigs, and fallen horses, while hunters and trappers supplemented the supply with skins from bears, deer, muskrats, and wolves. The little swamp's soggy ground made it easy for Crane and his diligent workers to sink near the stream the wooden vats in which crushed oak bark was placed for tanning the skins. The forests of oaks on Newark's bluffs, together with the clear waters and the abundant availability of animal hides, made tanning a flourishing industry.

By 1700, Newark's agrarian way of life already had begun yielding to the promise of a better life through the power of the proliferating waterwheels. Along with the tanners, the carriage and coachmakers were slowly laying the foundation for Newark's manufacturing prominence in the nineteenth century.

Newark also had earned a reputation throughout the colonies for making a truly fine cider. The pilgrims had planted apple trees brought over from Europe, and before the original settlers of Newark had died around the turn of the seventeenth century, they had perfected the art of cider making. Newark's delicious cider was shipped mostly to southern ports.

During most of the eighteenth century, Newark remained a pastoral rural village with pleasant homes, churches, businesses, and public buildings concentrated along Broad Street between High and Mulberry streets.

When the original 13 colonies declared their independence in 1776, Newark could look back proudly at its 110-year heritage and a sizable population of about 1,000 that lived in 141 dwellings.

Some of the notable events preceding the Revolutionary War were:

• The granting of a charter to Newark by Queen Anne on April 27, 1713.

• The opening of the first schoolhouse in 1714.

• Establishing a system in 1719 for assessing the residents for the support of the poor.

• The granting of a charter by King George II to Trinity Episcopal Church on February 10, 1746.

• The first commencement of the College of New Jersey on November 9, 1748 (now Princeton University).

• The birth on February 6, 1756, of Aaron Burr in Newark, where his father served as president of the College of New Jersey. Burr became vice president of the United States (1801-1805).

• The first lodge of Free Masons in New Jersey was organized in Newark on May 13, 1761, meeting at the Rising Sun Tavern.

• The beginning of formalized horse racing in New Jersey on September 9, 1767, with the first contest held in Newark.

• The founding of the Newark Academy in 1774.

THE REVOLUTIONARY WAR

The increasing tensions between the colonies and the British Crown over the destiny of the New World prompted the creation of the Newark Committee of Observation on December 7, 1774. Shortly after, the residents of Newark received news of the battles of Lexington and Concord. On April 24, 1775, the members of the Committee of Observation adopted a resolution that they were "willing at this alarming crisis to risk their lives and fortunes in support of American liberty."

On May 8, Newark's citizens enthusiastically greeted members of the Massachusetts, Connecticut, and New York delegations, including John Adams and John Hancock, as they made their way to Philadelphia for the opening session of the Continental Congress.

On June 25, George Washington rode through Newark on his way from Philadelphia, where he had been a delegate to the Second Continental Congress. Washington was to assume command of the Continental Army at Cambridge, Massachusetts.

More than a year later, Washington was forced to withdraw some 3,000 troops from Newark, where they had been stationed for six days, just hours before Lord Cornwallis and about 6,000 British troops marched into town. Washington's sudden retreat from Newark began on November 28, 1776.

The British occupied Newark for only five days, but in that brief time they were able, through their hostile actions, to convince many doubting colonists that the patriot cause was certainly the proper one. British troops harrassed residents and plundered their homes, giving Newarkers more than enough reason to want to eliminate the Crown's presence in the colonies.

Alexander Macwhorter, pastor of the Old First Presbyterian Church and a leader in the revolutionary movement, had accompanied Washington on his retreat south across New Jersey. Macwhorter sat in on the war councils planning the decisive

Above: A hub of commercial activity, Newark's old Center Market was located on the edge of Military Park, where the Morris Canal crossed under Broad Street. This illustration was made before the tower was removed in the 1860s, and shows the colonial flagpole (left) that still stands in the park today. Courtesy, New Jersey Historical Society

Right: A New Jersey Rail Road flagman stopped traffic for a train leaving Newark's Market Street Depot in this detailed circa 1840 illustration. When the station was constructed in 1838, the area experienced a surge of development. Courtesy, The Newark Public Library

battles of Trenton and Princeton, the turning point of the American Revolution.

Thomas Paine traveled with the Continental Army through Newark in November 1776. The famous first lines of his *The American Crisis*— "These are the times that try men's souls"—were reportedly written in Newark, acording to tradition.

British troops again attacked Newark on January 25, 1780, burning the Newark Academy where American troops had been quartered. Several leading residents were taken prisoner.

But the rebellious colonists perservered, and the first recorded Independence Day celebration in Newark took place July 4, 1788. The celebration included a parade honoring the city's trades—the tanners, weavers, carriage and clockmakers, and silversmiths.

A MODERN INDUSTRIAL CITY EMERGES

As any realtor knows, the value of real estate is determined by three factors: "Location. Location.

Location."

Just as Robert Treat had chosen that scenic location along the Passaic River as the home for his Puritan congregation, many others were also attracted to that promising land for the same reasons. Its growth was inevitable because of its close proximity to New York City and as a pleasant stopover for travelers on the way to Philadelphia.

The Indian trails adopted by the settlers as their pathways of travel and commerce became the connectors between New York and the City of Brotherly Love, but the trails always stopped at the waters' edge. By 1765, ferries were shuttling passengers, and barges were carrying goods across the Passaic and Hackensack rivers. They were flat-bottomed boats, or scows, which were pulled across the rivers by ropes attached to a treadmill on shore. At first, horses provided the power, but they were soon replaced by chains on a windlass.

In 1794, a sturdy wooden span went up across the Passaic River at Bridge Street. Other bridges were erected across the marshes, connected by "corduroy" roads made of logs laid down in the soft swamplands, allowing the uninterrupted flow of people and goods between Newark and New York City. By the beginning of the nineteenth century, Newark had become a main stop on the stage route between New York and Philadelphia.

Until 1797, Philadelphia had been the leading seaport in the new nation. New York Harbor assumed that distinction shortly after. Today, Ports Newark-Elizabeth handle more tonnage than New York. The ports are under the jurisdiction of the Port Authority of New York and New Jersey.

In 1798, a causeway was built over the marshes to the Hudson River, establishing the quickest overland route from New York to Philadelphia. The heavily used corridor bypassed Elizabethtown, making Newark the number-one stop along a transportation network rapidly reaching out in all directions.

It was Newark's easy accessibility and seemingly endless supply of water that drew entrepreneurs and inventors from all corners of the tri-state region. One of the first—and most gifted leaders in terms of future impact—was Moses Newell Combs. In 1780, Combs had opened a small factory near the "Watering Place," the center of

Newark's tanyards. A shoemaker, Combs' durable shoes were snapped up at 50 cents a pair by the locals and those outside Newark looking for a good buy. Word spread fast of Combs' well-crafted shoes, and within 10 years shoes made in Newark were worn by consumers as far away as Georgia. One order, for 200 pairs of sealskin shoes, was the largest of any footwear manufacturer at that time.

Combs was the first Newark manufacturer to capitalize on mass marketing. As his Newark products were peddled throughout the East and beyond, other shoemakers opened shops in that bustling town on the Passaic River. A map of Newark made in 1806 by Charles Basham of Newark Academy featured a picture of a shoemaker in the lefthand corner, paying tribute to a craft that employed "one third of Newark's inhabitants."

Combs has been credited by historians and social philosophers with promoting a universal education for industrial workers. He established the first Free School for youths working in his plant. They studied in the evening and trained as apprentices during the day. It was the genesis of the industrial and trade manual training school. Combs' innovative educational regimen instilled the Puritan work ethic in the youths, making them more productive in his factory. Combs' value system, which included emancipation and temperance, inculcated in the very young that pride in the product of one's labor was a recognized reward of achievement.

Newark and its productive workers were on the move. By 1804, the city had grown into an amalgamation of 844 houses, 207 craftsmen's shops, five public buildings, and a population consisting of 9 clergymen, 10 physicians, 14 lawyers, 16 teachers, 34 merchants, and 81 farmers. The latter

were gradually losing ground to the crafts and mercantilists.

Another catalyst for Newark's industrial growth was the War of 1812, when England imposed an embargo on trade with the upstart American enterprise system that dared to compete with the British Empire as the "workshop of the world."

Realizing the vast potential of the Passaic River, Alexander Hamilton, the first Secretary of the Treasury, had encouraged industrial self-reliance as the best way to remain free and less dependent on England's cheap, mass-produced goods flooding American markets. Hamilton helped set up The Society for Promoting Useful Manufactures in 1791, selecting high ground at the Passaic River Falls in Paterson as the site for industrial investment in America's future. Newark benefitted from Hamilton's vision of a great industrial nation as well. Under the Society's auspices, a paint factory was built in the city, increasing its industrial diversity and strengthening its position as the industrial leader in New Jersey.

By 1810, Newark's population had swelled to more than 8,000, an eight-fold jump in just three decades.

During the 1820s, Newark's businessmen got behind the building of the Morris Canal, which connected the coalfields of eastern Pennsylvania with the industrial cities of New Jersey. Built primarily by Irish immigrants, who, with the Germans, were the largest immigrant groups in the region, the canal was completed in 1831. The canal carried the fuel for the steam engines that were slowly replacing the water wheels powering the early industries. When the canal was ultimately replaced by the railroads, it became the roadbed for today's subway system.

Right: J.L. Hewes and J.M. Phillips were once apprentices of famous inventor Seth Boyden, and went on to develop a successful steam engine company based in Newark by the mid-1800s. Courtesy, The Newark Public Library

Facing page: Recognized as Newark's greatest inventor, Seth Boyden developed many wonderful and creative inventions, including patent leather and the process for making malleable iron. Courtesy, The Newark Public Library

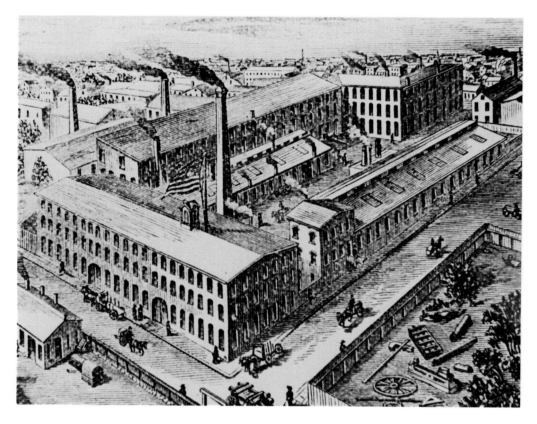

Newark's leading industries in 1830 were manufacturers of carriages, shoes, saddlery hardware, and hats followed by tanners, soapmakers, and iron and brass foundries.

By 1836, Newark's population had climbed to nearly 18,000, roughly 15 times more than at the outset of the Revolution. This time, however, Newark found itself in the forefront of another revolution—the American Industrial Revolution. And the father of Newark's industrial revolution—the one who literally shaped the rural farming/factory village into a modern industrial giant—was an unassuming genius named Seth Boyden.

Born in Foxborough, Massachusetts, on November 17, 1788, Boyden spent much of his youth farming his father's land and working occassionally as a woodstoker at an iron furnace owned by his maternal grandfather. His formal education had been limited to two months a year in the district schools, but Seth, like his father, possessed an inquisitive mind, and at age 15 was said to be have made a microscope, telescope, and air rifle between his chores. He impressed family and friends with a remarkable painting of himself on a small piece of ivory. At age 18 his reputation as a young

man of many talents had extended beyond Foxborough, where he fixed guns and watches without fee. His preoccupation with making things work or finding better ways of doing something may have been the reason he never received the proper credit or publicity for many of his practical and popular inventions.

Nevertheless, Seth Boyden was recognized in his own lifetime as Newark's greatest inventor. Boyden's work attracted considerable attention in the East among engineers, entrepreneurs, and inventors. Thomas Edison, who arrived in Newark at the time of Boyden's death in 1870, referred to the industrial giant as "one of America's greatest inventors." Young Edison, who set up his own workshop on Ward Street, was the first to recognize that Boyden "never received proper credit for his many great and practical inventions," which Edison regarded as "the basis of great industries which have spread over the entire world and give employment to millions of people."

Boyden moved to Newark in 1815 with his wife, opening a harness shop on Broad Street. But before he had left Foxborough, he had perfected his father's leather refining machine. The elder Boyden had devised a machine to smooth the under-

Above: The Ballantine brewery is pictured here along the Passaic River in Newark after its establishment in 1840. Courtesy, The Newark Public Library

Top: This bank note was issued by the State Bank at Newark in 1862. Located next door was the Old First Church, which is depicted alongside its Broad Street neighbor in the note's central engraving. Courtesy, Collection of the Newark Museum

surface of leather hides. His son made a few adjustments so that the machine could split the hides. The result was a lot more leather from the same piece of hide.

Seth selected Newwark as the best place to use his splitting machine because of its renowned leather business. He may also have been drawn to Newark by the educational opportunities for mechanics and apprentices launched by Moses Combs 20 years earlier.

Seth's splitting machine gave him the edge he needed, but the iron hardware he was using on his harnesses easily rusted when exposed to the elements. He fixed that problem by developing a silver-plating process, the first of many spinoff enterprises.

Nail production, a necessity for the manufacturing industry, was another time-consuming effort begging for Boyden's attention. They had to be hand-worked in a forge, one at a time. Boyden found another way: a machine to cut nails quickly and inexpensively.

A fire destroyed Boyden's harness shop in 1818. He immediately built another on Bridge Street. It was here Boyden developed two of his most famous inventions—patent leather and the process for making malleable iron. By drying successive layers of special varnish on a hide in the sun and the final coat in a warm room, Boyden created a new look called patent leather. It soon became Newark's biggest industry, with malleable iron running a close second.

Luck and memory played an important role in the development of malleable iron. While a youth in Massachusetts, Seth was probing through the debris of his grandfather's dismantled foundry. He came across what were probably the furnace's burned-out iron grate bars. He noticed they sagged in the center, much like wrought iron, where the fire had been the hottest. He tested a bar in his shop with a heavy hammer. The unscorched ends were brittle and broke, as cast iron was expected to behave. But what he discovered was that the sagging center was no longer brittle. Seth was able to bend or flatten it. The iron's properties had been changed by the intense heat of the fire.

In his Bridge Street shop, Boyden remembered how he was able to shape the iron bar from his grandfather's foundry. On July 4, 1826, he perfected the process by heating the pig iron to a high temperature over nine days and letting the iron slowly cool. His Newark experiment liberated America's iron industry from dependence on England's "run steel."

Boyden also has been credited with making the first Daguerrotype camera in the United States. Boyden's friend, Samuel Morse, helped him to cut the long exposure time from five minutes to less than a minute. Boyden also assisted Morse in developing telegraphy.

Seth Boyden's other achievements include the construction of an electric clock, electric fountain, and an electric barometer, improving the driving rods for locomotives, building the two locomotives for the Morris & Essex Railroad, the reduction of zinc ores, the production of oroide metal (an imitation gold made from copper and tin), a machine to form hat bodies, and his own variety of large strawberries, the "Hilton."

A letter Boyden wrote in 1863 in response to an inquiry about his patent leather invention perhaps best reflects his philosophy and personality and how he saw himself as the leading force in Newark's fledgling industrial revolution:

I introduced patent leather, but it should be remembered that there was nothing generous or liberal in its introduction, as I served myself first, and when its novelty had ceased and I had other objects in view, it was the natural course to leave it. When I had done so, and other more active and enterprising persons chose to supply the wants of the public, I wish them all prosperity and am happy to see it and to see patent leather useful and valuable, and as a business of first magnitude and to see a friendly social feeling, existing among all interested. May it be as enduring as the use of leather.

With factories springing up to profit from Boyden's inventions, Newark's population had climbed to almost 11,000 by 1830 and was approximately 20,000 a decade later.

On March 18, 1836, Newark was incorporated as a city.

When the Civil War broke out, Newark was a booming manufacturing hub with a population of more than 72,000, and the city did not want to get involved in any conflict between the North and the South. Newark industries had many customers in the South, and the business community did not want to lose its Southern profits. Newark was branded a "Copperhead City" by northern sympathizers opposed to the city's neutrality at the outset of the war. Newark's business leaders, however, were merely reflecting the will of many of the people. Although New Jersey did not vote for Abraham Lincoln in the 1861 presidential election, Newark did send its sons and manufactured goods off to war after Lincoln personally appealed to the citizens of Newark to support his mission to "Save the Union."

Another basic industry that increased Newark's numbers before and after the Civil War was beer. As early as the 1810 Census of Manufacturing, Essex County was producing 17,600 gallons of beer annually, most of it in Newark. The same clean water that served the Lenape for thousands of years and allowed Robert Treat to establish a new settlement also propelled Newark's leather and iron industries, and was the chief ingredient in good beer. By 1840, two Newark breweries were producing 54,000 gallons a year.

Peter Ballantine, a Scottish immigrant, had moved his business from Albany to Newark in 1840. He chose the site on High Street, where the first attempt at brewing had taken place in 1799.

Until 1840, only top-fermented beers such as

ale, porter, common, and small beer were produced in the United States. Then bottom-
fermented beer with a lighter body and more
carbonation became popular.

The lager beer industry was begun by John N.
Schalk of Baden, Germany. He came to Newark in
1849 and founded a brewery at Napoleon Street
and Hamburg Place, and was eventually succeeded by his sons. The Schalks brewed beer that
was "equal, if not superior, to the best manufactured even in Germany," according to Joseph Atkinson in *The History of Newark, New Jersey.*

Another brewer, Gottfried Krueger, arrived in
the United States in 1852 and joined with Gottlieb
Hill to form the Hill and Krueger Company, another Newark-based brewery.

Beer consumption coincided with the number
of Germans moving into Newark in the mid-
nineteenth century. In 1830, there were six Germans living in Newark. When the first city census
of Newark was taken in 1836, there were 300 Germans in a population of 18,000. As the German population rose, so did beer production. By 1870, the
native-born German population of Newark totaled
15,873, living in a German community of 35,000,

Right: Thomas Alva Edison is shown here as he recorded his voice on the wax cylinder of the "Ediphone," the precursor of the phonograph record. Originally designed in 1878 for business use, the phonograph was later developed for entertainment purposes. Courtesy, The Newark Public Library

Facing page top: This colorful trade card was distributed by Stoutenburgh & Co., in Newark during the many years of the company's successful clothing business. Courtesy, Special Collections, Alexander Library, Rutgers University

Facing page bottom: The Newark Jewelry Store cartouche is illustrated here, listing the names of early Newark silversmiths. The dates indicate the time their work was carried by the store. Operating from three Broad Street addresses, the Newark Jewelry Store provided a strong retail market for the area's silversmiths. Courtesy, Collection of the Newark Museum

or one-third of the city's population. By 1879, there were 26 breweries producing 412,000 barrels a year—280,000 lager and 132,000 ale.

The Germans made their presence known on the many street signs of Newark, with such names as Bismark, Berlin, Frankfort, German, and Hamburg. Those street names were later changed during World War I to Pershing, London, Rome, Belgium, and Paris.

Another mainstay of Newark's burgeoning economy was jewelry making. Epaphras Hinsdale pioneered the art of jewelry making in Newark by setting up a small shop in 1801 on Broad Street, north of Lafayette. Within five years, there were six employees and a partner, John Taylor. In 1810, Taylor formed a new partnership with Colonel

Isaac Baldwin. They were the first company to produce enough jewelry to be marketed outside of their own shop. By 1836, Taylor and Baldwin had 100 workers making fine jewelry. One apprentice, James Madison Durand, went out on his own and achieved a "high standard of excellence said to have set an example followed by American jewelry makers in general." By 1874, there were 50 factories producing elegant jewelry worth more than $6 million a year.

In 1860, Edward Balbach developed a process for separating gold and silver from base metals. Balbach patented his profitable process and Newark became a major smelting and refining center.

Aaron Carter's use of steam-powered machinery, built by Boyden, enabled the mass production of gold chains and watch cases. That technological advancement triggered an expansion of such allied trades as jewelry tools, clocks, and watches. By the 1890s, Newark was supplying almost all of America's watchcase materials.

George Krementz, a Newark jeweler, was credited with the invention of the one-piece collar button, which combined new technology with the latest fashions. The Krementz collar had gained worldwide recognition by 1884.

The world's greatest inventor, Thomas Alva Edison, started his career in Newark by manufacturing his stock tickers on the third story of a building on Ward Street (today's Edison Street). Edison employed 18 men during the six years he perfected duplex and multiplex telegraphy, from 1870-1876. It was Edison's first manufacturing establishment. He moved to Menlo Park in 1876, where he invented the incandescent light bulb, the phonograph, and created the world's first "invention factory," the forerunner of the modern research and development laboratory. The world's largest private R&D operation is now Bell Laboratories, situated not far from Edison's Menlo Park and later West Orange invention factories. Edison holds the

Left: The Phineas Jones and Company wheelwright yard is shown in this photograph as it appeared in 1915. Nationally known for its quality work, this company supplied the first tires for Henry Ford's automobiles as well as the heavy wheels needed to transport the wagons of the Ringling Brothers Circus. Courtesy, The Newark Public Library

Facing page: English native Edward Weston came to Newark in 1875 and soon established a name for himself with his inventive genius regarding the applications of electrical power and light. Weston Electrical Instrument Company went on to become one of the world's leading manufacturers of its kind. Courtesy, The Newark Public Library

MISSES C.F. & R. BUI
LADIES FINE FU
ORNAMENTAL HAIR

Left: The Newark Industrial Exhibition opened in August 1872, exclusively featuring Newark manufacturers and businesses. The exhibition lasted for seven weeks from August to September, attracting more than 130,000 visitors. Courtesy, The Newark Public Library

record for patented inventions—1,093—including the motion picture camera and the electric power grid. Edison Studios produced the first feature film, "The Great Train Robbery."

Industrial exhibitions in major cities were the showcases for America's inventions and products during the second half of the nineteenth century. Newark became the first to stage an industrial exhibition displaying only products made in the city. The Newark Industrial Exhibition opened on August 20, 1872; it was a bold and risky venture, but it paid off handsomely for all involved. By the time the exhibition closed on October 11, Newark's place as the manufacturing capital of the New World was secured. More than 130,000 people attended the exhibition over the seven-week period, including President Ulysses S. Grant and Horace Greely, editor of the *New York Tribune*. At least 876 companies and/or individuals exhibited their wares, ranging from iron, leather, machinery, rubber products, clothing, furniture, jewelry, shoes, hardware, carriages, and scores of other articles. The products were representative of the work being done by Newark's 1,500 trade and industrial factories.

The New York Times was impressed with what Newark had to offer, as reported in this article published during the exhibition:

With a population of 120,000, fully 30 percent of its inhabitants devote their attention to manufactures. It produces no less than 1,000 different articles representing 312 distinct branches of trade. For its population it is undoubtedly the largest manufacturing centre in the U.S. The trunk you travel with is, in 9 cases out of 10, of Newark manufacture; the hat you wear was made there, the buttons on your coat, the shirt on your back, your brush,

Left: Workers assembled electrical equipment in the Westinghouse Electric factory on Orange Street in Newark around the turn of the century. Courtesy, The Newark Public Library

Below: Prior to 1886, the Prudential Insurance Company insured only industrial workers whose small premiums were collected on a weekly basis by Prudential agents. The agent depicted in this 1883 trade card appears to be paying a claim to this woman and her small children. Courtesy, Special Collections, Alexander Library, Rutgers University

*the tinware you use in your kitchen, the oil-cloth
you walk on, the harness and bit you drive with,
all owe Newark their origin; and as to your wife's
chain, bracelets, ear rings and pendants, they have
been fashioned by some cunning Newark goldsmith.*

The success of Newark's go-it-alone exhibit was
repeated over the next three years.

At the time the exhibit was proudly showing
the world what Newark was capable of doing, two
brothers, John Wesley and Isaiah Hyatt, opened a
celluloid factory in Newark. Wesley, born in 1837,
was an Albany printer who responded to a $10,000
offer by a New York City firm for anyone who
could develop a substitute for ivory for use in billiard balls. He heated up a soupy formula that he refined into celluloid, the foundation for a new
industry called plastic. From his plastic billiard
balls he devised the famous roller bearings and
founded a company to turn them out by the millions. Before his death in 1920, Hyatt had invented
a superior sugar cane mill, a sewing machine capable of making 50 lock stitches at once, and, of
course, a machine for making billiard balls.

Another inventor who elevated Newark to even
higher technological heights was Edward Weston.
Born in England, Weston was in America only five
years when he arrived in Newark in 1875. He
came to the city with incredible credentials: He
was an authority on dynamos and an expert in electroplating. Weston worked out of a makeshift laboratory in his house on Eighth Avenue, and before
long, manufacturers of metal art objects called on
Weston to produce electroplating machines. Weston was on the cutting edge of electrical instrumentation, and, as such, was in constant litigation in a
competitive, cutthroat industry. Weston Electrical Instrument Co. became one of the biggest manufacturers of specialized equipment in the world.

A public spirited person, Weston was one of
the principal organizers of the Newark District Telegraph Co., a leading investor and promoter in the
Newark Domestic Telephone & Telegraph Co.
Upon his death in 1936, Weston left his laboratory
apparatus and equipment, drawings, and legal and
scientific papers to the Newark College of Engineering (New Jersey Institute of Technology). He endowed the college with enough money to maintain

his collected works in perpetuity.

Further enhancing Newark's reputation as a
city of remarkable inventiveness were the Reverend Hannibal Goodwin, rector of the House of
Prayer, who produced the first flexible photographic film, which, with Edison's camera, formed
the basis of the motion picture industry; Louis Aronson, who designed the Ronson lighter; Richard
Ranger, who invented the photo-radiogram and electric organ chimes; Winfield Scott Sims, who originated the dynamite breach gun used at the Battle
of Santiago in the Spanish American War, as well
as a submarine boat and electrically propelled torpe-
does; and George Murdock, who developed self-
sealing fuel tanks for war planes.

With enough water from the Passaic River to
keep their factories humming around the clock,
Newark's ambitious entrepreneurs increased the
number of industrial buildings from 765 in 1860 to
3,339 by 1910, and aggregate value of output rose
from $28 million to $127 million during that
50-year period of unprecedented growth. Some
two dozen Clark Company factory buildings in Newark and East Newark were spinning out cotton
thread onto spools carrying the famous ONT
("Our New Thread") labels throughout the world.
Newark had reached its zenith as an industrial
mecca, setting the economic stage for America's entry into the global marketplace.

The makers of many of America's goods made
it possible for Newark to become a flourishing center of mercantilism. Julius Hahne was one of the
first to see the opportunities of meeting new consumer demands on a large scale. In 1858 Hahne, a
pocketbook maker, opened a little bird cage store
at the corner of Broad Street and Central Avenue.
Soon his stock of birds and cages expanded to Christmas toys and pocketbooks. Deliveries were made
in a wheelbarrow. As business picked up, Hahne enlarged his quarters and took in a partner. The company was known as Hahne & Bloch. It was
Newark's first real "department store." A new, elegant establishment opened on Broad Street on Labor Day in 1901, with birds and their cages still in
stock. It was "the place" to shop at the turn of the
century.

L. Simon Plaut, the son of a Connecticut
grocer, came to Newark in 1870 and opened a dry

goods store near the Morris Canal at 721 Broad Street. The "Bee Hive" thrived. Plaut, following Hahne's success, had brought Newark into a new age of merchandizing.

Louis Bamberger, a pushcart peddler, went from the streets of Newark to taking over one foundering store after another. Building on a string of successes, the resourceful merchant opened a fashionable, landmark store at 147 Market Street in 1893. The 50 employees included a corps of sales ladies in long, black aprons, floor walkers in Prince Albert coats, and a flock of 13-year-old boys and girls to run errands.

Bamberger filled up all six floors of his building by 1898 and had to take over floor space in an addition built on the corner of Market and Halsey streets. By 1912, L. Bamberger & Co. had to erect a new building at its present site at the corner of Market and Washington streets.

When Louis Bamberger was 74, his company was acquired by R. H. Macy & Co., which operated the world's largest department store in Manhattan's Herald Square. Bamberger's today is Macy's, the largest department store chain in the East.

It was Bamberger who directed his crystal sets salesman, Jack Poppele, to start a radio station on the roof of the Newark store in 1922. Poppele, a wire-

Above: Louis Bamberger and his sister Mrs. Caroline Fuld endowed the Institute for Advanced Studies in Princeton, and helped convince Albert Einstein, pictured here in 1939, to accept the first teaching position at the prestigious institute. Courtesy, The Newark Public Library

Right: An ideal picture of happy life in 1920s Newark, this contented family was tuned into radio station WOR, which had been created in 1922 by Louis Bamberger. WOR radio was the sixth commercial radio station to be established in the nation. Courtesy, Bamberger's Archives

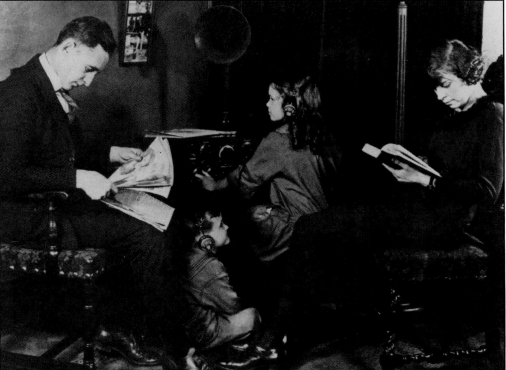

less operator and a native of the Ironbound, erected two poles and strung a wire between them and the station went on the air as WOR. It became the most powerful broadcast frequency in the New York metropolitan region and was an early pioneer of television (WOR-TV, Channel 9) in the late 1930s.

Bamberger and Hahne also left their mark on the city's cultural scene. Bamberger furnished the funds for the building of the Newark Museum, supported the New Jersey Historical Society, and, along with his sister, Mrs. Caroline Fuld, brought cherry trees from Japan for the city's beautiful Branch Brook Park.

Hahne generously supported the many civic projects of the Federation of Women's Clubs and contributed to the city's swiftly expanding social and cultural institutions.

Bamberger and Mrs. Fuld also endowed one of the world's premier "think tanks"—the Institute for Advance Studies in Princeton. They convinced Albert Einstein to accept the first teaching post at the Princeton institute. The famed theoritical physicist settled in Princeton in 1933 and spent the last 22 years of his life in that quiet ivy league town, refining his theory of the origins and fate of the universe.

Ohrbach's and Kresge's—also popular department stores—also attracted customers from the North Jersey area before suburbia and the shopping malls sprung up on the countryside in the late 1950s and 1960s.

By 1916, when the First World War was at full tilt, Newark enjoyed the status of its role as a world-class city comparable to Hamburg, Milan, and Manchester. It had achieved the distinction of a manufacturing-mercantile center of unlimited promise and potential.

A map of Newark commissioned by the Presbyterian Church in 1910 showed the city comprising eight ethnic groups dominated by Italians and Jews, with Germans and Irish constituting the next largest population mix. The city's population of 347,469 consisted of 50,000 Italians, 50,000 Jews, 40,000 Germans, 30,000 Irish, 20,000 Slavs, 11,000 blacks, and 34,000 others, including several thousand Chinese and Greeks, as well as Poles.

America's involvement in the first global war

brought about a significant change in Newark, according to William Ashby, as blacks came up from the south to work in the factories that had been manned by whites drafted into the "war to end all wars." Ashby, founder of the Urban League and now approaching his 100th birthday, helped the city's business leaders in recruiting labor from the south to keep Newark's factories running during the five years of war. With the northward migration begun, the black population nearly quadrupled to 38,880 in 1930, and doubled to 75,000 by 1950. By the time of the Newark riots in 1967, the black population was well over 200,000 out of total of about 300,000.

In May 1970, Newark elected its first black mayor, Kenneth Allen Gibson, a civil engineer and steady saxophone player—the first black mayor of a major city in the Northeast.

Like earlier periods that assumed new identities to reflect the changing times, Newark is undergoing yet another metamorphosis mirroring today's ethnic heritage. High Street has been renamed Dr. Martin Luther King, Jr., Boulevard, and Waverly Avenue is now named for Muhammad Ali, the great world boxing champion. South Side High School is now Malcolm X Shabazz High School, and Robert Treat Junior High School is now Marcus Garvey Junior High School, named for the black nationalist leader. South 10th Street School bears the name of Harriet Tubman, a former slave who became a famous abolitionist, and Waverly Avenue School now honors the name of Rosa Parks, the Alabama woman who decided she would not sit in the back of a bus.

The city's growing Hispanic population is also making its presence felt. The Summer Avenue School has been designated the Roberto Clemente School in honor of the Baseball Hall of Fame Pittsburgh Pirate player from Puerto Rico.

The post-World War II Newark has all but disappeared for those who grew up when the city was a dynamic mix of just about every nationality that passed through the Ellis Island immigration clearinghouse at the turn of the century. Raymond J. Tuers, senior managing editor of the *Asbury Park Press*, recently recalled his childhood years in Newark during the 1940s and 1950s before the downturn of the 1960s:

I remember Newark, my hometown, as a glorious, sweaty city in the summers of the '40s and '50s, when glistening boys, stripped to their waists, played stickball on cobblestone streets in polyglot neighborhoods.

I remember the winters, when an unaccustomed silence settled upon those same streets with every snowfall.

They were ethnic enclaves, those Newark neighborhoods . . . miniature foreign homelands on the rim of a wheel whose hub was Broad and Market streets, an intersection as American as a Saturday matinee. At that center, illuminating shadows cast by buildings that seemed to a small boy to clutch the clouds, was the Paramount Theater. There we saw Casablanca *before it became a classic. And the Adams, where The Count [Basie]—"The Kid from Red Bank"—played. And Loew's, where we were terrified by the Wicked Witch of the West. And Minsky's burlesque, even then hanging by its garish, aging fingernails to an era already past.*

I remember Nedick's hot dog stand, with its famous orangeade, right at the corner of Broad and Market. The Newark News on sale at every peeling newstand. Bamberger's. Ohrbach's. Kresge's. Hahne's. And their Christmas dressings each December.

I remember the St. Patrick's Day Parade on Broad Street each spring. And how the aroma of fresh-roasted peanuts and green balloons became forever entangled with each other in my mind. I remember Mulberry Street, with its Chinese restaurants and sinister alleys. I remember the smoke-belching buses. How they squished through the translucent winter slush taking us up South Orange Avenue on Sundays to the Jewish bakeries along Prince Street . . .

. . . There are no bakeries any more on Prince Street, no windows filled with rum cakes and strudel . . .

. . . Ah, and Down Neck! The Ironbound section. There, no renaissance has ever been wanted nor needed. It remains as it was when I lived there. Most of the Przemelewskis and the D'Angelos, the Berkowitzes and the O'Sullivans are gone. But city officials say there are still some 40 ethnic groups living in the Ironbound. One dominates now, though: Portuguese.

. . . Ferry Street [Ironbound], a carnival of shops when I was a boy, is even more so today, lined with signs in Portuguese. It teems with shoppers, browsing among the stalls and shop windows piled with fruits and vegetables, socks and sweaters . . . The old neighborhood, never peaceful, is more raucous than ever: 600 feet overhead, 747s now lumber across the sky on a flight path into Newark Airport. I think of the lumbering sounds of another era, when Ballantine trucks, their solid rubber tires hammering the cobblestones, rumbled down Hawkins Street . . .

From the ashes, blight, and despair left behind by the 1967 riot, Newark today is inexorably rebuilding, block by block: a mighty phoenix, even grander and more appealing than that which emerged from the great melting pot of the late nineteenth and early twentieth centuries.

The story of twenty-first century Newark, where the best of the old and the treasured will stand graciously with the new and the bold, is just beginning.

Facing page: These four young women received the first contribution for the USO in Newark during World War II from the general chairman of the Newark United Service Organization, and from the vice president of Bamberger's Department Store. Courtesy, The Newark Public Library

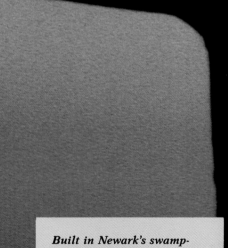

*Built in Newark's swamp-
land in 1928, the Newark International Airport has developed into one of the nation's
busiest transportation centers. Photo by Bob Krist*

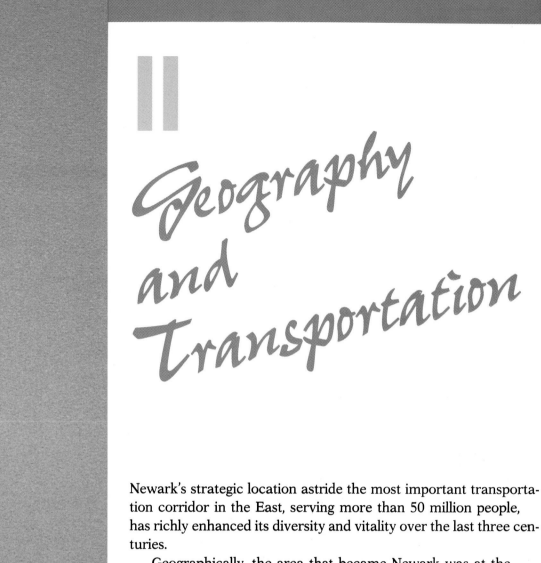

II

Geography and Transportation

Newark's strategic location astride the most important transportation corridor in the East, serving more than 50 million people, has richly enhanced its diversity and vitality over the last three centuries.

Geographically, the area that became Newark was at the right place at the right time when the New World was discovered and developed.

The land the Puritans settled owes much of its variegated appearance to the great glacial age that swept across North America some 12,000 years ago, about the same time as the emergence of man on this continent. As the sea withdrew, the forces of erosion removed the sediments of the coastal plain and etched out the larger topographic features we see today. When the great glaciers receded, or melted, a general rise of sea level at the close of the Pleistocene epoch flooded low areas along the coast, forming Newark Bay at the junction of the Hackensack and Passaic rivers. Over the millenia, meadows were shaped by stream deposits, only to be "reclaimed" by the settlers and those who followed over the last 320 years.

NEWARK INTERNATIONAL AIRPORT

One of those man-made areas created by filling in swampland became the world's first modern airport. As early as 1919, Newark boasted its own airport on property belonging to the Forest Hill Golf Club a good distance from the forbidden swamps. But Heller Field, as the locals referred to their little landing strip, was abandoned by the U.S. airmail service in May 1920 because of its small size and hazards that caused many accidents.

After World War I, however, aviation literally took off, with flying buffs and daredevils seeking thrills with their rickety canvas contraptions. The Aeronautical Club of New Jersey saw a definite, "serious" need for a major airport at Newark, the state's leading city and transportation/financial/cultural hub. At a dinner in 1925, John J. Bergen, the club's president, and Colonel Clarence Chamberlin, vice president and a famous aviator, urged the construction of Newark Airport.

At first, City Hall didn't want to turn over valuable acreage along its waterfront intended for future industrial use. After all, this fledging industry had yet to get off the ground in terms of long-term profit for investors.

But the citizens of Newark, always ready to seize an opportunity, rallied around the idea of having those wonderful flying machines swooping around their booming city; aviation was an exciting new form of entertainment for a prospering people ready to exploit a new technology. They wanted to be ahead of this trend toward "air-mindedness."

Aware of Charles Lindbergh's planned solo flight across the Atlantic in May 1927, the citizens of Newark wanted to beat Lindy to the starting line with their own Port-of-Newark-to-Paris non-stop flight. But the "Lone Eagle" went off in his *Spirit of St. Louis* before the Newarkers could put their own Navy speed fliers, Noel A. Davis and Frank H. Conant, in the cockpit for the trans-Atlantic flight.

Lindbergh, who later lived in New Jersey after marrying a young woman from Englewood, Anne Morrow, became an instant celebrity.

Newark city government was finally convinced that a large airport was in its best commercial/transportation interest. On July 11, 1927, Mayor Thomas L. Raymond publicly announced his support for the construction of a municipal airport in Newark's "wasteland" by the city's bustling port on Newark Bay. City Engineer James W. Costello prepared plans for a $6 million project. The plan was approved by U.S. Secretary of Commerce Herbert Hoover, who headed a fact-finding commission to site the metropolitan region's first commercial airport.

In a remarkable engineering feat, more than 2.5 million cubic yards of fill were placed on the original 68 acre site, beginning in January 1928. Eight months later, a 1,600-foot asphalt-topped runway, the first hard-surface strip in the country, was laid down on the man-made land.

In August 1928, a small four-passenger Ryan monoplane from Washington, D.C. made the first landing on a completed section of the tarmac. With the inauguration of Newark-to-Washington service, and a passenger flight from Montreal, Newark Airport was in business. A 120-foot hangar was built to house 25 planes. By the fall of 1930, Newark Airport was the world's busiest place for air traffic. The famed air center embraced 420 acres, with another 500 acres awaiting further expansion.

The airport's activities became the most popular pastime for area residents. Every Sunday through 1930, more than 50,000 people visited the airport to watch the planes take off and land.

Newark's fascination with aviation resulted in many "firsts." The first all-air passenger service to the West Coast was started in 1930. The trip took 36 hours. Other "firsts" included the first airport

Right: Newark International Airport is bathed in moonlight as evening settles over the city. Photo by Michael Spozarsky

Below: Sunlight streams through the windows of Terminal C at Newark International Airport. Photo by Michael Spozarsky

Above: Newark's skyline creates a striking backdrop for the activities of the airport. Photo by Michael Spozarsky

Left: The taxiway lighting and signing operations at Newark Airport, designed by the Port Authority of New York and New Jersey, are now used as a standard for airports worldwide. Photo by Michael Spozarsky

Facing page: Nearly 30 million airline passengers were served by Newark International Airport in 1988. Photo by Michael Spozarsky

weather bureau, night lighting, airport post office, air traffic control, and even the rare artistic modern murals of Archile Gorkey done during the Depression years in the airport's main administration building. The building, which stands today, is itself a true Art Deco masterpiece.

During the 1930s, one-third of the world's air traffic traversed the Newark facility. It was the beginning and focal point of commercial aviation for 10 years after the Lindbergh flight.

On a clear day in 1934, World War I ace Eddie Rickenbacker landed at Newark after a record-breaking passenger transport flight from Los Angeles in 13 hours and two minutes. On a snowy February 21, 1934, the Army Air Corps delivered the first airmail to Newark, the metropolitan area's official "air center."

A year later, on May 15, 1935, the first central terminal was opened for passengers. Also in 1935, Amelia Earhart flew nonstop from Mexico City to Newark in 14 hours and 19 minutes.

Howard Hughes, movie tycoon and perhaps aviation's greatest eccentric, kept up Newark's record of great flight milestones when he landed in 1936 after establishing a new transcontinental speed record of nine hours and 26 minutes.

By 1937, Newark was shipping 34.8 percent of America's airmail. The city's airport also accounted for 27.1 percent of the passenger traffic.

On September 25, 1938, following a hurricane, the number of scheduled flights for one day skyrocketed to a record mark of 476. By 1940, Newark Airport was serving almost 500,000 passengers a year and handling nearly six million pounds of mail.

In 1948, the City of Newark turned over the operation of the airport to the Port Authority of New York and New Jersey, the world's largest transportation authority. Within five years, the Port Authority had increased the airport's total area to 2,300 square acres—four times the size of New York's La Guardia.

In recent years, Newark International Airport has become the fastest-growing airport in the greater New York metropolitan region. The Port Authority reported more than 368,000 plane movements in 1988, serving nearly 24 million passengers and generating gross revenues in excess of $175 million. Some 325,000 tons of air cargo and almost

More than 2,750 ships arrive in Ports Newark and Elizabeth each year. Photo by Michael Spozarsky

50,000 tons of airmail are processed annually at the Newark facility. There are 16 certified commercial airlines, seven commuter airlines, and six cargo airlines.

The Port Authority has invested nearly one billion dollars in Newark Airport since 1948, adding new runways up to 9,200 feet in length and 150 feet wide, an air cargo center, and three huge oval terminals. There is parking for approximately 20,000 motor vehicles. Some 15,000 people are employed at the airport.

The Port Authority designed the taxiway lighting and signing that have become the standard for airport operators around the world. For its pioneering role in aviation, the Newark International Airport has been designated a National Historic Engineering Landmark.

The authority, which was established on April 30, 1921 as the first bistate operation of its kind in the Western Hemisphere, was the first interstate agency ever created under that clause of the Constitution permitting compacts between states with Congressional consent.

The Port Authority operates within the "Port District," a roughly defined circle with a 25-mile radius, centered on the Statue of Liberty just off the shores of the Jersey City waterfront.

PORTS NEWARK-ELIZABETH

The Port Authority of New York and New Jersey developed the concept of containerized shipping and built on Newark Bay the world's first and still largest containerport. Today, Ports Newark-Elizabeth handle approximately 18 million long tons a year, the biggest maritime operation in the East, with more than 2,750 ship arrivals annually.

The City of Newark first developed its port on the bay in 1915. On March 22, 1948, the Port Authority leased the facility from Newark. The authority acquired the adjacent United States Naval Industrial Reserve Shipyard in 1963 and opened a new 40-foot-deep channel on the south side of Port Newark adjoining the Elizabeth Marine Terminal. The Newark Port covers 930 acres, with 23,600 linear feet of berthing space along the wharf. More than 3,100 employees earn more than $76 million a year at the Newark port.

The Port Authority has invested about $240

million in the Newark Bay site since 1948.

Two of the major containership facilities at Port Newark are the Maersk Line and Universal Terminal. Maersk operates two 30-ton container cranes to service its 764-foot-long berth and 61-acre terminal. Next door is the 85-acre Universal Terminal, which is equipped with three 40-ton cranes to serve a berthing space of 3,058 feet.

Port Newark is one of the most flexible multipurpose cargo centers in the United States. The leading port for the importation of products ranging from automobiles to bananas, Port Newark's diverse facilities also support the Elizabeth container complex by providing efficient methods of "stripping," or unloading, containers.

Among the major facilities at Port Newark are a 125,000-square-foot refrig-

erated warehouse that includes a 20,000-square-foot cooler section capable of handling a variety of products such as meats, seafood, and cheeses. Also at Port Newark are a bulk liquid handling facility for the warehousing of refined and edible grades of fats and oils; a high-tech copper rod production plant that processes about 60,000 tons of copper rod annually; a 281,000 square-foot gypsum importing and processing facility; two orange juice concentrate storage and blending facilities capable of storing 6.5 million gallons of Brazilian orange juice concentrate; several auto preparation centers; a 45-acre lumber terminal; a special heavy lift berth; two scrap terminals; and a cement terminal.

The Ports Newark-Elizabeth Marine Terminal is also designated as a foreign trade zone. The zone, which encompasses

Right: Sunset blazes over Port Newark's container facilities. Photo by Rich Zila

Facing page top: Port Newark handles a wide variety of cargo, from orange juice and seafood to lumber and automobiles. Photo by Michael Yamashita

Facing page bottom: The Maersk Line operates one of the largest containership facilities at Port Newark. Photo by Michael Spozarsky

the entire 2,100-acre marine facility, enables tenants to take advantage of such zone benefits as the deferral, reduction, and possible elimination of U.S. customs duties on imported goods. Merchandise brought into the zone may be stored, tested, relabeled, repackaged, displayed, manipulated, mixed with domestic and/or foreign materials, and used in an assembly or manufacturing process.

The Elizabeth port, located on the western shore of Newark Bay, has been transformed into "America's Container Capital" by a cumulative investment of $278 million by the Port Authority, which assumed responsibility for the Elizabeth port in 1958.

With 16,934 linear feet of wharf along the Elizabeth channel and Newark Bay and a mean low water depth of 35 to 40 feet, Elizabeth provides modern, efficient facilities for steamship lines and export-import shippers.

Within the 1,170 acres of the terminal are 23 container cranes serving 22 fully equipped containership berths, 15 distribution buildings with over one million square feet of space, eight cargo buildings, and 54 miscellaneous service structures.

Sea-Land Service, Inc., the pioneer container shipping company that commenced operations at Elizabeth during the summer of 1962, opened an entirely new terminal in 1974. Sea-Land's container facility covers 232 acres, including 4,519 feet of

Above: The skyline of New York City can be seen in this view looking northeast from Ports Newark and Elizabeth. Photo by Michael Spozarsky

Left: Ports Newark and Elizabeth handle a combined 20 million long tons annually. Photo by Bob Krist

wharf. The terminal is equipped with six container cranes.

The combination container and roll-on/roll-off ships of Atlantic Container Line, Ltd., began ACL's transatlantic operation from Elizabeth in 1967. Today, ACL has three container cranes, 2,100 feet of wharf, and 102 acres of upland area.

Maher Terminals, Inc., the Port Authority's largest terminal operator with facilities at both ports, maintains terminals totaling 7,350 feet of berthing space, approximately 537 acres of upland area, 15 container cranes, and miscellaneous buildings. Maher's 371,000 square-foot stuffing and stripping building is the largest at the Elizabeth Marine Terminal. A new "transtainer" system, which uses wheel-mounted cranes to automate the handling and storage of individual containers, was installed in 1987.

To accommodate the needs of shippers, carriers, warehousers, distributors, and manufacturers, an additional 237 acres of property in Elizabeth, immediately adjacent to the twin seaport complex, have been purchased by the Port Authority for its marine terminal expansion and industrial development programs.

Modern, single-story buildings of up to 300,000 square feet are being constructed and leased to various users of the port. East Coast Warehouse and Distribution Corp. is one of the first tenants to occupy the new warehouses, which provide ambient and cool storage for food products.

About 3,250 people work at Port Elizabeth, whose annual payroll is more than $87 million.

PENNSYLVANIA STATION

It is the anchor of downtown Newark, the magnet that draws millions of people to and through New Jersey's transportation hub.

Located only two blocks from the crossroads—Broad & Market—and along the Ironbound, Penn Station is a remarkable, pulsating monument to America's commuters and travelers along the great Boston-to-Washington megalopolis. It is both uniquely attractive and conveniently serviceable, a stunning Art Deco mix of old and new. More than 60,000 commuters rush though its busy corridors each workday.

Thomas N. McCarter, the first president of Public Service Electric & Gas Co. (PSE&G), New Jersey's largest and the nation's third-largest combined utility, led the campaign to convince the Pennsylvania Railroad to improve service in Newark by concentrating a variety of services in one handsome station. After many years of negotiations, the city and the railroad, then known as Standard Railroad, agreed in 1928 to build a new station to replace the outdated castle-like configuration one block west on Market Street.

Erected during the depths of the Depression, the magnificent marble and granite station was the newest showcase of Standard Railroad when it opened on March 24, 1935. At 10:17 P.M., an express train from New York City to Philadelphia stopped at the $42 million Newark station—at that time an astronomical amount of money—signaling the opening of New Jersey's greatest

↑ TRAILWAYS   ↑ GREYHOUND   ↑ BUSES

Inlaid red terrazzo floors and carved marble entranceways enhance the architectural beauty of Pennsylvania Station. Photo by Rich Zila

Facing page: A N.J. Transit train pulls out of Pennsylvania Station. Photo by Rob Kern

transportation center serving trains, buses, and subways with connections to New York and beyond in all directions.

In the year that Penn Station opened, Newark ranked first in the nation in industrial production per square mile and first in the diversity of manufacturing. Every day, 232 trains passed between Newark and New York, operated largely by a single private railroad. No two cities the size and prestige of Newark and New York had more, Standard Railroad boasted.

When built, Penn Station sent repercussions throughout the state and influenced 100 square miles of development, according to New Jersey historical specialist Lynn Drobbin, of the State Department of Environmental Protection.

The Newark station was visibly impressive, a one-of-a-kind structure. Large, classically inspired limestone pilasters and granite archways make up the facade of the 46-foot-high waiting room lined with rose yellow travertine marble from Montana. Across the floor, brown walnut benches with specially carved armrests inlaid with aluminum are positioned atop red terrazzo floors inlaid in black and yellow and embedded with brass.

If that weren't enough to dazzle the eye, the insignia of the Pennsylvania Railroad, and intricate carvings of proud eagles surrounded by stars and sunbursts, are embedded in aluminum marquees and marble entranceways throughout the grand, museum-like station.

In the evening, commuters are bathed in light from four large overhead globes circumscribed with finely crafted white bronze figures depicting the signs of the zodiac. Sunlight slips through sheets of orange, translucent Alabama marble mounted on the western wall.

Listed on the National Historic Register as one of the finest examples of the Art Deco style in the United States, Penn Station underwent a $20-million facelift after it was taken over by New Jersey Transit on August 1, 1984. The state's public transportation agency acquired the station from Amtrak, which had assumed ownership in 1971 after the Pennsylvania Railroad and New York Central Railroad merged and later went bankrupt as the Penn Central Transportation Company. Conrail was formed from the ruins of the once-thriving railroad barons.

New Jersey Transit infused new life into the neglected station, displaying bright banners from the ceiling proudly showing the agency's colors of

burnt orange, magenta, and reflex blue. Green plants have been strategically placed to spruce up the interior. Modern artworks have been installed, including a large triptych painting soaring above the waiting room, which, when activated by a photovoltaic cell, electronically opens and closes its wings as the sun rises and sets outdoors.

Most of the functional decorations, like the elaborate aluminum grillworks hiding the heating system, or the specially designed water fountain at the eastern end of the station, are taken for granted by the thousands of commuters darting in and out of the station and through the corridors to the escalators that lift them to their waiting trains.

Few travelers stop to meet others by using the conveniently numbered benches, or take the time to notice the large round reliefs encircling the waiting room that depict the history of transportation from the canoe to the airplane.

Even fewer look up to see the huge round head of an oxen that stares down from the ceiling above the main entrance. The ox was one of the earliest forms of transportation.

Within Penn Station is a busy mini-mall; some 13 stores occupy 13,000 square feet of retail space, represent 180 jobs and pay one million dollars in yearly rents to the state's transportation agency.

N.J. Transit invested another $12 million to install television security cameras, air conditioning systems, and new doors and elevators, making Penn Station the best of both worlds by resurrecting a bygone era when rail was king and then enhancing it with the electronic marvels of the Space Age.

A total of 219 trains serve Newark's Penn Station each weekday, in addition to 112 on Saturday and 99 on Sunday. The Northeast Corridor trains stop in Newark, as well as N.J. Transit's Raritan Valley and Jersey Coast lines. Some 22,500 N.J. Transit rail riders utilize Penn Station each weekday.

At the western end of Broad Street, N.J. Transit's terminal serves the Morris & Essex lines—a total of 187 trains operating on weekdays, 75 on Saturdays, and 60 on Sundays. The Broad Street Station serves approximately 2,000 rail riders each weekday.

There are also 360 N.J. Transit buses serving

Above: The N.J. Transit light-rail system serves the Newark community with 11 stations and more than four miles of track. Photo by Rich Zila

Facing page: Just 35 cents will take you between stations on the N.J. Transit light-rail subway in Newark. Photo by Rich Zila

Newark during the weekday peak periods. Many of these buses operate multiple trips during each peak period. There are 70,000 bus riders each weekday in Newark—those traveling to and within the city. Almost a quarter of the ridership is concentrated in the Newark area.

N.J. Transit provides a shuttle to Newark Airport, known as Airlink. About 1,200 riders use this service each weekday. An express bus line shuttles another 1,775 riders each weekday between the airport and the Port Authority Bus Terminal in midtown Manhattan.

'SECRET' SUBWAY

One of Newark's best-kept secrets is N.J. Transit's subway, a 4.3-mile, light-rail system with 11 stations connecting Newark and the city's border at Belleville. The line serves Penn Station, the city's central business district, the university complex, Branch Brook Park, and parts of the North Ward. The subway consists of four underground, four depressed-grade, and three at-grade stations.

The 15,000 riders pay only 35 cents between stations to move quietly and efficiently on 24 passenger cars through the city's subterranean tubes.

N.J. Transit recently spent $20 million improving the tracks, switches, signals, stations, and passenger cars, which were built in 1946 and purchased in 1953 from Minneapolis. They were completely reconditioned and restored in 1986.

The subway replaced the city's first major transportation system—the Morris Canal. After lying idle for years, PSE&G President Thomas McCarter proposed the use of the old canal bed in 1903. But it wasn't until 1924 that New Jersey closed the unused, dilapidated canal, which had lost its freight business to the railroads. By then, trolley lines, street cars, and auto traffic were congesting Newark's seemingly shrinking wide streets.

In 1929, Newark obtained title to the canal property and construction began a year later. In 1935, the Newark City Subway opened between Broad Street and Heller Parkway. Newark artist Domenico Mortellito designed and installed the decorative tile murals in the underground stations, which depicted his boyhood days when he swam in the narrow, murky waterway, watching mules pull canal boats often lifted by inclined planes.

Left: Built in the early 1930s, the Pulaski Skyway spans the Passaic and Hackensack rivers. Photo by Michael Spozarsky

Facing page: More than 200,000 people ride PATH each day during the workweek. One of the PATH trains is shown here along McCarter Highway in Newark. Photo by Mary Ann Brockman

The Literary Digest, in its January 9, 1932, edition noted that the canal "will be widened, and into it will be directed more modern torrents—streams of loaded trolley cars, whose passengers, saving from 10 to 20 minutes each, will be emptied out at the new Pennsylvania Station, soon to be begun."

The *Digest* described the water-to-rail transition in one poetic caption: "Where the whiz of the trolley will replace the swish of the stately canal boat."

Welcomed as the "biggest improvement in rapid transit since the introduction of the bus," the city's subway was the first step toward rapid transportation to the surrounding suburbs.

In 1937, the subway was extended to the new Penn Station and a year later the subway was leased from the city by Public Service Coordinated Transport, a subsidiary of PSE&G.

By 1952, the subway became Newark's only remaining trolley line. Currently the Newark subway system employs 25 drivers and 31 mechanics and maintenance personnel.

PATH

"Eight minutes to New York" is about as quick as anyone can go between Manhattan and Jersey City, New Jersey's first stop on the PATH line. Newark is about a 15-minute ride. All fares are one dollar, after years of being heavily subsidized at only 30 cents.

PATH is a primary transit link between Manhattan and New Jersey's urban and suburban commuter railroads. PATH carries more than 70 percent of all passengers entering New York City by rail from New Jersey. Approximately 203,600 passengers travel PATH each weekday, more than two-thirds of those during the morning and evening peak hours.

Opened in 1908 as the Hudson and Manhattan Railroad, a privately owned corporation, PATH has been been a rail subsidiary of The Port Authority since 1962.

PATH (Port Authority Trans Hudson) began life on November 17, 1874, when "death-defying" construction got under way on the train tunnels under the Hudson River between midtown Manhattan and Jersey City. It was touch-and-go all the way as the human moles with their cutting blades carved out the holes under the Hudson River, boring inch by inch, deeper and deeper through the soft, sticky mud. The unprecedented project was not without the usual fatalities for such risky, pioneering work.

The Hudson and Manhattan Railroad operated the rapid transit system from its opening on February 25, 1908, until the Port Authority made PATH an integral part of its vast transportation network on September 1, 1962. It modernized the 14-mile

line, which carries more than 70,000 commuters between the two Hudson River states. Ticket booths and token clerks were replaced with coin-operated turnstiles and closed-circuit television cameras. The security force was increased from 15 rail security personnel to more than 90 Port Authority police officers.

Since the Port Authority assumed control, PATH ridership has nearly doubled, from 29 million in 1962 to 58 million in 1988, and the 313 sleek PATH cars clock 280 million passenger miles a year. Meanwhile, the number of employees—1,143—remains virtually the same as in 1962.

Ridership on the transit line peaked at 113 million in 1927. A year later, the Holland Tunnel was opened to motor vehicles, the first trans-Hudson toll crossing that brought about a decline of mass transit, a trend the Port Authority has been aggressively trying to reverse for a half-century.

A new 207,000-square-foot rail yard costing $205 million has been built in anticipation of improved ridership in the 1990s. The steel/masonry facility is located on 57 acres just across the Passaic River in Harrison.

One of the early mechanical wonders on what became the PATH line was the "world's greatest railroad lift bridge," erected during the same time as Penn Station. Although there were several two-track lift bridges of greater length, the lift bridge

built in Newark by the Pennsylvania Railroad was the longest three-track railway lift span to be built up to that time—230 feet between end bearings. The towers on each end were 67 feet long. Together with the approach spans, the entire bridge was 528 feet long. The moving weight of the span was 2,100 tons, and 2,100 tons for the two counterweights. About 5,000 tons of steel went into the superstructure.

ROADS

Newark is served by the nation's two busiest toll roads—the New Jersey Turnpike and the Garden State Parkway.

The Turnpike is the only major thoroughfare in the world that provides buses and trucks with their own north/south lanes, while automobiles and motorcycles have their own triple lanes in both directions. The Turnpike provides direct access to Newark Airport, Ports Newark and Elizabeth, and downtown Newark.

Over the last 30 years, the Parkway has widened into an eight-lane engineering marvel through the most densely populated place in America. Motorists can get in and out of Newark easily through its wide main streets that connect to both the Parkway and Turnpike and the more recently built interstates 78 and 280.

Route 1, once the most heavily traveled corridor in the United States, remains a critical artery paralleling the Turnpike, giving motorists in the greater Newark area an alternative to the north-south flow of vehicles, especially during the congested peak periods in the mornings and late afternoons.

When the Pulaski Skyway was built over the Passaic and Hackensack rivers in the early 1930s it became New Jersey's first superhighway and its most spectacular elevated road. The Skyway (Route 1) became the fastest route from Jersey City to Newark and the most critical link in the New York-to-Washington corridor. The imposing viaduct extends 3.7 miles over the two rivers, and marshes, meadows, and swamps. The skyway consumed 88,461 tons of structural steel, or 20,000 tons more than were used to build the George Washington Bridge. The price tag for the Depression-era span was a bargain $20 million.

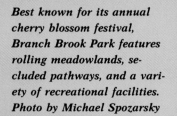

Best known for its annual cherry blossom festival, Branch Brook Park features rolling meadowlands, secluded pathways, and a variety of recreational facilities. Photo by Michael Spozarsky

III

Parks and Recreation

No city in America of comparable size can match the number of Newark's resplendent green acres and historic sites utilized as parks and public recreation areas. Within the nation's first smallest major city are no less than 44 designated parklands, two of which are the nation's first and second county parks—Branch Brook and Weequahic.

When the Puritans laid out their virgin settlement in 1666, they assured future generations there would be plenty of open spaces for a growing population. Along every stretch of roadway they set aside the public squares and commons for people to gather in the shade of the tall trees. The Puritans were conservationists first, and then hardworking farmers and businessmen.

As the landscape was modified by successive generations, so were the common grounds. Today, the city's parks range from the cozy, well-preserved Arlington Terrace Steps, taking in only 100 square feet, to the largest park in Essex County, Branch Brook, at 486 acres. Within this multifaceted spectrum of vest-pocket parks and almost rural-like gardens and farm settings are Newark's more typical parklands: the 6-acre Military Park and 3.4-acre Washington Park along Broad Street in the heart of the downtown district, and the 4.4-acre Lincoln Park on the eastern end of Broad Street adjacent to an elegant brownstone neighborhood. Lincoln Park features monuments to the Indians and to the soldiers of World War I, while Washington Park pays tribute to the father of our country, befriended by statues of Christopher Columbus, an Indian and Pilgrim, and the city's most prolific inventor, Seth Boyden. Military Park contains the massive and impressive block of granite and bronze "Wars of America" monument created by Gutzon Borglum, best known for his gigantic Mount Rushmore carving of Washington, Jefferson, Lincoln, and Theodore Roosevelt. The war memorial honors not only those who went off to fight, but to those who stayed at home and worked. The memorial depicts an airplane navigator bidding goodbye to his mother, the tragic face of an old father whose sons have all gone to war, and another father urging his son to do his duty in the Navy. There are some recognizable local faces of the early 1920s: benefactor Amos Van Horn as a Union soldier, and Borglum himself and his son, as the young sailor and his father.

Borglum also fashioned the bronze, brooding figure of Abraham Lincoln that sits solemnly on a park bench in front of the Essex County Court House, the site of familiar scenes for several motion pictures made in Newark over the last 75 years.

But the most spacious treasures of all the city's recreational resources are Branch Brook and Weequahic, the nation's oldest county parks.

Named for the branch of a brook flowing through the valley and emptying into the Passaic River, Branch Brook Park had been known as the Old Blue Jay Swamp, a dismal marsh that had been an army training camp during the Civil War. The soggy area was also called Reservoir Park, for it was the walled containment for the city's supply

Above: A father takes his children for a brisk winter walk through Washington Park. Photo by Barry M. Winiker

Left: Washington Park is situated in the heart of Newark's downtown district. Photo by Carol Kitman

Facing page: More than four acres make up the grounds of Lincoln Park, which feature stately memorials to native Americans, and to the soldiers of World War I. Photo by Rich Zila

of drinking water. Before Essex County began acquiring the first 60-acre tract for recreational purposes in 1895, that northern area of Newark had become a neglected eyesore, an open dump. Gradually, the forbidding swamp with its unsightly litter and swaying cattails was turned into undulating lawns and fields of laurels and sparkling waterways. The genius behind that remarkable transformation was Frederick L. Olmsted, the distinguished landscape architect who had designed Manhattan's Central Park and Brooklyn's Prospect Park.

Branch Brook, under Olmsted's watchful eye, grew to more than eight times its original size. In addition to fishing and boating, facilities were installed for all major sports, including 37 tennis courts, baseball diamonds, bicycling and cross-country running pathways, bocce alleys, cricket crease, horseshoe pitching, soccer fields, and a Gaelic football field. A 24-acre lake, once rated as good largemouth bass water, was one of four Essex County lakes and ponds stocked with trout. In the winter, the frozen lake comes alive with ice skaters. In warmer weather, paddle boats are available.

Branch Brook Park is two miles long and averages about a quarter-mile wide. Its dominant features consist of a combination of open meadowland and small patches of woodland on gently rolling terrain. There is a large band concert area where musical festivals are staged from spring through fall.

Branch Brook is especially known for its annual cherry blossom festival, the largest such display in the world according to the Japanese American Association. More than 2,200 ornamental cherry trees of four different species provide a spectacular, colorful display each April, one even larger and more beautiful than that during the cherry blossom festival in Washington, D.C. The trees, planted from 1927 through 1933, were a gift of Mrs. Caroline Fuld and her brother, department store magnate Louis Bamberger.

The entrance to Branch Brook Park off Lake Street is known as "Ballantine Gateway" in honor of the Ballantine family, Newark's most famous brewers, who donated a replica of a gate house in Scotland.

Branch Brook was the first county park to be

Left: A child rides along the pathways of Military Park in the spring. Photo by Rich Zila

Facing page: Families enjoy the peaceful beauty of Branch Brook Park. Photo by Michael Spozarsky

The imposing granite and bronze "Wars of America" memorial monument is the central focus of Military Park. Photo by Joseph DeCaro

opened for public use in the United States.

Weequahic, named after the Indian word for "boundary" or "the end," is the nation's second-oldest county park. It is the second largest park in the Essex County park system, with 311.3 acres. The Lenni Lenape called this watery nook in the southwestern corner of Newark "the head of the cove."

Acquired by the county in 1897, the area had been a blend of farmland, swampland, and fairgrounds for city events. Originally, the county intended to use the Weequahic tract as a reservation for future population growth, and residents were living around the borders of the new preserve.

Weequahic Park's 80-acre lake is only five feet above sea level. The park's topography includes wooded, rocky hills and wide grassy plains. Divident Hill was used by the early settlers as a means of setting the boundary between Newark and Elizabeth. Among the trees growing in Weequahic are American Beech, Osage, Orange, Cucumber, and Japanese Cherry. Azaleas line the park road.

Weequahic features an 18-hole golf course, ball diamonds, football fields, soccer fields, lighted basketball courts, tennis courts, playgrounds, picnic grounds, fishing, boating, ice skating, a cross-country run, and a rose garden.

PASSAIC RIVER

The Passaic is New Jersey's longest and most important river. "It turns more mills, operates more factories and furnishes more water power for the uses of man than any other stream of its size," wrote John Whitehead in his account, *The Passaic Valley*, published in 1901.

Although only 90 miles in length from its source in the Mendham swamps of Morris County to where it flows into Newark Bay, the Passaic drains more than 800 square miles in seven counties whose boundaries are formed by its serendipitous course. In descending order, those counties are Morris, Somerset, Union, Essex, Passaic, Bergen, and Hudson.

Since the mid-seventeenth century, the grand ole Passaic has been "cribbed, confined and made

Above: From ice skating in the winter to summertime paddle boats, the 24-acre lake in Branch Brook Park is a great source of recreation. Photo by Alan L. Detrick

Right: Branch Brook Park provides a great source of fun for adventurous children. Photo by Michael Spozarsky

Facing page top: A father and son enjoy an afternoon of fishing in Newark's Branch Brook Park. Photo by Mary Ann Brockman

Facing page bottom: The Cherry Blossom Run through Branch Brook Park draws thousands of participants each year. Photo by Michael Yamashita

Left: Weequahic Park encompasses more than 300 acres and is the second oldest county park in the nation. Photo by Carol Kitman

Below: Scullers skim along the waters of the Passaic River. Photo by Rich Zila

to play a critical part as an appliance in ministering to the wants and demands of modern civilization," Whitehead reported.

When Henry Hudson cruised into New York Bay on September 9, 1609, and discovered the river that now bears his name, he dispatched a small crew up through the narrow Kill van Kull to explore what is now Newark Bay and the Passaic River. Later, Newark's founders realized that this noble river with its protected bay would always serve as a highway out of the wilderness through which there were no other paths except those made by the Indians.

The river served the Indians for several thousand years before European settlers moved in and, within 200 years, harnessed its waterpower and ignorantly and carelessly polluted the greatest natural resource in the Passaic Valley.

During the American Revolution, General Washington's army camped along the Passaic and crossed it several times in the long New Jersey battles that were the turning point in the Revolutionary War.

While it was still relatively clean, Washington Irving, one of the nation's greatest literary figures, spent his vacations in the 1840s on the banks of the gently looping Passaic.

By 1912, the river and the bay, nearly to the city line, had a channel 300 feet wide, a depth of

16 feet at low water and 21 feet at high tide. Newark Bay and the lower Passaic River have a wharf frontage of nearly 11 miles.

Today, a "Riverlands Renaissance" is reshaping the Passaic River waterfront into a fresh and vital marine community that will help return Newark to its preeminence among America's great historic cities.

NEWARK WATERSHED

Nearly three times larger than the city itself, the Newark Watershed is North Jersey's "last frontier" —a rare, pristine oasis in the great metropolitan sprawl. Located 35 miles northwest of Newark, it is regarded as one of New Jersey's greatest natural resources; an invigorating public wilderness owned by the people of Newark.

The city acquired this vast wooded lake region

in 1900 from farmers and other local landowners. For an investment of $6 million, the city assured future residents of a constant and lasting supply of the cleanest water to be found anywhere.

When Alexander Hamilton was secretary of the treasury, he set out to find where the purest and softest water in the colonial states was waiting to be tapped. Hamilton wanted to promote manufacturing. Pure, soft water was essential to the manufacture of the best leather.

Under Hamilton's direction, the new republic engaged a number of American and English chemists to travel the entire former 13 colonies, examining stream water. The chemists found the purest in what was called the Pequannock Watershed. The Indians called this area "Paau quun auke," which means "land naturally clear or open."

The Pequannock takes in approximately 63.7 square miles and comprises about 86 percent of an entire drainage area, or 35,000 acres. Newark's property is situated in six separate municipalities: Rockaway, Jefferson, and Kinnelon in Morris County, Hardyston and Vernon in Sussex County, and West Milford in Passaic County.

The watershed is located in the Atlantic flyway and migratory birds temporarily stop over near the mirrored ponds and lake-like reservoirs to replenish themselves. Fish teem in the feeder streams and reservoirs, including bass, perch, pickerel, and trout. The watershed contains some of the last streams in New Jersey with a naturally regenerating trout population.

The watershed's scenic beauty is an exquisite natural mosaic of clear lakes and ponds, green valleys, manificent rock outcroppings, gorges, mountains, and forested ridges of oaks, maples, birches, and other hearty hardwoods.

The watershed boasts some of the few elevations in the New York-New Jersey region that require hours to reach by trail. The Empire State Building can be seen on a clear day from the watershed's lofty peaks.

The Pequannock also has more acreage that is inaccessible by automobile than any other place in northern New Jersey.

A maze of woodland trails take a hiker to the early years of America. The pathways were initially used to transport iron ore from mines to area furnaces. The trails and a number of abandoned mine shafts, along with an iron furnace near the Clinton Reservoir, are the only remnants of a bygone era. The remains of a castle built at the end of the nineteenth century can also be seen on a hill overlooking Hanks Pond. On Green Pond Road a house with a cornerstone dated 1773 continues to be used by a city employee.

The Pequannock consists of a surface water supply system of five major reservoirs: Oak Ridge, Clinton, Canistear, Echo Lake, and Charlottesburg.

Oak Ridge Reservoir encompasses 482 acres and has a capacity of 3.9 million gallons. It is 846 feet above sea level. The tributaries flowing into Oak Ridge wind through 21.7 square miles.

The Clinton Reservoir sits 992 feet above sea

Left: An Oak Ridge Reservoir tributary runs alongside Route 23, providing motorists with a picturesque scene. Photo by Rich Zila

More than 60 square miles make up the gentle terrain of the Newark Watershed, which was originally purchased by the city in 1900. Photo by Rich Zila

Left: The Newark Watershed is rich with natural wildlife, crystalline lakes, and rolling green valleys. Photo by Rich Zila

Above: The combined resources of the watershed's five major reservoirs amounts to nearly 10 million gallons of water. A section of the 482-acre Oak Ridge Reservoir is shown here in its natural splendor. Photo by Rich Zila

Facing page: Refreshing waterfalls and shimmering ponds can be seen while experiencing the beauty of the Newark Watershed. Photo by Rich Zila

level and has a capacity of 3.518 million gallons within its 423 acres of containment. Its tributaries flow through 10.5 square miles.

The Canistear Reservoir, at 1,086 feet, can touch the clouds on some days. Canistear contains 2.4 million gallons within its 350-acre wedge in a valley. Its tributaries trickle through 5.6 square miles of rocky woodlands.

Echo Lake Reservoir embraces 300 acres at an elevation of 894 feet. The streams running down into the cool waters of the lake pass through 4.6 square miles of virgin wilderness, supplying Echo Lake with 1.7 million gallons of spring and snow-melt water.

Charlottesburg Reservoir contains 3 million gallons within its 375 acres, furnished by a network of gushing streams rushing through 18.4 square miles of wildlife habitat. Charlottesburg is 743 feet above sea level.

The five reservoirs can collect and hold 14.4 billion gallons of water for Newark and the eight municipalities that draw from the city's precious Pequannock reserve. The daily safe draw is between 50 to 55 million gallons. The communities served by Newark's watershed are Pequannock, Lincoln Park, and Wayne townships in Passaic County; Nutley, Belleville, and Bloomfield in Essex County; and Elizabeth and Hillside in Union County.

The New Jersey Training School in Totowa and the Essex County Hospital in Cedar Grove also depend on Newark's water, which is exceptional in quality.

In 1971, the city decided to explore the possibility of opening its vast landholdings to limited development as a means of generating revenue for a financially strapped urban center. The proposal aroused the citizenry both in Newark and around the periphery of the watershed. Although concerned citizens and environmentalists warned city officials not to degrade the last clean body of land and water in the most densely populated and developed state in the nation, plans are still being studied to accommodate additional recreational, commercial, and residential development.

In 1974, the city permitted the first commercial activity within the watershed—the Craigmeur Ski Area in Rockaway Township. The second intrusion was a tree-high microwave tower for cable TV transmission.

One popular use of Newark's watershed is as an open classroom for the study of ecology and the relationship between nature and humankind. Thousands of Newark students take trips each year to their wide-open backyard about an hour's drive from their homes and schools.

As North Jersey becomes covered with wall-to-wall development, the Newark watershed becomes ever more valuable, not as a piece of real estate to raise taxes, but as a peaceful sanctuary for the city's 325,000 residents seeking a quiet place to get away from the din of modern society.

As a recreational retreat, the Pequannock Watershed can continue to provide Newark and its environs with a plentiful and healthful supply of water. Any permanent development can only lessen the refreshing quality of life in this final frontier that has survived settlement and remained virtually intact for three centuries.

Above: A game of bocci ball in Branch Brook Park provides an afternoon of outdoor recreation. Photo by Linda Zila

Facing page: Blooming tulips produce a splash of springtime color in Newark. Photo by Linda Zila

The magnificent Sacred Heart Cathedral, with its handcarved Italian marble altar and finely detailed woodwork, is just one of many remarkable landmarks to be seen in the city of Newark. Photo by Rich Zila

IV
Landmarks and Historic Sites

As the third-oldest major city in America, Newark today stands as a unique living testament to more than three centuries of American history. A remarkable number of the city's buildings, districts, and historic sites mirror the incredible story of America's colonial roots and a new nation's fight for freedom and independence.

From the Revolutionary and Civil wars to the Industrial Revolution that transformed America into a vibrant melting pot, through two world wars, the Depression, and the cultural convulsions of the 1960s, Newark always adapted and survived, creating an unprecedented historical legacy in the process.

That cherished endowment is preserved in the 53 historic landmarks and sites and two historic districts that constitute a considerable amount of Newark's comparatively small cityscape.

Luck and chance played fortuitous roles in determining what remains today of Newark's variegated past. While the founding fathers laid out the basic, efficient design of their new Eden along the Passaic, successive generations imbued their own spirit and vision into the structures and neighborhoods that evolved into what Newark is today—an eclectic amalgamation of architecture and individualistic expressions representing hundreds of years of human ingenuity and inquisitiveness.

Strolling the streets of Newark, one can come across just about any kind of form and style, from Arabasque to Romanesque. From its simple beginnings as a theocracy, Newark never lost its deep religious heritage. Many of the most impressive edifices designated as national historic landmarks are the religious institutions that have become the one constant in the

development and refinement of New Jersey's premier city.

SACRED HEART CATHEDRAL

The most inspiringly visible manifestation of Newark's religious tradition is Sacred Heart Cathedral, appropriately situated in the heart of the city overlooking the refreshing Branch Brook Park. It is one of the Western Hemisphere's best examples of French Gothic architecture and was built in the grand cathedral tradition of Rheims, Chartres, and Lyon. Its diagonally positioned towers are reminiscent of those intended for the abbey church in Rouen. A magnificent fleche marks the crossing and rises to a height of 260 feet aboveground. A structural masterpiece whose elaborate spires soar higher than the Notre Dame Cathedral in Paris or Westminster Abbey in London, Newark's Cathedral of the Sacred Heart is the honored seat of Catholicism in New Jersey, the state's dominant religion. The Archdiocese of Newark encompasses more than 40 percent, or 1.4 million, of the state's 2.8 million Catholic population.

Sacred Heart is the home of the Archbishop, the highest ranking Catholic priest in New Jersey. The state's first Catholic diocese, or jurisdiction, was established by Pope Pius IX in 1853. The first bishop, installed in 1859, was James Roosevelt Bayley, a convert from the Anglican Communion and nephew of St. Elizabeth Ann Seton, after whom Seton Hall University in South Orange is named.

The Archdiocese of Newark serves more than one million parishioners in Essex, Bergen, Hudson, and Union counties, a rainbow collection of 125 municipalities, 241 parishes, and 189 Catholic elementary schools and 40 high schools with a total enrollment exceeding 63,000 students.

Although the Newark Archdiocese is geographically the smallest in the nation, covering only 541 square miles, it is served by one Catholic university (Seton Hall), three colleges (St. Peter's in Jersey City, Caldwell College, and Felician College in Lodi), as well as the Immaculate Conception Seminary in South Orange.

The archdiocese also serves the medical community with eight Catholic hospitals ranging from

Right: Sacred Heart Cathedral is a stunning display of French Gothic architecture. Photo by Rich Zila

Facing page: The spires of Sacred Heart Cathedral rise over the Newark skyline. Photo by Sharon Sullivan

Holy Name in Teaneck to St. Michael's in Newark.

The Newark Archdiocesan network is made up of 1,160 priests, 220 deacons, 156 religious brothers, and 2,128 religious sisters.

Sacred Heart remains an active urban parish for some 500 families in Newark, but its breathtaking grandeur has made it a spectacular showcase for the arts in recent years. The Cathedral Concert Series is a popular attraction featuring organ recitals, choirs, the Newark Boys Chorus, the Archdiocesan Festival Chorale, a candelight carol sing, hand-bell ringers, original dance presentations, and premiere performances such as "Dreamscapes" by the Caldwell College Theater.

Newark architect Jeremiah O'Rourke drew the original plans for Sacred Heart Cathedral, which were later revised by Isaac E. Ditmars, who succeeded him as cathedral architect. Paul C. Reilly was the architect for the completion of the cathedral. He designed the interior, the plaza, and the

Right: A mass for 50th wedding anniversaries is held amid the splendor of Sacred Heart Cathedral. Photo by Mary Ann Brockman

Facing page top: The exquisite stained-glass windows of Sacred Heart Cathedral are made of antique Bavarian glass. Photo by Rich Zila

Facing page bottom: Easter Sunday at Sacred Heart Cathedral brings little girls dressed in bright springtime colors. Photo by Michael Yamashita

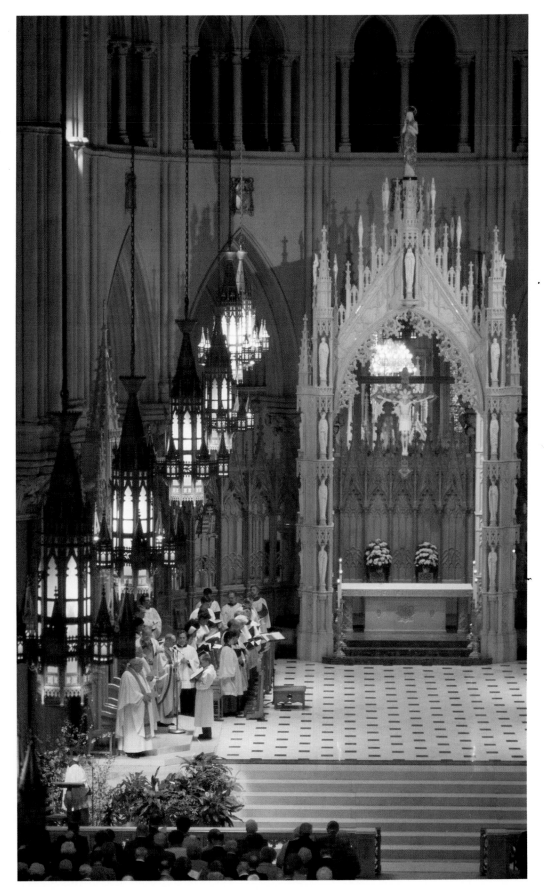

Archbishop's residence.

This irreplaceable monument to faith measures 365 feet in length, with a width of 165 feet in the transept. Originally conceived in the English-Irish Gothic style, the Newark cathedral gradually evolved on the drawing boards into a French neo-Gothic creation. The 200-by-800-foot plot for the new church was purchased on January 2, 1871, for $60,000.

The cost of the cathedral was not to exceed one million dollars, but it multiplied ten-fold over the 75 years it took to complete.

The cathedral's incredible weight, including a steel-supported slate roof, is held up by 24 nave and ambulatory columns. The vaulting and clerestory rest on the giant pillars.

The altar, handcarved from Italian Pietra Santa marble, is topped by an imposing Botticino marble canopy standing 39 feet high. A figure of the cathedral's patron, the Sacred Heart of Jesus, appears the apex of the canopy.

The focal point of the altar complex is the burnished brown crucifix with light-green onyx marble inlays and lifelike figure of Christ carved from a sold block of Portuguese light rose marble, with garments of Carrara marble.

Ringing the main altar are five chapels dedicated to national saints representing the various ethnic groups that make up New Jersey's Catholic population.

The scores of stained-glass windows, considered among the rarest in the world, were designed by renowned artisan Franz Zettler of Munich. The 200 windows are made from antique glass manufactured in Bavaria, and follow the color scheme used for the windows of Chartres. The great rose window of the south front is 35 feet in diameter, and is the second largest rose window in the United States. The transept roses are each 32 feet in diameter. These windows, designed by Karl Jung of Munich, each contain 1,000 square feet of glass.

The thick bronze doors were made in Rome and installed in 1954, the year the cathedral was completed. The altars are made of Botticino and Carrara marble, the chandeliers of Czechoslovakian cut glass, the carved screens, statues, and pews of Appalachian white oak, and a spacious crypt is appointed with handsome bronze gates.

The pealing of the bells is a familiar sound in the city's North Ward and to visitors of Branch Brook Park, which serves as a lush green backdrop and glassy lake reflector for the magnificent Gothic structure. There are 14 bells in the west tower, all cast in Padua, Italy, and tested by Vatican bell experts. The bells can be played from a small keyboard next to the master organ console in the south gallery, or automatically from a panel in the main sacristy. The altars, mosaics, and wood

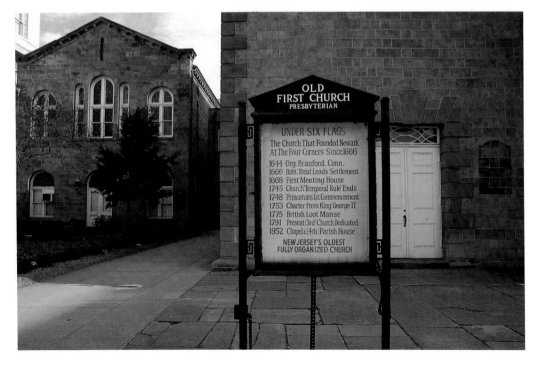

Left: Dating back to 1791, the third and present Old First Church stands at the corner of Broad Street and Branford Place. Photo by Carol Kitman

Facing page: The four clocks on each side of the Old First Church tower can be seen from all directions. Photo by Carol Kitman

and stone carvings of New Jersey's most beautiful cathedral are not merely decorations displaying man's handiwork and ingenuity; they are, according to the Catholic church, "statements of an ageless Faith which continues to transcend the test of time . . ."

THE OLD FIRST CHURCH

When Sir Isaac Newton was contemplating his epochal discovery of the law of universal gravitation, one of Newark's founders, the Reverend Abraham Pierson, established the Congregational or Independent Church, later referred to as the First Presbyterian Church, on a piece of land that became the center of this new Puritan settlement. The year was 1666. Today, the Old First Church is Newark's most venerated landmark, standing solidly on Broad Street at Branford Place, its thick main tower displaying four octagonal-shaped clocks that face north, south, east, and west.

The Presbyterians renamed the church 50 years after it was organized by Pierson, whose son was one of the founders and the first president of Yale University.

Around 1715, a second church building replaced the original gabled house of worship that had also served as the town's first and only main meeting center for more than 40 years. In 1791, the second Old First Church site was converted into a courthouse.

In September 1787 the cornerstone of the third and present church was laid. It was opened for worship and dedicated on January 1, 1791. After nearly two centuries, the Old First Church is considered a splendid example of early church architecture, with fine stonework, heavy oak timbers to support the gambrel roof, and an interior retaining all of the charm of the eighteenth century.

JAMES STREET COMMONS

The James Street Commons, one of Newark's oldest and finest areas, became the city's first official landmark district in 1977. It contains a remarkable mix of residential, cultural, and commercial constructions within a 20-block area on the edge of the city's downtown business district.

The city's first market place in 1669 was the "Upper Commons," now the site of Washington Park. This tree-shaded oasis, once surrounded by magnificent mansions, is now engulfed by modern office towers.

Lining both sides of James Street are a choice variety of town and rowhouses, of which the most architecturally significant are: 37 James Street, a Federal-styled structure now used as a restaurant; 49 through 61 James Street, an exceptional row of red-brick Queen Annes; 44 through 48 James Street, a series of brick rowhouses with ground-to-roof curved bays; and 50 James Street, an orange-brick townhouse with rare ogee arches.

On the west side of Dr. Martin Luther King, Jr., Boulevard (High Street), harmony and adherence to scale give this 1880s-1890s cluster of three-story, red-brick dwellings a strong sense of neighborhood. Shop owners occupied these fashionable homes during the Victorian era, viewing their businesses down below from their front windows.

Across the street, St. Michael's Medical Center, Newark's oldest medical facility, blends in compatibly with its striking red-brick exterior and multiple gables and mansard roof, featuring rock-faced stone lintels and a Gothic arched entranceway. Built in 1871, the fortress-like edifice appears to be guarding the entrance to the Commons.

In 1888, a red-brick and brownstone firehouse was built for Hook & Ladder Company No. 2 on High Street with its panoramic view of downtown Newark. Now used by meatpackers, the two-story, gable-roofed building is trimmed in brownstone.

The red-brick townhouse at 43 Bleecker Street is one of the oldest and finest in the commons district. Constructed in 1849, it is believed to have served as home to the first Catholic bishop of Newark. The two-story house with wood-finished basement and fireplace was also one of the stops in the famed Underground Railroad.

St. Patrick's Pro Cathedral Complex is a modified and elaborate French and English Gothic structure completed in 1850. This church served as the official Archdiocesan cathedral until Sacred Heart was opened in 1954.

On a bluff commanding a view of the city's downtown district stands Eberhardt Hall, an impressive red-brick and brownstone Elizabethan-Collegiate Gothic edifice built in 1856-1857 as the Newark Orphan Asylum. It became the home of

Newark College of Engineering (NCE), now the New Jersey Institute of Technology (NJIT). An octagonal turret about six stories high and enclosing a spiral staircase is situated to the left of the central battlement tower. Both the north and south wings of the building are marked by curved gables suggesting a Flemish influence. The roofs are pierced by many triangular dormer windows, while the facade, wings, and corners are braced by a variety of buttresses. Like a baron's castle protecting the village below, the NJIT administrative headquarters, which cost $31,000 when constructed, was designed by John Welch, a founder of the American Institute of Architects who emigrated to Newark from Scotland in 1850. The building, with 23,000 square feet of floor space, is named after Frederick L. Eberhardt, a Newark industrialist and a president of NCE.

The Polhemus House was one of the earliest red-brick mansions built near Washington Park. Completed in 1859 by Eliza Polhemus, widow of the pastor of the nearby North Reformed Church, the elegant home was fashioned in the early Victorian and Empire styles. An underground tunnel in the basement leading to University Avenue served as both a transport stop in the Abolitionists' underground railroad and as an early, primitive air conditioning system. The Polhemus House was one of the first in Newark to have indoor plumbing, gas-

lights, and a dumbwaiter.

The 1870s French Chateau, Romanasque-styled Fewsmith Mansion was built by the pastor of the Second Presbyterian Church. The round-arch style is evident throughout in the arches and lintels.

Perhaps the most striking structure within the commons is the Ballantine Mansion, an eclectic Victorian-Edwardian mansion built for John H. Ballantine, son of Peter Ballantine, founder of the famed brewery. The 1885 domicile shows off the wealth that was prevalent in Newark in the late nineteenth and early twentieth centuries. The Ballantine Mansion ranks as the most spectacular restoration performed in the city. The 21-room mansion features stained-glass windows, huge fireplaces, intricate paneling, ornamental plaster, and embossed leather wallcovering. Displayed throughout the house are many original furnishings, period paintings, and antiques from the Newark Museum's extensive collection. Rotating exhibitions in the Music Room Gallery depict aspects of the nineteenth century decorative arts.

Next door is the Newark Museum, built in 1926 in the Second Renaissance Revival tradition with funds furnished by Louis Bamberger. Regarded as the preeminent museum in New Jersey, the Newark facility, currently undergoing a $17.5 million renovation by Princeton architect Michael Graves, houses treasures from every part of the globe, with its Tibetan collection the most noteworthy. The lovely, spacious garden behind the museum contains contemporary sculpture, the Fire Museum, and the historic Lyons Farms Schoolhouse. Once located on Elizabeth and Chancellor avenues, the one-room schoolhouse was built in 1784. It was the first public building in the state built from brownstone quarried in Newark. Washington talked with pupils in the little schoolhouse during a visit to the city.

On the next block is the Newark Public Library, the state's largest, designed by Rankin &

Above: The North Reformed Church, which was the last church built in Newark without steel or iron, dates back to the late 1850s. Photo by Rich Zila

Right: A detail of the Newark Public Library shows the intricate design and craftsmanship which went into the creation of this Italian Renaissance structure. Photo by Rich Zila

Kellogg. An excellent example of the Italian Renaissance style, the granite and marble building was completed in 1901. The magnificent interior features an open center court extending to the fourth floor, topped by a stunning stained-glass skylight. Marble arches and mosaics enhance the first floor. The Newark Library system is New Jersey's largest, boasting more than 1.25 million volumes.

Outside the Commons in the downtown area, there are the oldest houses of worship in the city. The North Reformed Church, erected in 1857-1859, was the last church in Newark built entirely without the use of steel or iron. The brownstone Gothic structure once housed the largest Reformed Church congregation in America—1,800 parishioners.

Trinity Cathedral, Newark's second-oldest church, was built in 1809-1810, replacing a building constructed in 1743-1746 and damaged by the British during the Revolutionary War when it was used as a hospital. The original tower was retained in today's structure. Twenty feet square with walls five feet thick, the tower still stands as the oldest piece of public masonry in Newark.

Members of the Episcopal faith had been holding services in Newark since 1729, having broken away from the Old First Church. King George II of England granted the original charter for the

Above: Classical mounted figures adorn the facade of the New Jersey Bell Telephone building on Broad street, which was built in the American Perpendicular style in the late 1920s. Photo by Rich Zila

Left: Constructed of pink granite in the Romanesque style, the First Baptist Peddie Memorial Church has been part of Newark history since the 1890s. Photo by Carol Kitman

church in 1746. Parts of the original structure were incorporated in the present site, making the existing building a hybrid of architectural styles.

Continuing in chronological order (listing the oldest landmarks first), the Symington House follows Trinity Cathedral. A quaint Federal-style structure built in 1808 as the rectory for Trinity Church, it served as the headquarters of Newark's 300th anniversary celebration in 1966. Also known as the Continental House when it was owned by the Continental Insurance Company, the downstairs doors are braced with double-cross panels used by the original superstitious inhabitants to bar the entry of witches. Rare solid mahogany floors in the front parlor and library show almost no wear. Every room in the house has its own mantel, including the basement. The front parlor fireplace is covered with carved Italian marble.

The Romanesque-styled First Baptist Peddie Memorial Church is a pink granite Byzantine building featuring an outstanding 80-foot-high dome inspired by the Baths of Pisa in Italy. It was paid for by former Newark mayor and philanthropist Thomas Peddie, who gave the architect, William Halsey Wood, "a blank check" in 1890 to design a church with a unique 600-light gaslight system on the interior and a large seating capacity relative to its outward appearance. With its rich paneling, 200 doors, and 173 windows, it is the "international" of parishes in Newark, a city of more than 200 houses of worship, many of them of recent storefront vintage.

The Veterans Administration Building was the original headquarters of the Globe Indemnity Insurance Company. The limestone, Second Renaissance Revival structure was completed in 1920. The building is similar in character, materials, workmanship, and style with other institutional structures in the Washington Street commons, such as the library and museum.

In the downtown business district, the New Jersey Bell Telephone Company occupies a special skyscraper facing Washington Park. Erected in 1927-1929 in the American Perpendicular style, the building's facade is covered by magnificent classical mounted figures.

The American Insurance Company building is the finest example in Newark of the Georgian Re-

vival style applied to skyscraper dimensions. Built in 1929-1930, it was acquired by Rutgers University in the 1970s and dedicated as the Samuel I. Newhouse Center for Law and Justice. Newhouse was the founder of a chain of newspapers and magazines and publisher of *The Star-Ledger*, New Jersey's largest newspaper.

The Second Presbyterian Church, within the Commons, was built in 1932 and is the third religious center on its site. The first went up in 1811 and was replaced by a brownstone in 1888. The present building is made from limestone and fieldstone and is dominated by a 110-foot tower and detailed stained-glass interior.

LINCOLN PARK HISTORIC DISTRICT

A 15-minute walk from the Commons down Broad Street is the city's second designated historic district—Lincoln Park. At Broad Street and Clinton

Right: Stunning townhouses, rich with architectural detail, line Spruce Street along Lincoln Park. Photo by Rich Zila

Facing page: Constructed in 1932, the Second Presbyterian Church features a magnificent tower that rises 110 feet into the air. Photo by Barry M. Winiker

Avenue, this more than four-acre park was laid out in 1850. Opposite it is Clinton Park, where stands a copy of the Colleoni equestrian statue, the original of which is in Venice.

Surrounding this oasis on the border of the business district are the sturdy brownstone mansions built in the mid-nineteenth century as the homes of the city's elite. Among these are the Dorothy Ball House at 103 Lincoln Avenue, the Community Center of the Arts at 89-95 Lincoln Park (occupying two former private dwellings and a carriage house), and a row of attractively renovated buildings run by Integrity House, from 37 up to 103 Lincoln Park.

INDIVIDUAL LANDMARKS

The Plume House at 407 Broad Street is a Dutch Colonial farmhouse built around 1710 and is believed to be one of the oldest buildings in Newark. The stone house, rich in lore about visits by Washington and his army, has served as the rectory of the House of Prayer since 1850. The Reverend Hannibal Goodwin invented flexible film—the basis for the motion picture industry—in an attic laboratory in 1887.

The city's oldest private home is the Sydenham House on the Old Road to Bloomfield. Built in 1712 as a gift for Susannah Sydenham, the daughter of Edward Hancock, the house was enlarged

four times through the 1700s, with the last structural change occurring about 1800. The house is regarded as a prime example of early American architecture of the salt-box type. The foundation and walls are of stone, principally sandstone, put in place without the use of cement or plaster.

The William Clark Mansion at 346 Mount Prospect Avenue is an imposing 28-room structure built in the 1870s at a cost of $200,000 by the founder of the Clark Thread Company in East Newark. It was billed as one of the handsomest homes in the country at the turn of the century. The interior is lavishly decorated in orangewood paneling and mantels, with a large stained-glass window and opulent ceiling. Guests are greeted by a giant staircase winding to the second floor.

The Krueger Mansion at 710 Martin Luther King, Jr., Boulevard (High Street) is considered the most expensive home ever built in Newark. The 40-room Baroque mansion was constructed in 1888-1889 at a cost of $250,000, an amount equal to several million dollars today. Gottfried Krueger, whose fortunes flowed from his Newark brewery, ensconced himself in his five-story tower with its thick, sweeping arches.

Newark's second Episcopal congregation was organized in 1837 as the Grace Episcopal Church. Its present building at 950 Broad Street held its first service in 1848. The English Gothic structure was

designed by Richard Upjohn and incorporated many splendid details. A hymn tune composed in 1882 by a Grace Church organist, Samuel A. Ward, is the widely sung melody of "America the Beautiful," with words by Katherine Lee Bates.

The distinctive twin towers and barrel-vaulted ceiling are the standout features of the nineteenth century Greek Revival-styled church at Broad Street and Lincoln Park dedicated in 1855. Owned by the Presbyterian Church, the building is now occupied by the Lighthouse Temple Church of Christ.

Newark was a Presbyterian community in 1826, barely tolerating Episcopalians and looking with profound Calvinist suspicion on the handful of Roman Catholics who had just organized their first New Jersey parish, St. John's, on Mulberry Street. Of stone and brick composition, set off by early English-style buttressing, St. John's had the distinction of having the first chimes installed in a city church in 1859. It was also the first Catholic church in the state to have a resident pastor.

Today, St. John's walls enclose part of the original structure, completed in 1828. Its proudest possession is the altar, carved with jeweler's hammer and penknife by an early pastor more than 150 years ago. For New Jersey Catholics, St. John's symbolizes the root of a mighty oak.

On September 4, 1854, the old Benedictine Church at Court and Howard streets was burned by rioters from the "Know Nothing" party, which preached a doctrine of "Protestant Native Americanism" and opposed immigrants and Catholics. A memento of the riot, a battered statue of the Virgin Mary, is still preserved in a glass case at St. Mary's Abbey Church on High Street. St. Mary's Abbey relocated to Morristown in 1956.

The first Benedictine came to Newark in 1838, leading to the establishment of St. Benedict's Preparatory School next to the abbey. The Benedictine Order was founded near Monte Cassino, Italy, about A.D. 526, by the hermit monk who became St. Benedict. The order was instrumental in colonizing and converting to Christianity the migrant Teuton nations and it became an integral part of German Catholicism in Newark.

The present rectory and abbey were dedicated in 1872. The abbey was founded as a monastery and priory. It took on abbey status in 1884 when Father James Zilliox became the first abbot. The Benedictine monks founded St. Benedict's Preparatory School in 1868. Although St. Benedict's received a college charter by a special act of the state legislature on March 25, 1881, it expanded so rapidly that it never was in a position to enter the field of higher education.

Christ Free Mission was the name given when Christ Episcopal Church held its first service on Feb-

Right: The English Gothic Grace Episcopal Church has been an active part of the Newark community since its first service was held in 1848. Photo by Rich Zila

Facing page: The elegant William Clark Mansion on Mount Prospect Avenue dates back to the 1870s. Photo by Rich Zila

The stately Essex County Court House, built between 1902 and 1907, is the result of the combined efforts of architect Cass Gilbert and sculptor Andrew O'Connor. Photo by Rich Zila

ruary 20, 1848. There was no building for nearly two years and parishioners alternately met in rooms at Grace and Trinity churches. The present structure was built in 1850 on Congress Street and enlarged in 1871.

An almost exact copy of the Royal Chapel at the Palace of Versailles in Paris, St. Columba's Church, near Lincoln Park, has changed little since its founding in 1871. It still serves Catholic immigrants, mostly Hispanic in recent years.

A graceful portico is the dominant feature of the French-styled edifice built to serve Irish immigrants. Originally, it was to have been the site of a cathedral in the Irish quarter of the city. Bishop Michael Corrigan laid the cornerstone for a cathedral chapel in 1869. But a modest wooden shelter arose instead, eventually giving way to the present Stockton graystone church in 1899. The church organ was purchased in 1901 from the First Presbyterian Church.

Many of Newark's worshippers worked at Murphy's varnish factory, whose protective veneer product was known around the world. Started in 1865, the factory grew to the size of two city blocks. The six buildings that comprised the Murphy Varnish Company were built during a 30-year period and embodied the architectural styles of the times: a two-story 1870s factory in the Italianate style, followed by Newark architect James Lindsey's build-

ings in the 1880s inspired by the Richardsonian Romanesque, then an 1890s Victorian Renaissance firehouse, and architect Howard Chapman's reinforced concrete factory. A carving of a Roman chariot carrying a can of Murphy varnish is the only architectural feature intact on the remaining building on the west side of McWhorter Street, near Vesey Street.

The New Jersey Historical Society, founded in 1845, occupies a three-story Georgian Colonial limestone and brick structure built in the 1930s. It houses the society's collections of books, pamphlets, paintings, furniture, and memorabilia about the Garden State.

In the core of the business district stands the 24-story, gleaming white marble Prudential Insurance Company tower. Opened in 1960, it is the headquarters of the world's largest insurance organization.

ESSEX COUNTY COURT HOUSE

The exterior of the Essex County Court House is 98 percent marble quarried in Berkshire County, Massachusetts. Designed in modern Renaissance style and embellished with neo-Classical touches, the seat of Essex County was the work of renowned architect Cass Gilbert and sculptor Andrew O'Connor. Together, they created the 180-foot-long, 160-foot-wide courthouse that rises 64 feet.

Built between 1902 and 1907 at a cost of

The exquisite bronze statue of Abraham Lincoln, created by sculptor Gutzon Borglum in 1911, is located in front of the Essex County Court House. Photo by Rich Zila

nearly $2 million, the courthouse is guarded by two bronze statues, *Truth* and *Power*. Over the main entrances, the words "Law," "Justice," and "Peace" are inscribed. Above them is the inscription, "Truth is the handmaiden of Justice." Above that, O'Connor's family of allegorical statues represents "The Power of Law," "The Reason of Law," "Statutory Law," "The Victory of Law," "The Shelter of Law," and "The Authority of Law." They are nearly eight feet high and are cut from 10-ton blocks.

Inside, a solemn rotunda rises three stories above the main floor. Two grand staircases ascend at either side, each covered with its own vaulting. On the four pendentives (supports for the dome) are life-sized paintings of four female allegorical figures painted by the mural artist Edwin Blashfield and representing Wisdom, Knowledge, Power, and Mercy.

The various courtrooms include an extraordinary collection of murals. Each room was designed by Gilbert to accent a different ancient architectural style. The paintings portray significant events in the history of Newark and Essex County, such as the landing of the Puritans on the banks of the Passaic River and the landing of Lord Carteret.

Seated on a bench in front of the courthouse is a bronze statue of Abraham Lincoln, executed by noted sculptor Gutzon Borglum and unveiled in 1911.

NEWARK CITY HALL

One of New Jersey's best examples of the Beaux Arts influence in American public architecture is Newark City Hall on Broad Street. Opened in 1906 at a cost of $2.5 million, the five-story domed structure features a central skylight flanked by columns and twin atriums, a magnificent staircase set off by the Great Rotunda, and an ornate municipal council chamber with historical murals.

Made of steel, bronze, and granite from New Hampshire and Italy, the city's seat of government stands 97 feet from its basement to the dome. It measures 240 by 140 feet, with ceilings ranging from 15 to 19 feet high on the various floors.

The Newark Preservation and Landmarks Committee describes the seat of city government thusly:

The flamboyance of the Beaux Arts is there in its fanciful Ionic capitals atop pilasters and engaged columns, in its abundant carvings and in its fluted Ionic columns which serve as lampposts as well as perches for bronze eagles. The interior is even more emphatically Beaux Arts with its Great Rotunda and grand staircase which call to mind the Paris Opera House. The arcade panels along the second story, frescoed with scenes important in the

Newark City Hall was designed in the elaborate and lively Beaux Arts style, featuring Ionic columns, elegant carvings, and frescoed murals. Photo by Rich Zila

The dominating focus of Newark Ciy Hall, which opened in 1906, is the stunning central skylight. Photo by Rich Zila

city's long history . . . the mayor's suite panelled with African mahogany, carries through the chair rails and transomed doors found throughout the office spaces in the building.

NEWARK SYMPHONY HALL

Newark Symphony Hall is New Jersey's largest and oldest showplace, attracting more than 200,000 patrons a year in the arts, education, and entertainment. Seating 2,825, the theater is bigger than Carnegie Hall, Lincoln Center's Metropolitan Opera House, or Philharmonic Hall in New York City.

Tests by Bell Laboratories in 1965 put Newark Symphony Hall's acoustics on a par with Boston's acclaimed Symphony Hall.

The Newark hall was built in 1925 at a cost of $2.2 million by the Ancient Order of the Nobles of the Mystic Shrine, a Masonic order commonly known as the Shriners. The theater in the temple was known as "The Mosque." It was a famous showcase for classical, jazz, and popular artists, from Judy Garland and George Gershwin to Arthur Rubenstein and Arturo Toscanini.

Originally called the Salaam Temple, the elegant edifice was designed by three architects—Frank Grad, Henry Baechlin, and George Backoff. The style they selected was Neo-Classic Revival. The design motifs are an eclectic mix, primarily inspired from Greek and Egyptian examples, with some Roman influence. The 70-foot stage is flanked by two huge baroque doorways, each framed by two wide, spiral-fluted Ionic columns supporting an elaborately ornamented and statued acroterion. The walls enclosing the orchestra are rimmed by arcades, which are surmounted by balconies with colonnades of Corinthian columns. Medallions grace the walls between the arches. The colonnade supports a full entablature, whose frieze is decorated with angelic figures separated by scrollwork and panels. Between the columns hang exquisite art nouveau-style chandeliers. From the center of the ceiling hangs the palatial, 3,000-crystal chandelier.

The friezes, capitals, and most inside ornamentation are gold-leafed, and the balustrades and columns are carved from white marble. With the lush red carpeting, the total effect is luxurious and agreeably opulent.

LANDMARKS COMMITTEE

The Newark Preservation and Landmarks Committee, founded in 1973, has rescued and restored a growing number of historic buildings and sites throughout the city. The 20-block James Street Commons Historic District became the first such preserved area in 1977, followed by the 10 blocks around Lincoln Park in 1983.

In 1986, the committee launched its most ambitious project: the creation of a 55-block historic district in the Forest Hill section of the North Ward. It was nominated as a National Historic District in 1988.

Between 1880 and 1925, many notable Newarkers built their fashionable residences in Forest Hill, exemplifying the full range of architectural design and degrees of opulence. Situated on a ridge amidst dense forestland, the hill area commanded an enviable view of New York City.

Forest Hill has retained its charm and desirability as a residential enclave with wide, tree-lined thoroughfares near Branch Brook Park.

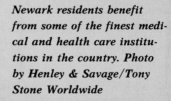

Newark residents benefit from some of the finest medical and health care institutions in the country. Photo by Henley & Savage/Tony Stone Worldwide

V

Health Care

The residents of Greater Newark are served by several of the nation's finest medical and health care facilities. More than a dozen major hospitals and medical centers are situated within the Greater Newark area, including six within the city itself.

UMDNJ

UMDNJ are the familiar call-for-help letters that spell out the largest free-standing health sciences university in the United States—the University of Medicine & Dentistry of New Jersey. Unlike most medical universities in America, UMDNJ's free-standing status allows it to function unattached to another university.

The university, which comprises six health sciences schools, occupies campuses overlooking the downtown business district, Piscataway-New Brunswick, and Camden-Stratford in South Jersey. The institution is unique for being the only one of its kind in the U.S. that educates D.O. (doctors of osteopathic medicine) students and M.D. students in the same classes.

With its schools, four core teaching hospitals, two mental health centers, and a network of 128 affiliated education and health institutions in 19 of New Jersey's 21 counties, UMDNJ touches the life of every New Jersey city, according to Board Chairman Herbert A. Roemmele.

UMDNJ's schools enroll some 3,000 students in medical, dental, and allied health programs, 90 percent of whom are New Jersey residents. Another 1,100 study in 53 medical and dental residency programs sponsored by the university. More than 8,100 health professionals have graduated from UMDNJ's schools, and half of those now practice in the Garden State.

With 5,800 employees and a total annual payroll of $135 million, UMDNJ's Newark campus is one of the city's largest employers.

University Hospital, UMDNJ's Newark-based teaching hospital, is a pacesetter in New Jersey in several medical specialities, including neurology and neurosurgery, cancer, liver disease,

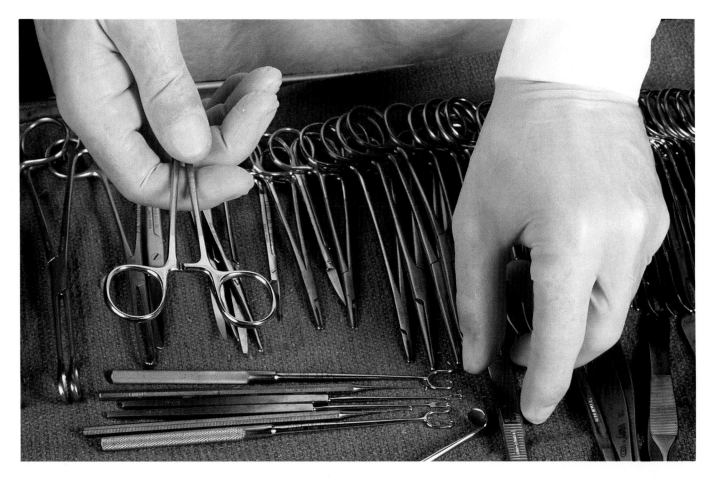

Above: General surgery plays a major role in the services of Newark's many hospitals. Photo by Pete Saloutos/Tony Stone Worldwide

Right: University Hospital is the central teaching facility for the University of Medicine and Dentistry of New Jersey. Photo by Rich Zila

Facing page bottom: The Martland Building is just one of the many facilities that comprise the University of Medicine and Dentistry of New Jersey. Photo by Carol Kitman

reproductive medicine, and cystic fibrosis. The hospital records more than 100,000 outpatient visits and 17,000 admissions annually.

Nearly 100,000 patients each year are admitted to University Hospital and the university's three other core affiliates—Robert Wood Johnson University Hospital in New Brunswick, Cooper Hospital/University Medical Center in Camden, and Kennedy Memorial Hospitals/University Medical Center in Stratford, South Jersey.

Emergency and outpatient services register half a million visits annually at these hospitals. Through university-operated ambulance services in Newark and Camden, UMDNJ emergency medical

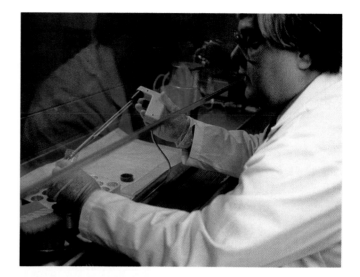

Above: One of the nation's leading centers for research into Acquired Immune Deficiency Syndrome (AIDS) is the University of Medicine and Dentistry of New Jersey (UMDNJ) Medical School, with more than $30 million in federally-funded projects underway. Dr. James Oleske, one of the first researchers in the country to identify AIDS in children, focuses his studies on the means by which pregnant women with AIDS transmit the virus to their babies. Courtesy, University of Medicine and Dentistry of New Jersey

technicians respond to some 100,000 calls a year.

UMDNJ's two community mental health centers, which are among only a handful of centers in the nation with university affiliations and accreditation by the Joint Commission of Accreditation of Health Care Organizations, offer the state's residents exceptional quality care. The Community Mental Health Center in Newark accommodates 4,000 clients with 40,000 visits each year, while the Piscataway facility on the Rutgers University campus receives 4,000 clients with 55,000 visits each year.

With a 1988 funding level of $37 million in sponsored research programs, UMDNJ has attracted more than $200 million in grants and contracts to New Jersey since its inception.

Under the leadership of President Dr. Stanley S. Bergen, Jr., UMDNJ has expanded and improved upon its extensive medical programs and activities since its founding by an act of the state legislature in 1970.

The university's goal, with the support of New Jersey Governor Thomas H. Kean, is to make UMDNJ one of the top 25 academic health science universities in America. With 19 breakthrough patents for new technological advancements, UMDNJ is off to an auspicious start. Among the University's accomplishments up to 1988 are:

• Center for Advanced Biotechnology and Medicine. A developing world-class research institute with a growing staff of noted scientists conducting investigations into such areas as molecular genetics, molecular pharmacology, structural biology, and cell and development biology. Based in Piscataway, it is a joint venture with Rutgers-The State University.

• Environmental and Occupational Health Sciences Institute, New Jersey's developing center for the study of environmental and occupational health issues. The institute's three-pronged focus involves educational programs for health care professionals, research into environmental health problems, and monitoring hazardous waste workers and environmental conditions in the state. Based in Piscataway, EOHSI is a joint project with Rutgers-The State University.

Today's state-of-the-art health care services range from laser surgery and artificial implants to trauma care and preventative medicine. Photo by Diana Rasche/Tony Stone Worldwide

• Sammy Davis, Jr., National Liver Institute. With the support of the world-renowned entertainer, UMDNJ is building its noted liver unit into a major national center for the study and treatment of liver and related diseases. In 1988, the state's first liver transplantation facility opened at University Hospital in conjunction with the Newark-based Liver Institute.

• Dental Research Center. Opened in May 1988 at the Newark campus, this state-of-the-art facility is directed by biochemist Dr. Bronislaw Slomiany. He and his nationally renowned dental research team specialize in the study of salivary glands and gastrointestinal secretions.

• Sickle-cell Anemia. One of the nation's first institutions to offer a prenatal test for detecting sickle cell anemia. The diagnostic procedure is one of the first made possible through recombinant DNA technology.

• Parkinson's look-alike. Some individuals, mistakenly diagnosed as having Parkinson's disease, actually are victims of a nervous disorder that mirrors Parkinson's. The discovery was made by

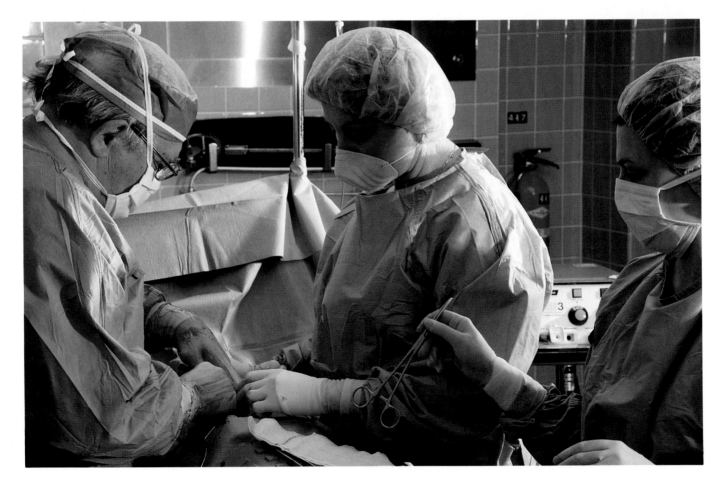

Dr. Roger Duvoisin, a UMDNJ neurologist known for his role in the development of L-dopa, a drug used to control the involuntary symptoms of Parkinson's disease.

● Diagnosing heart disease. A painless technique for diagnosing heart disease was developed by a UMDNJ cardiovascular specialist working with a team of engineers at Rutgers University. The key to the procedure is a computerized electronic monitoring system that amplifies and analyzes the sound of blood flowing through coronary arteries. The procedure was refined at the university's Piscataway campus in 1982.

● Protecting artificial implants. Death from infection is the most significant problem associated with artificial implants such as heart valves and arteries. UMDNJ researchers discovered that synthetic replacements can be protected if bonded with antibiotics before being implanted.

● Bone marrow infection. University researchers found two new drugs—one a penicillin derivative—effective in treating bone marrow infection in laboratory animals. The bacteria responsible for such infection gradually has become resistant to regular antibiotic treatment.

● Lasers and glaucoma. A University ophthalmologist, one of the New Jersey's laser surgery pioneers, adapted laser technology to treat the most common form of glaucoma, known as open angle glaucoma.

● Diabetes and exercises. Another UMDNJ researcher found that a regular program of physical training among males who became diabetic as adults can reduce some of the risk factors that make them susceptible to premature atherosclerosis, a disease of the arteries that can lead to heart disease. The findings led to a first-of-a-kind program in the state several years ago, offering diabetics an intensive exercise and education regimen aimed at improving health and self-care.

● Laser acupuncture. The University Pain Center is developing laser acupuncture to alleviate pain.

● Urodynamics Laboratory. The first facility of its kind in New Jersey to offer a complete spectrum of testing for bladder muscle and nerve abnormalities.

● New Jersey Regional Comprehensive Hemophilia Care. One of the nation's largest, the Hemophilia Care Program is available under the auspices of the UMDNJ-Robert Wood Johnson Medical School at two primary centers: Robert Wood Johnson University Hospital in New Brunswick, and St. Michael's Medical Center, Newark. Comprehensive, multidisciplinary care is provided to patients suffering from bleeding disorders.

● Connections. UMDNJ is rebuilding ligaments and tendons with a patented carbon fiber material.

● The Neville tube. This prosthetic trachea is saving lives around the world by creating a new air pas-

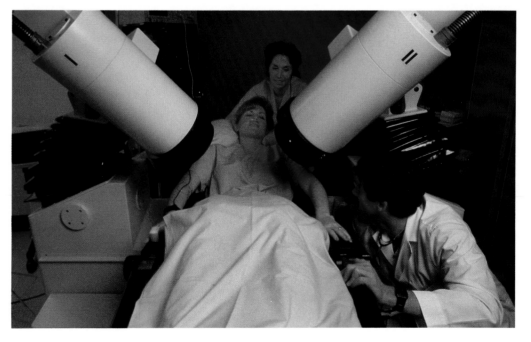

The Stone Center of New Jersey, at the University of Medicine and Dentistry of New Jersey (UMDNJ) University Hospital in Newark, is equipped with the most advanced lithotripter available in the United States. Since its opening in 1988, the center has treated more than 400 patients for kidney stones without surgery. Courtesy, University of Medicine and Dentistry of New Jersey

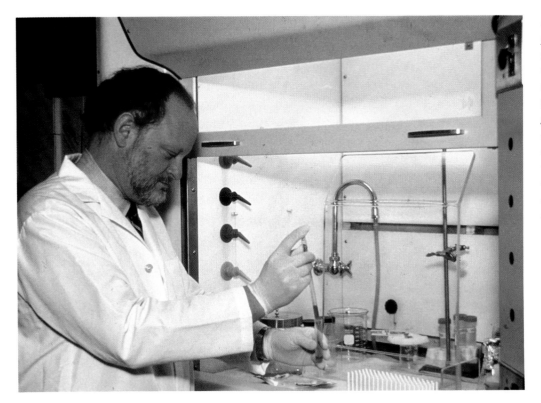

University Hospital's Center for Fertility and Reproductive Medicine, headed by Dr. Gerson Weiss, offers one of the nation's most advanced in vitro fertilization programs. Dr. Weiss' team has achieved successful pregnancies from donated eggs as well as from frozen embryos. Courtesy, University of Medicine and Dentistry of New Jersey

sage for the lungs.

• The New Jersey larynx. This device was developed by the medical center for victims of throat cancer and other severe illnesses who otherwise would not be able to vocalize again.

• Radioactive antibodies. UMDNJ established a high technology center in Newark involving the use of radioactive antibodies to seek and destroy cancer cells.

UMDNJ-UNIVERSITY HOSPITAL

A 518-bed teaching facility for the New Jersey Medical School, University Hospital is located on the 63-acre Newark campus of UMDNJ. The hospital is the center of referral for many of the state's newest and most advanced medical services and specialized programs made possible by the teaching and research environment of the university. At the same time, the hospital is the major source of primary care in the immediate community, acting as the "family physician" to thousands of men, women, and children who have no other means of medical treatment. University Hospital's commitment to medical education, primary care, and specialized referral services has produced the most extensive array of inpatient and outpatient services available in New Jersey.

Each year, University Hospital registers some 17,000 admissions, 2,200 births, 54,000 emergency room visits and 100,000 outpatient visits. A large part of this utilization is attributable to the hospital's multidisciplinary centers of excellence programs and services that provide unique levels of care to patients from the local community, from every county in New Jersey, from several states, and from throughout the world.

Notable programs and facilities include:

• The New Jersey State Trauma Center. In recognition of University Hospital's expertise in treating all forms of trauma on an immediate basis, the New Jersey Department of Health designated the Newark Center as the Level I Trauma Center in northern New Jersey. Serving a region of nearly 6 million people, the Trauma Center provides an unparalleled level of on-site emergency treatment, including a limb replantation surgical team. Accessiblity to the Trauma Center's life-saving services was greatly enhanced when the hospital initiated its emergency medical helicopter transport program in conjunction with the New Jersey State Police in late 1988.

• The New Jersey Cancer Center. Established in 1985, the hospital's center provides a focal point for the clinical and research activities in cancer conducted throughout University Hospital and the New Jersey Medical School. The center prides itself on providing an organized, single-site, multidisciplinary system of cancer prevention, detection, and treatment, which includes radiation therapy programs and participation in experimental drug studies.

• The Center For Fertility and Reproductive Medicine. Through the diagnostic and treatment services offered by the center, couples who have previously been thought of as hopelessly infertile now have an excellent chance of conceiving and carrying a child. Taking the still new procedure of *in vitro* fertilization one step further, the center has begun a donated-ovum program, in which a donated egg is fertilized by the male partner's sperm and is then implanted in the female partner's uterus to be carried to term. This program provides hope to women who do not produce their own eggs and therefore could never hope to give birth. Research utilizing new drugs and techniques to maximize success is undertaken at the center.

• The Statewide Perinatal Services and Re-

search Center. In conjunction with Children's Hospital of New Jersey, also in Newark, University Hospital has been designated as a Level III Perinatal Center, a regional resource for the most sophisticated services for high-risk pregnancies and newborns. Thanks to the specialized care of the Perinatal Center, babies with birth weights of as little as one-and-one-half pounds are now thriving.

• The Stone Center of New Jersey. This state-of-the-art facility is equipped with a $2-million lithotripsy system that utilizes shock waves to crush kindey stones without resorting to painful and expensive surgery. This project is a joint venture with UMDNJ and St. Barnabas Medical Center in Livingston.

These programs and others, including sports medicine and orthopedics, neurology and neuro-

An EKG technician talks with a patient in the intensive care unit. Photo by Diana Rasche/Tony Stone Worldwide

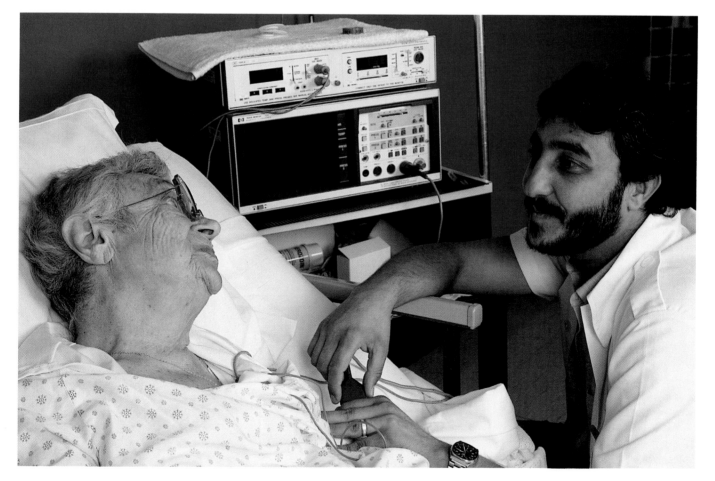

surgery, and pain management and spinal cord injuries, provide New Jersey residents with the most advanced medical care available anywhere. The research facilities, innovations in technology, and levels of care at University Hospital equal or exceed those found at other university medical centers throughout the United States.

CATHEDRAL HEALTHCARE SYSTEM

In 1987, the Health Corporation of the Archdiocese of Newark was renamed the Cathedral Healthcare System to reflect its association with Sacred Heart Cathedral.

The system is comprised of St. Michael's Medical Center, located right on the rim of the academic-commercial district; St. James Hospital in the multi-ethnic Ironbound community behind the Penn Station transportation hub; and St. Mary's Hospital in nearby Orange, serving many patients in Newark. With 2,500 employees, Cathedral Healthcare is one of the city's largest employers.

In 1988, Cathedral Healthcare opened a health and fitness center in the lobby of Gateway One, a modern commercial complex opposite Penn Station that employs more than 12,000. It is a model for health promotion by encouraging exercise and a healthy lifestyle.

The archdiocese, through its Catholic Community Services, also operates The Inpatient Pavillion of The Mount Carmel Guild on Mulberry Street. This hospital maintains a 20-bed, short-term evaluation and crisis stabilization psychiatric unit. It is geared to individualized treatment planning, team case review, and supervised milieu therapy. One unit offers safe medical detoxification of opiates, sedatives, hypnotics, and alcohol for users 16 years of age or older. The maximum stay is three weeks. Another unit offers a comprehensive treatment for patients with a wide range of psychiatric problems, and supervised by a 24-hour nursing staff. The maximum possible stay in this unit is three to four weeks.

St. Michael's Medical Center was founded in 1867 as a 13-bed health care facility, and has become one of the leading centers of health treatment in New Jersey and the Northeast. St. Michael's today has 411 licensed beds, 2,000 employees, and the very latest technological apparatus and medicines. It was the first hospital in the state to open a cardiac clinic (1937) for treatment of heart patients by medical means.

In 1949, St. Michael's established the nation's first cardiac catheterization laboratory in a community hospital. That same year, Dr. Charles P. Bailey performed the first operation on a diseased heart valve. In 1959, surgeons at St. Michael's performed the first open heart operation in New Jersey.

The first stroke unit in a community hospital

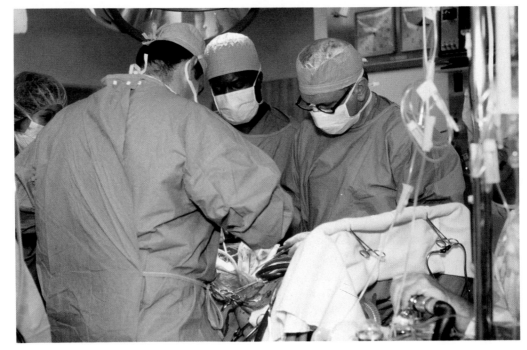

The cardiac care program at Saint Michael's Medical Center has been consistently recognized and highly respected for more than 40 years. While many open-heart operations are performed, so too are many non-surgical procedures, including cardiac catheterization, balloon angioplasty, and valvuloplasty. Courtesy, Saint Michael's Medical Center

was opened in 1966 under the direction of full-time psychiatrists. In 1975, the state designated St. Michael's as a regional center for cardiovascular surgery. A year later, New Jersey's first immunology and virology laboratories opened at St. Michael's.

The hospital remains a highly respected referral and teaching medical center, with tertiary care services in hematology, cardiology, and infectious disease. St. Michael's is the site of one of the state's two hemophilia care centers, and is a statewide referral and research center for clotting disorders and other blood-related problems.

Its infectious disease program has an international reputation and is known for its numerous clinical trials for antibiotics. St. Michael's patients have access to the latest, most promising drugs before they are available to the general public. Its professional and humane care of AIDS victims has been a hallmark of the infectious disease service since the advent of the deadly virus in the early 1980s.

St. Michael's various teaching affiliations link it with UMDNJ, Rutgers University, Seton Hall University, and many other institutions of higher education in Newark and throughout New Jersey.

In 1988, St. Michael's became a major teaching affiliate of the New England College of Osteopathic Medicine and added an osteopathic intern rotation to its medical education program.

Some 20,000 area residents also avail themselves of St. Michael's impressive list of outpatient clinic services. Clinics cover general medicine, pediatric and maternity care, and such specialty services as podiatry, chest diseases, gynecology, orthopedics, neurology, rheumatology, cardiology, and infectious diseases.

The 400 members of St. Michael's medical staff are primarily located in Essex, Hudson, Middlesex, Passaic, and Union counties in northern and central New Jersey.

Since 1900, St. James Hospital has proven extremely flexible in serving the needs of a changing community. It shares the stability and devotion to family, work, and neighborhood that characterizes its multi-ethnic community in the city's Ironbound district. Trilingual literature, a trilingual guest relations program, and a proactive community relations department ensure that St. James serves the

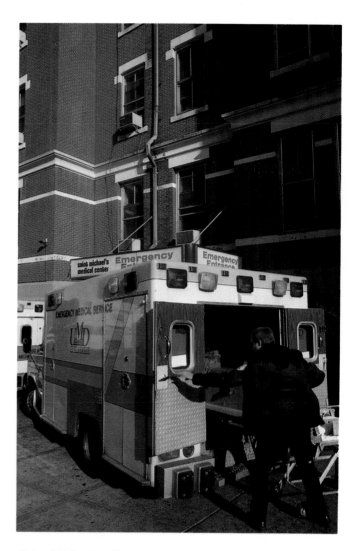

Saint Michael's offers emergency medical care. Photo by Carol Kitman

Above: The Beth Israel Medical Center is at the forefront of modern health care. Photo by Rich Zila

Top right: A nurse checks her young patient in preparation for release from the hospital. Photo by Charles Gupton/ Tony Stone Worldwide

Facing page: Because of the department's highly developed laboratory facilities and research orientation, Saint Michael's infectious disease research program is often used to test drugs before other hospitals. Here, Dr. Ed Johnson and Dr. George Perez are shown at work. Courtesy, Saint Michael's Medical Center

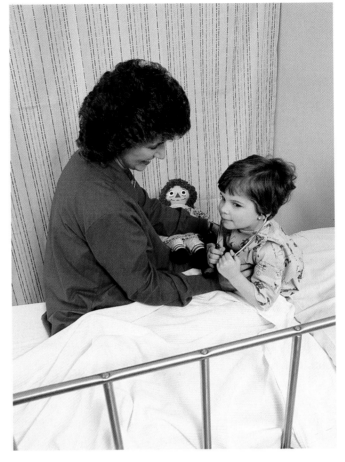

special needs of the Portuguese and Spanish families in the Ironbound.

St. James' emergency department plays a significant role in the vitality of the heavily industrialized community, which, with a population of 50,000, could be a major New Jersey city by itself.

Some 16,000 people were treated in the emergency room in 1988 and about 9,000 were treated as inpatients. Shaping its facilities to the area's special needs, St. James offers an occupational health services program, a maternity clinic, and outpatient diagnostic services. St. James today has 206 beds, 200 physicians, and a staff of 600 medical, technical and support personnel.

St. Mary's Hospital, founded in 1906 in Orange, is a voluntary community hospital of 202 beds with 600 employees, 150 volunteer workers, and a medical staff of 290 physicians.

Each year St. Mary's serves approximately 7,000 inpatients and 18,000 outpatients from Newark and the Oranges, with more than half from neighboring towns from the Caldwells and Livingston to Short Hills and Verona.

St. Mary's particular strengths are in gastroenterology, orthopedics, vascular surgery, and general surgery. Its computerized laboratory is among the most advanced in the state.

A staff led by the Felician Sisters of nearby Lodi, Bergen County, the hospital personnel are busy providing services in a same-day surgery unit, a minor surgery suite, a main surgical suite featuring athroscopic, laser, and microsurgery techniques, an oncology unit, telemetry unit, radiology department with ultrasound mammography and CAT scanner, a nuclear medicine department, a laser center, a cardiac laboratory with stress testing and echocardiography equipment, a specialized laboratory for sickle-cell anemia, Cooley's anemia, and drug testing, a physical therapy department with Cybex rehabilitation and testing equipment, a pain management center, and two in-house television channels for patient and staff education.

St. Mary's also provides a number of community services, among them an award-winning television series, "Healthscope," which is cablecast throughout New Jersey, and maintains a working relationship with the New Jersey Department of Health whereby St. Mary's serves as a training site for substance-abuse counselors, for courses in CPR and diabetes control, and a breast cancer screening program in cooperation with the American Cancer Society. St. Mary's has an arrangement with the Tri-State Ambulance Company through which the City of Orange is provided with ambulance service.

The hospital also participates in the training of nurses from Rutgers University, Seton Hall University, Felician College, and Essex County Community College.

BETH ISRAEL MEDICAL CENTER

In its nearly 90-year history, Beth Israel has been responsible for many New Jersey medical "firsts,"
including the implantation of the first American-made nuclear-powered pacemakers and the first liver-kidney transplant, performed in 1968.

Beth Israel was also the first hospital in the state to perform special radioimmunoassay procedures in its endocrine laboratory, thus laying the groundwork for the hospital to become a "core" laboratory for special endocrine procedures involving the analyses of tissue samples.

Beth Israel was one of the nation's first blood banks, established in 1937.

A dynamic health community of 2,300 specialists and staff working in a 545-bed medical center, Beth Israel today performs around 80,000 diagnostic radiologic examinations a year, nearly 20,000 of which are emergency room procedures.

More than 6,500 kidney transplants and 10,000 open-heart operations have been performed at the renowned medical center. Beth Israel ranks in the top 5 percent of the nation in the number of open-heart surgeries performed annually.

Beth Israel rarely uses freshly drawn whole blood, preferring to meet the needs of open-heart surgery by using blood components entirely. The hospital's "washing machines" were responsible for more than 27,000 blood-cleaning treatments for hemodialysis-dependent patients in 1988.

The hospital performs more than 86,000 diagnostic radiologic examinations a year, nearly 16,200 of which are emergency room procedures.

Beth Israel and Deborah Hospital in South Jersey are the only two state-designated Tertiary Care Cardiac Centers at the present time. The Beth Israel Center is doing more than 3,000 cardiac catheterizations and about 1,100 open-heart cases a year.

Beth Israel has built a reputation on specialized services, four of which best typify the kind of hi-tech medical equipment available at the Newark center:

• The Flo Okin Oncology Center. Long a leader in cancer treatment and research, Beth Israel offers this multidisciplinary oncology center, housing the treatment and administrative areas for medical, surgical, and radiation oncology under one roof.

The oncology division handles more than 3,000 active cancer patients and adds approximately 1,100 new patients a year. When the division was created in 1970, it was the only fully operational oncology service of its kind in New Jersey. The staff works with clinical research groups at Memorial Sloan-Kettering Cancer Center and Mount Sinai Hospital, as well as the National Cancer Institute.

In addition, vibrant colors, exciting lighting treatment, exquisite woven graphics, and a tree-filled atrium have been thoughtfully provided for those who, in a time of illness, become more sensitive to aesthetics.

• Renal Treatment Center. Renal medicine has been at the forefront of the multitude of special services provided by Beth Israel since 1963, when the first acute dialysis treatment in the state was performed there. The renal center offers a complete range of services, including inpatient and outpatient dialysis, home dialysis training, pediatric hemodialysis, and an inpatient nursing unit for renal patients. Organ procurement and research and educational activities are constantly being accelerated.

• The Ruth Gottscho Kidney Foundation's "Operation Lifeline" provides an organ procurement telephone hotline. The Gottscho Foundation also set up New Jersey's first children's dialysis unit in 1973 at "The Beth."

• The Nuclear Medicine Center. The diagnostic core of the Nuclear Medicine Center enables exploration into areas of nuclear radiation that had been formerly unavailable. There are now three cameras (including a portable camera), a stationary computer, and a portable nuclear medicine computer which allows the staff to do comparison studies at bedside and provide computerized images in color. Active clinical research in nuclear cardiology and in the evaluation of new pacemakers powered by radioisotopes is being pursued, as is the daily use of another isotope that seeks out working muscles.

• The Radium Therapy Center. A vital component in the expanded, multidiscipline Oncology Center is the radiation therapy facility, which features a megavoltage linear accelerator. With it, more than 7,600 procedures were performed in one year. The cost of the acclerator was assumed by the Auxiliary, the only major fund-raising arm of the medical center.

UNITED HOSPITALS MEDICAL CENTER

UH Medical Center is a unique 429-bed teaching hospital formed in 1959 when the following four Newark hospitals merged to achieve greater levels of excellence and efficiency:

• Presbyterian Hospital, founded in 1909, forms the cornerstone of today's UH Medical Center. Presbterian Hospital has become the community's "family doctor" and the provider of essential medical services. Because there are fewer physicians in private practice, more city residents are seeking primary care at Presbyterian than ever before, availing themselves of a highly sophisticated health care system providing quality medical care where the people live.

• Children's Hospital of New Jersey is essentially a "hospital within a hospital." Founded as Babies Hospital in 1894, the Children's Hospital is now a complete diagnostic and treatment center for infants, children, and adolescents. This 135-bed unit provides the most comprehensive pediatric services in New Jersey and offers subspecialty programs in all major pediatric disciplines, including cardiovascular surgery, newborn intensive care, and hematology/oncology. The Children's Hospital serves as the major teaching site for the department of pediatrics at the UMDNJ. As a statewide resource center for children with complex illnesses, Children's Hospital has outgrown its current facilities and plans to build a new free-standing facility on the UMDNJ campus. The new center will continue to provide New Jersey with superior programs in pediatric medicine, teaching, and research.

• United Hospitals Orthopedic Center was founded in 1892 as Crippled Children's Hospital. Today, this unit provides comprehensive orthopedic care to adults and children from throughout the state. The center provides a unique environment for diagnosing and treating a wide range of musculoskeletal problems, including joint reconstruction and replacement. The center also serves as the major orthopedic teaching hospital for UMDNJ and offers highly specialized services for arthritis, scoliosis, muscular dystrophy, and sports medicine.

• The Newark Eye and Ear Infirmary, founded in 1880, and the Eye Institute of New Jersey, established in 1970, are committed to the preservation and restoration of sight, sound, and speech. As the only such specialty facilities in the state, the Eye and Ear Infirmary and the Eye Institute serve as the major teaching sites for UMDNJ's departments of ophthalmology and otolaryngology. These units utilize the latest technologies to diagnose and treat disorders of the eyes, ears, nose, and throat.

COLUMBUS HOSPITAL

Since its beginning in 1934, Columbus Hospital has served the densely populated northern corner of Newark and its neighbors in Bloomfield, Belleville, and East Orange.

Founded by a small group of Italian-American business and professional men, Columbus Hospital opened with 45 beds and expanded to the present 206-bed capacity. The non-profit community hospital is licensed and accredited by the state to provide general care for medical, surgical, orthopedic, obstetric, and pediatric patients.

The outpatient department offers a full range of medical services at low cost for those without a private physician. In addition to a new low-dose film screen mammography installed in the radiology department, there are nine outpatient clinics: diabetic, medical, ob/gyn, pediatric, urology, prenatal, podiatry, pulmonary, and surgical. At the heart of the activities at Columbus Hospital is its 15-bed combined intensive/coronary care unit. State-of-the-art equipment is readily available at each patient's bedside for cardiac monitoring with a central computerized station located at the nursing desk.

A 16-bed telemetry unit serves as a "stepdown" for patients transferred from Intensive Care. The cardiac status of every patient on the telemetry system is monitored 24 hours a day through a central station manned by telemetry technicians.

Cardiac patients also have access to the latest advances in medical technology, including a color-flow doppler echocardiography unit that does

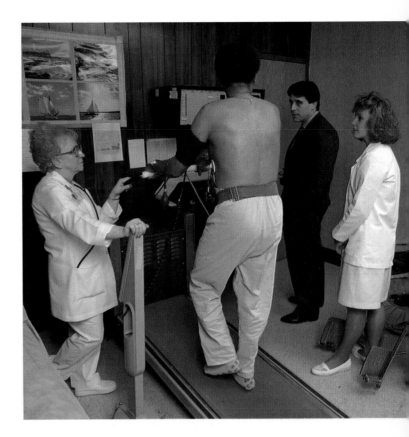

A cardiology patient undergoes a stress test at Columbus Hospital in Newark. Courtesy, Columbus Hospital

non-invasive testing to track ventricular outflow. Preventive medicine is accomplished through health fairs, free health screenings, and literature promoting physical fitness and general well-being.

GREATER NEWARK

Beyond the city proper are several major medical institutions, including Clara Maas Hospital, which began in Newark and relocated to Belleville, Montclair Community Hospital, Overlook Hospital in Summit, East Orange General Hospital, The Hospital Center at Orange, the Kessler Institute in East and West Orange, and St. Barnabas Medical Center in Livingston, the largest medical facility in New Jersey.

Students take a break between classes at the New Jersey Institute of Technology. Courtesy, Gordon B. Bishop

VI
Education

By 1713, more than a half-century before the American Revolution, Newark's first schoolhouse was preparing the children of the small village in language, mathematics, the arts, and the basic skills needed for a challenging and fulfilling life.

The first commencement of the College of New Jersey—later renamed Princeton University—took place on November 9, 1748, in Newark. The prestigious school moved to Princeton in 1756 and secretly served as the nation's capital during the Revolutionary War. The new colonial government met in the university's Nassau Hall.

The Newark Academy was founded in 1774, and the first free vocational school in the United States was started in 1794 by Moses N. Combs, the father of Newark's shoemaking industry.

Within those eight decades, Newark had laid an enduring foundation for one of the most progressive and academically advanced educational systems in the New World, where learning and faith were the hallmarks of an enlightened society.

New Jersey's first—and the nation's third—high school was opened in 1838. Newark's population had then grown to more than 18,000.

Newark High School—later Barringer High, named after the city's first school superintendent—became the beloved academic breeding ground of scholars, statesmen, doctors, star athletes, and many other distinguished alumni, among them U.S. Supreme Court Chief Justice and presidential candidate Charles Evans Hughes (1862-1948), New Jersey Supreme Court Chief Justice Arthur Vanderbilt (1888-1957), composer Jerome Kern (1885-1945), U.S. Supreme Court Justice William Brennan, former Newark Congressman Peter Rodino, who presided over the Watergate hearings as chairman of the House Judiciary Committee, and retired New Jersey Chief Justice Joseph Weintraub.

That tradition of excellence continues today with Newark's Arts High, Science High, University High, the Newark School of Fine and Industrial Art, St. Benedict's Prep, the New Jersey Institute of Technology, Rutgers University, Seton Hall University,

Above: The New Jersey Institute of Technology (NJIT) is currently expanding its resources with the construction of new laboratories, research facilities, and technology centers on its 36-acre campus. Photo by Rich Zila

Facing page top: Nearly 8,000 students attend the New Jersey Institute of Technology, one of the country's leading engineering and technical schools. Courtesy, Gordon B. Bishop

Facing page bottom: Newark offers a strong educational environment, promoting a wide spectrum of learning opportunities from the fine arts to the study of criminal justice. Photo by Bob Krist

Essex County College, the Newark Community School of the Arts, the Ironbound Educational & Cultural Center, and the University of Medicine & Dentistry of New Jersey.

NEW JERSEY INSTITUTE OF TECHNOLOGY

In 1881, the Newark Board of Trade decided the city needed its own technical school to serve a booming manufacturing industry. The Newark Technical School evolved into one of the best engineering schools in the country, constantly expanding its horizons from the Newark College of Engineering (NCE) to the New Jersey Institute of Technology.

Graduates of the New Jersey Institute of Technology (NJIT) hold impressive technological and managerial positions in all 50 states. In New Jersey alone, more than 25 percent of engineers are graduates of NJIT.

With a current enrollment exceeding 7,700, of which one-third are graduate students, NJIT offers a rich diversity of training, including architecture, engineering, computer science, actuarial science, management, mathematics, science, and the humanities.

Since computers now play a critical role in the fields of engineering, design, and manufacturing, students of the New Jersey Institute of Technology have access to more than $6 million of donated equipment, providing them with the training of competitive skills. Courtesy, Gordon B. Bishop

Each incoming freshman is provided—free of charge—with the components to build his or her own personal computer (PC) in a supervised setting. NJIT is one of the few institutions of higher learning in the nation to provide students with their own PCs. The "build your own" PC is unique to NJIT.

New Jersey's premier technical institute has taken the lead in offering programs in the emerging fields of computer-integrated design and manufacturing, bioengineering, biotechnology, hazardous and toxic substances management, microelectronics, and computerized communications.

NJIT is the home of two advanced technology centers of the New Jersey Commission on Science and Technology—the national hazardous substances management center and the computerized manufacturing systems center.

Approximately one quarter million square feet of new facilities to house these and other research centers and laboratories are under construction on NJIT's 36-acre campus within the city's expanding educational community. The structures are part of a $100-million expansion program.

NJIT, under the visionary direction of its energetic president, Dr. Saul K. Fenster, is committing its significant human and institutional resources to-

ward strengthening the community. Its pre-college programs for inner city youth have become a model for national emulation. Through its involvement in the Newark Collaboration Group and, in particular, University Heights, NJIT is helping to keep Newark in the vangard of America's urban renaissance.

Just as Thomas Edison chose Newark as the place to incubate his ideas and launch his patented inventions, NJIT today is preparing itself to be the "Factory of the Future."

InfoTech—the Information Technologies Building—brings under a single roof NJIT's expertise and equipment in manufacturing and information sciences. InfoTech's mission is advancing the frontier of knowledge through research, fostering further integration across disciplines, stimulating industry-university interaction, and facilitating the transfer of new technologies to the marketplace. Newark's Edisonian "Factory of the Future" will provide unprecedented opportunities for education, research, and development in manufacturing.

This futuristic factory consists of a CAD/CAM-Robotics Consortium supported by Public Service Electric & Gas Co., Singer-Kearfott, Westinghouse Electric, and AT&T. Its concern is increasing productivity through factory automation and

Students conduct an experiment at the New Jersey Institute of Technology. Courtesy, Gordon B. Bishop

computer-assisted design. More than $6-million worth of hardware, software, and equipment in advanced manufacturing has been donated by McDonnell Douglas, Mentor Graphics, Calma-GE, Convergent Technologies, Auto-Trol, AT&T, Westinghouse, Ingersoll Rand, and Digital Equipment Corporation.

The Center for Microwave and Lightwave Engineering was established in 1986 to foster curriculum development and research in the millimeter and microwave areas of optoelectronics. Prominent scientists from industry and government serve on the board of advisors.

The Technology Extension Center (TEX) in Information Services was established under a grant awarded by the New Jersey Commission on Science and Technology. The center is an outgrowth of NJIT's successful Center for Information Age Technology. The TEX Center helps small- and medium-sized businesses and organizations in New Jersey develop their capabilities to apply information technology.

As part of NJIT's "Science, Technology, and Society" initiative, the university has established the Center for Technology Studies, which in its first year concentrated on fostering programs in technology literacy and science in schools and colleges. The center is also developing a series of presentations on ethics and technology.

NJIT is not only a bastion of science and technology, but it has earned a well-deserved reputation as a patron of the arts. The nation's first—and still only—Literary Hall of Fame was organized at NJIT in 1976, honoring prominent New Jersey authors from Walt Whitman and Stephen Crane to William Carlos Williams and Robert Ludlum.

New Jersey elementary, junior high, and high school students are also honored at NJIT's annual poetry and writing competition. The Van Houten library theater has also been the showcase for the world premiere of the black musical, *CRISPUS*, the historic saga of Crispus Attucks, the first native son (half American Indian, half black) killed in the American Revolution, at the Boston massacre. The musical was staged by New Jersey's oldest black theater, the Newark-based Theater of Universal Images. NJIT has also hosted "Ballet-O-Mania," a series of four free dance performances given by the Garden State Ballet for the school and the community.

RUTGERS-NEWARK

The Newark campus of Rutgers-The State University accounts for 20 percent of the nation's eighth-oldest institution of higher learning, founded in 1766 as Queen's College.

Of Rutgers' 48,000 students, some 10,000 are registered in the seven schools at the Newark campus: Newark College of Arts and Sciences, the College of Nursing, University College, the Graduate School, the Graduate School of Management, the School of Law, and the School of Criminal Justice.

Campus resources include special divisions such as the Institute of Animal Behavior and the Institute of Jazz Studies. A new $11-million Center for Molecular and Behavorial Neurosciences opened in 1989. A 350-bed housing facility for nursing and graduate students opened its doors in 1987.

Rutgers' nearly 10,000 graduate and undergraduate students is the highest number of enrollees of the four institutions of higher learning in Newark. NJIT follows with nearly 8,000, with the newest addition to the academic community—Essex County College—at approximately 6,000 students. UMDNJ has 1,200 students, and Seton Hall Law School, 1,300.

Rutgers-Newark traces its origins to the New Jer-

Right: The Paul Robeson Campus center at Rutgers-Newark is a hub of activity. Photo by Carol Kitman

Facing page: These Rutgers-Newark students enjoy a warm and sunny walk as they make their way to the next class of the day. Photo by A.J. Sundstrom/The State University of New Jersey/ Rutgers

sey College of Pharmacy, established in 1892. The New Jersey School of Law opened in 1908, followed a year later by the Newark Institute of Arts and Sciences. In 1927, the pre-legal undergraduate school of the New Jersey School came into being at the same time the New Jersey College of Pharmacy merged with Rutgers University, based in New Brunswick. Dana College and the Seth Boyden School of Business were formed from the law school's pre-legal unit in 1929-1930, and during 1934-1936 all of the various schools were merged to form the University of Newark, which became the Rutgers campus in 1946.

In the 1960s, a campus was constructed, replacing scattered brewery, factory, stable, and brownstone facilities earlier used for classes. The Paul Robeson Campus Center, named after the famous actor-singer (Rutgers Class of 1919), was built in 1966.

In 1978, the School of Law and the School of Criminal Justice moved to the S.I. Newhouse Center for Law and Justice. The Justice Henry Ackerson Library serves two professional schools—the School of Law and the Graduate School of Criminal Justice. Over the past three decades, the distinguished library has grown from a collection of 14,500 volumes in 1946 to more than 320,000 volumes, including 35,000 microfilm volume equivalents. A strong emphasis in the development of this collection has been the acquisition of primary legal materials from the common law world.

The library has been designated a selective depository for publications of the U.S Government Printing Office. The library also was designated some 25 years ago as a double depository for New Jersey documents, and has maintained a superb collection of materials over this period of time.

Also available are the statutory codes and current revisions of all 50 states, the Canadian provinces, and Australian states, and extensive holdings of earlier codes and session laws from most of these jurisdictions. The field of primary authority is rounded out by a complete collection of all available American state administrative codes and administrative registers. Federal and New Jersey administrative decisions are held completely insofar as available in print. The collections are arranged to permit students direct access to almost all materials.

The College of Arts and Sciences, with an enrollment of more than 3,800, offers more than 30 fields of study, ranging from Afro-American/ African Studies, to biology, chemistry, computer science, finance, geology, Hebraic studies, music, physics, Slavic studies, zoology, and physiology.

University College has a dual BA/MBA program with the Graduate School of Management, a dual BA or BS/MA with the School of Criminal Justice, and a certificate program in public administration. Among the more than 20 majors available are

Left: Seton Hall University School of Law, housed in the campus Law Center, currently enrolls more than 1,200 students. Photo by Barry M. Winiker

University Green is the centerpiece of Seton Hall's 58-acre campus. Courtesy, Seton Hall University

accounting, economics, labor, marketing, mathematics, political science, and urban studies.

The College of Nursing enrolls more than 500 students, 95 percent of them women. A typical course of study includes chemistry, English, anthropology or cultural studies, trends in health care, anatomy and physiology, microbiology, humans and the environment, nursing process, nutrition, humanities, and Life Span—a holistic approach to medicine.

The graduate school offers programs of study leading to doctor of philosophy degrees in biology, chemistry, criminal justice, management, psychobiology, and psychology. Master's programs lead to degrees in biology, chemistry, economics, English, geology, history, liberal studies, nursing, political science, psychology, and public adminstration. An MA in criminal justice is available through the School of Criminal Justice and an MBA through the Graduate School of Management.

Opportunities for post-doctoral work are available in biology, chemistry, psychobiology, and psychology.

Fewer than one-third of the nation's programs in management are accredited at the graduate level by the American Assembly of Collegiate Schools of Business. The Graduate School of

Management at Rutgers has been part of this select group since 1941.

Executive surveys by the Standard and Poor's Corporation, involving more than 55,000 high-level managers, rank Rutgers among the top 10 graduate programs supplying executive talent to U.S. companies. Among state universities, Rutgers ranks second nationally.

Rutgers MBA program has supplied chief executive officers to such companies as the Prudential Insurance Company of America, the world's largest insurance company; Hoffmann-LaRoche; Bristol Labs of Bristol Meyers; and Public Service Electric & Gas Co.

MBAs are offered in management and professional accounting, and the "Executive MBA" program for midcareer managers sponsored by their employers allows potential high-level executives to continue their education without interrupting their professional careers.

SETON HALL LAW SCHOOL

Miriam Rooney became the first woman dean of law in the United States when the Seton Hall University School of Law was established in 1951. Shortly after, Seton Hall University opened on Clinton Street in Newark with the physical assets, including the legal library, of the John Marshall School of Law, Jersey City.

In 1972, the law school moved to temporary quarters on Raymond Boulevard until the present law center, which opened in 1976, was constructed. It is the only law school in New Jersey operated by a private university, and, as its founders intended, it continues to offer a kind of legal education not otherwise available in the Garden State.

The law school's programs have two basic aims: to delineate and underline the foundation of America's common law and the Judeo-Christian principles on which it is based, and to challenge the critical powers of the student in order to develop the analytical and creative skills required in resolving contemporary legal issues through the application of sound rules of law.

Seton Hall's law school has been on the approved list of the American Bar Association since 1954 and a member of the Association of American Law Schools since 1959.

The law school's curriculum has grown to a total of 120 courses covering all of the major legal areas. It has had a writing program since 1974, requiring writing activity throughout the full term of the student's stay at the school.

The Legislative Bureau publishes one of only five law school journals on legislative law in the United States. The Women's Law Forum, begun in 1972, has addressed legal issues affecting women. More recently, the Environmental Law Society and the Sports Law Forum have dealt with issues in their respective areas.

The school's Hispanic clinic was the first evening clinic and one of the first bilingual clinics in the country. The unique Juvenile Justice clinic not only has two divisions—one working with prosecutors, the other with public defenders—but it is also involved in preventive law as students counsel young people who seem to be headed for serious trouble.

Students study for their midterm exams in Seton Hall's McLaughlin Library, a facility which contains a collection of more than 300,000 books and 1,800 periodical titles. Courtesy, Seton Hall University

Courses in computers and the law, and statistics and the law, have been added to the broadening curriculum.

In 1980, the Richard J. Hughes Chair for Constitutional and Public Law and Service was established. Hughes was the only elected official in the history of New Jersey government to serve as both governor and chief justice of the state supreme court.

The law school currently has an enrollment of approximately 1,235, making it one of the largest in the nation. The faculty comprises 41 full-time members and an almost equal number of judges, private practictioners, and other specialists who serve as adjuncts.

In 1988 students from nearly 360 undergraduate and graduate schools in 33 states and 10 foreign countries were represented in the applicant pool of 1,850. Approximately 400 students from 156 colleges and universities were enrolled.

Also in that year the "most up-to-date academic and library facilities in the country" were being planned by Seton Hall School of Law and the City of Newark, with an estimated price tag of close to $30 million. The new law school will have ap-

proximately 200,000 square feet of learning and research space.

SETON HALL UNIVERSITY

Founded in 1856 in Madison and relocated to South Orange four years later, Seton Hall University is the only Catholic university in New Jersey and the eighth-largest in the U.S. It was established by James Roosevelt Bayley, the first Bishop of Newark, and named after his aunt, Elizabeth Ann Seton.

Seton Hall became a university in 1950, became fully coeducational in 1968, and counts more than 50,000 people among its alumni.

The South Orange campus houses the College of Arts and Sciences, the W. Paul Stillman School of Business (Stillman founded what is today New Jersey's largest bank, First Fidelity), the College of Nursing, Immaculate Conception Seminary and School of Theology, University College, and the recently created School of Graduate Medical Education.

Present enrollment totals around 9,000 students, including undergraduates, graduate students, and law students. The university expects to have more than 60 percent of its undergraduates living on campus within the next few years, making it a primarily residential school.

The university offers more than 40 undergraduate and more than 43 graduate majors. Cooperative education, internships, and study-abroad programs are available, as is ROTC.

ESSEX COUNTY COLLEGE

Newark's newest addition to higher education is Essex County College, an "open door" institution that started with 3,400 students, a faculty of 90, and 100 staff members in September 1968. The first commencement, for 214 graduates, took place in May 1970.

In the past 20 years, Essex County College has given thousands of students from Newark and its environs an opportunity to earn two-year, four-year, and postgraduate degrees in technical and professional fields of their choice.

Essex County College (ECC) boasts the largest physical education megastructure in the state's most populous county. In addition to provividing a home court for exciting "Wolverine" basketball action, the 20,000-square-foot gymnasium can accommodate countywide tournaments and an impressive array of athletic events, including gymnastics and boxing exhibitions. Health club facilities featuring weight rooms, sauna, a hydro-fitness unit, and training labs are open for membership.

Cultural events at ECC span the arts and reflect the ethnic diversity of Essex County. A new artist-in-residence program with the acclaimed Gallman's Newark Dance Theatre provides a yearly showcase of dance talent. The college also hosts major observances during the year to celebrate the rich cultural heritage of the community.

From its 4,500-seat gymnasium and 300-seat lecture halls to the intimacy of The Art Gallery, ECC provides a collegiate setting for numerous public forums and countywide events. Performances by such noted artists as Lou Rawls and Ashford and Simpson typify the quality of productions staged at ECC. Events as varied as a concert by internationally renowned composer/pianist Abdullah Ibrahim to a master class by the Alvin Ailey Repertory Dance Ensemble reflect the range of programming.

From public hearings on state and national issues to the Teen Arts Festival for more than 1,000 aspiring high school artists, ECC provides a unique setting appropriate to each individual program. Full multimedia services and on-campus catering facilities make the college an outstanding conference location.

Essex County College offers business and industry a convenient, low-cost approach to upgrade employee skills. Customized training is usually conducted at the work site on a flexible schedule to meet specific employment demands. Programs have been developed for such employers as AT&T, the Internal Revenue Service, Prudential Insurance Company, Foster Wheeler, the New Jersey Division of Labor and Industry, and the Veterans Administration. Academic programs are offered through nine separate divisions and departments:

● The Bilingual Education program enables students to develop their English language skills while enrolling in selected courses offered in several native languages.

● The Division of Biology, Chemistry, and Health Technologies offers programs in biology/premedicine, chemistry, health service management, ophthalmic dispensing, physical therapist assistant, and radiography. Two additional allied health programs—dental hygiene and emergency medical technology-paramedic—are offered jointly with the University of Medicine and Dentistry of New Jersey.

● The Department of Nursing offers a highly selective two-year degree program that trains students to become licensed registered nurses. The curriculum features a strong clinical component, with students serving practicums at various medical centers in Essex County.

● The Division of Business prepares students for a wide array of positions in business and industry through career and transfer programs. Degree offerings include accounting, business administration, business education, and office systems technology.

● The Department of Computer and Information Sciences provides the most up-to-date training in computer science, computer information systems, and business application programming.

● The Engineering Technologies and Physics Divi-

These two students take a moment to review their class assignment on the campus of Essex County College. Photo by Rich Zila

sion prepares students for transfer to four-year institutions or technical positions in industry. Degree offerings include engineering, electronic engineering technology, architectural technology, civil construction engineering technology, and fire and safety science.

• The Department of Mathematics offers a degree program for students intending to transfer into baccalaureate study in math and math education. The department also provides basic and advanced courses required for other academic majors.

• The Humanities Division offers degree programs in liberal arts, art, music/music education, and television production. There is also a liberal arts degree in technical writing or journalism specialization.

• The Division of Social Sciences offers transfer degree programs in liberal arts, criminal justice and education, and career options in such fields as social work, mental health, gerontology, and substance abuse.

Essex County College also has a number of outstanding applied degree programs designed to develop "hands-on" competencies in some of the

most marketable professions.

The Architectural Technology program prepares students for various careers in architecture. Building upon general education skills during the first year, including math and physics, the second-year curriculum emphasizes intensive coursework in architectural drawing, construction methods and materials, and building equipment.

Students in the Civil Construction Engineering Technology program take a portion of their classes at the New Jersey Institute of Technology. Graduates can transfer directly in their junior year to NJIT or enter the civil construction field as engineering technicians.

The Media Production and Technology (MPT) Center coordinates a program in television production that includes specializations in management and technology. A regional production and distribution center with state-of-the-art facilities and video hardware, MPT has a teaching faculty with extensive experience in the industry as writers, producers, directors, and engineers.

Students enrolled in the Ophthalmic Dispensing program are trained for careers in opticianry. The curriculum includes extensive theoretical training in the anatomy and physiology of the eye and in applied math and physics. Second-year students work closely with experienced practitioners in the laboratory techniques of measuring and grinding eyeglasses to prescription, and the fitting and final adaptation of eye wear.

The Emergency Medical Technology-Paramedic program, offered with UMDNJ, trains students to attend to critically ill or injured patients prior to and during transport to the hospital. Program graduates qualify to take the New Jersey State EMT-Paramedic Certification Examination.

The Dental Hygiene program, also offered jointly with UMDNJ, prepares students for employment in all aspects of dental hygiene. Graduates qualify for the National Board Examination for Dental Hygiene.

The Radiography program trains students to become licensed X-ray technicians.

Graduates of the Physical Therapist Assistant program are eligible for licensure as physical therapy assistants. In addition to classroom instruction, students receive supervised clinical training at local hospitals and health centers.

The Alcohol and Substance Abuse option within the Human and Social Services program provides comprehensive training in substance abuse treatment. Students may concurrently pursue New Jersey Alcoholism Counselor certification. Essex County College is one of only five centers in New Jersey to offer courses in alcoholism counseling.

ECC's Career Training Institute specializes in intensive short-term training to meet current needs in business and industry.

The Dislocated Worker Training Resource Center provides testing, academic and personal counseling, and placement and educational assistance for individuals released from employment due to technological changes and business relocations or closings.

NEWARK SCHOOL OF FINE AND INDUSTRIAL ART

Founded in 1882, the Newark School of Fine and Industrial Art (NSFIA) is the only postsecondary professional art school in the United States sponsored by a local board of education.

The school's building is a recognized Art Deco structure built expressly for this unique institution in 1931. The edifice is currently shared by Arts High, a "Fame" type high school for students with talents in the visual and performing arts.

The fine arts school hires only professional artists to teach either one, two, or three days a week, permitting them the time they need to be active in their fields. A faculty of 40 for a student body of 125 gives the school an enviable teacher/student ratio of almost 1:3. Many of the faculty also teach at Pratt, Parsons, Fashion Institute of Technology, SVA, and other art institutions. They are recognized experts in their particular areas of creativity, who have been chosen for their inspirational as well as technical qualifications.

Students attend a full five-day-per-week program for three years to receive a diploma. Students may also choose to attend part-time during the day or evening. The first year foundation curriculum includes courses in basic materials, methods, skills, and creative attitudes. The second- and third-year students choose specialized courses in advertising art, fashion illustration, fine art, interior design, pictorial illustration, or textile design. A work-study program provides professional experience for some senior students.

Historically, NSFIA places 100 percent of its interior design and textile design graduates, and more than 90 percent of advertising art graduates. Fashion illustration, fine arts, and pictorial illustration either become self-employed or continue their studies.

One of the school's recent projects was the creation of seven plaster sculptures at Newark's Penn Station. Called "The Commuters," the project involved sculpting seven figures representative of the 1930s when Penn Station was built. Nine first-year and graduate students made up the master sculpture class that executed the sculptures under the direction of Grigory Gurevich. The seven life-sized sculptures are a young girl with her mother, an artist, a young couple from out of town, a newsboy, and a ticket agent. Each figure is symbolic, Gurevich points out. The young girl symbolizes the beauty of youth and energy; the newsboy represents America; the couple represent the first travelers to arrive in Newark; the ticket agent is a necessity; and the artist is the "soul" of society.

Right: Built in 1931, this landmark art deco structure is home to the Newark School of Fine and Industrial Art. Photo by Rich Zila

Below: Education provides young people a solid base from which to pursue lifetime goals. Photo by Carol Kitman

SPECIALTY HIGH SCHOOLS

Newark has been endowed with three special high schools that allow the city's public, parochial, and private school students to become the best and the brightest on their way to college and career. Those three special public high schools are Arts High, Science High, and University High.

Arts High School was the first high school of its kind in the United States, founded in 1931 to encourage and develop the artistic, dramatic, and musical talents of students who demonstrate a potential in those areas.

Graduates from Arts High include singers Sarah Vaughan, Melba Moore, and Connie Francis; jazz artists Wayne Shorter and Woody Shaw; Philadelphia Orchestra trumpeter Seymour Rosenfield; musical director Mort Lindsey; and actor Taurean Blaque.

A college preparatory pattern of studies is offered in conjunction with the art, music, and dramatics major programs. Arts High espouses the premise that artists, musicians—singers and instrumentalists—and persons engaged in any aspect of threater production must be well-educated and well-rounded individuals. Over 90 percent of Arts High graduates pursue postsecondary education in professional schools and colleges.

The first year of the Fine Arts program focuses on basic drawing and painting. In the second and third years of study the curriculum is arranged to allow for concentration in a number of art areas. Half of the second year is devoted to three-dimensional work in sculpture and ceramics—the other half to two-dimensional design and development of painting and drawing at a more mature level. Similarly, half of the third year is devoted to work in graphics and photography, and the other half to painting and drawing, with special attention given to expression representative of contemporary movements in art. Students select their area of specialization in their senior year: fine arts, commercial art, costume design, or illustration.

A music student customarily takes two, sometimes three, different music classes a day. Theory, harmony, and appreciation classes are given for both vocal and instrumental students. Students opting for the vocal program participate in the glee club, choir, and student-directed gospel chorus. Individual vocal training is also available. Instrumentalists develop their skills in private practice and in the band and orchestra.

An instructor with a professional background and experience in theater conducts the Dramatic program one double period a day. All aspects of theater are considered in the training of an actor: speech, voice, diction, movement, facial expression, and the art of pantomime. Lighting, makeup, costuming, and design and construction of sets are explored in the preparation of effective theater presentation, and management and publicity concerns are studied in theatrical production. Study of the history of theater and careful analysis of the contributions of major playwrights complements work experience. Students, in turn, are asked first to write short skits and then, as they progress, move on to larger works.

Science High School is one of the three "-schools operated by the Newark Board of Education, and ranks at the top in numerous statistical categories, including college acceptances, proficiency tests, basic skills, and attendance.

Conceived in 1974 under the leadership of Morris Lerner and Sister Shirley Corbliss, a structured science program was developed at Central High School. The curriculum stresses all fields of science and math, along with the humanities. There is also an advanced computer training program that introduces students to the use and programming of various computers. Science High alumni have graudated from Princeton, Harvard, Yale, MIT, Rutgers, Howard, Pennsylvania, and many other leading colleges and universities.

One of the more notable achievements at Science High is Coach Brent Farrand's Debate Team, which notched its unprecedented sixth consecutive state championship and attained a national ranking. Mr. Ferrand has developed similar debating programs throughout Newark.

Science High also has an athletic tradition dating back to the school's inception. In football, Michael Charles attained All-State honors at Central while attending Science High. He was named to a number of All-American teams at Syracuse and played for the Miami Dolphins in the Super Bowl in 1984. Eleven Science High players, including All-City selections Greg Clark and Claude Sivels, contributed to Central's last City League championship in 1984.

In track, George Chambers and Joe Strickland helped Central to win the prestigious Penn Relays, while Evangeline Grover, Angie Pulliam, Leticia Beverley, and Renee Carr contributed to city and state championships.

In 1985, Clarence "Teddy" Allen was named to the All-County and All-State baseball teams.

University High School, the "School Within A School," was founded in 1968 to nurture and serve the academically talented child. The program was housed in South Side High School (now Malcolm X Shabazz High School), where Dr. Leo Litzky was principal and Seymour Speigel, director. (Dr. Litzky's nephew, poet Allen Ginsberg, was born in Newark's Beth Israel Hospital in 1926). An interdisciplinary team concept of instruction was employed. Students were recruited from the eighth grades of Newark's elementary schools. University High began with an initial class of 116 students. The students all read at grade level, or above, were leaders of their elementary classes and wanted to attend. The present enrollment is 528.

The curriculum remains four years of a correlated humanities program (English, history, arts, and music), four years of mathematics, integrated science with strong emphasis, one modern foreign language for three years, and electives that include advanced placement courses in calculus, biology, English, and U.S. history, with courses in computer programming, western civilization, law-in-action, creative writing, and journalism.

University High is served by an advisory board made up of members from Newark's leading businesses—Prudential Insurance Co., Mutual Benefit Life, Howard Savings, AT&T, and Public Service Electric & Gas Co.

University High occupies a former junior high school on Clinton Place equipped with state-of-the-art science laboratories, a computer lab, gymnasium, music suite, a spacious library, auditorium, and cafeteria.

Over 95 percent of University High's graduates pursue higher education. Alumni have succeeded as physicians, attorneys, engineers, social workers, teachers, accountants, nurses, and many other fields and professions. While University High prepares its current generation of students, its alumni are becoming a vital force in the greater Newark community.

NEWARK PUBLIC SCHOOL SYSTEM

The Newark School District with its 82 schools and 51,000 students is the largest school system in New Jersey. The student population by race is approximately 33,000 black, 13,000 Hispanic, and 5,000 caucasion. The average age of the schools is 72 years.

The Newark School District has developed partnerships and collaborative programs with local businesses and community groups, as well as with local colleges and universities, to augment and enrich public school programs for students. Among the many enrichment programs are:

● Artists-in-Education—a program that strengthens the artistic skills of students and teachers in dance, theater, and playwriting, in collaboration with the New Jersey State Council on the Arts.

● Fashion and Design—a project with the West Ward Cultural Center designed to provide 200 Newark students with marketable skills in dressmaking, fashion design, modeling, and fashion show commentary.

● Leadership Development/Drop Prevention—a program in collaboration with Aspira, Inc., to encourage and successfully enable dropouts to reenter educational programs and complete high school.

● Educational and Video Training—a project in collaboration with the Theater of Universal Images to train students to create and manage television programs with "hands-on" experience in all areas of video and theater production.

● The Melting Pot: A Cultural Course for Young Newarkers—in collaboration with Special Audiences-New Jersey, this program helps Newark students (1,200 from elementary and intermediate schools and 300 from high schools) to dispel ethnic

and racial stereotyping.

● Project Pride Foundation—six corporations created this program in 1983 to sponsor debate projects in eight high schools. The funding allows students to participate in summer debate institutes at prestigious colleges and universities nationwide. Newark's Science High School Debating Team has won the New Jersey State Forensic Championship for the sixth consecutive year, an unprecedented record.

● Close Up—a seminar program cosponsored by the Sealand Corporation to encourage in-depth study of government policy and practice and provide "hands-on" knowledge of the workings of government at the local, county, state, and federal levels. The Newark Municipal Council sponsored "Newark Close Up Day" during the 1987-1988 school year.

● Saturday Academy—a program offered in col-

Above: The Vailsburg School is centrally located near the corner of Ivy Street and Richelieu Terrace. Photo by Rich Zila

Facing page: Ridge Street School is located in the North Ward. Photo by Rich Zila

laboration with Rutgers-Newark to provide positive educational experiences in a college setting for 100 students, with the purpose of improving SAT scores.

• Choices—sponsored and funded by the New Jersey Bell Telephone Company, this program is targeted at ninth-grade students to make them aware of the "key" choices by which they control the level of success in later life. Bell employees trained in critical thinking skills visit ninth-grade classes to convince students of the importance of education. The program is directly linked to student attendance improvement and dropout reduction.

• Pre-College—sponsored by the New Jersey Institute of Technology to increase the number of students seeking higher education and to expose students to higher-order skills and careers related to mathematics and science. Programs include urban engineering, experimental math, communications, computer science, and integrated calculus/physics.

CATHOLIC SCHOOLS

There are 17 parochial schools in Newark with a total student population of more than 6,000, of which approximately 5,300 are enrolled in elementary schools and 700 in secondary schools.

Perhaps the best-known Catholic school in Newark is St. Benedict's Preparatory School at 520 Dr. Martin Luther King, Jr., Boulevard (formerly High Street). Established in 1868 on its present site, St. Benedict's prides itself on educating successive generations of the ethnic groups that came to Newark—Germans, Irish, Italians, Slavs, and, more recently, blacks and Spanish-speaking peoples. St. Benedict's believes firmly in the value of learning from the human and cultural diversity to be found in Newark today.

The urban campus consists of eight buildings, including a monastery, located on about eight acres within two blocks of the business district. Some of the buildings with Victorian red-brick facades date back to the 1850s and '60s.

The more than 400 students come from 36 towns and about 160 schools; two dozen are citizens of other countries. About 13 of the 32 faculty members are alumni of St. Benedict's, as is the school's headmaster since 1972, The Reverend Edwin D. Leahy, O.S.B., a graduate of Union Theological Seminary and Seton Hall University.

Some of the colleges at which recent graduates are enrolled are Rutgers, Holy Cross, Boston College, Purdue, Moorehouse, Belmont Abbey, and St. Peter's College.

Student life is what separates St. Benedict's from other private and public schools. Each student and faculty member belongs to one of 14 groups that assemble together for the morning convocation, and meet for 40 minutes of study, tutoring, and counseling each day. Group members are responsible for one another's progress, for the clean-up of some area of the school building, and for the general good order and morale of the school. Groups compete in academics, attendance, intramural sports, school service, and other activities. A comprehensive honor code of covenant sets high standards of responsibility for personal honesty and integrity.

The group system fosters many of the school's ideals by helping the student to feel at home as a

A young boy rides by the entrance of Central Street School in the city's Central Ward. Photo by Rich Zila

member of a small supportive group, to work with and be responsible for others, to exercise leadership, and to have some sense of responsibility for the running of the school.

As one student observed on life at St. Benedict's: "It's sort of an island in the middle of the city, and it's really a symbol of what can be if everybody—blacks, whites, Hispanics—pulls together."

Catholic Community Services (CCS), the largest private, nonsectarian, nonprofit provider of human services in New Jersey, also provides educational and spiritual support and opportunities for the handicapped through the Apostolates for the Retarded, for the Deaf, and for the Hearing Impaired. The CCS also provides programs for the preschool child, the exceptional child, the child in need of placement, the emotionally distressed, the sensorially impaired, newly arrived immigrants, and the elderly.

NEWARK COMMUNITY SCHOOL OF THE ARTS

New Jersey's largest school of the arts, the Newark Community School, is a success story built upon the shared vision of two creative schoolteachers who believed that the arts should be an integral part of their lives.

Stella Lass and Saunders Davis, who founded the school in 1968, held their first classes in a church basement with 75 local children. The school's philosophy is "Quality arts instruction for all who seek it." The school, with a professional faculty of 65, is committed to the cultivation of an informed audience, which understands and appreciates the arts.

The Newark arts school's most visible and creative undertaking to date has been to commission a new ballet, *And Still the Snowflakes Fall.* The ballet is based on a series of haiku, with orchestra and children's chorus (about 30 minutes long). The music of the opening carries the audience into the magic of a bonsai garden, where a geisha welcomes everyone to the "service of the tea"—the symbol of an ancestral culture. An almost miraculous live parade of thoughts, characters, and personalities follows, inviting the audience to contemplate, analyze, and compare the various American points of view about Japan (and subtly about the inner city). The ballet reaches a climax with the integration of three important theatrical elements— music, chorus, and dance—ending with the promise of a new day in Japanese style: the rising sun

The Newark Community School of the Arts received the 1988 National Education Association Challenge Grant, the 1987 Distinguished Artistic Award, and the 1986 New Jersey Governor's Arts in Education Award, presented to the school's director, William Reeder. Scott McVay, executive director of the Geraldine R. Dodge Foundation, sees the school as "a beacon for what is possible . . ."

Established in the late 1960s, the Newark Community School of the Arts is now the largest school of its kind in the state. Photo by Carol Kitman

Greater Newark is a melting pot of some 50 different nationalities, giving the city a colorful and diverse flavor. Street markets are a common sight throughout Newark's many neighborhoods, each with their own ethnic specialties. Photo by Jane Van Wert

VII
Ethnic Newark

Greater Newark is entering the twenty-first century as a modern "melting pot" embracing some 50 nationalities, from Aleuts and Filipinos to Samoans and Vietnamese.

As blacks and whites gradually mix into numerically equal proportions, Greater Newark will reflect a truly balanced American community mirroring a complete spectrum of ethnic cultures and traditions, from American Indian and African-American to Asian Indians and Europeans.

In the City of Newark, there are native organizations for peoples from all over the globe, bearing such proud and unmistakable names as the Independent Irish Societies, the Brazilian Center, the New Jersey Haitian/American Cultural Foundation, Ukrainian Chornomorska Sitch, United Afro-American Association, La Casa de Don Pedro, the Puerto Rican Political Association, B'nai Brith, the United Spanish Association, Newark Cubanos, Newark Portuguese, and Newark Pan-American, in addition to such ethnic newspapers as *Luso Americano* and *La Tribuna.*

A survey in 1982 of the ethnic mix of Essex County found that caucasions consisted of Polish, Irish, Italian, Jewish, and German descent, while blacks were African-American, Jamaican, and Haitian. Hispanics were identified as Cubans, Puerto Ricans, Mexicans, and Dominicans. In addition to the Portuguese there are the Pacific Islanders, including Japanese, Vietnamese, Korean, Chinese, and Filipinos; and the Indians, including American Indians and East Indians. There are also Guamanians, Eskimos, Aleuts, and Samoans in very small numbers.

The original natives of Newark and Essex County, the Lenni Lenape, were long ago displaced by white settlers, dominately European.

Newark's surging ethnic activism has resulted in the nation's only tri-lingual community newspaper, *Ironbound Voices*, for readers of English, Spanish, and Portuguese.

129

And the largest event of its kind for Portuguese people worldwide, other than the May 13 tribute to Our Lady of Fatima in Portugal, is the Portugal Day festival in Newark, now a weeklong series of events attracting more than 250,000 people from as far away as Massachusetts and Connecticut and featuring soccer games, track and field events, dancing, music, roller skating, and Portuguese-style feasts.

The festival commemorates the death of Portugal's epic poet and historian Luis de Camoes, who chronicled the discoveries of the great Portuguese explorers and their discoveries in the fifteenth and sixteenth centuries. Portugal may be the only country in the world that honors a poet with a national holiday.

Newark's leading ethnic-educational-cultural organizations form an integral part of the city's character and fabric. They are the source of hope and inspiration within their neighborhoods, the spiritual glue that keeps the city together as critical pieces in the larger mosaic of urban life.

THE NORTH WARD CENTER

The Center is a special place where people come together to solve problems, as well as to share good times and culture. It's one of a kind.

U.S. Senator Bill Bradley

The North Ward Educational and Cultural Center began as an idea in 1970 in the heart of the home—the kitchen. Around a kitchen table and over numerous pots of coffee, the concept was hammered out: It was simply that the urban ethnic working class, which makes up the backbone of many communities, deserved particular attention—attention that would originate in a true feeling for the circumstances of the urban ethnic.

From that kitchen table in the home of Steve Adubato, a Newark schoolteacher and community leader, the North Ward Educational and Cultural Center was born.

After the 1967 riots, deteriorating conditions and increasing racial tensions pressed in around the North Ward, which was facing extinction as a family neighborhood. Before the riots, it was a place of small frame houses and tiny gardens, and mansions that had been built by the economic elite of the city. The smaller homes were each an

achievement of generations of effort by immigrants. North Ward was gradually building into a middle-class community as the younger people went on to higher-paying professions. Its people loved their neighborhood. They loved their churches. They wanted simply to raise their children in peace.

But for a frightening period of time, the residents of the North Ward could see nothing between themselves and a rising tide of poverty and crime that would make their homes worthless and their achievements empty.

The response to keep North Ward a decent place where people could live, work, and share their dreams was the educational/cultural center. It was the vision of a remarkable clergyman, Monsigor Geno Baroni. He preached that urban neighborhoods could be saved if the people would band together and make them work. Baroni founded the National Center for Urban Ethnic Affairs and was called to the nation's capital to be the Undersecretary of Housing and Urban Development. His vision led community leaders, such as Steve Adubato, to create a community center that would unite the North Ward and turn the tide of despair into confidence.

And it worked. Former Congressman Peter Rodino said, "I can truly say that without the North Ward Center, there would be no North Ward as we know it today." Today, the Center is the nucleus of neighborhood support by major national and business organizations. It has grown far beyond a narrow ethnic response to an overwhelming problem; its doors are open to all the community and all the city. Its staff is a reflection of all who comprise the city's population. Its services are provided across the board, virtually from birth through senior citizenship. It is a success story. It is a model for all community centers.

Adubato believes the private sector and free marketplace are the most efficient mechanisms for supplying goods and services. But the voluntary, nonprofit sector enjoys a pivotal role in the North Ward: It can accomplish effectively what government cannot and private business finds unprofitable.

Senior citizens' services, recreation, day care, and job training are the cornerstones of the North Ward Center's success. It is involved in youth

Left: Ferry Street becomes Portugal Street during the annual Portugal Day festival. Photo by Carol Kitman

Below: Music, dancing, and delicious Portuguese food are just some of the many delights to enjoy during Newark's annual Portugal Day festival. Photo by Carol Kitman

Above: The Portugal Day festival, held in the Ironbound district of Newark, attracts more than 250,000 people to its festivities each year. Photo by Carol Kitman

counseling, housing, community rehabilitation and stabilization, health care, and partnerships with other organizations, notably the Boys' and Girls' Clubs of Newark.

Newark Mayor Sharpe James has noted: "The North Ward Center has an exemplary record of providing programs and services for senior citizens, preschoolers, young people, and adults, and works to preserve and celebrate the rich cultural heritage of the Newark community."

The Center's headquarters is a landmark mansion that once represented the power and prestige of the mill and factory owners who controlled Newark at the turn of the century. This majestic home is now in the hands of the descendants of those people who had worked in those mills and factories.

Above: The North Ward Educational and Cultural Center was formed in the early 1970s in response to the concerns of the area's residents and businesses. Photo by Rich Zila

Facing page top: With the help of active community organizations, such as the North Ward Educational and Cultural Center, the North Ward is experiencing an exciting rebirth, once again creating an enlightened sense of neighborhood and family life. Photo by Rich Zila

Facing page bottom: Two young entrepreneurs, with a brightly colored catering truck, ply their trade in the Park Avenue area of Newark. Photo by Mary Ann Brockman

One of the Center's first priorities was to launch an anti-crime program. That was followed by equivalency classes to help people acquire high school diplomas. A secretarial skills training program was also started for area residents seeking placement in the business world.

From the beginning, the Center was committed to restoring the old, neglected, and sometimes abandoned houses awaiting reoccupancy and a new lease on life.

In 1980 the Center began its Meals on Wheels program; signed its "sister city" agreement with Guaynabo, Puerto Rico, in 1981; established a hypertension screening program in 1982, with free examinations and follow-up care; and received a federal grant in 1983 for a senior citizen employment project.

If the North Ward were a separate political entity, it would rank as New Jersey's twelfth-largest city, with a population of 70,000. The North Ward represents a cross-section of American society: Italian-Americans, blacks, a rapidly growing Puerto

Rican population, and immigrants from the Caribbean and Latin America.

Adubato says that "the purpose of the Center is to defuse racial conflict through advocacy of common goals, predominately by acting as an organizational link between the community and the public and private sectors."

Over the years, the Center has evolved as perhaps the most racially integrated organization in New Jersey. The numerous ethnic, racial, and cultural events held annually at and through the Center are a major part of this effort and a tribute to its success.

Reaching out and affecting the lives of thousands of people each year, the North Ward Center knows no racial barriers, no ethnic differences. For the inner city boy and girl, the advantages are few and the pressures many. To give these youngsters an opportunity to channel their energies and get involved in participatory sports, the Center developed a recreation program that has grown into the largest in the state, outside of government-sponsored operations. With 10,000 youngsters, it may be the largest privately operated recreation program in the country.

The exchange agreement with the City of Guaynabo in Puerto Rico means that recreation teams from Newark and the island trade visits. That has meant an unusual educational experience for city youth who have the opportunity to fly to Puerto Rico, stay with families there, and gain an insight into another culture.

The Women's Softball League also has international connections. Team Canada and Team Venezuela are among those who have visted Newark, along with teams from other parts of the Northeast.

The Rick Cerone Little League is sponsored by the Center. Project Pride, a private group committed to providing programs for Newark students with the objective of building pride in their schools, sponsors one major fund-raiser each year—the Pride Bowl, in which New Jersey colleges play for the benefit of Newark students.

An important dimension of the Center's activities is the Summer Arts Festival. Each year, outstanding performances are provided by such groups as the New Jersey Ballet, the Garden State Concert Band, the New Jersey School for the Arts, the New

Jersey Opera Institute, the Whole Theatre Company in Montclair (founded by Academy Award-winner Olympia Dukakis), the George Street Playhouse in New Brunswick, the New Jersey Shakespeare Festival under the auspices of Drew University, Madison, the New Jersey State Opera, and McCarter Theatre in Princeton.

The Center has also held special events annually or for singularly noteworthy occasions. The annual activities include: a celebration of Martin Luther King, Jr.'s, birthday; participating in the Columbus Day Parade with a contingent of more than 1,000; sponsoring a Puerto Rican scholarship dinner and participating (with the largest contingent) in the Puerto Rican statewide parade; a St. Patrick's Day recognition dinner; a Christmas tree lighting ceremony; the Division of Youth and Family Services Christmas party, matching adoptable children with prospective parents; and sponsoring the annual picnic for the John F. Kennedy School for Special Children.

Among the individual special events and celebrations held at the Center have been: a simulated

Right: The North Ward Center has developed a major recreational program for the area's youth, instilling a sense of competition and sportsmanship in sporting activities. Here, a group of boys practice shooting baskets on the grounds of Ridge Street School in the North Ward. Photo by Rich Zila

Below: The North Ward Center is represented in the annual Cherry Blossom Run in the city's Branch Brook Park. Photo by Michael Yamashita

More than 50 different ethnic groups live in Newark's Ironbound, the largest group being Portuguese, accounting for approximately 40 percent of the community. Photo by Mary Ann Brockman

peace treaty signing on March 21, 1979, between an Israeli and an Egyptian family living in the North Ward; a fund-raising event celebrating Italy's "Little Christmas," for the victims of the 1980 earthquake in southern Italy; and a fund-raising event for Ethiopian Famine Relief in conjunction with UNICEF.

Another special activity of the North Ward Center is the production of the highly-acclaimed cable television series entitled "Roots and Wings," which focuses on issues, people, and topics important to the City of Newark. Fran Adubato hosts the TV program.

THE IRONBOUND

Like the North Ward, the Ironbound's 50,000 residents comprise what could be a sizable city that shares a common bond: the enrichment of a compact neighborhood, by the Portuguese, and, recently, Hispanics. Ironbound got its name from the fact that it is bounded by iron rails that still remain from when the train was the king of transportation.

Since the late 1960s, thousands of immigrants of Portuguese and Spanish descent have settled in the 1,000-acre neighborhood known as the Ironbound. City residents refer to the area as "Down Neck" because it is shaped like a horse's neck as it bends around the lower Passaic River. During the peak of the Industrial Revolution, "Down Neckers" boasted they made everything from a tiny pin to a powerful locomotive.

The recent arrivals into the Ironbound joined their neighbors of German, Irish, Italian, Polish, Jewish, Slavic, and Lithuanian ancestry. In total, there are 52 ethnic groups residing harmoniously in the Ironbound.

The largest ethnic group is Portuguese, with some 18,000, or just less than 40 percent of the population. Those of Spanish origin make up about 15 percent, or roughly 7,000 people, with Puerto Ricans comprising 10 percent and Cubans 5 percent. Over half of the population is foreign born.

The Ironbound has experienced little physical change in recent times. The rows of small, two- and three-story, well-kept houses are still some of the best in the city. The narrow, clean streets still have mixed residential, industrial, and commercial activities thriving side by side. Such practices are, academically, against all tenets of "good" urban planning, which calls for rather strict segregation of competing urban necessities. Many streets are flanked with mature trees, softening the potentially harsh realities of truck, bus, and automobile traffic.

The Ironbound is known throughout the metropolitan region for its fine restaurants serving Hispanic cuisine.

The Ironbound continues today, as it has for the past 150 years, a classic paradox violating all of the conventional wisdom of the "good life." The hearty working class of Newark's East Ward have reversed the trend toward urban extinction, and through hard work, community pride, the family, and church, have preserved its tradition as a seedbed out of which social, economic, and political urban growth have prospered.

The Ironbound is not only a polyglot, a genuine cosmopolite, but it is also the true spirit of America. Two invaluable ethnic-cultural organizations have helped to maintain that special quality and flavor unique to the Ironbound: the Ironbound Community Corporation and the Ironbound Educational & Cultural Center.

The Ironbound Community Corporation (ICC) was founded in 1969 by community residents to assist neighborhood people in developing community-based programs. The 46 staff members of the community corporation are residents shaping their future for their families and neighbors. ICC activities include: a preschool/day care-center for 75 children; an open-classroom elementary school for 40 students in Kindergarten through the eighth grade; an adult college program for 150 adults; a health project with health screenings for children and organizing on health issues; a senior citizen advocacy and service project with homemaker, transportation, and meals-on-wheels programs; and a commu-

nity information center that offers neighborhood organizing, social services, information and referrals, and a community newspaper. The ICC also produces "Ironbound Insights," Newark's only community-based public-access cable television show, which features half-hour discussions on local topics each week.

The establishment of five family day-care homes in the community is the type of care being promoted as the wave of the future, with the Ironbound as the leader.

The ICC has also established the "Brown Bag Clubs," in which more than 400 senior citizens participate and receive a 15-pound bag of groceries each month. These "self-help" clubs are operated directly by the senior volunteers who collect funds, load and unload the cartons of food, and prepare bags for distribution.

With dense, heavy industrial operations in the Ironbound, including its biggest neighbor, Newark International Airport, the Ironbound's Community Health Project has taken a pioneering role in organizing residents on the questions of toxic waste, worker safety, noise pollution, and zoning violations that result in health hazards. The Health Project believes in the strength of coalitions, and works with community groups in other towns to improve the quality of their neighborhoods.

The Ironbound Educational & Cultural Center (IECC) is the force behind New Jersey's first multi-ethnic heritage museum and theater. The multimillion-dollar Ironbound Gateway Development Project is committed to the restoration of the historic landmark Second Dutch Reformed Church and rectory for use as a neighborhood community center to house the theater and museum, while also providing space for commercial rental property and the Glockenspiel International Cuisine.

The IECC logo consists of a shield that symbolizes tradition and culture, clasped hands that demonstrate unity, oak leaves to signify the strength and renewing powers of education, and stars that represent the dreams and aspirations contained within the American flag. A dome in the logo's background, which in reality sits atop the 1848 Church of Our Lady of Mount Carmel, is visible throughout Newark's Gateway district. Erected as the Second Dutch Reformed Church, the rock-solid edifice is the home of the new museum and theater.

The cupola and portico supporting the dome is itself a miniature, mechanical theater, certainly the most unusual free hometown entertainment attraction in the United States. Every day at noon and 5 P.M., leading New Jersey historical figures, from the Lenni Lenape Indians and Newark founder Robert Treat to today's various nationalities, appear in a spectacular, revolving musical dramatic show, reminiscent of the finely tuned and crafted German cuckoo and weather clocks, but on a grand, towering scale. As different ethnic songs sound out on carillon chimes throughout the Gateway at Newark's Penn Station, the Disney-like carousel figures perform on their various instruments or do their native dances, accompanied by a booming taped narration explaining their individual cultural contributions to the Ironbound, Newark, and New Jersey.

It's an old-fashioned show stopper as pedestrians and even motorists stop to gaze up curiously at the lofty show in the church portico and cupola. A huge illuminated clock also rings as the hours change.

The museum features artworks and crafts and sundry artifacts of the ethnic groups of the Ironbound and Newark. The theater provides a forum for ethnic folkloric music and dance performances, as well as modern music, dance, and drama. There is also a facility for teaching dance and other ethnic cultural art forms. The theater's stage is foldable and portable for easy removal and storage. The main level of the museum is used as a luncheon club on business days to generate additional revenue to support the museum and theater. During the week, dance and gymnastic instruction is available to area residents.

An International Palace Restaurant adds the final, magical touch to this unforgettable Gateway experience.

The church rectory houses not only business offices, but art galleries as well. An outdoor cafe at the front and to the side of the rectory is designed in the European style—glass enclosed with a multitude of hanging plants. The cafe complements Peter Francisco Park, a triangular-shaped oasis between the museum/theater and Penn Station, the transportation hub of Newark.

The IECC was founded in 1975 by Richard Pereira, former chief building cost estimator for the City of Newark. Pereira, a gifted developer and builder, sought a multipurpose center to serve the East Ward residents. Its services include youth development and family crisis intervention, as well as advocacy services for senior citizens and the disabled. A firm believer in "the best way to do it is to do it yourself," Pereira set up a tool-lending library (both power and manual) so residents can upgrade their residential properties. More than 100 borrowers are facelifting many of the deterioriating homes—floor by floor, structure by structure, block by block. Pereira calls such commitment "sweat equity" that pays off handsomely: Newark's real estate escalates in value as more and more do-it-yourselfers and upscale professionals discover the real potential of America's third-oldest major city.

LA CASA DE DON PEDRO

The "Newark house" of Don Pedro Albizu Campos, the patriarch of the Puerto Rican independence movement in the 1940s and 1950s, was opened in 1971 when a group of 10 families met to discuss the issues and concerns affecting the residents of the North Ward. Today, La Casa has grown into a multi-service agency that serves thousands of families through a comprehensive network addressing every aspect of the "Life Cycle."

La Casa's "Life Cycle" begins with the early developmental phases of preschoolers and continues with programs and services tailored to meet the needs of adolescents, adults, senior citizens, and the overall improvement of family life and community development.

La Casa strives to create an atmosphere of hope and optimism. The strategy developed at La Casa involves motivating individuals to utilize all of the resources within its network to develop self-sufficiency and resourcefulness. This development of upward mobility, motivation, and self-sufficiency permeates all of La Casa's programs, which seek to break the cycle of poverty and despair that bind the poor and undereducated to emotional and financial dependency on welfare and other assistance programs.

La Casa sponsors housing programs, senior citizen and youth projects, a leadership training program and various initiatives such as a credit union, legal aid, and economic development.

Newark Deputy Mayor Luis Quintana says La Casa was "very helpful to me as a young man growing up in the city, serving as a role model. And today it helps us in City Hall in locating housing and helping our citizens in other ways."

BLACK HERITAGE

With Newark's population composed of about 75 percent blacks (1988), the city each year celebrates a nationally prominent Black Heritage Day weekend with parades, speeches, workshops, and ethnic festivities.

More than 40,000 people turn out to see and be a part of the Black Heritage Day Parade held in early June, which features brightly decorated theme floats and flashy marching bands. The Masjid Muhammad in East Orange has a vast contingent and a moving display of past and present black leaders.

With one of the largest African-American populations in the United States, Newark was the first to sponsor a black ethnic parade, originally named in honor of Crispus Attucks, the first American to die in the American Revolution. The Crispus Attucks Parade was conceived in 1966 by John Thomas, who was then a teacher at the former Central High School. One day he was telling his students how Newark was a great melting pot in which various ethnic groups continued to honor their respective heritages. A black student responded: "But Mr. T,

Above: The Senior Citizens Project was started in 1976, offering support and services to local seniors and to the concerns which affect their lives and neighborhoods. Senior Ride, which provides transportation services, is just one of the many helpful programs of this Ironbound Community Corporation project. Courtesy, Ironbound Community Corporation

Facing page: One of Ironbound Community Corporation's six major programs is the Children's Center, a state licensed preschool, serving children ages three to five. Established in 1969, the center provides a nurturing and educational environment in which parents play a significant role. Courtesy, Ironbound Community Corporation

Above: A soft sunset illuminates Riverbank Park in the Ironbound. Photo by Rich Zila

Top right: An attitude of optimism and growth pervades La Casa de Don Pedro, as individuals develop a sense of self-esteem and inner strength through the assistance of La Casa's resources and services. Courtesy, La Casa de Don Pedro

Above: La Casa de Don Pedro serves thousands of Hispanic families in Newark, seeking to improve the quality of family life and to promote a strong sense of community. Courtesy, La Casa de Don Pedro

we don't have such a day."

For 10 years, The Crispus Attucks Parade joined the impressive list of other ethnic parades that marched down Broad Street in front of City Hall. It was disbanded in 1976 and two years later resurrected as the Black Heritage Day Parade.

Mayor Sharpe James proudly points out that no other city in America stages such elaborate ethnic parades honoring Puerto Rican Day, St. Patrick's Day, Columbus Day, Portuguese Day, and Black Heritage Day. Newark is truly the "All-American City!" James proclaims.

For the annual black event, Newark is turned into a playground of black culture and pride, the biggest-ever local tribute to African-American culture. The formal ceremonies are conducted in conjunction with the Prince Hall Mason's "National Tribute to Black Heritage." Among the many distinguished blacks honored is a New Jersey native, Paul Robeson, the famous actor-singer born in Princeton and the first black student at Rutgers University (Class of 1919). Robeson was an All-American athlete and star of stage and screen.

Congressman Donald Payne, the first black representative from New Jersey, finds that Newark is "moving towards a great future," adding that "We will see a great metamorphosis from despair and decay to hope and a new beginning."

THE URBAN LEAGUE

The Urban League's roots go back to 1910 when the Committee on Urban Conditions Among Negroes was established in New York City to help black migrants from the rural South find jobs and housing, acquire more education, and adjust to the rigors of an urban environment.

The Urban League of Essex County was founded in 1917 by William Ashby of Newark. Ashby turned 100 years old in 1989.

During an interview, Ashby recalled how he was asked by the Newark-Essex business community to recruit blacks from the South to man the area's factories during World War I. Thus began the northern migration to Newark and Essex County of southern blacks seeking opportunities in prospering urban America.

The Urban League today is a national interracial nonprofit community service organization using the tools and methods of social work, economics, law, business management, and other disciplines to secure equal opportunities in all sectors of society for black Americans and other minorities. The Urban League is also a nonpartisan organization.

Its mission is the elimination of racial discrimination and segregation in America and achievement of parity for blacks and other minorities in every phase of American life. Each year the Urban League publishes its highly regarded report, *The State of Black America.*

The Essex-Newark agency focused in 1988 on maintaining and building the "Black family," with services and programs geared toward preservation of the family. "The family will be seen as an association of persons by blood or otherwise who recognize themselves as a unit with a common interest to financially and emotionally support each other," the Essex agency announced in 1988. Comprehensive assistance is being provided to family members to ensure stability. Advisory councils were developed to establish a stronger presence in Montclair, Irvington, East Orange, and Orange. Programs for the homeless, AIDs victims, and the single parent are constantly being improved.

The Urban League "Sunday concept" was originated to bring about a greater relationship between the League and religious institutions. Community festivals are scheduled for the summers and Urban League Sundays during the fall.

Two new auxiliaries, the Pacemakers and the Montclair Youth Council, were created in 1987, reinforcing the Urban League Guild and the Day Care Parents Associations. Auxiliaries formed in 1988 include the Urban League Friends, a fundraising arm; the Newark Youth Council; ULtra Go, a word- and information-processing training center for unemployed and underemployed Essex residents; the graduate organization of the ULtra Center; and the Guild Gallery Advisory Council. The IBM Corporation is a partner with the ULtra Center, providing hardware and technical assistance. New program training thrusts have been added, such as video production and other office skills.

The ULtra Center has produced more than 399 graduates and boasts a 91 percent placement rate for its graduates; it placed 97 percent of its gradu-

These gentlemen enjoy a bit of conversation and friendship in the refreshing surroundings of Branch Brook Park. Photo by Linda Zila

ates in the past year alone. More than 75 percent of the clients are from Newark and 60 percent of the work trainees are women.

The Essex agency also offers a Community College scholarship program to mature adults who are, in most instances, heads of households. An annual conference in collaboration with the Newark NAACP and Rutgers University is held to assist in identifying and meeting the pre-college needs of Essex County students.

"Operation Brightside" is a summer youth-employment program. In 1987, the program created its own urban garden in which youth grew vegetables and flowers. An educational component, cultural activities, and an orientation to the world of work are part of "Operation Brightside."

UNIFIED VAILSBURG

The Unified Vailsburg Services Organization (UVSO) is a coalition of some 20 congregations, civic groups, and block associations that represent one of Newark's finest neighborhoods. Its mission is "Creating a Stable and Compassionate Community." Services are provided in several languages, including Ukrainian, Spanish, Italian, and English. A quarterly newsletter, *Vailsburg Voices*, currently has a press run of 6,000 copies.

UVSO was founded by the Reverend Burton Vincent, pastor of Advent Chapel, Holy Trinity Lutheran Church; the Reverend John Sharpe, pastor of Kilburn Presbyterian Church; Father Miles Varley,

pastor of Sacred Heart Church; and Rabbi Julius Eidenbaum of Beth Israel Synogogue.

Among its extensive services are:

* A Senior Center for exercise, choral groups, speakers, crafts and other projects, and bus trips.

* Youth and family services, including crisis response and intervention, job development and placement, league sports, tutoring, summer day-camp, a day-care center, and special events such as an annual youth talent show, community awards banquet, and trips to parks, beaches, and major league ball games.

* Neighborhood preservation, involving technical assistance and training to local block clubs and the Central Block Association Council.

Unified Vailsburg's membership roster for 1988 was made up of the Alexander Street Block Club, the Beth David Jewish Center, the Ellery Block Association, the Holy Trinity Lutheran Church, the Ivy Hill Neighborhood Association, the Kenmore Avenue Block Club, the Kilburn Memorial United Presbyterian Church, the Lions Club of Vailsburg, the Father Vincent Monella Center of Italian Culture, the Pine Grove Terrace Block Club, the Sacred Heart Church of Vailsburg, the St. John's Ukrainian Catholic Church, the Sanford Heights Presbyterian Church, Seton Hall University, South Orange-Vailsburg United Methodist Church, Vailsburg Businessmens Association, Vailsburg Clergy and Laity Association, Vailsburg Interested People, and Zion United Church of Christ.

Left: Ivy Hill Park in the Vailsburg district provides both children and adults a great place to enjoy the out-of-doors. Photo by Rich Zila

Below: Vailsburg is one of Newark's finest neighborhoods. Photo by Rich Zila

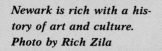

Newark is rich with a history of art and culture. Photo by Rich Zila

VIII
Culture

According to Rand McNally, Newark ranks tenth among American cities in the quality of its cultural and performing arts institutions, as measured by indicators such as the number of patrons, revenue, and the number of institutions. In Newark, more than 40 such institutions, with a combined operating budget in excess of $25 million, attract more than 500,000 people a year.

For many performing artists, Newark—only a few minutes from Broadway by train across the Hudson River—is a promising "off-Broadway" location of elegant showcases, experimental theaters, popular nightclubs and bistros, and pace-setting radio/television studios and productions.

There are WNET/Thirteen TV, the pioneering Newark-licensed flagship of the national Public Broadcasting System (PBS); WBGO, the most listened to public radio station in the country; the *home*-state-of-the-art New Jersey Network (NJN) studios; Newark Symphony Hall, one of the largest and acoustically finest concert halls in America; the Newark Museum, rated as one of the best collection/display houses in the nation; the Newark Public Library, one of the greatest bibliographic treasures in the land; the New Jersey Historical Society, with one of the oldest and most valuable collections of antiquities in the New World; the Institute of Jazz; the Black Film Festival; the New Jersey Television and Motion Picture Commission; New Jersey Symphony Orchestra; the New Jersey State Opera; the Garden State Ballet; the Theater of Universal Images and ETC (Ensemble Theatre Company), the oldest and newest black theaters in New Jersey; the Ironbound Theater; the New Jersey Literary Hall of Fame, the nation's first and still only institution of letters honoring authors, writers, and artists/illustrators; Newark Festival of People; DanceAfrica; and a dozen ethnic radio and TV stations and newspapers, including the national-prize-winning *Star-Ledger*, New Jersey's largest newspaper, the eleventh-largest Sunday and fourteenth-largest daily paper in the United States, and the biggest in the Newhouse newspaper chain.

Newark is also the home of several art galleries, including the prominent City Without Walls and Aljira Arts.

Add to this a growing number of historians, sculptors, crafts people, filmmakers, and visual and performing artists, and Newark is more than a culturally enriching off-Broadway venue—it is also the metropolitan region's latest haven for artists and writers living and working only a short rail ride from the center of the entertainment/communications capital—the Big Apple.

And if plans for a $200 million New Jersey Center for the Performing Arts materializes, Newark will be the home of a five-theater, state-of-the-art showcase.

THE NEWARK MUSEUM

The Newark Museum is New Jersey's largest cultural institution and a pioneer among collectors of American art. It was the first to hold museum exhibitions of American folk art in the landmark shows of 1930 and 1931. Other "firsts" include exhibitions of industrial design, both American and European.

The museum is known around the world for its collection of Tibetan art and artifacts. The initial holdings were received in 1911 and active collecting continues to this day. The importance of the museum's Tibetan collection and research has been highlighted by historic visits from His Holiness, the XIV Dalai Lama. The oriental department also includes significant Japanese collections, as well as notable Chinese, Korean, and Indian holdings.

The museum's exhibitions and activities today attract more than 350,000 people a year. Since its founding in 1909, the Newark Museum has achieved national and international renown in such areas as American painting and sculpture, African art, Oriental and Tibetan art, classical art, coins and currency, New Jersey decorative arts, and the natural sciences.

Museum pioneer John Cotton Dana envisioned the Newark facility as "first of all an institution of and for active service to the people of the community." It was Dana's philosophy that a "good mu-

seum attracts, entertains, arouses curiosity, leads to questioning, and thus promotes learning." Dana, who became director of the Newark Public Library in 1902, first started exhibiting pieces in the library and held 56 exhibitions between 1902 and 1908. The museum's first home after it moved out of the library in 1909 was to 49 Washington Street. The new building was the gift of Newark merchant Louis Bamberger.

Dana's first important art acquisition when the museum opened in 1909 was George T. Rockwell's collection of Japanese art. The initial acquisition of scientific materials came in 1912 when the library donated the collection of Newark physician, Dr. William S. Disbrow. The City's first annual appropriation for the operation of the Newark Museum was made in 1911. In 1969, the State of New Jersey became a one-third partner in the operating budget.

Above: This portion of the Newark Museum Sculpture Garden shows an aspect of the space that is informal, inviting, and open. Pictured here to the right is an untitled group of five sculptures by artist Grace F. Knowlton. Courtesy, The Newark Museum

Left: Cotton-top tamarins, a species of small monkeys unique because the males take an active role in caring for their young, help the Newark Museum Mini Zoo to focus attention upon the critical issue of the threatened rain forest. Visitors are able to view the animals through glass-fronted enclosures, which have duplicated their natural habitat. Courtesy, The Newark Museum

The Newark Museum is a leader in the collecting of American decorative arts. The centerpiece of that department is the Ballantine House, a lavish Victorian mansion restored in 1976 to its original grandeur, giving Newark a new link to its illustrious nineteenth-century past.

The museum's Classical collection displays objects from Egyptian, Greek, Etruscan, and Roman antiquity, including the outstanding Eugene Schaefer collection of ancient glass, among the best of its type in the United States.

The ethnology department concentrates on objects of material culture from peoples native to the Americas, Africa, and Oceania. The African collections are especially rich and are some of the museum's earliest acquisitions.

The sculpture garden showcases contemporary works and provides focus for many of the museum's summer programs, including noon-hour jazz concerts and children's theater presentations.

Collections in the science department, oriented toward educational use, are strongest in geology, earth science, and botany, and include a popular "Mini-Zoo." A planetarium offers programs for the general public, as well as for school groups throughout the state.

The museum library holds 26,000 volumes on art and science and a photographic archive documenting the collections.

More than 300 programs are presented each year, attracting more than 100,000 people to the many educational activities readily available to the public. They include concerts, lectures, films, gallery talks, and special activities for senior citizens and the handicapped. Museum-quality objects borrowed from the Lending Department's 10,000 items enable students and other community groups to enjoy and learn from museum resources on a personal level.

The 15-year-old Newark Black Film Festival, an annual six-week series, is heralded as the best festival of its kind by film critics and historians. The Newark Museum's celebration of Black History Month each February is considered one of the most comprehensive in the metropolitan area.

Samuel C. Miller, director of the museum since May 1, 1968, is one of the leaders of the Newark cultural revolution. He arrived after the summer riots in 1967 and faced his first crisis in February 1969 when he learned the Newark City Council had voted to close the library and the museum. He went to Trenton, and, for the first time, the state stepped in to save New Jersey's finest cultural institution.

Miller took it upon himself to bridge cultural differences and bring all the people together by making a "statement" to cement community relations. To do so he mounted a nine-month "Art of Africa" exhibition in 1969, accompanied by a two-week festival of African culture. In 1971, he presented a five-month show of Afro-American art, combining works from a landmark 1944 Newark Museum show with contemporary pieces. In 1975, Miller established a permanent gallery of African Art on the museum's first floor.

By the mid-70s, Miller and his museum were fully assimilated into the Newark culture. Not ignoring the museum's many other prized ethnic pieces, he showcased for the first time in 1973 the famed Tibetan collection, which toured the United States in 1978-1979.

Another Miller coup was the acquisition in 1985 of the "Portrait of Mrs. Charles Thursby," painted in 1898 by John Singer Sargent.

Miller's steady and energetic presence resulted in the $17-million master plan for renovation and expansion, which will double gallery space, improve climate control, and create greater public accessibility, in addition to providing new educational facilities.

Under the gifted eye of Princeton architect/ artist Michael Graves, the museum is being dramatically remodeled in the spirit of an American renaissance. The five-story South Wing will house a 300-seat auditorium for concerts, films, lectures and children's theatrical programs, and will accommodate the educational department, Junior Museum, Arts Workshop studios and classrooms, the Junior Gallery, Mini-Zoo, administrative offices, and the 26,000-volume research library. The master plan involves the adaptive re-use of the former YMCA and Rutgers Law School.

The North Wing, a three-story atrium, is the focus of Graves' brilliant master plan. The stunning atrium will serve as the hinge between the North Wing, the main building, and the Ballantine House,

The Newark Public Library, serving the community since 1888, offers an entire world of history, music, science, and art, including more than a million volumes in its main Newark building and 11 branches. Photo by Rich Zila

coordinating four disparate structures into a unified complex.

Before the expansion, only one-third of the museum's permanent collection could be displayed at any one time.

THE NEWARK LIBRARY

Organized in 1888, the Newark Public Library recently celebrated its centennial year with a major renovation and restructuring—recapturing its old glory while developing its resources and services to meet contemporary needs and standards. The library possesses 1.3 million volumes housed in the main building in downtown Newark and at eight branches and three other outlets.

As the largest public library in New Jersey, located in the state's largest city, the Newark library has been designated as a statewide resource center and as a researh center in the fields of business and "Jerseyana." It is New Jersey's largest repository of print and electronic information at the community level.

The development of the Newark Public Library reflects the interests and energies of its past directors, especially John Cotton Dana, probably the most famous librarian in American history. When Dana arrived from Denver in 1902, he presided over a newly opened Italian Renaissance-style building, one of the city's architectural gems. It was under his long and visionary directorship that many

of the special features of the library were introduced.

Dana made the public library accessible to the public—a "people's" library for all the citizens of Newark. He set aside a section for youngsters, where they could browse and read at their own leisure. Dana introduced the system of library branches, bringing the resources of the Newark Public Library to the many communities in the city.

Under his supervision, the library issued booklets, articles, bookplates, and all sorts of publications that he thought might be of interest to the city's residents. Newark was one of the first libraries to feature the works of American artists.

A library print shop influenced the quality of local commercial printing. Pictures and reproductions of paintings were made available for loan, and delivery service of library materials to schools was arranged with the local board of education.

The Newark Public Library is the repository for every patent entry listed by the United States Patent Office—some 4.5 million to date. The city is a logical place to house this information. Thomas Alva Edison, still the patent record-holder, began his career in a four-story building in Newark in the 1870s.

One of the most significant innovations for Newark's thriving business community was the opening of the first business library in the country in 1904. The Business Library, which has had its own building in the heart of the commercial-financial dis-

Eugenie Grunewald and Peter Graham perform in the Opera/Music Theatre Institute production of **Bilby's Doll** *at the Newark Public Library. Photo by Carol Kitman*

trict since 1927, underwent major renovation in recent years, making its large collection of reference material, often electronically controlled, readily accessible. Among other information, the Business Library has the names and addresses of all businesses in the United States, together with financial and administrative information for thousands of these companies.

During its recent restructuring, the library's resources were organized into major divisions. In addition to the Business Library are the New Jersey Division, Humanities, the Pure, Applied, and Social Sciences, the Popular Library, Art and Music, and the branches and extension services.

The New Jersey Division, which celebrated its 50th anniversary as a separate department in 1988, has the largest collection in the state, which includes Jerseyana information, books, government documents, pictures, archives, maps, periodicals, real estate data, and microfilm collections.

In 1972, the library inherited the "morgue" of *The Newark Evening News*, the newspaper of record in New Jersey for almost a century. The library has been indexing *The Star-Ledger*, New

Jersey's largest daily and Sunday newspaper, in recent years.

The Humanities Division and the Pure, Applied, and Social Sciences Division have been building their collections for decades. In addition to thousands of circulating books on language and literature, travel and sports, biography, and geography and history, the Humanities Division has a broad selection of basic reference sources and reviews.

The Sciences Division contains more than 500 current and back-issue periodicals, subscriptions, books on pure sciences, technical subjects, health and home matters, as well as the various social sciences. Library patrons can find government materials, college catalogs, statistical and technological references, as well as tax and consumer information.

The Art and Music Division contains more than 100,000 fully catalogued items, forming a core collection surrounded by a number of special collections. The art section is located on the third floor of the main library building and includes exhibition galleries, original prints, the picture collection, and a number of special collections. The large picture collection, begun in 1902, is one of the oldest picture files in the United States. There are slides, postcards, posters, a history of fine printing, the autograph collection, and prices and sales records for fine arts and collectibles.

The music section reflects Newark's tradition as a musical city, known in the nineteenth century for its large resident choral groups. The three principal focuses are music literature, music collection (scores), and music phonograph albums and tape recordings.

The Popular Library, which now occupies much of the first floor of the refurbished building, has separate browsing areas for both black and Hispanic studies and materials, as well as an area for special community services such as job and vocational training information and information for special groups, like the handicapped, teens, and seniors.

The library has entered the modern era with a variety of new materials and services. Audiocassettes, CDs, and videocassettes may be borrowed by cardholders. Computer searches are available. The Newark Library is able to tap the resources of other libraries in the region and its materials may be lent to other libraries.

The restored Centennial Hall with its gilt ceilings and wide, wood-burning fireplaces is a vast public room for music, drama, and the arts. The hall features a rare mural by R.H. Ives Gammel, painted in 1927 and uncovered during the restoration.

NEW JERSEY HISTORICAL SOCIETY

The Society's invaluable holdings range from the 1777 *New Jersey Gazette* to today's preeminent statewide newspaper, *The Star-Ledger*. More than one million items are organized in approximately 1,300 distinct manuscript groups. The approximately 65,000 books date from the earliest printed in New Jersey to the state's most current titles.

Founded in 1845, the New Jersey Historical Society occupies a three-story square structure at 230 Broadway, built in 1931. The Society has outgrown the 31,000-square-foot building and is now searching for new quarters with at least 200,000 square feet of storage, display, and working space. The present site is two miles north of the city's center. The Society operates on an annual budget of just over $1 million dollars, with 27 full-time employees.

The Society's first organizational meeting was held in Trenton on a cold and snowy January 13, 1845, and its constitution was adopted at a second meeting in February at City Hall. The constitution proclaimed the Society's purpose "to discover, procure, collect and preserve and make available to its members and to the general public whatever relates to any department of the history of New Jersey . . . and to disseminate knowledge concerning the education and the moral and mental improvement of men, women and children, without pecuniary profit and solely for the benefit of the public."

The Society's photographic collection consists of more than 100,000 pieces, from daguerreotypes of the 1840s to modern color transparencies. The photos are primarily of New Jersey people and places.

About 22,000 prints, or engravings in steel, copper, and wood, as well as mezzotints, aquatints, etchings, and lithographs tell the visual history of New Jersey back to the seventeenth century.

There are more than 2,000 maps, plus broadsides, pamphlets, rare books, and printed ephemera. Paintings number more than 300 oils and watercolors, including portraits, landscapes, and marine views, many by noted American and New Jersey artists. There are also hundreds of original drawings, including landscapes, portraits, illustrations, and architectural and technical drawings.

The costume collection consists of several hundred changes and thousands of accessories from the mid-1700s to the mid-1900s. In the textile collection are samplers, quilts, coverlets, and fine linens.

In decorative arts, several hundred examples of

American furniture, silver, glass, and ceramics, as well as thousands of utilitarian objects of everyday use, are available for scrutiny by scholars, Society members, and citizens.

The Society publishes a quarterly journal devoted to the state's history. The scholarly publication has been in continuous existence since 1845, making it one of the oldest historical journals in the United States.

Jersey Journeys is a monthly reader for students with themes geared to the social studies curriculum. A bimonthly newsletter for members is titled *Messenger*.

Within the Society's headquarters is The History Shop, featuring reproductions of historic documents and maps, and posters, publications, and educational items for children. The shop is open during museum hours, from 10 A.M. to 4 P.M.

Among the Society's selected book titles are: *The Lenape: Archaeology, History and Ethnography*, by Herbert C. Kraft; *New Jersey from Colony to State*, by Richard P. McCormick; *Freedom Not Far Distant: A Documentary History of Afro-Americans in New Jersey*, by Clement A. Price; *Pictorial Guide to Victorian New Jersey*, edited by Robert B. Burnett; and *Pleasures of Colonial Cooking*, prepared by the Miller-Cory Museum and the New Jersey Historical Society.

NEWARK SYMPHONY HALL

New Jersey's largest, oldest showcase enjoys record-setting seasons as more than 200,000 people attend cultural, educational, and entertainment events throughout the year. Symphony Hall audiences have welcomed such famed artists as Isaac Stern, Barry White, Victor Borge, Yehudi Menuhin, Millie Jackson, James Cleveland, and John Amos, plus the regular productions of the New Jersey State Opera, the New Jersey Symphony Orchestra, the Garden State Ballet, the Newark Boys Chorus, and the Theater of Universal Images.

Newark Symphony Hall occupies a "central place in the cultural history of New Jersey," according to architectural historian Donald Geyer, whose investigation of the hall led to its listing in the National Register of Historic Places in 1975. The historian found Symphony Hall to be "one of the few surviving creations of an important era in Ameri-

can cultural development."

Seating 3,365, the Newark theater is larger than Carnegie Hall, Lincoln Center's Metropolitan Opera House, or Philharmonic Hall in New York City. AT&T Bell Laboratories, the world's largest private research organization, tested the acoustics of Symphony Hall in 1965 and put it on par with Boston's renowned Symphony Hall.

The landmark Salaam Temple on Broad Street, as the hall was originally called, was designed by three architects—Frank Grad, Henry Baechlin, and George Backoff—for the Ancient Arabic Order of the Nobles of the Mystic Shrine, commonly known as the Shriners. Groundbreaking for the new temple took place in April 1922. The inaugural performance was held September 8, 1925. The theater in the temple, known as "The Mosque," was a famous attraction during the vaudeville era.

Among the historic figures who have performed at New Jersey's venerable hall have been Sergey Rachmaninoff, Arthur Rubenstein, Vladimir Horowitz, George Gershwin, Arturo Toscanini, Eugene Ormandy, Lily Pons, the Columbia, Boston, and Cleveland symphony orchestras, the Metropolitan Opera National Company, and the Ballet Russe de Monte Carlo.

Symphony Hall is either the home of or the popular venue for New Jersey's premier musical and artistic ensembles: the New Jersey Symphony Orchestra, the Newark Boys Chorus, the New State Opera, the Garden State Ballet, the New Jersey Ballet Company, and the Theater of Universal Images.

The New Jersey Symphony Orchestra traces its roots to 1846, when the Eintracht Orchestra and Singing Society of Newark was founded. Incorporated as the New Jersey Symphony Orchestra (NJSO) in 1928, it has been fully professional since 1968 and was named one of America's major symphonies by the American Symphony Orchestra League in 1972. The New Jersey Symphony has performed at Lincoln Center, Carnegie Hall, the John F. Kennedy Center for the Performing Arts, the United Nations in New York, and at the Wolf Trap Farm Park in Virginia.

Reaching an audience of approximately 200,000 people, the New Jersey Symphony today consists of 85 members. The orchestra performs in

Left: The 85-member New Jersey Symphony Orchestra performs more than 150 concerts each season. Photo by Arthur Paxton/New Jersey Symphony Orchestra

Facing page, far right: The landmark Symphony Hall hosts a wide spectrum of entertaining and educational events throughout the course of the year. Photo by Michael Spozarsky

Below: The Newark Symphony Hall, which seats more than 3,300 people, is larger than the Metropolitan Opera House in New York City. Photo by Sharon Sullivan

more than 150 concerts each season, from New York City's Harbor Festival and the Philadelphia Academy of Music to the Garden State Arts Center in Central Jersey and the Waterloo Village Festival in North Jersey.

The orchestra hosts summer pops concerts, an annual Young Artists' Audition Program, and presents a far-reaching educational program with over 60 full orchestra, chamber orchestra, and ensemble concerts in all of New Jersey's 21 counties. It also gives performances with the New Jersey Ballet, the New Jersey State Opera, the Garden State Ballet, and the June Opera Festival.

The New Jersey Symphony has been on three PBS-TV specials: "Gershwin and Song" (1980), "Luciano Pavarotti at Madison Square Garden" (1984), and "Contemporary Classics" (1986).

Hugh Wolff, appointed music director in 1985, joins a list of distinguished conductors who have led the symphony. Kenneth Schermerhorn took the orchestra to full professional status in the 1960s, and was succeeded by Henry Lewis, who

brought the NJSO into the first rank of American orchestras and expanded its geographic outreach from New Jersey to New York and Washington, D.C. Max Rudolpf was music advisor in 1976, and Thomas Michalak served as music director from 1977 to 1983.

In 1986-1987, his first full season, Hugh Wolff already had the orchestra playing "with something very much like world-class musicianship," according to the *New York Times*.

Almost every great artist of international stature has appeared with the New Jersey Symphony Orchestra, from opera great Luciano Pavarotti to the legendary Sarah Vaughan.

The world-renowned Newark Boys Chorus began as the New Jersey Symphony Chorus, organized in 1966. The chorus has been heard and applauded by audiences throughout the world. With more than 40 recital and orchestral engagements each season, the Newark Boys Chorus has come to be regarded as New Jersey's "Cultural Ambassador." In the spring of 1985, its reputation gained national and international attention when the chorus toured the People's Republic of China—the first such Western organization to do so in modern Chinese history. Other international appearances have included tours to Japan and the Vatican.

The Newark Boys Chorus appears regularly with the New Jersey Symphony and has been

Above: The New Jersey State Opera production of Giuseppe Verdi's La Traviata *features the talents of Adriana Maliponte. Courtesy, New Jersey State Opera*

Facing page top: Based in nineteenth-century Japan, the three-act opera Iris, *which premiered in 1898, was composed by Pietro Mascagni. Jerome Hines stars in this New Jersey State Opera performance. Courtesy, New Jersey State Opera*

Below: Choreographed by Peter Anastos with an unusual blend of music from the court of Louis XIV in combination with the style of Minimalism, Contredanse *has proved a delight to Garden State Ballet audiences. Courtesy, Garden State Ballet*

spotlighted in performances with the Baltimore Symphony Orchestra, the American Symphony Orchestra, and Newark's Cathedral Symphony Orchestra, under the direction of such outstanding conductors as Gunther Schuller, David Zinman, and NJSO's Henry Lewis. The chorus has performed with the New York Philharmonic conducted by Leonard Bernstein and Pierre Boulez, the Philadelphia Orchestra with Eugene Ormandy, the Atlantic Symphony with Robert Shaw, and the New Jersey Symphony with Henry Lewis. It has also participated in a number of notable world premiere performances, including Gian Carlo Menotti's "The Trial of the Gypsy," and, more recently, Randall Svane's "Songs of Innocence."

All Newark Boys Chorus members attend the Newark Boys Chorus School, a full-time academic school for grades five through eight located at Symphony Hall. Academic potential and musical aptitude are the principal criteria for admission to the chorus school. Once admitted, the 45 vocalists from diverse socioeconomic and religious backgrounds are nurtured in an educational experience so intensive that by the eighth grade the students test two to three years above their peers nationwide.

Their repertoire is eclectic, ranging from renaissance, classical, popular, and spirituals, to folk, African, jazz, and show tunes. Contemporary works are commissioned specifically for the Newark Boys Chorus by various composers.

The New Jersey State Opera began as a workshop in 1964, calling itself the Opera Theatre of Westfield. A young conductor named Alfredo Silipigni was engaged in 1965 and, a year later, the company changed its name to the Opera Theater of New Jersey. Its performances were presented in the Westfield and Scotch Plains-Fanwood high schools until November 1968, when it presented *Faust* at Newark Symphony Hall. Outside of Newark, the New Jersey State Opera has performed at the Garden State Arts Center, the Trenton War Memorial, Glassboro State College, Paper Mill Playhouse, the landmark Asbury Park Paramount, Waterloo Village, and Princeton's McCarter Theater.

The roster of stars in New Jersey's grand opera productions have included Jose Ferrer, Beverly Sills, Placido Domingo, Roberto Peters, Robert Merrill, Richard Tucker, Anna Moffo, Jerome Hines, Birgit Nilsson, Magda Olivero, Leyla Gencer, Franco Corelli, Victoria de los Angeles, Ferrucio Tagliavini, Licia Albanese, Dorothy Kirsten, Giuseppe Taddei, Samuel Ramey, Gilda Cruz-Romo, Theresa Kubiak, John Alexander, Sherrill Milnes, James McCracken, and Adriana Maliponte.

The State Opera's education programs reach some 10,000 students each year in their schools across the state. "We see education programs, both teaching about opera and using opera—the queen of the arts—to teach other subjects, reaching as many as 100,000 students a year," says Silipigni, who has been with the company since its founding nearly a quarter-century ago.

The Garden State Ballet, which originated in Newark, is one of New Jersey's oldest dance companies. It specializes in the works of master choreographer George Balanchine and Peter Anastos, founder of Les Ballets Trockadero de Monte whose free-lance ballet creations are staged in Pennsylvania, Dallas, and San Antonio. Anastos designed the routine for one of Baryshnikov's television specials and choreographed a full-length *Cinderella* for the American Ballet Theatre.

The Garden State Ballet concentrates on contemporary dance and revivals of early American ballet from the 1930s and 1940s by such choreographers as William Dollar, Lew Christensen, and Eugene Loring.

The creative force behind the Garden State troupe has been Fred Danieli, who moved to Newark in 1950 after a brilliant career as one of the first to champion the cause of a uniquely American style of ballet. During the 1930s and 1940s Danieli danced with small touring companies that evolved into America's finest ballet troupes—The American Ballet Theatre and the New York City Ballet.

Just before World War II, Danieli formed his own small troupe, El Ballet de los Americas. After the war, he performed in a CBS television dance series that included a production of *Crime and Punishment*. In 1959, Danieli decided to organize his own ballet school in Newark. Each year, thousands of children attend Garden State Ballet's *Nutcracker* and spring repertory performances in their community; for many, it is their first experience viewing a live professional ballet performance.

The New Jersey Ballet Company gave its first performance in 1958 to a small band of believers who nurtured it into a reputable troupe with the help of internationally acclaimed dancer Edward Vilella, who serves as the company's artistic director. Vilella creates some of the choreography for the company and takes part in special galas.

New Jersey Ballet reaches out to the people not only through its masterful performances, but through workshops, classes, lecture-demonstrations, residencies, and teacher training in theaters, high schools, and colleges in New Jersey and at a festival in West Virginia.

The New Jersey Ballet has developed a broad repertoire of contemporary ballet and jazz works, from the traditional pas de deux to abbreviated presentations of *Swan Lake, Don Quixote,* and *Peter and the Wolf.*

Carolyn Clark, born in East Orange and raised in Livingston, has helped make the New Jersey Ballet Company an artistic success. A member of the American Ballet Theatre, Clark has toured North America, Europe, Africa, and the Soviet Union. In 1959, Clark left the ballet stage to appear in Broadway musicals and television productions, including the prestigious Bell Telephone Hour. As a teacher-dancer, Clark brought dance—the most universal of the arts—into the community through mini-concerts featuring classical and jazz pieces.

New Jersey Ballet has performed at the prestigious Jacob's Pillow Dance Festival, the University of Tennessee, the University of Pennsylvania, Iona College, Brooklyn College, and the Virginia Festival of the Performing Arts.

With a repetoire of more than 60 works by eminent traditional and contemporary choreographers, and a company of 16 professional dancers, New Jersey Ballet is recognized nationally as a major dance company.

TUI—the Theater of Universal Images—has staged more original works by promising new playwrights than any other professional theater in New Jersey, according to founding producer-director Clarence Lilley. Founded in Newark in 1970, New Jersey's oldest black theater has staged many memorable productions, including a revival of Eugene O'Neill's *Emperor Jones,* starring John Amos, and

Newark poet Amiri Baraka's play, *Dutchman*, starring Antonio Fargas.

TUI presented the world premiere of *Crispus*, a black historical musical on the life of Crispus Attucks, who was killed at the Boston Massacre and is considered the first person to fall in the American Revolution.

In addition to its regular theatrical season, TUI has produced a touring series, children's plays, festivals, concerts, radio dramas, and film and video productions. It also operates a casting service for local professional talent.

The theater occupies the former television studios of WNET/Thirteen.

THE NEW JERSEY LITERARY HALL OF FAME

Founded in 1976 by English Professor Herman Estrin of Scotch Plains, the Literary Hall of Fame is the only institution of its kind in America that honors writers, authors, and published artists and illustrators.

No student of American literature needs to be told that Stephen Crane's *The Red Badge of Courage* or Walt Whitman's *Leaves of Grass* are timeless classics. Crane, of Newark, and Whitman, from Camden, are among the many New Jersey authors whose portraits hang on the Literary "Wall of Fame" at the New Jersey Institute of Technology in Newark, home of the Literary Hall of Fame. From James Fenimore Cooper of Burlington, America's first novelist, to President Woodrow Wilson, former Princeton president, New Jersey governor, and Nobel laureate, to Pulitzer Prize-winning historians Will and Ariel Durant of Jersey City, who wrote the multivolume *Story of Civilization*, New Jersey authors have written about history, science, medicine, education, animals, and war and peace.

Readers of popular fiction know well the books of Belva Plain, Mary Higgins Clark, Robert Ludlum, and Phyllis Whitney, all of whom were (or are) New Jerseyans. Yet who knows that America's first playwright was William Dunlap of Perth Amboy, or that the nation's first widely acclaimed serious writer was John Woolman of Mount Holly, or that William Henry Herbert (alias Frank Forester) was North America's first author of books dealing with outdoor sports?

Few minor poets ever have won wider affec-

tion than that given to Joyce Kilmer of New Brunswick, whose short poem "Trees" is among the most widely reproduced pieces ever written. No author of dog stories is ever likely to win more readers than Albert Payson Terhune of Pompton Lakes. The "standard" study of life in the early nineteenth century was *Hans Brinker* or *The Silver Skates*, written by Mary Mapes Dodge of Newark. All the volumes concerning the Bobbsey Twins, Nancy Drew, and the Rover Boys were written in East Orange.

John McPhee, Judy Blume, William Carlos Williams, Peter Benchley, Allen Ginsberg, Joyce Carol Oates, Thomas Fleming, Sidney Kingsley, Jim Bishop, and New Jersey Governor Thomas H. Kean (1982-1990), author of *The Politics of Inclusion*, are a mere sampling of the many hundreds of noted authors associated with the Garden State, many of whom have been inducted into the Hall of Fame.

Renowned Princeton architect-artist Michael Graves designed an original, classical disc-shaped Hall of Fame award known as the "Michael," named after its creator. Each year, a handful of New Jersey authors and published artists are presented with a "Michael" when they are inducted into the Literary Hall of Fame. There are plans to widen the scope of the Hall of Fame by making it national sometime in the early 1990s.

WBGO

Newark radio station WBGO (88.3 FM) celebrated its ninth birthday in 1988 by becoming the most listened-to public radio station in the country, according to Arbitron ratings. The standard rating service for radio stations throughout the U.S. reported that WGBO had 360,700 listeners per week in the greater metropolitan region of New York, New Jersey, and Connecticut.

"What we are doing here is creating a jazz institution, a premier institution that encompasses all the things we are doing to present jazz in different settings," enthuses Anna Kosof, WGBO's station manager, who succeeded Robert Ottenhoff, head of New Jersey Network, the state's public TV outlet.

WGBO sponsors and cosponsors a variety of live jazz, from intimate brunches in the performance studio in Newark, to concerts at a variety

WBGO radio in Newark has recently developed into the most popular public radio station in the country, featuring a complete program of jazz for its loyal listeners. Photo by Carol Kitman

of Manhattan locations. In the summer of 1987, the Newark station cosponsored the first jazz series ever presented at and by Lincoln Center, a series that was expanded into a full week in the summer of 1988. The station also presents the "Jazz Fridays" series in the Terrace Ballroom of Newark Symphony Hall.

WBGO's program director Wylie Rollins says, "We are very broadly defining jazz because it gives the music more justice in terms of getting out there to a wider public, rather than just a narrow audience who have developed ears for hard-core jazz." Rollins wants jazz to be "a lot more palatable for more people."

According to jazz critic George Kanzler, WBGO is "now a national force, the country's most listened to public radio station, an achievement that should make all New Jersey jazz fans especially proud."

THE INSTITUTE OF JAZZ
The Institute of Jazz is the foremost archival collection of jazz and jazz-related materials under university auspices. Housed in spacious quarters at Rutgers/Newark, the institute's collection consists of more than 50,000 phonograph records, numerous tapes, cylinder recordings, and piano rolls; a library of more than 5,000 books on jazz and related subjects, including an extensive reference component and large holdings in jazz periodicals from throughout the world, many of them ex-

tremely rare; record catalogs and sheet music; exhaustive research files; photographs, films, and videotapes; and memorabilia and a collection of antique phonographs.

The Institute of Jazz was founded in 1952 by Dr. Marshall Stearns, a professor of medieval English literature at Hunter College and the author of the two basic studies, *The Story of Jazz* (1956) and *Jazz Dance* (1968), the latter coauthored with his wife, Jean Stearns. In 1966, the institute's board selected Rutgers as its permanent academic home. On April 20, 1980, then Newark Mayor Kenneth A. Gibson, a former alto saxophonist, declared a Jazz Week in Newark. The major impetus for the annual affair was Jazz 88, Newark's public radio station, WBGO.

Both Rutgers/Newark and Essex County College in Newark regularly present free jazz concerts. Arts High School sponsors a jazz big band, and drummer-pianist Chick Wing and others teach jazz to children in the community.

Jazz talent of major stature continues to emerge from Newark. Trumpeter Woody Shaw has toured Europe with his own concert ensemble. Organist Rhoda Scott is another major attraction in Europe. The list is impressively long, with names like Schnitter, Davis, Gladden, Johnson, and Thomas keeping the jazz beat alive around the world.

The Newark Jazz Society, started in 1984, also plays a signficiant role in the dissemination of this truly American musical form.

WNET/THIRTEEN

Channel 13 began life at 8 P.M., September 16, 1962, with its first broadcast. The famed broadcast journalist Edward R. Murrow opened the program with these words: "Tonight you join me at the birth of a great adventure."

That adventure initially was identified as WNDT—New Dimensions in Television. Its call letters became WNET as a result of the Ford Foundation's national educational television programs aired on Channel 13 since the foundation acquired the station in 1952. The Ford Foundation continued its generous support of public television through the late 1970s with grants that eventually topped $300 million. Without the Ford Foundation, there would be no Channel 13.

Today, the Newark-licensed television station produces 40 percent of PBS national programming and has been responsible for such presentations as "The Brain," "Heritage: Civilization and the Jews," "Live from Lincoln Center and The Met," "Great Performances," "The Adams Chronicles," "Jewel in the Crown," and "An American Family." Add to that impressive list the financial advice of "Adam Smith," the stark beauty of "Naturewatch," the powerful, haunting images of "Frontline," the unforgettable series "Upstairs, Downstairs," and the entertainingly informative "Sesame Street" and "Mister Rogers," and what you have is an around-the-clock people's television outlet, without interrupting commercials.

WNET/Thirteen, under the direction of New Jersey native President John Jay Iselin (1973-1988), launched "The MacNeil/Lehrer Newshour," still the only full-hour primetime TV newscast. Iselin also helped provide WNET with a base of operations for his informative "Journals" and various specials.

With more than 300,000 members, WNET/Thirteen is the nation's largest and most productive PBS channel. "Great Performances" is the longest-running performing arts series on television. Dramatic productions have featured such noted actors as Laurence Olivier, John Gielgud, Richard Burton, Vanessa Redgrave, Alec Guinness, Leo McKern, Jason Robards, and Jerome Robbins. The works of dancers Mark Morris, Alvin Ailey and Agnes DeMille were highlighted, as was the music of Leonard Bernstein, Zubin Mehta, Itzhak Perlman, Miles Davis, Placido Domingo, Seji Ozawa,

A WNET camerawoman prepares for a station taping. WNET is the country's most productive PBS channel. Photo by Carol Kitman

Steve Reich, Regine Crespin, and Vladimir Horowitz.

Other specials included Robert MacNeil's nine-part series, "The Story of English," and Bill Moyers' 11-part series "In Search of the Constitution."

A regular feature of WNET/Thirteen is the popular "Nature" series, in which host George Page takes viewers to such places as Alaska, Mexico, Brazil, Japan, and the Galapagos Islands to explore the mysteries of the natural world.

NEW JERSEY NETWORK

New Jersey Network (NJN) is New Jersey's only statewide public television system and is viewed by more than one million households weekly, which makes it one of the most-watched PBS systems in the nation. Almost one-fourth of NJN's broadcast inventory is produced in studios in Newark and Trenton. Consequently, NJN is one of the largest public television producers of local programming in the country.

NJN is one of the few public television systems in the United States to produce a full-fledged newscast, the award-winning "New Jersey Network News." Other local programs provide an insight

*Above: The New Jersey Net-
work studios in Newark handle a variety of programming
from special performances to
daily and weekly news segments. Photo by Rich Zila*

and involvement into the life of New Jersey and
Greater Newark matched by no other TV station
in or outside the state. Among the regular local pro-
grams are: "State of the Arts," "Sports People
Play," "New Jersey Outdoors," "Front Page: New
Jersey," "Another View," "On the Record," "New
Jersey Bowl," and "Images/Imagenes."

NJN also has a full-time documentary unit
called "Target New Jersey," which originates several one-hour programs each year.

More than 40,000 teachers use NJN's programming each school week to instruct more than one
million students in more than half the state's
school districts. On weekends, NJN airs adult and
continuing education college credit courses.

NJN's Newark studios, under the direction of veteran station manager and award-winning producer
Jeffrey N. Friedman, shoots a variety of programming, from the 24 episodes of "Another View" and
special performances by the Garden State Ballet,
to daily segments and pieces for "New Jersey Net-

work News" and weekly segments for "Front Page."

The Newark station also stages the live "New Jersey Bowl," produced in cooperation with Rutgers University, as well as the children's talent showcase special, "Images/Imagenes."

The Newark facility at 980 Broad Street is always available for student tours. The station normally averages two groups a month. Friedman's Newark operation also reaches out to colleges for career days and other activities that help the young. During the past year, NJN has visited Montclair State College, Kean College, Wagner College, Essex County College, Rutgers/Newark, and Project Co-ed in Newark.

GATEWAY CABLE

The goal of Gateway Cable is to allow the Newark community to see itself through the cable medium. Viewers enjoy on a weekly basis more than 80 hours of diverse programming, ranging from video music and public affairs to local topical events, high school sports, and even parades. The station covers a gamut of all sectors of the Newark community, including programming from the African-American, Hispanic, Italian, and Portuguese communities.

Gateway Cable's programming department is referred to as TUI/Gateway Cable TV. Theater of Universal Images (TUI) founder Clarence Lilley is the artistic force behind Gateway Cable's programming. Gateway Cable's public access channel (26) and local origination channel (3) have filled the void in media coverage by reaching out to the residents via the system. Residents are able to experience the growing concerns of others by viewing local programming such as City Council meetings and other community affairs.

Since January 1, 1987, Gateway Cable has been serving neighboring South Orange.

A Gateway special in 1988—"Comic Relief in Newark"—was created specifically to raise funds for Newark's homeless people. It was taped at Mr. Wes' Lounge on Broad Street and featured comedians from such popular local clubs as Catch a Rising Star, Rascals, and The Comic Strip. The fund-raiser was a cooperative venture with Gateway Cable, Home Box Office, and Suburban Cablevision.

GALLMAN'S NEWARK DANCE THEATRE

The dancers in this exciting performing company are from New Jersey's inner cities, and each have trained under the urban youth scholarship program at Gallman's school at 303 University Avenue.

In 1978, Alfred Gallman, artistic director and chief choreographer, opened his unique dance theater with a repertory of original works blending technical skills in ballet, modern dance, and jazz dance. The dancers' "high-voltage" performances have brought audiences young and old to their feet in concert appearances in the tri-state area, including programs at Essex County College, Montclair State College, Williams College in Massachusetts, the Newark Museum, Morgan State University in Maryland, Rutgers, the Celebrate Brooklyn Festival, Symphony Space in New York, Newark Symphony Hall, Lincoln Center Out-of-Doors, Riverside Dance Festival, Dancemobile Winter and Summer Series, Solos and Duos at St. Anne's Church, and Men in Dance at the Brooklyn Academy of Music.

During the summer of 1986, Gallman, a member of the national touring company of *The Wiz* was commissioned to choreograph "Miss Liberty Rag" with original music by conductor Peter Howard for the New Jersey Statue of Liberty Celebration. In 1987, Gallman's dance theater was appointed artist-in-residence at Essex College, with plans for a two-year associate degree program.

The New York Times says "Gallman's works are heart felt." *The Village Voice* finds Gallman's "stocked with talent . . . a spine-tingling high." *Dance Magazine* recognizes that Gallman "knows what he is doing," while dance critic Valerie Sudol of *The Star-Ledger* comments: "Gallman's young dancers are impressively strong, with the enviable 11 o'clock extensions and rock-solid balance . . . a bright spot in the city's cultural life. They're giving New Jersey plenty of reason to be proud!"

ART GALLERIES

Newark's most prominent smaller art galleries are City Without Walls and Aljira.

City Without Walls (CWW) is New Jersey's most visible art gallery, with more than 12,000 commuters and visitors passing its wide windowed space each day at Gateway One in the heart of the downtown business district, across from Penn Station.

Founded in 1975 by young artists from high schools around Newark, City Without Walls is a community-oriented gallery with more than 1,000 square feet of prime urban space in which 10 major art shows are handsomely exhibited each year for young, fresh talent. The gallery has presented the works of hundreds of fine art creators over the past two decades.

An artist advocacy organization, CWW is committed to the physical rejuvenation of Newark. Its first book, released in 1982, details "Newark's Architecture: A Study of Steel and Stone."

An urban artist collective, the Newark group launched a major exhibit with Rutgers University titled "North of New Brunswick, South of New York." Among the local artists City Without Walls has helped promote are Frank Palaia of Elizabeth, a multi-media artist; Barry Blair of Hoboken, a sculptor; and Bisa Washington, a new sculptor and fiber specialist.

More recent exhibits have been a series called "Urban Contexts," featuring "Summer Cityscape and Its Permutations," and Manuel Acevedo's "A Window Installation." An earlier show by Acevedo

was titled "Off the Walls."

The name "Aljira" comes from the Australian aborigines and refers to a utopian "dream-time." True to the vision of its cofounders, this world encompasses a concept of timelessness and open possibilities—ideas inherent in the creative process. Aljira remains committed to serving artists and those who appreciate contemporary art.

A center for contemporary art, Aljira began in 1983 as a collective of artists seeking to share inexpensive studio space. Inspired by the visions of artists Victor Davson and Carl Hazlewood, Aljira evolved into an exhibit space for New Jersey artists. Today, Aljira has secured a special place in the cultural life of the Newark area by supporting both emerging and established artists from a variety of national and ethnic backgrounds.

Since 1984, Aljira has presented the work of more than 250 artists from New Jersey and across the United States and Canada. It has also been home base for such emerging dance companies as Gallman's Newark Dance Theatre and the Maimouna Keita School of West African Dance.

Aljira is committed to issues of interest to the immediate neighborhood, as well as to the diverse communities of art enthusiasts from throughout the

Artist Mike Murphy poses at the entrance to the City Without Walls gallery, which is strategically situated in the Gateway One center. Photo by Carol Kitman

metropolitan area. In addition to its activities as an information and resource center, Aljira also works with other organizations on cultural, educational, and artistic projects.

In 1988, Aljira presented "Art from the African Diaspora," a series devoted entirely to contemporary African art, featuring works by artists of African descent from throughout the world. Another recent show was "Transparent/Translucent," which investigated the formal and metaphorical qualities of transparent materials used in art.

DANCEAFRICA . . . FESTIVAL OF PEOPLE

DanceAfrica is a festival of African-American dance companies that performs at Symphony Hall and other Newark venues. Among the various dance troupes are Les Guirivoires, Sabar Ak Ru Afriq, and Urban Bush Women, all of which perform traditional dances of Africa and the Caribbean.

"Newark is a heartland of African-American culture," says Chuck Davis, founder and artistic director of DanceAfrica. "It is really a happening that the companies involved and the people of Newark will not soon forget." Davis taught dance at Central High School and at Jersey City State College before studying and choreographing in Europe and Africa. He organized DanceAfrica in 1978.

Performances begin with a "Council of Elders," choreographed by Davis and comprised of Newark community leaders, which leads a procession and traditional "Dance of Welcome" through the audience and on to the stage.

In addition to performances, DanceAfrica is accompanied by a food and crafts bazaar featuring exhibits and sales of arts and crafts, as well as ethnic foods.

Festival of People was organized in 1985 by a volunteer committee of community and corporate representatives. The weekend festival in mid-September features a wide variety of attractions, including an international marketplace running the length of Park Place, several types of music and dance, arts and crafts, exhibits and a Healthy Heart Festival sponsored by HealthFare USA and Prudential.

The festival's menu is as diverse as the crowd of people, which numbers from 30,000 to 50,000.

The festival signals the close of the summer season. Hot and spicy Indian dishes, traditional "soul food," zeppoles, Ethiopian dishes, smoked sausages, and other ethnic foods please the palates of those who gather in and around the PSE&G Plaza and Military Park in the heart of the business district.

In 1987, the Newark Jazz Festival was added to the lenghtening list of festivities.

"Every ethnic group has something to offer," says Maxwell Jumah, a native of Ghana who brings his three children to the cultural and educational carnival. *Star-Ledger* writer Angela Stewart sums up the spirit of the Festival of People this way: "It is a time for people, all kinds of people . . . sharing a unique experience in which cultural distinctions are 'embraced' and unity prevails over division."

ENSEMBLE THEATRE COMPANY . . . IRONBOUND THEATRE

Following the seminal Theater of Universal Images, founded in 1970, was the Ensemble Theatre Company (ETC), which debuted in 1981, and the Ironbound Theatre, organized in 1983.

ETC specializes in black drama. The troupe's choice of shows and dramatic interpretations are quite unlike most of the fare being offered elsewhere.

"Our mission is to show the complexities of black people," says co-artistic director Marvin Kazembe Jefferson, "to place Afro-Americans in various situations—some that we're familiar with, some not—to enhance our humanity. And, by enhancing it, to get people of different cultures to share in our humanity."

Jefferson's collaborator, Reginald C. Brown, directs such off-beat plays as Jean Anouilh's *L'Ermine.*

ETC's regular home is the tiny Newark Community School of the Arts/Stella Lass Theater, at 186 Clinton Avenue. The Ensemble also performs in larger settings, including the Crossroads Theatre in New Brunswick.

Over the past few years, ETC's "statewide, multi-regional impact" has brought it increased attention and potentially higher funding. But the company, which operates on "less than a shoestring and pours a raw intensity into any material it touches," will remain rooted in Newark, where several of its members grew up, reports drama critic Bob Campbell.

Most company members are graduates of the Mason Gross School of the Arts at Rutgers, New Brunswick. That city is the Ensemble's second home.

ETC is now forming a unified front with TUI and Ironbound to forge a new audience in Newark.

The Ironbound Theatre is also imbued with "a mission"—to provide an affordable, accessible, and quality theatrical experience in a city in the process of renewing itself.

The Ironbound Theatre was conceived by a group of New Jersey theater artists trained at nearby Montclair State College in Upper Montclair. What they all shared was a "respect for each other's work," according to Paul Whelihan, managing director, and Gregg Thomas, editor of *Prologue*, a publication of Ironbound Theatre. They came together and performed several evenings of one-act plays. They were enthusiastically received by full-house audiences in a small basement in the Ironbound section of Newark. "We knew from the magic of those evenings that what we had was right," Whelihan recalls of their first production year. They moved out of the cellar and over the next two years played in various spaces throughout the city before settling into its current home, Trinity Reformed Church on Ferry Street, one of the main arteries through the Ironbound.

Among the theatre's more recent productions have been *Once Upon a Time There Was a Family*, *The Birds*, *Master Harold . . . and The Boys*, and *The Golden Handshake*, an original drama by Robert Sturmer.

Ironbound Theatre's boosters include the New Jersey State Council on the Arts, Public Service Electric & Gas Co., New Jersey Bell, Mutual Benefit Life Insurance Company, NJIT, Rutgers, Newark Public Library, Montclair State College, and Middlesex County College.

FESTIVAL OF THE ARTS

Every third Tuesday of the month, the Festival of Arts at the Second Presbyterian Church presents a distinctive program focusing on the arts of both the black and Hispanic cultures, including solo in-strumental and vocal recitals, vocal and instrumental ensembles, dance, lectures, and exhibits.

Depending upon the character of the individual programs being offered, events are held in the Great Nave (1,500 seats), Hunter Hall (an 1880s, more intimate Victorian performance room), or Clee Auditorium (800 seats). Programs are preceded by a light buffet supper available at a nominal cost.

The first Sunday of each month all programs are preceded by a buffet luncheon and guided interpretive tours of the Nave and magnificent stained glass art. Tours are free.

The surrounding business community may enjoy the Festival of Arts every Wednesday from 12 noon to 1 These programs offer a refreshing interlude to the working day. They feature vocal and instrumental solo and ensemble performances, dance, film series, and lecture demonstrations. Admission is free and audiences may bring their own brown-bag lunch.

Previous lunchtime programs have included "Organ Music From Spain," "Contemporary Black Composers and Their Music," "Spanish Art as Religious Expression," "The Life of Black America Through Writings and Photography," "Flemenco!," and "Street Corner Gems!"—black performers who have performed on street corners and out-of-the-way cafes with a wide range of styles from blues and jazz to pop and rock.

Dr. J. Richard Szeremany is director of the Festival of the Arts.

SUMMER EVENTS IN ESSEX

Some 60 free events are sponsored each summer by the Essex County Division of Cultural Affairs. A typical calendar looks like this:

The 40-piece New Jersey Pops Orchestra kicks off the summer with concerts and festivals in the parks, starting with Newark's Branch Brook Park. The Metropolitan Opera performs in various parks, followed by an "American Celebration" with rides, clowns, a petting zoo, food stands, and family entertainment, including fireworks and an appearance by the U.S. Air Force Band.

The National Gilbert and Sullivan Playhouse, a repertory company, stages excerpts from such popular works as "The Pirates of Penzance."

Craft shows and concerts are common fare, including the senior citizens' "Art Alfresco" and performances in the Turtle Back Zoo in West Orange.

Big Band Nights feature performances by many popular local and regional bands. The Starlight Jazz Band, the Duke Stabile Orchestra, the Swing Renaissance, and the Garden State Brass Ensemble are among those featured.

There are classical groups, blues, country, pop, and folk sing-a-longs in the parks. Other events include: Gallman's Dance Theatre, the American Arts Ensemble, a gospel festival, children's festival, India festival, international jazz festival, American Indian festival, and bluegrass concerts.

The season usually ends with the Newark Festival of People in Military Park.

CELEBRITIES

No story of any community can be complete without a list of its more famous residents, those who have either been born and raised in Newark, or have chosen Newark as the place to work and apply themselves. Since its inception, Newark has spawned some of the finest minds and talents in American history. Whether composers, inventors, or political leaders, Newark can claim its share of the best.

The Newark Public Library has, over the years, compiled a list of various personages who have distinguished themselves in their respective fields, be they educators or business people. Although the city's most illustrious "Who's Who" is still growing—with some names inadvertently omitted due to imperfect record-keeping—herewith are those who have been identified as being among the most gifted products of Newark:

Entertainers include singers Sarah Vaughan, Melba Moore, Connie Francis, The Ritz Brothers, and Viola "Miss Rhapsody" Wells; musician/conductor Mort Lindsey; comedian/actor Jerry Lewis; actresses Eva Marie Saint, Vivian Blaine, and Gloria Gaynor; and actors John Amos and Jack Warden.

The various writers include Stephen Crane (*The Red Badge of Courage*), Philip Roth (*Goodbye, Columbus*), poet/playwright Amiri Baraka (*LeRoi Jones*), playwright and movie mogul Dore Schary,

Mary Mapes Dodge (*Hans Brinker*), animal writer Albert Payson Terhune, Washington Irving, Henry William Herbert (the first sportswriter), Howard Garris (the *Uncle Wiggily* stories), playwright Richard Wesley, Nathan Heard (*Howard Street*), and columnist Russell Baker (of *The New York Times*).

And there are composers Jerome Kern, Samuel A. Ward (who wrote the music for "America the Beautiful"), and Alex Bradford of gospel fame.

The four most prominent inventors have been Thomas Edison, who started his first production factory in Newark; Seth Boyden, who invented patent leather; the Reverend Hannibal Goodwin, whose flexible photographic film made the motion picture industry possible; and Edward Weston, whose innumerable electrical devices advanced America's Industrial Revolution.

In industry and business, there have been John Dryden, founder of Prudential Insurance Company; brewer Peter Ballantine; Louis Aronson of Ronson lighter fame; William Mennen and his hygenic products; and merchant Louis Bamberger (Bamberger's is now Macy's).

In government, the notables are New York Mayor Edward I. Koch, Vice President Aaron Burr, Jr., Congressman Peter W. Rodino, Jr., (who chaired the "Watergate" hearings), United States Senator Frederick Frelinghuysen, and three New Jersey governors: Franklin Murphy, Marcus Ward, and William Pennington.

In the annals of jurisprudence, three figures stand out—U.S. Chief Justice Charles Evans Hughes, U.S. Supreme Court Justice William J. Brennan, and New Jersey Chief Justice Arthur Vanderbilt.

Newark's luminaries also include Aaron Burr, Sr., founder of Princeton University, the legendary nurse Clara Maass, educator James M. Baxter, and Newark's own founder, Puritan leader Captain Robert Treat, who went on to serve as governor of Connecticut.

And, of course, there are many sports greats: boxing champions "Marvelous" Marvin Hagler and Abie Bain, Olympic fencer Peter Westbrook, world-class cyclist Frank L. Kramer, track star Renaldo Nehemiah, baseball players Jim Bouton, Rick Cerone, Lary Doby, and Ray Dandridge, Sr., and basketball players Al Attles and Edgar "E.J." Jones.

Newark's community organizations have helped to create a renewed sense of spirit and pride in the city and in all it has to offer. Photo by Michael Spozarsky

IX
Organizations

Newark survived the riots in the summer of 1967 after the black, Hispanic, and white communities realized that without cooperation and commitment, their city could never be reunited and rebuilt as their *home*, their extended-family neighborhood where they could live, work, play, and pray individually and collectively.

That hope, that elusive dream, has been painstakingly slow in coming to fruition. But after more than two decades of false starts and tough trial-and-error, a feeling of community spirit is starting to take root through several organizations that strive to keep the 'family of Newark' together, spiritually and materially.

These groups quietly go about their business by developing "networks" and "linkage strategies" and "collaborations" and "consensus" to stabilize and rejuvenate homes and workplaces, blocks and neighborhoods, historic sites and institutions, and to provide for jobs, health care, and educational opportunities.

They include The Leaguers, the NAACP, the Newark Coalition for Neighborhoods, the Newark Collaboration Group, Catholic Community Services, New Community Corporation, Protestant Community Centers, FOCUS, and many other organizations dedicated to improving a rainbowed quality of life in New Jersey's largest city.

NEWARK COALITION FOR NEIGHBORHOODS
The operative word for The Newark Coalition for Neighborhoods (NCN) is "work"—working for people, for neighborhoods, and for Newark by forging a unity for urban survival.

The Newark neighborhoods coalition works to provide a "strong, intelligent voice for community advocacy and neighborhood policy development," according to its executive director, Richard Cammarieri. Its mission is to provide services "to all without regard to race, religion, sex, age, national origin, or citizenship."

NCN, founded in 1977, represents major community-based organizations located through the city. Their reason for being is "self-improvement" through housing, tenant support, employment training, economic development, property tax reform, voter registration, education, welfare reform, correctional services, and monitoring of government bodies.

The coalition's activities include task forces for arson prevention, housing and economic development, as well as for advancing collective community development block grants, neighborhood cleanup, health screening, and a public access television program.

Its associate and member agencies read like a "Who's Who" of Newark's grass roots constituencies: St. Ann's Learning Experience, Mount Pleasant Community Development Corp., Peoples Energy Cooperative, Independence High School, Newark Emergency Services for Families, Ironbound Community Corp., La Casa de Don Pedro, The Leaguers, NewArk School, Newark Tenants Organization, North Ward Center, Protestant Community Centers, Roseville Coalition, St. Columba's Neighborhood Club, Tri-City Peoples Corp., Unified Vailsburg Services Organization, and Youth Consultation Services.

The coalition's Linkage Strategy Project addresses broad policy issues in housing and employment opportunities for residents. NCN's participation in organizing the Fair Banking Initiative Coalition focuses on providing more immediate resources to individual residents in terms of credit and banking needs.

NCN's work with the New Jersey Community Loan Fund and NCN's Capacity Building activity relates primarily to assisting nonprofit groups to take part in the development process in ways that best suit their needs and interests.

"The ultimate goal is to empower community groups and residents they represent so they have a meaningful role in the revitalization of Newark," NCN states in its "Activities" objectives. "Linkage strategies have been used in various cities throughout the country. They work on the principle of 'linking' approval of development plans with developers contributing in some way to pressing local needs like housing and employment."

Above: The young people of Newark benefit from the concern and support of the city's many community-oriented programs. Photo by Mary Ann Brockman

Right: With the support and assistance of many community programs, Newark proudly acknowledges that it is a city on the move. Photo by Rich Zila

Availability of clean and comfortable housing, such as these charming family units in the Central Ward, is a basic concern of Newark's many community groups. Photo by Rich Zila

Examples of linkage include negotiating with developers to provide a certain percentage of housing for low-income units, or "first source" agreements which involve companies using city residents as their first source for employment needs.

Responding to Newark's resurgence, NCN is working with the public and private sectors to ensure that revitalization provides "balanced development" and "equitable benefits" for all residents.

"Without these efforts and support, low-income people are in an extremely vulnerable position, at the mercy of speculative forces which lead to displacement of poor people at all costs," Cammarieri stated.

Balanced economic development efforts, planned and implemented by low-income people and representatives, provide a means to seize the opportunity we have today to guide Newark's renewal so that it does offer equitable benefits, provide a fair share and opportunity for those most in need and contributes to the long-term stabilization of the social fabric and quality of life for our city.

NCN's efforts in economic development and unemployment are planned in concert with the Metropolitan Ecumenical Ministries, a coalition of church groups.

NEWARK COLLABORATION GROUP

The Newark Collaboration Group (NCG) was born out of a meeting of 40 business, community, religious, and educational and governmental leaders in May 1984. They convened with a common purpose: To chart a course for Newark's revitalization and unite those forces interested in working toward that goal.

Today, membership in the nonprofit organization has swelled to more than 200 members. The mayor, city council president, county executive, and chairman of the Greater Newark Chamber of Commerce serve as members of its executive committee, along with 11 other persons representing various sectors of the city.

More than 20,000 hours of voluntary time have been committed, not to duplicate the functions of existing organizations, but to serve as a facilitator and coordinator of various efforts already underway while helping to spark new initiatives.

Gregory S. King, managing director of NCG, says the collaboration is not meant to be a community organization, but a "business-driven" organization working as a facilitator and convener.

Recognizing that people are the city's most important resources, the NCG has become the "principle vehicle for an expression of hope and progress," according to Dr. Robert Curvin, dean of the Graduate School of Management for New Jersey for Social Research in New York City. Curvin headed the group's task force that analyzed what its role in Newark would be. He also organized Newark's first black and Puerto Rican political convention in 1970 that led to the election of the city's first black mayor, Kenneth Allen Gibson.

Behind closed doors at meetings of the NCG's 19-member executive committee considerable give-and-take is apparent and often some strong difference of opinion. But it is all done in a polite, nonconfrontational manner, according to NJIT President Saul Fenster, chairman and one of the driving forces behind the Collaboration.

As an organization, the NCG operates on the principles of openness, inclusiveness, and consensus. Tangible evidence of that can be found in the "City Life" document, a set of 29 initiatives for Newark's future developed by a strategic planning committee that included more than 250 volunteer members from the public, private, nonprofit, and local community sectors.

Initially, the NCG made housing, employment, and training its top priorities. As the group matured, it targeted other concerns: education, recreation, infrastructure, small and minority business, community development, disposition of publicly held land, the city's image, and culture and the arts.

One of NCG's first undertakings was the establishment of the Newark Housing Partnership, a collaborative effort among financial institutions, government, and a national nonprofit housing organization to provide more than $35 million for the construction or rehabilitation of more than 600 dwelling units. It represents the largest single commitment of public and private funds for housing regeneration in New Jersey's history. At least 20 percent of the funds are set aside for single- and multi-family homes for low- and moderate-income families. The remaining units are being sold at market rates.

The group has been directly involved in the University Estates project of Vogue Housing Connection, Inc. The project is a development of 40 two- and three-bedroom townhouses for families of moderate incomes built in the Central Ward.

"Our intent," said Donald Harris, president of Vogue Housing, "is not just to build housing, but to build a comprehensive community." Vogue set out to build the community as a "first among equals, one that will set the tone for all developments in the area."

The NCG has attracted national groups to invest their resources in Newark. Among them are

Youth-oriented services are a priority at La Casa de Don Pedro. Courtesy, La Casa de Don Pedro

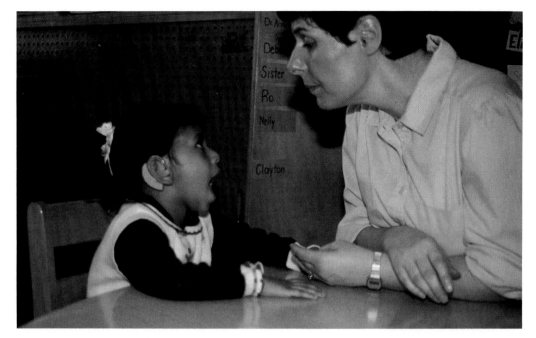

A speech and language pathologist from the Catholic Community Services Communications Disorders Program is shown here in therapy with a four-year old child. Slated to be one of the best programs for speech and learning in the state of New Jersey, the Communication Disorders Program serves more than 100 Newark residents annually. Photo by Kimberly A. Watson/Catholic Community Services

the Enterprise Foundation and the Ford Foundation's Local Initiative Support Corporation.

The La Casa/Enterprise Foundation partnership developed a 39-unit project of tri-level, three-bedroom condominiums for low-income families.

Robert O'Brien, chairman of Carteret Savings Bank, observes: "Two important goals of the housing partnership are to allow nonprofit organizations to take a greater role in responding to the housing needs of their communities and to boost the number of minorities in the housing business."

The NCG's Incubator Training Fund, developed with funding from the Gannett Foundation's Community Priorities Program, supports training for some 100 local residents in high-demand job skills as it assists job-creating business incubators—facilities where rents are low, and staff, expertise, and other services are shared. Through the Training Fund, more and more unemployed residents of Greater Newark are trained for tooling and machining. New companies in "incubators" also receive on-the-job training subsidies for additional workers in the project.

TAPCO—the Training and Placement Correlation Organization—convened by the Newark Private Industry Council, is one of the first initiative working groups to be launched as part of the implementation of the "City Life" plan. It exists to increase communication and coordination among the city's job training and placement agencies.

TAPCO is organized into three committees: the Job and Training Opportunity Network, Transportation, and Coordination of Training Programs with Job Opportunities.

Neighborhood-based organizations active in the NCG are Tri-City Peoples, the Central Ward Coalition of Youth Agencies, Unified Vailsburg, Clinton Hill Home Owners Association, La Casa de Don Pedro, North Ward Center, North Ward Property Owners Association, and the Ironbound Educational & Cultural Center.

Citywide groups include Aspira, the Newark Coalition of Neighborhoods, and the Rutgers Urban Gardening Program.

The Newark Collaboration Group is also involved in the $500 million "riverlands renaissance," attracting developers from Taiwan and Port Liberte in Jersey City. The waterfront property runs from Bridge Street south along McCarter Highway to River Bank Park in the Ironbound section.

CATHOLIC COMMUNITY SERVICES

Catholic Community Services (CCS) evolved from the Mount Carmel Guild, which was the vision of Bishop Thomas J. Walsh, who organized the original Guild in Buffalo, New York, in 1911. Its purpose was two-fold: to benefit aid recipients through spiritual, mental, and physical relief, and to benefit the association's own corps of Catholic women volunteers.

A staff member of the Frail Elderly Program in Newark is pictured here offering support and guidance to one of the program's clients. A special component of this program, offered by Catholic Community Services, is the availability of Braille typing and electronic visual aids. Photo by Kimberly A. Watson/ Catholic Community Services

Walsh's 1918 consecration as third Bishop of Trenton brought about a Guild in the state's capital in 1920, followed by a Camden branch. After Walsh was appointed to Newark's Episcopal See in 1928, he established a Guild for the Greater Newark area two years later—at the onslaught of the Depression. Services for the deaf were instituted in 1937, for the blind in 1940, and for the learning-disabled in 1965.

In the 1960s, the CCS founded the first community health center in Newark, as well as the first vocational rehabilitation center.

Today, CCS administers 42 programs within the Archdiocese, ranging from adoption services to counseling for the elderly.

The workers of the Catholic Community Services have sometimes been called "Angels—a gift to Church." The "Angels" are often the help of last resort, the only hope in a community, as evidenced by the comprehensive array of critical services made available by the CCS. A partial listing of these programs include Afterschool Program, Campaign for Human Development, Family/Children Counseling Services, Foster Grandparents, Hispanic Resource Centers, Immigration Assistance, Ministry to the Deaf, New Jersey Boystown, Refugee Resettlement, Shelters for the Homeless, Substance Abuse Counseling, and Unwed Mothers' Services.

NEW COMMUNITY CORPORATION

Founded in 1968 by a group of residents from the city's Central Ward, the New Community Corporation's (NCC) mandate is to improve economic development in Newark. Although it is not an Archdiocesan organization, the NCC is run by an Archdiocesan priest. The NCC has more than 700 employees from communities it has developed in the Central and West wards of the city. It owns more than 2,300 units of housing in those wards. As such, it is the largest nonprofit housing corporation in New Jersey and one of the largest in the nation.

Spurred to action by the pressing crisis of urban poverty, the Central Ward citizen activists sought to create a new community that would allow them to determine their own destiny by making the housing, educational, economic, and political decisions that would govern their lives.

New Community today is proud of its part in Newark's renaissance. It has a real estate investment in the city of more than $100 million, and every year it pays more than $1.7 million in real estate taxes to the city.

New Community acts as an umbrella corporation for a group involving itself in real estate planning and development, construction, finance and asset management, and public relations. It oversees housing ventures, day care, an employment cen-

Left: A physical therapist works with residents of the New Community Corporation extended care facility. Courtesy, New Community Corporation

Below: The elegant St. Joseph's Plaza offers an idyllic luncheon atmosphere. Photo by Carol Kitman

ter, commercial real estate, health care, and business development.

NCC provides its services to the community through a "cooperative network" that includes the housing corporation and its components—Babyland Nursery and St. Rose of Lima Parish.

Babyland is the first and finest nonprofit, interracial, and nonsectarian day-care center in New Jersey for children from age two-and-a-half months to five years. It is the third-largest day care operation in the nation.

St. Joseph's Plaza is also a product of New Community's leaders. A brownstone church listed on both the National and State Register of Historic Places was converted into a unique center housing New Community's headquarters on the third level of an atrium, plus the Priory Restaurant, a spa, medical offices, lounge, sandwich shop, credit union, and conference center.

NCC's network, in addition to offering a federal community development credit union, includes a health care center with medical group practice, an extended health care facility, protective services for children, a family violence shelter, nutrition and food services for young and old, a privately owned nonprofit construction company, a monthly newspaper (the *Clarion*), and a computer system.

Among other projects, the NCC is involved in a joint venture with Pathmark to build a new super-

market in Newark. The benefit to the community that the supermarket brings is immeasurable, since most residents are low-income families and senior citizens who do not have cars.

There are 8,000 homeless families in Newark and about 107,000 whose income falls below the federal poverty level. These are the most needy, the ones New Community is trying to bring into the mainstream of Newark's gradually improving socioeconomic system.

New Community's philosophy can best be expressed with the organization's own words: "All

Right: A safe, clean, and comfortable life is the guiding vision of community-oriented citizens. Photo by Mary Ann Brockman

Below: Newark is making great strides in changing the city into a safer place for children. Here, a group of young friends buy a treat from a local neighborhood vendor. Photo by Michael Yamashita

persons, as children of God, are entitled to and capable of confirming their own dignity and determining their own destiny."

NCC's goal is to improve the quality of life of Newark to "reflect individual dignity and personal achievement" by "concretizing the need and value of working and living together with mutual respect and courtesy."

PROTESTANT COMMUNITY CENTERS

Out of the vision of some members of Old First Church and South Park-Calvary Church, a committee was formed in the spring of 1964 to implement a summer program for children and youth residing within the communities surrounding the two churches.

One phase of that program was located in a storefront in a run-down building at 313 Mulberry Street. In one of the poorest, most neglected areas in the city, its doors were opened to both the young and the old. This storefront operation quickly became known as "The Center." Arts and crafts, games, music, reading, understanding, and friendship were offered to those who walked into the Mulberry center. Teen canteens were held in the evenings and the small quarters were always overflowing with local residents. The center was on duty day and night for months that summer. Its doors officially closed on Labor Day weekend, but the people kept coming and the center unofficially continued during the winter months, expanding activities along the way.

On February 19, 1965, five persons met at the South Park-Calvary Church to make "The Center" a formal organization, incorporated as a nonprofit, interdenominational community service project to "broaden and enrich the lives of inner-city families," according to Dorothy J. Knauer, associate director for programs.

The signers of the papers that established the Protestant Community Center were Dr. Conrad H. Massa of Old First Church, Dr. Norman A. Wilson, Richard Corriden, and Margaret G. Burns of South Park-Calvary, and Richard H. Wood, who still serves as executive director. As the center matured and its activities reached out to the larger community, its name was changed to the Protestant Community Centers (PCC).

Since then, PCC has diversified into an educational, cultural, and recreational operation helping the needy, the destitute, and the misfortunate youth in Newark and in the surrounding Essex County communities through its residential program known as Cross Counter. "Self-help" and "maximum growth" are the foundation on which PCC and its sister agency offer their services to the Greater Newark community.

In July 1981, PCC—with assistance from Blue Cross/Blue Shield, Mutual Benefit Life, New Jersey Bell, Prudential, and PSE&G—opened the James Street Neighborhood House Child Care Center. The center was created to provide quality child care benefiting those parents working in the immediate downtown business district. Parents can even have lunch with their children because the center is within walking distance of the major supporting companies. Workshops are addressed to the parents of infants, toddlers, preschoolers, prekindergarteners, kindergarteners, and first-graders enrolled in the center.

The "Parent Linking Project" was established to help teenage mothers meet their emotional, developmental, and economic needs, as well as the needs of their children. The teen mother is given an opportunity to develop her vocational and job-search skills to allow her to become self-sufficient.

Three recent programs at the James Street Neighborhood House are the Micro-Computer Course, which teaches youth the basic hi-tech skills needed in an automated society; English-As-a-Second-Language, which teaches adults new to this country the necessary communication skills to survive and flourish; and the Business Volunteer Tutorial Program, which gives business employees the opportunity to volunteer their time and talents to students enrolled in the Newark public school system.

The Suburban Cultural Educational Enrichment Program (SCEEP) has been a major activity of PCC since 1971, offering remedial/tutorial education to students of the Newark school system (grades three to six) who are recommended to the program by their teachers and, in some cases, by their parents. SCEEP currently has 16 on-site locations where students can develop their basic skills. From October to May of each year, more than 500 suburban volunteers from the 16-plus churches participating in the program donate their time and talents to help the youngsters in fulfilling their educational goals by providing supplementary instruction in math and reading on a one-on-one basis, as well as training in arts and crafts.

The on-site SCEEP locations are Basking Ridge Presbyterian Church for the Bragaw Avenue School; Chatham United Methodist Church for the Peshine Avenue School; Livingston Presbyterian Church for the Warren Street School; Morristown Presbyterian Church on The Green for the South 17th Street School; First Presbyterian Church in Sparta for the Bergen Street School; First Presbyterian Church of Orange for the Warren Street School; Morrow Methodist Church in Maplewood for the George Washington Carver School; Christ Church in Summit for the Bergen Street School; Calvary Presbyterian Church in Florham Park for the Chancellor Avenue School & Annex; Presbyterian Church of Madison for the Madison Avenue School; Community Church of Mountain Lakes for the George Washington Carver School; Union Congregational Church in Upper Montclair for the Sussex Avenue School; Ogden Memorial Presbyterian Church in Chatham for the Chancellor Avenue School & Annex; First Presbyterian Church in Mendham for the South 17th Street School; First Presbyterian Church in Cranford for the Dayton Street School; and Chatham Township Presbyterian Church for the Dayton Street School.

THE LEAGUERS

Founded in 1946 by educator and civic leader Dr. Mary B. Burch, The Leaguers has, since its inception, been dedicated to stimulating "opportunities for youth through education and community participation." Its constitution sets forth six fundamental principles: To develop a spirit of community cooperation among youth; To promote a strong leadership imbued with civic responsibility among youth; To stimulate and assist all beneficial, social, cultural, and educational activities; To provide effective guidance in vocational education and employment qualifications; To awaken a sense of economic security resulting from efficient self-realization, diligence and mature citizenship; To motivate the community toward making necessary provision for its youth—that they may achieve these goals.

The primary objectives of The Leaguers, headquartered at 731 Clinton Avenue, are to provide high school-age youth with supplemental educational opportunities while in school and to prepare them for careers following graduation, and to generate college scholarships and other assistance for those aspiring to higher education. To date, the Leaguers has realized more than $1 million in college scholarship funds.

In response to the needs of the Newark community, The Leaguers has expanded its programming and broadened its scope. The organization now serves children at the preschool and primary grade levels. At the Leaguers' Community and Youth Development Center on Clinton Avenue, programs and services are also offered to adults and senior citizens.

NAACP

The National Association for the Advancement of Colored People was founded in 1909 and is the oldest civil rights organization in the world, with almost 400,000 Americans of all races as members.

The NAACP has provided and trained more leaders for the black community than any other single organization. Virtually every black American leader, public and private, learned the spirit of public service and the techniques of leadership through the NAACP. Roy Wilkins, Vernon Jordan, Julian Bond, Andrew Young, Thurgood Marshall, Ralph Bunche, and many others served their apprenticeships in the association's youth councils and college chapters. There are more than 500 local youth councils and college chapters throughout the country, making the Youth and College Division the largest secular youth organization in America.

The NAACP is the national voice for black Americans and other minorities, and for those who support civil rights objectives in America. The NAACP articulates the grievances of black Americans and protects their rights by whatever legal means necessary.

With offices at 1028 Broad Street, the NAACP is actively involved in areas of preeminent concern to minorities, indeed, to all Americans, as its slogan makes clear: "Toward One Society." Among its priorities are voting rights, economic advancement, criminal justice and "The Black Family and the Urban Challenge."

In 1984, the NAACP was heartened by the success of its first statewide Urban Program Office in New Jersey, a program initiated in late 1982 with the aid of the state's 36 local branches. Since then, the New Jersey Office has developed a successful job skills/availability bank with area corporations, resulting in numerous job placements. It has also launched its SAT (Scholastic Aptitude Test) programs at four sites, negotiated several new "Fair Share" agreements, sponsored statewide conferences to improve black-Jewish relations, and bolstered its voter registration capacity. The Urban Program is a model the NAACP is extending to other states.

The NAACP's agenda includes public information, curriculum improvement, school desegregation, SAT test preparation clinics, open housing, Back-to-School/Stay-In-School programs, voter education, civil rights internships, "Overground Railroad Marches," prison programs, equal

Left: Community spirit, career guidance, and the promotion of civic responsibility and leadership are among the basic principles and goals of The Leaguers organization. Photo by Rich Zila

NAACP Newark Branch president Keith M. Jones spoke to the public over the air at WNJR radio, during the NAACP 1988 Radiothon, regarding the importance of membership. Radiothon hostess Margaret Mitchell (far left) and other NAACP members looked on. Courtesy, NAACP Newark Branch

A community garden in the city's North Ward adds a touch of loving care to the neighborhood. Photo by Sharon Sullivan

The refreshing spray from a fire hydrant helps to keep temperatures down during the hot summer months in Newark. Photo by Bob Krist

employment activities, health fairs, affirmative action, a resume retrieval project, and promoting black entrepreneurship.

FOCUS

FOCUS started in 1968 to help train and find jobs for Spanish-speaking residents in Newark and the surrounding urban Essex area. The acronym stands for Field Orientation Center for the Underprivileged Spanish, and the organization was so named "to show the way and what we're attempting to do," says founding chairman Jose Rosario.

The multipurpose agency offers guidance and training to the city's growing Spanish population. It serves more than 8,000 Hispanics a year. (More than 50,000 Puerto Ricans, Cubans, and Latin American Hispanics live in Newark.) The agency occupies the FOCUS Victoria Center, a large, stylistic office building at 443-449 Broad Street. A new annex for the handicapped at 441 Broad Street was opened in 1988.

"Here we see the beginning of something by the poorest people in the city toward living together in harmony," Rosario says. "Such an intercultural activity can help eliminate misunderstandings, lack of communication, and ingrained discrimination leading to tension which can have catastrophic consequences."

FOCUS sponsors cultural forums to demonstrate the artistic achievements of youngsters. It tutors high school students, aids juveniles, offers counseling to parents and young people with emotional problems, and is also active in legal aid and solving housing problems.

FOCUS has its own language skills laboratory where two levels of English instruction are offered for adults. The agency also maintains an ongoing literacy program that teaches reading and writing skills to adults who are illiterate.

SALVATION AND THE "Y"

A pair of venerable institutions—the Salvation Army and the YMWCA—need no introduction, for their presence is evident everywhere.

The nucleus of all Salvation Army activity is the local Corps Community Center. This place of worship and neighborhood activity provides people of all ages with spiritual guidance, recreation, or material assistance through a variety of human services and social adjustment and development programs.

In 1988, more than 117,000 individuals and families were assisted by Corps Community Centers in Newark, Kearny, and the Oranges/Maplewood through human service and character-building activities. Of those, some 33,000 young people and adults attended about 1,300 religious services and programs at the local centers.

The Salvation Army's New Jersey Divisional Headquarters are at 80 Washington Street, Newark.

Approximately 2,800 firefighters, victims, and emergency personnel in Greater Newark have been served by the Salvation Army's Emergency Disaster Services. Whether it was a fire, flood, hurricane, or other disaster, the Army's mobile canteen was there providing hot food, sandwiches, beverages, and other related services to those individuals. Through the assistance of dedicated volunteers, the Army is able to be there when disaster strikes to "meet the need at the point of need."

Compassion and mercy best describes the League of Mercy volunteer. The mission of this one-on-one companionship program is to bring a friendly smile, a warm greeting, and a practical gift to shut-ins, hospital patients, the incarcerated, and nursing home residents. More than 5,000 people were recipients of the volunteers' greatest gift of all—love—in 1988.

The mentally ill homeless, the incarcerated mother anticipating her release from prison, the family with no heat or hot water—these are just a few of the many personal and family crisis needs seen every day in the Newark Social Service and Corrections Bureau. Around 18,000 individuals and families each year receive emergency housing, food, and other forms of assistance, as well as counseling, advocacy, and referral services. Programs such as the Mother/Child retreat for women prisoners, Project Volunteer for Energy (an energy assistance program in conjunction with PSE&G), and the Mentally Ill Homeless Program for helping this specific population readjust to society, are just some of the ways the bureau is meeting needs of people in Greater Newark.

The Service Extension Program at the Salva-

Organizations such as the Salvation Army and the Boys' Club of Greater Newark provide many recreational opportunities for the area's youth. Photo by Linda Zila

tion Army is just that: extending its services by way of local volunteer committees to communities not having a building-centered program. About 400 people are assisted by the service units in Belleville, Bloomfield, and Nutley. The service units provide food vouchers, lodging, energy assistance, and many other types of aid to their communities on behalf of the Salvation Army. Many units also provide local scholarships to youth accepted into college who cannot afford to go without aid.

The Adult Rehabilitation Center is a place where purpose is put back into a life devoid of meaning, hope, and a future. Alcoholics and drug addicts are given another chance through counseling, work therapy, and spiritual instruction. Challenged to appreciate their own worth as human beings, these persons are also provided with the basic necessities of food and shelter. More than 400 people are helped each year at the Newark center.

Camp Tecumseh is where the lives of many youth each year are renewed in mind, body and spirit. Those seniors who are "young at heart" also find Camp Tecumseh a place to see old friends and to make new ones. About 450 campers, young and old, experience the wonder of God's creation during a week-long encampment at the Salvation Army's camp on 392 acres of rolling hills in Pittstown, Hunterdon County. Hiking, crafts, swimming, boating, music, and games are some of the activities enjoyed by visitors to this serene setting.

The Boys' Club is one of the Salvation Army's institutions and services in Greater Newark. The Boys' Club is more than just a place for recreation, it is a program through which each child receives day-to-day guidance from qualified and dedicated supervisors. Every child has a chance and is encouraged to develop to his fullest capacity, obtain health care and develop physical fitness, acquire mental and manual skills, and grow spiritually and morally. Membership is open to any boy or girl between the ages of seven and seventeen.

The YMCA/YWCA is another integral part of Greater Newark's urban-suburban life. The Young Men's and Women's Christian Association grew out of a need in the latter half of the nineteenth century to provide fellowship and spiritual guidance to young people. The women's branch was formed and founded in Newark in 1871, followed a decade

The rambling homes of South Ward come alive with the scent of springtime flowers. Photo by Sharon Sullivan

later by the men's branch.

In 1954, the YMCA and YWCA merged at a time when both associations needed additional space to house their programs. The move was the first of two "revolutionary" changes; the second was the placement of a black executive director/CEO—Robert Wilson—of a major urban "Y" in 1968.

Headquartered at 600 Broad Street, today's "Y" provides a wealth of programs for most age groups, with recreational and aquatic programs for youth, after-school programs for youngsters, and day care for preschoolers. Through its three branch offices in Harrison, Clinton-Hill, and Irvington, the Y reaches out to thousands of residents in Belleville, Bloomfield, East Orange, Hillside, Harrison, Nutley, Irvington, and Kearny. Through the three camps in Sussex County, the YMWCA promotes spiritual, physical, and intellectual wellbeing, as well as providing a forum for teens to air their views. Job fairs and special achievement programs have also been in operation for several years to help unlatch the creative potential awakening in youth.

In the throes of a critical housing shortage in North Jersey, the YMWCA has effectively provided shelter for more than 4,000 individuals since the inception of its Emergency Residency Program (ERP) in 1981. The ERP assists its clients by advocating for and assisting in the acquisition of transitional housing. A separate day care facility is available for youngsters of the residents; moving and relocation assistance is also provided.

Physical fitness and medically balanced nutrition counseling is also available at the YMWCA for adults, busy business executives, young careerists, and local residents.

The "Y" serves in excess of 36,000 people annually and operates on a budget approaching $5 million a year.

As a major transportation hub, strategically located on the Passaic River, the city of Newark continues a long and thriving tradition of business and industry. Photo by Bob Krist

X
Business

Newark's new-found popularity can be attributed to the fact that it is New Jersey's premier center of commerce, culture, finance, learning, trade, and transportation.

"Where else will you find five colleges and universities in one town with deep-water ports, railroads, an international airport, and major highways?" asks Newark Mayor Sharpe James.

Add to that lengthening list of amenities the city's efficient subway system and gracious Victorian homes, and what Newark has going for it is an incredible "critical mass"—a kind of socioeconomic fusion reaction igniting and attracting one exciting, productive, and creative activity after another.

That critical mass consists of a rare combination of extraordinary capital resources infusing fresh life and ideas into Newark and Metro New Jersey—led by Prudential Insurance Company of America, Mutual Benefit Life Insurance Company, First Fidelity Bank, New Jersey Bell, and Public Service Electric & Gas Co.

Anchored by the City of Newark, Metro New Jersey—Essex, Union, Bergen, Morris, Middlesex, Hudson, and Passaic counties—is the twentieth most populous market in the nation, with the fifteenth-highest "Effective Buying Income."

Newark, the nucleus of Metro New Jersey, placed eighteenth out of 74 American cities ranked for their "business climate" by *U.S. News and World Report* in late 1985. In a survey by *Money Magazine* in summer 1987 of the top 100 "most desirable places to live" in the United States, Newark placed 68th—14 ahead of New York City. The core of Metro New Jersey, with Newark as its focal point, is the sixth-largest population center in the United States.

Almost all of the nation's 100 largest corporations either have an office or their headquarters in Metro New Jersey.

Serving this prospering, compact community is the Greater Newark Chamber of Commerce, with 2,500 members based in 18 of New Jersey's 21 counties. The Greater Newark Chamber is the largest, full-service chamber in the state. The Metro region represents 87 percent of the chamber's membership.

In Newark, 3,000 retail firms—ranging from Macy's (the

Above: Computer technology plays an important part in Newark's business and manufacturing communities, from word processing and communications to engineering and design, providing a wide range of capabilities. Photo by Bob Krist

Top right: From telecommunications to insurance, the Newark area boasts a wide variety of business and employment opportunities. Courtesy, La Casa de Don Pedro

Facing page: More than $2.5 billion has been privately or publicly invested in Newark since 1980, creating a surge of development and economic activity. Photo by Michael Spozarsky

world's largest department store) to Woolworth's (America's "five & dime" and *everybody's* store)—are actively participating in the city's revitalization. And Harry Grant's Newark Renaissance Mall, the newest jewel of the downtown shopping district, has added a half-million sparkling square feet of retail space along the city's "Main Street."

More than $2.5 billion has been invested in Newark since 1980, in both private and public funds.

Within the city are 36,000 manufacturing jobs—the result of such thriving operations as Anheuser-Busch, Seton Leather, Krementz and Company, Victory Optical Manufacturing, Stanley Tools, the Penick Corporation, and Englehard Industries.

A random sampling of Newark companies reveals a profile of everything from nuts and bolts and mattresses to fruit juices, and the finest diamond/gold/platinum jewelry to some of the world's largest steel and paper recyclers. Various typical operations include the Natural Juice Company . . . Faitoute—the second oldest steel service center in New Jersey . . . Hurley's metal forgings for the space program and the nation's first nuclear project . . . Ace's plastic molds for toys, industry, and more than 150 million nylon upholstery buttons . . . Naporano, one of the world's largest recyclers of scrap metals recovered from the hulks of discarded trains, buses, and cars . . . the Newark Group's vast paper recycling system . . . Jersey Millwork's production of doors, windows, and mould-

Right: Though the work force of Metro New Jersey is primarily service oriented, manufacturing and industrial positions comprise approximately 25 percent of the region's jobs. Photo by Bob Krist

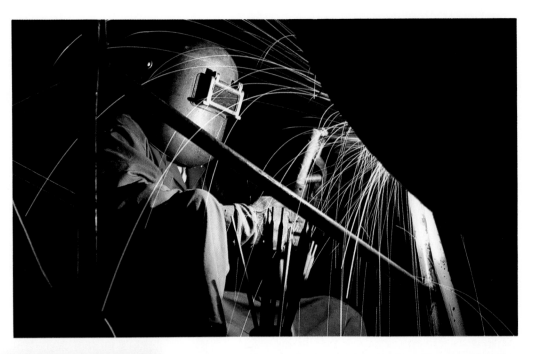

Below: Johnson & Johnson is one of the top employers in the Metro New Jersey region. Here, a technician conducts pharmaceutical research. Photo by Bob Krist

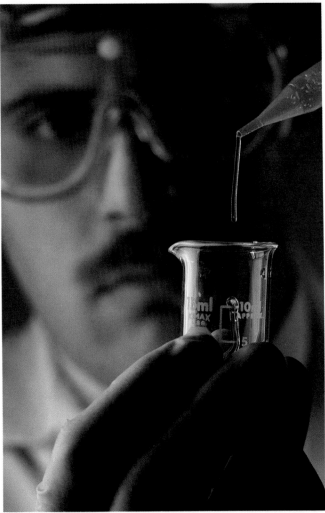

ings . . . National Magnetics pioneering powdered iron core and ferrite industry, tooled to shape more than 6,000 products . . . Serta and Continental mattresses . . . Dura-Flash bulbs, lighting, and starters for flourescent lighting . . . Country Workshop's crafting of such assorted items as ammunition boxes and wooden toys to swivel-top television tables and contemporary furniture . . . THIRD POWER marketing for promoting ideas, events, and products . . . plus chemicals, plastics, energy, and trucking—to name only a few of the hundreds of small-, medium-, and large-sized firms doing business in Newark.

In banking, there are 15 commercial banking institutions and 23 savings and loan associations in Essex County alone. Total bank deposits in the City of Newark exceed $22 billion.

In insurance, Prudential and Mutual Benefit Life make Newark the the third-largest insurance center in the country. Additionally, Blue Cross and Blue Shield and many regional HMOs provide a variety of medical coverage plans.

In real estate, such major firms as Archie Schwartz, Helmsley Spear, Feist and Feist, Cushman Wakefield, and Trammell Crow serve as innovators in packaging sizable real estate deals in Metro New Jersey.

In telecommunications, such prominent corporations as New Jersey Bell, AT&T, IBM, GE, and Hewlett-Packard lead the way, employing more than 150,000 workers in telecommunications, including teleconferencing, computer operations, satellite communications, and electronic mail.

In utilities, PSE&G, with nearly 14,000 employees around the state, makes sure that area residents and businesses are efficiently supplied with energy resources at competitive prices—and at the flip of a switch.

In the legal field, Metro New Jersey is home to federal, state, county, and municipal courts, and serves as a base of operations to the state's most prestigious law firms, including Kraft & McManimon; Clapp & Eisenberg; Sills, Cummis; McCarter & English; and Riker, Danzig.

In the media, Metro New Jersey is the base of operations for all statewide media, including WWOR (Channel 9) owned by MCA; *The Star-Ledger,* New Jersey's largest newspaper; New Jersey Network and WNET/Thirteen, the public television outlets; and public radio station WBGO and the commercial WHTZ-radio.

In accounting, both large and small public and private accounting firms are available to serve the region's business and individual needs. Arthur Andersen; Arthur Young; Coopers & Lybrand; Deloitte, Haskins and Sells; Ernst & Whinney; Samuel Klien; Peat, Marwick and Mitchell; and Touche Ross are just a few of the firms located in the region.

Metro New Jersey offers a labor force that in 1988 was 73 percent employed in service activity, currently producing state-of-the-art electronics, much of America's fine gold jewelry, more of the nation's pharmaceuticals than anywhere else, a wide variety of telecommunications and services, medical instrumentation, engineered plastics and electroplating, and a range of electrical and machine products.

Top employers include AT&T; New Jersey Bell; Supermarkets General (Pathmark/Rickel); Prudential; RCA; Sears, Roebuck; Johnson & Johnson; Public Service Electric & Gas; R.H. Macy; North American Phillips; A&P; First Fidelity Bancorp.; Midlantic Banks; Marriott Corp.; Acme Markets; Allied-Signal; Hoffman-LaRoche; K-mart; UPS; IBM; Exxon; ITT; DuPont; GPU; and J.C. Penney.

RENAISSANCE NEWARK

This privately funded, non-profit organization has invested considerable resources in bringing about a position change to Newark's central business district. Formed in 1980 by the chairmen and CEOs of five of Newark's major corporations—Mutual Benefit, Prudential, PSE&G, First Fidelity, and New Jersey Bell—Renaissance Newark today boasts dozens of contributing business members. The organization provides a wide range of services, including feasibility studies, market research, marketing materials, files on development activities, and inventories of available sites and properties. Renaissance Newark has become a driving force behind the city's redevelopment effort.

One of the Renaissance's priorities is the *Newark International Airport Access Study: Newark-Elizabeth.* It represents the work of a public and private interest group appropriately named the Growth Connection. Everett Shaw, president of Renaissance Newark, is chairman of the Connection. The Connection is bringing together support for the development of an improved modern transit system to move people to and from the Broad Street Station in Elizabeth, Penn Station in Newark, and Newark International Airport.

The Port Authority of New York and New Jersey has committed $60 million of the capital improvement budget to the design, development, and implementation of the project. The entire system has a projected cost of $180 million and could take anywhere from four to twelve years to complete.

PRUDENTIAL

Headquartered in the heart of Newark, Prudential Insurance Company of America protects more than 27 million people around the world through various life, health, home, and auto insurance coverages. With assets approaching $200 billion, Prudential reigns as the world's largest insurance company and provider of other financial services.

In recent years, Prudential—known to investors everywhere as "The Rock"—has branched into such areas as property and casualty insurance, health care, leasing, investment banking, securities brokerage services, and real estate. More than 6,000 Prudential agents are licensed to sell mutual funds and other investment-oriented products.

In 1981, Prudential acquired Bache, one of the

oldest and largest investment brokerage firms in the world. Prudential-Bache Securities, Inc., provides clients with stocks, bonds, options, commodities, tax-favored investments, and a personal asset management service called the Command Account.

Prudential-Bache received top billing in the "most improved" category in *Financial World* magazine's 1987 poll of 150 top investment officers. The company also ranked among the top 10 brokerage firms in executing orders, research, and overall service. A Dutch subsidiary was formed in 1987, and Prudential-Bache purchased a seat on the Tokyo Stock Exchange in 1988.

In life insurance, more than 80 percent of Prudential's 22,000 agents are registered with the National Association of Securities Dealers—and that credential became a prerequisite for all agents hired as of 1988.

The Prudential Health Care System is serving several million people across the country. Its largest group health insurance client—the American Association of Retired Persons (AARP)—grew from 5.4 million insured individuals at the end of 1986 to more than 6 million in 1988.

Soon after Prudential's Dental Management Organization (DMO) topped the 1 million-member mark, AT&T contracted Prudential to offer coverage to its 1 million active and retired employees and families, beginning January 1, 1988. It was the first such nationwide plan for Prudential and the DMO industry as a whole.

In April 1987 the Prudential Bank and Trust Company started offering home equity loans through agents in more than 30 states.

At the end of 1988, The Prudential Realty Group managed more than $40 billion of real estate assets.

Since 1977, the Prudential Foundation has selectively awarded grants totaling tens of millions of dollars to hundreds of organizations and institutions. The grants are for business and civic affairs, culture and the arts, education, health and human services, urban and community development, minority purchasing and business development, and local organizations. Grants can range from $368,000 to the Second Harvest in Chicago for equipment purchases for local food banks throughout

the United States, to $10,000 to the Tri-City Citizen Union for Progress in Newark for economic development. William H. Tremayne, senior vice president of communications for Prudential, has been chairman of the foundation since its inception.

MUTUAL BENEFIT LIFE

Mutual Benefit was formed in 1845—the first life insurance company in New Jersey and fourth in the United States. In 1879, Mutual Benefit became the first insurance company to formally assist policyholders who missed premium payments by documenting how long such coverage would be continued after missing payments. Called a "nonforfeiture plan," the system was adopted by other companies and later it became law that all life insurance contracts must include such a plan.

Founded by Robert Patterson and 11 associates, Mutual Benefit has insured several U.S. presidents since 1885. Grover Cleveland, a New Jersey

Left: As the world's largest insurance company, Prudential is involved in many areas such as property and casualty insurance, health care, investment banking, and real estate. Courtesy, Prudential Insurance Company of America

Below: Adopted when the Mutual Benefit Life Insurance Company was founded in 1845, the official company symbol depicts a "pelican in her piety." An ancient legend holds that in time of famine, a mother pelican will pierce her breast to feed her nestlings with her own blood. Courtesy, Mutual Benefit Life

Left: Originally established as The Prudential Friendly Society in the basement of the National State Bank in 1875, Prudential Insurance now serves a worldwide community, with its main headquarters located on Broad Street in the heart of Newark. Photo by Rich Zila

Above: Mutual Benefit's present headquarters, located across from Washington Park, is much different from the company's original $25 per month office space in a three-story building at Broad and Market streets in 1845. Mutual Benefit today is a diversified financial services organization with more than $10 billion in assets. Photo by Barry M. Winiker

Right: A single toll-free number provides quick and accurate answers for any Mutual Benefit policyholder in the country. Approximately 20,000 such calls are processed each year. Courtesy, Mutual Benefit Life

native, was the first president to hold one of the company's life insurance policies. William F. McKinley, William Howard Taft, and Warren G. Harding followed his lead.

When Mutual Benefit obtained its charter in 1845 from the New Jersey State Legislature, few people knew about life insurance. But Patterson and his associates believed that life insurance was necessary for families who would be destitute at the loss of a wage earner.

Rather than create a for-profit business, the founders formed a company "dedicated to the good of all" and selected the name "Mutual Benefit" to reflect that objective. The idea of a mutual company whose policyholders were its owners was original at the time. To demonstrate this dedication, the founders chose part of Mr. Patterson's family crest—the pelican—to serve as the company's

symbol. According to ancient legend, in times of famine a pelican will pierce its breast to feed its young. Through the years, Mutual Benefit has maintained that philosophy of caring for its policyholders.

Headquartered at 520 Broad Street since 1957, Mutual Benefit today provides financial opportunities to millions of individual and group policyholders and investment clients. The company's expanding insurance lines include increasing premium life insurance and "interest-sensitive" whole-life products like variable annuities and universal life, which provide policyholders with unparalleled flexibility.

Mutual Benefit's Group Life and Health Division is headquartered in Kansas City and, since the mid-1950s, has provided group life and health insurance, disability and income protection, and rehabilitation services.

Mutual Benefit is an acknowledged leader in the field of 401(k) and salary savings plans and administration. Specialists in Mutual's Pension Division design and administer group pension plans and tax-sheltered annuity programs for small businesses and FORTUNE 500 companies, as well as for statewide employee systems, hospitals, educators' groups, and the military.

At the Providence, Rhode Island, headquarters of Mutual Benefit Financial Service Company, financial professionals research, design, and develop unique investment opportunities for individuals. These include mutual funds and tax-advantaged investments in real estate, gas and oil, equipment leas-

ing, gold and silver certificates, and arts and entertainment. For example, the company's arts and leisure opportunities have made possible the London and New York productions of "Les Miserables," the magazine *Arts & Antiques*, and the Broadway production of "Into the Woods."

Investments in real estate joint ventures are made by Muben Realty, a rapidly growing company affiliate. Muben works closely with Mutual's Financial Service Company to develop limited partnership programs suitable for pension fund

The New Jersey Bell building, located on Broad Street across the way from Washington Park, was designed in a striking Art Deco style. Photo by Rich Zila

and individual client investments. Investment opportunities range from Marriott hotel properties in Richmond, San Francisco, and Palm Springs to New Jersey's Princeton Forrestal Village to Williams Island and Fisher Island in Florida, and a number of residential communities around the country.

In recognition of its dedicated volunteer service in Newark and Kansas City through education, social services, and neighborhood improvement, Mutual Benefit became one of a select group of national companies to receive President Ronald Reagan's "C" Flag. The "C," which standards for "We Can, We Care," is a fitting expression of Mutual Benefit's commitment to volunteerism throughout the nation.

NEW JERSEY BELL

This communications provider grew out of the Delaware and Atlantic Telegraph and Telephone Company, incorporated in 1904, and a subsidiary of the New York Telephone Company operating in northern New Jersey. Both were operating facilities of the American Telephone and Telegraph Company (AT&T). On November 1, 1927, Delaware and Atlan-

tic was officially incorporated as New Jersey Bell.

Two men were responsible for creating AT&T: Alexander Graham Bell, whose invention became a practical reality with the help of the "Wizard of Menlo Park,"—Thomas Edison—and Theodore Vail, a resident of Morristown, who established the basic framework of the Bell System, a structure that began in the 1880s and continued largely untouched until the great divestiture on January 1, 1984. At that time, New Jersey Bell became a wholly-owned operating company of Bell Atlantic Corporation.

The bare copper wires that once were New Jersey Bell's single-channel pathways have evolved into coaxial cable, microwave and other radio links, and fiber-optic channels. Using new technology in both fiber and lasers, New Jersey Bell can send data at a rate of 1.7 billion bits per second.

Based at 540 Broad Street in a standout Art Deco-style high-rise, New Jersey Bell today serves more than 3.2 million residential and business customers with the lowest basic residential service rate of all Bell companies in the country—an average of about $7.86 a month.

Left: Today's telecommunication networks rely on the technology of cables, lasers, computers, and fiber optics. Photo by Bob Krist

Facing page: PSE&G has been serving the Newark community since 1903. Photo by Rich Zila

With net income of $372 million, New Jersey Bell's total operating revenues moved toward the $3 billion mark in 1987. With approximately 19,600 employees, the company operates some 4.5 million network access lines.

Each year the telephone company spends about $600 million to improve the statewide telecommunications network. More than 85 percent of its switches are now electronic or digital electronic. Other computerized systems are constantly being installed to improve service and to control costs. They include systems to eliminate written service orders, to design, assign, and keep track of circuits, to speed the answering of directory assistance calls, and to enable customers at certain locations to pay their bills in person at local retail establishments.

New Jersey Bell has introduced several new services in recent years. The *New Jersey Bell Yellow Pages* has been redesigned to make it even more useful to customers and more attractive to advertisers. The new format has full-color Community Interest Showcase pages with local sports sched-

ules, mass transit information, and local street maps. A new Blue Pages section provides listings of federal, state, and local government offices, including schools. A Green Pages section has discount coupons from local merchants.

In Hudson County and Atlantic City, the company launched CLASS Calling Service—seven convenient calling features for residential and small business customers.

In Monmouth and Ocean counties, New Jersey Bell and Monmouth Cablevision Associates are testing "Request TV"—a pay-per-view service that enables the cable company's customers to request, over the phone, in-home viewing of recently released movies.

In Holmdel and Red Bank, Monmouth County, trials have begun of Integrated Services Digital Network (ISDN), an innovative technology that lets customers send and receive voice, data, and video signals simultaneously over existing telephone lines.

Hundreds of miles of highly efficient fiber optic cable are being installed statewide. In 1988, NJ Bell ran fiber optic cable directly to 104 South Brunswick homes to determine the feasibility of using fiber, rather than copper wire, to serve residences.

New Jersey Bell, under the presidency of Anton J. Campanella, also participated in the restructuring of the Bell Atlantic Corporation, its parent company. The ongoing restructuring provides Bell customers with a more complete selection of options, including telecommunications equipment and services, computer leasing and maintenance, and financing.

PUBLIC SERVICE ENTERPRISE GROUP INC.
This group is the parent holding company of Public Service Electric & Gas Co. (PSE&G) and five non-utility businesses. PSE&G, the principal subsidiary, provides safe, dependable, and competitively priced electric and gas energy to its two million customers (seven out of 10 residents of the Garden State).

Community Energy Alternatives, Inc., is an investor in and developer of cogeneration and small power projects.

Public Service Resources Corporation is an investment subsidiary dedicated to earning a reasonable return to enhance the parent group's overall financial strength and to provide a source of funds for future needs.

Energy Development Corporation is involved in gas and oil exploration and production and the acquisition of gas and oil reserves.

Enterprise Group Development Corporation engages in real estate investment and development ventures focusing on income-producing properties in New Jersey.

PSEG Capital Corporation is a funding subsidiary providing financing to and raising required capital for the parent holding company and the other non-utility businesses.

Public Service grew out of Thomas Edison's invention of the incandescent light bulb and the subsequent electric power grid in 1882 as a reliable source of energy for lighting. It brought together under one corporate symbol hundreds of small gas and electric firms and 99 trolley companies operating at the turn of the century. When PSE&G went into business in 1903, it had less than 19,000 electric meters in service, compared with nearly 2 million today. The company's payroll lists more than 6,500 employees.

Edison's creative spirit still permeates the company today. The giant utility was the first to feed power from a fuel cell into a power grid. It has supported fusion research at Princeton University's Plasma Physics Laboratory since 1970. It also built the pioneering Battery Energy Storage Test Facility in Hillsborough in conjunction with the U.S. Department of Energy and the Electric Power Research Institute.

By 1990, around half of the electricity produced for Public Service's customers will be furnished by nuclear power reactors which do not generate air pollution or ash waste from burning coal.

As a gas company, PSE&G was something like an older, bigger brother to the electric industry. In 1903, there were 187,000 gas meters in service in its territory. Today there are more than 1.5 million meters in use. In 1903, the capacity of PSE&G gas plants was less than 23,000 cubic feet a day. By 1990, that figure will exceed 200 billion. The 1,494 miles of gas mains in use in 1903 will be extended to more than 13,000 miles by 1990.

In 1974, PSE&G built the nation's first synthetic natural gas plant in Harrison. It can produce 20 million cubic feet of gas a day. In 1974, the utility built another "syngas" plant in Linden with a capacity of more than 125 million cubic feet a day.

FIRST FIDELITY

As one of America's 20 biggest banks, with assets of approximately $30 billion, First Fidelity can trace its roots to the State Bank of Newark, founded in 1812, making it one of America's earliest banking companies. While that first bank was being built at the corner of Broad and Mechanic Streets (now Edison Place), newly enlisted troops occasionally tramped by in drill on Broad Street, preparing for the expected military conflict with England.

Within a year of its founding, the bank paid its first dividend, the first in a series of regular dividend payments that have continued uninterrupted to this day. Today, First Fidelity places fifth among all American corporations for having recorded the longest, unbroken string of regular dividend payments.

The bank's first president was William S. Pen-

Right: Businessmen enjoy a working lunch at the St. Joseph's Priory Restaurant. Photo by Carol Kitman

Facing page: The Wilson Towers development in the Ironbound is being financed by First Fidelity and the Banco Portugues Do Atlantico. Photo by Rich Zila

nington, a Revolutionary War captain who later became governor of New Jersey. He was succeeded at the bank by his son, William, who also followed in his father's footsteps as governor of New Jersey.

In 1865, the bank obtained a national charter, becoming the National State Bank of Newark.

With assets of more than $10 million, National State Bank of Newark rode out the storm of the Great Depression, during which time withdrawals were never halted.

In 1931, W. Paul Stillman, then 34 , became president and chief executive officer—the youngest bank president in America at that time.

In 1966, Robert R. Ferguson, who presides over First Fidelity's operations today, succeeded William H. Keith as president. Ferguson, an intense workaholic, set into motion the preparation process for the coming interstate banking era.

First Fidelity's 18-story headquarters at 550 Broad Street were occupied in 1967.

Succeeding Stillman as chief executive of the parent company in 1973, Ferguson engineered the historic merger between First National State Bank of New Jersey and Fidelity Union Trust Company in April 1984—the biggest ever in the nation's banking history at the time. It brought together New Jer-

sey's largest and third-largest banking organizations and created a $10 billion banking institution that has tripled in assets since then.

Overall, the First Fidelity system through its affiliates operates more than 500 branch offices throughout New Jersey and in the 14 easternmost counties of Pennsylvania, as a result of the merger in February 1988 of Fidelcor in Philadelphia with First Fidelity. Its employee force has grown to more than 15,000.

NATIONAL WESTMINSTER BANK

Known almost all of its life as First National and then First Jersey, the merger between First Jersey and National Westminster (completed on February 1, 1988) created a super-regional banking organization with combined assets of $16 billion and over 250 offices in New Jersey, on Long Island, and in New York City and Westchester.

Organized under the National Bank Act of 1864, the original bank was chartered on February 18 of that year as the First National Bank of Jersey City. Two months later, on April 16, it open its doors for business at One Exchange Place in the bustling waterfront hub of Jersey City, the "backdrop" of the Statue of Liberty and Ellis Island, the legend-

ary immigration clearinghouse that gave America its reputation as a mighty "melting pot."

In 1971, the then First Jersey became the first bank outside New York City to be approved by the New York Stock Exchange Board of Governors as a transfer agent. The bank, through its Jersey National Securities Transfer Corp. subsidiary, established an office in New York's financial district. That same year, the bank's Wall Street Division, consisting of the Mutual Fund, Stock Transfer, Special Services, and Stock Bookkeeping Departments, became First Jersey Financial Services Company, an autonomous division of the bank.

In 1986, the organization embarked on a major retail promotion to introduce the GEORGE Money Management system statewide. The system is one of the most comprehensive, inexpensive, benefits/ full cash management accounts ever offered by a bank to retail customers. By using electronics such as automated teller machines, direct deposits of checks, and the telephone, customers can handle all their routine banking—even paying bills— without having to visit a bank office.

As National Westminster, the Jersey City based bank maintains a significant position in the nonbanking financial area, notably as one of the nation's leading processors of mutual funds through its Financial Services Industry Group. And, through

Tilden Management Corporation, financing is available to automobile and equipment leasing companies in the New York, New Jersey, and Fort Lauderdale, Florida, marketplaces.

BROAD NATIONAL BANK

Broad National Bank began life on June 25, 1925, as the Labor Co-Operative National Bank, a name that was later changed to the Union National Bank. Among the 27 original incorporators were William J. Brennan, Newark police commissioner and father of U.S. Supreme Court Justice William J. Brennan, Jr.; Melinda Scott of the Organized Textile Workers of America, the first woman to serve as a bank director in New Jersey and perhaps in the country; and Arthur A. Quinn, the bank's first chairman and president.

The individuals who took the initiative to create a bank were mostly Newark labor leaders interested in bettering the lives of the working people in the area. Their purpose was to establish a bank to serve all the people and to provide financial services not otherwise available to them.

From original assets of $1 million, Broad National Bank has expanded into a nearly half-billion dollar banking institution with 240 employees and 11 offices in Essex, Bergen, Union, and Middlesex counties.

In 1960, ground was broken at 905 Broad

Above: Since it was established in 1866, Krementz & Co. has been creating fine gold jewelry. Photo by Michael Spozarsky

Facing page: Sunset colors the Broad Street skyline. Photo by Mary Ann Brockman

Street (opposite City Hall) for the bank's present headquarters.

KREMENTZ & COMPANY

Much of America's finest jewelry is designed and crafted at this firm, and sold at stores of distinction everywhere, including Tiffany's. Krementz & Co. operates two jewelry factories, in Newark and Pleasantville, New York. It is a wholly owned family operation based at 49 Chestnut Street in the city's oldest manufacturing district. With a quarter-million square feet of production, sales, and administrative space, Krementz is one of Newark's biggest employers. The company employs around 800 workers in the city and at Pleasantville.

Krementz describes itself as "manufacturers of fine jewelry in karat gold and 14 kt. gold overlay and dealers in gemstones."

The story of the company began in 1866 when five men made a decision to form a partnership for manufacturing jewelry, according to Richard Krementz, Jr., grandson of the founder, who has chronicled the fabled history of one of America's greatest jewelry makers. Although the partnership was short-lived, two of the men—George Krementz and Julius Lebkeucher—remained as partners and formed their own company. The company began production in a former tannery.

One of the most significant developments made in the company's formative years was that of the collar button. In 1876, the Centennial Exposition was held in Philadelphia. Displayed there were the inventions that were soon to usher in the Industrial Revolution. The methods of manufacturing brass cartridges for bullets, which involved the drawing and hammering of sheet metal to produce a relatively complex shape, caught the eye of George Krementz, who applied the technology to produce a collar button from a single piece of metal. Over the next 10 years, Krementz developed sophisticated equipment to produce an inexpensive and high quality collar button. By 1900, most of the collar buttons produced in the world came from the Krementz plant in Newark.

Krementz was issued a patent, but it was contested in court and the case went all the way to the United State Supreme Court. Krementz won—but the Supreme Court decided then it would take no more patent lawsuits. Since then, all patent cases have been handled at the lower court level.

The success of the clad metal collar buttons led to the development of a complete line of men's clad metal jewelry. Cufflinks and dress sets were widely distributed to haberdashers, and that division become the forerunner of the Krementz 14 kt. Gold Overlay Division.

Perhaps no other style in the company's line is more synonymous with Krementz Overlay than the rose. Today the rose parts are produced on an automatic press that performs all the detailed operations in one step. A Krementz rose can become a pendant, earring, brooch, stick pin, or bracelet. Diamonds and stones can be added to compliment and highlight the rose's beauty.

Over the decades, Krementz has acquired several jewelry companies, including Abelson & Braun in 1940, producers of wedding and engagement rings; Allsopp-Steller in 1950, a gold manufacturing company featuring colored stones; and Jones & Woodland in the 1960s, which added gold wedding bands and a new division named "Diana by Krementz." In 1965, Krementz purchased George Schuler & Co., which was geared toward making expensive, handmade jewelry. This was followed by

the acquisition of Herbert Cockshaw & Co., which merged with the Shuler line.

In 1975, Krementz & Co. became the first American jewelry manufacturer to have space at the Basel Fair in Switzerland. As a result, a German and a Belgian company were formed, based in Frankfurt and Brussels, respectively. Also in 1975, Krementz brought McTeigue & Co. into its everexpanding organization. McTeigue manufactured fine 18 kt. gold, platinum and diamond jewelry in a small factory in New York City.

BAMBERGER'S

Newark was the place where Louis Bamberger started what was to become America's fourthlargest department store—Bamberger's (now Macy's). On December 11, 1892, Louis Bamberger paid cash for his first advertisement in the *Sunday Call*, announcing the opening of a new retail dry goods business on Market Street, west of Broad Street.

Reserved and unassuming, Bamberger always maintained a formal manner with business friends and employees. Born May 15, 1855, in Baltimore, Maryland, the rather shy salesman who left school at 14 seemed destined to become one of America's greatest retail merchants. His mother's family (the

With almost one hundred years of retail experience and tradition, Macy's has endured as an integral part of the Newark lifestyle. Photo by Carol Kitman

Hutzlers) was well known in Baltimore where the Hutzler Brothers' organization was and still is a major retailer. In fact, when Bamberger's opened two stores in the Baltimore area in 1891, the Hutzlers and their native son's legacy were in direct competition.

Louis and his brother Julius took over their father's wholesale notion business in the 1880s until Louis left in 1887 to become a buyer in New York for a San Francisco notion house, learning all there was to know about retailing.

Louis was then prepared to open his Newark store by himself, but was later joined by his brothers-in-law, Louis M. Frank of Philadelphia and Felix Fuld of New York. A partnership was formed under the name L. Bamberger & Co. Louis depended heavily on Fuld for staffing and other day-to-day details. Upon Fuld's death in 1929, Bamberger decided to sell his company to his then arch-rival, Macy's, known throughout the world for its Thanksgiving Day Parade. Bamberger was 74, but not yet ready for retirement.

It was under Louis Bamberger's direction that WOR was licensed as the nation's sixth radio station, eventually becoming the cornerstone of the Mutual Broadcasting network, the forerunner of today's "networks"—ABC, CBS, NBC, and CNN. WOR went on the air February 22, 1922, broadcasting Al Jolson's "April Showers" from the roof of the Market Street store. The station was organized by one of Bamberger's salesmen of crystal sets, Jack Poppele, a German native of the Ironbound District. That 250-watt transmitter sent signals as far away as Staten Island, Brooklyn, and Asbury Park. By October 1922 the Newark station was transmitting to England, and by 1923 to Tokyo. The world's first trans-oceanic fashion show was broadcast from Paris to Bamberger's via WOR in 1933.

In February 1924 Bamberger published *Charm* magazine, a fashion and general interest publication that anticipated America's emerging "culture of consumption." *Charm*, an 88-page glossy magazine, was distributed to Bamberger's 80,000 charge account customers. In New Jersey, *Charm* was as popular as the *Ladies Home Journal*, which had a statewide circulation of 83,000. *Charm* reigned as the shopper's magazine of choice until 1932, when the Depression took its toll on it and other promi-

nent publications of the day.

In 1930 Louis Bamberger founded the Institute for Advanced Studies at Princeton, with the cooperation of his sister, Mrs. Felix Fuld. Albert Einstein, one of the first to be hired on the faculty, spent the last 25 years of his life refining his theories of relatively at the Princeton institute.

Over the years, Louis Bamberger collected signatures of the signers of the Declaration of Independence, a hobby that he pursued doggedly until he completed the set sometime around 1920. Among the many treasures he presented to the Newark Museum, which got its start with Bamberger's assistance, was a page from the first Gutenberg Bible, printed in the mid-1440s.

Louis remained chairman of the board of Bamberger's until April 1939, when he officially retired at the age of 84. He died in his South Orange home on March 11, 1944.

Today there are 25 Bamberger's stores (14 in New Jersey) selling under the name of Macy's.

* * *

Through its many economic changes over the past two centuries, Newark remains the law center of New Jersey, with the largest and the smallest law firms handling everything from wills and accidents to giant corporate accounts and criminal trials, as well as taking on considerable volunteer public service work.

In 1989 a towering triangular edifice, connected to Penn Station by a pedestrian skybridge, opened as the Legal and Communications Center. With such amenities as a first-class restaurant and retail shops and services, the center fills the personal needs of the legal profession. By providing everything from computerized legal research to printing and typesetting, from paralegals and word processing to messengers, this modern center supplies every service essential to a successful law practice. This project is a joint development effort of the Newark Economic Development Corporation and the Port Authority of New York and New Jersey.

MCCARTER & ENGLISH

New Jersey's largest law firm opened its 100,000-square-foot office on five floors of the Gate-

way Four building in the spring of 1988. Governor Thomas H. Kean, at the reception for public officials and clients in the library atrium of the law office, noted it was appropriate that the state's oldest and largest law firm be based in its largest city. "The firm served the public through 25 presidents, seven wars and all kinds of fads," Kean recalled.

The McCarter family founded the firm in 1844 in Newton, Sussex County. The practice was moved to Newark in 1865, the year the Civil War ended. A merger in 1905 brought in the English family.

Among the law firm's more storied clients were Thomas Edison and Annie Oakley. Today, McCarter & English specializes in corporate, tax, trust and estate, real estate, bankruptcy, securities, merger and acquisition, copyright, and environmental law.

Above: The Legal and Communications Center tower, pictured here in the final stages of construction, was designed to meet the professional and personal needs of Newark's legal community. Photo by Alan L. Detrick

Right: Impressive additions to Newark's changing skyline, the glass-adorned Gateway buildings are major centers of business and commerce. Photo by Michael Spozarsky

The firm has 38 partners, 135 associates, and more than 400 employees, with offices in Cherry Hill; Wilmington, Delaware; and Boca Raton, Florida.

SILLS CUMMIS ZUCKERMAN RADIN TISCHMAN EPSTEIN & GROSS

In just 18 years, one of New Jersey's premier law firms has grown from five lawyers to more than 115, making it the third-largest law firm in the state. Sills Cummis provides the range and depth of legal counsel formerly available only in New York. One of the dozen law firms occupying the new Law Center, it counts among its clients the Government of the Philippines. It was responsible for recovering some of the state-owned assets of former Philippine ruler Ferdinand Marcos.

Founder and managing partner Clive S. Cummis began assembling the extraordinary talent needed to create the firm in 1971. Prior to that year, Cummis had been appointed by Governor Robert B. Meyner as chief counsel to the County & Municipal Law Revision Commission. Effecting long overdue revision of county and municipal law, Cummis also laid the groundwork for New Jersey law firms to gain entry into the business of writing bond opinions. In addition, Meyer serves as trustee of the Newark Museum and as chairman of the board and trustee of the Center for Molecular Medicine and Immunology of the University of Medicine and Dentistry of New Jersey.

Sills Cummis retains satellite offices in New York City, Hackensack, and Atlantic City.

TOUCHE ROSS

Counted among the "Big Eight" accounting firms in the United States, this national partnership holds the second-best litigation record among that prestigious group. In 1988, the firm assisted more companies with their initial public offerings than any other accounting firm in the nation.

Touche Ross' New Jersey's roots were planted in 1900 when Scottish-born John Ballantine Niven and George A. Touche banded together to open a public accounting practice in the U.S. Niven went on to become president of the New Jersey Society of Public Accountants in 1916; it is he who is credited with establishing a company tradition of active participation in professional affairs.

The national firm boasts more than 800 partners, 8,500 other professionals, and more than 100,000 clients. The international firm is the result of three public accounting practices that merged in 1947 to create Touche, Niven, Bailey & Smart.

More than 33 partners and 300 other professionals are based at the Touche Ross Headquarters in Newark's Gateway Center and at its Trenton Office, a landmark brownstone opposite the State Capitol.

Accounting and auditing, tax consulting, and management consulting services are provided to all segments of the business community, including banking, construction, education, finance, food, health care, high technology, insurance, manufacturing, media, real estate, retail, savings and loan, securities, services, transportation, the wholesale industries, and the non-profit public sector.

Among Touche Ross' expanded services for special needs are actuarial, benefits, and compensation consulting, the Financial Services Center, the Washington Service Center, the Garr Consulting Group (retail and distribution management consulting), litigation support, the Corporation Financial Group, reorganization advisory services, industry specialization, Touche Ross International (worldwide resources), Braxton Associates (strategy management consulting), and valuation engineering and appraisal services.

Through its contributions of money and manpower, Touche Ross has maintained an unbroken tradition of supporting organizations that serve the public interest. The practice's senior partner, Robert M. Berkowitz, is a board member of Renaissance Newark and also serves on the Governor's Cultural Center Task Force. Partner Joel J. Rogoff served as president of the New Jersey Society of Certified Public Accountants in 1988. Other Touche Ross partners have also been selected to hold the top posts in United Way of Essex and West Hudson, the Hospital Finance Management Association, the New Jersey Historical Society, the New Jersey Public Broadcasting Authority, and the Association of Government Accountants. Touche Ross also participates in Leadership New Jersey, as well as other civic and community groups.

While the service industry dominates Greater Newark in the 1980s, manufacturing remains on the com-

petitive "cutting edge" in the city and its environs.

DURA ELECTRIC LAMP COMPANY

Founded in 1925, Dura pioneered the first wire-filled, synchronized flashbulb in 1936. The company is the leading manufacturer of fluorescent fixtures and fluorescent lamp starters, and its product line includes general service incandescent light bulbs and mobile power converters.

Among Dura Electric's products for the nation's defense are glassworking devices, miniature lamps, glass switches, time-delay devices, small shells, parts made on screw machines, and products requiring vacuum and gas fill.

ACE TOOL & MANUFACTURING COMPANY

Ace Tool opened its doors in 1929 to provide the plastics industry with quality molds. From the 1950s up until the early 1970s, 95 percent of Ace Tool's business was from a major plastics company that needed durable molds for the toy industry. In the 1970s, Ace Tool began producing molds for engineered products producers like Stanley Tools. Today, there are 16 presses custom molding engineered plastics. Ace Tool builds and runs gear

molds, component molds, molds for the medical industry, and various industrial molds. Ace Tool is one of the world's largest custom manufacturers of outdoor nylon buttons, having produced more than 150 million to date.

FAITOUTE STEEL

As New Jersey's second-oldest steel service center, Faitoute Steel has supplied steel products for many of the state's most important structures, from roads and bridges to buildings and dams. Organized in 1904 by Moses Wilfred Faitoute and James A. Coe, Faitoute has historically been a supplier of steel for New Jersey's Standard Oil (Esso/Exxon), the Mutual Benefit Life Insurance building in downtown Newark, and viaducts and bridges on the entire New Jersey Turnpike.

As a steel service center, Faitoute is essentially a "lumberyard" for steel, cutting raw steel into various shapes and forms according to customer specifications for construction and other uses. Faitoute's products are hot-rolled and cold-finished bars, bar shapes and sheets, reinforcing bars, structural shapes, plates, strip, expanded metal, flexangle, and bar grating.

Above: Brewing has been part of Newark industry since the early 1800s, and the Pabst Brewing Company continues that tradition today. Photo by Jane Van Wert

Facing page: The container tanks of MacArthur Fuel Oil and Solvents create a pleasing industrial image. Photo by Rich Zila

During the 1940s, when milk bottles were being replaced by paraffined cardboard containers, Faitoute handled orders from American Can Co. for welded steel shapes that were formed and assembled to make frames for the first paraffining machines.

During World War II, Faitoute became a valued supplier to the U.S. Army arsenal, supplying parts for tanks and munitions. Faitoute was a key source of parts for production of the then-secret M7 "Tank Killer." The company also fabricated for munitions elevators.

HURLEY FORGE
Hurley Forge began business in a barn in the Ironbound section in 1923, forging high quality well-drilling equipment. Hurley advanced to open-die forging, pioneering many new industry developments such as forging stainless steel and making important contributions to the Manhattan Project,

which accomplished the first atomic chain reaction. Hurley is also a contractor for the nation's space program.

Today, Hurley Forge occupies seven buildings plus storage yards on five acres at an appropriate address—70 Manufacturers Place. Hurley Forge provides a fully integrated service with complete facilities for forging, heat treating, machining, and testing to virtually all specifications.

NATIONAL MAGNETICS GROUP INCORPORATED
This affiliation of three companies and two product lines traces its beginnings to the birth of the powdered iron core and ferrite industry in the 1940s. National Moldite Co. is the oldest at 47. National Magnetics is tooled for making more than 6,000 parts, ranging from antenna rods and shield beads to inductors and transformers.

JERSEY MILLWORK COMPANY
Jersey Millwork is New Jersey's largest and most varied lumber and building material wholesaler and distributor. Founded in 1927, Jersey Millwork employs some 270 people and operates a fleet of 35 trucks. The company deals in specialized products. For example, Jersey Millwork provided the custom-made windows to refurbish the Easton, Pennsylvania YMCA, a stylishly sophisticated building listed in the National Register of Historic Places. The company also supplied the back windows of the renovated Berkeley Carteret Hotel in Asbury Park, a national landmark owned by singer Johnny Cash and the Vaccarro brothers, developers at the Jersey Shore.

NAPORANO IRON & METAL/NIMCO SHREDDING COMPANY
These two firms are a "scrap supermarket" for steel mills around the globe. Naporano started dealing in scrap metals in 1907, evolving into one of the largest, most technically advanced scrap processors in the United States. Recycling everything from cars and buses to locomotives and turbines, Naporano processes nearly 80 grades of ferrous scrap, 29 grades of alloy scrap, and more than 120 grades of nonferrous scrap. At its 20-acre recycling center at Newark Bay, Naporano provides a parts inventory for the transportation industry unequalled in the United States.

City Hall is the center of activity for Newark's government.
Photo by Barry M. Winiker

XI
Government

The official theme in city government is, "Newark puts people first!"

For Newark Mayor Sharpe James, it all begins with people—people born in Newark, people living in Newark, people working in Newark, people raising children in Newark, people attending school in Newark, people with the greatest stake in Newark.

As chief executive, Sharpe James presides over the nation's 46th largest city having the fifth-highest population density. Blacks comprise about 70 percent of the 325,000 residents, and Hispanics, about two-thirds of which are Puerto Rican, about 15 to 20 percent. Portuguese, Italians, and eastern Europeans have sizable representations, followed by Asians and people from the Caribbean and Latin America.

With approximately 4,000 employees, the city government operates with an annual budget approaching $400 million.

Organized as a city in 1836, Newark has been governed since 1954 by an elected mayor and council similar in structure to most large business corporations. The mayor is elected by the voters and becomes the city's chief executive, just as a corporation selects a chief officer—the company president. The voters also elect the nine members of the City Council, just as stockholders of a corporation elect a board of directors. The council names one of its members as president, just as a corporation board names its chairman. The mayor appoints department directors, while a corporation president selects his managerial executives to conduct the business affairs of the company.

First elected to public office as South Ward councilman in 1970 as part of the "Community Choice" ticket headed by Mayor Kenneth A. Gibson, Sharpe James was elected mayor on May 13, 1986, the 35th person to hold that public office since 1836. For 18 years prior to his election as mayor, James was a professor of behavorial science at Essex County College. At the college, he was the first black to serve as department chairman and director of athletics within the state college system. He also was the first black to serve as president of a state college athletic conference.

James credits his predecessor with restoring calm to the community after the 1967 riots and instilling a sense of confidence in City Hall. Gibson, the first black to be elected mayor of a major northeastern city and the longest to serve in that office, began the exhausting task of rebuilding a politically corrupt city that had been racially, economically, and culturally divided.

The campaign stage was set for James, who responded to the Gibson legacy by first setting up a new Office of Citizen Services within the mayor's office as a "one-stop complaint and information center," so that people with problems and questions would not be shuttled all over City Hall.

An Office of Affirmative Action, another first within the mayor's office, sought increasing shares of jobs and business for blacks and Hispanics. A companion unit was created later to carry out the city's Minority Set-Aside Program, which guarantees that at least 25 percent of all city contracts for goods and services go to firms actually controlled by minorities.

James believes the city must "redirect a substantial amount of profits back to the black community through vigorous enforcement of our affirmative action goals." The goal of the James Administration is "to see that blacks share in the profits of the economic resurgence at all levels."

To set a faster pace for affirmative action, James has named Newark's first Hispanic department director, its first female deputy mayor, and the first black heads of several key agencies. He

has moved to assure that other segments of the people—including a sizable concentration of Portuguese—are represented in jobs and on various governmental boards.

To fill the second-highest executive post in city government, James conducted a nationwide professional search for a business administrator. The job went to Richard A. Monteilh, who had built a reputation as assistant city manager of Savannah, Georgia, and then as deputy finance commissioner in Atlanta. Monteilh became Newark's first black administrator to supervise all municipal operations.

Under the James Administration, evidence of a turnaround are appearing on several fronts:

* Reported crime, probably the most urgent concern of residents and commuters, has decreased 14 percent within one year. The police department has been expanded by 80 positions after years of shrinkage, and is experimenting with more flexible shifts, mini-stations, downtown street booths, and special squads to combat crack use, truancy,

Right: Mayor Sharpe James, pictured here on the steps of City Hall, is a leading force in the renaissance of Newark. Photo by Rich Zila

Facing page top: City Hall echoes with the voices of government. Photo by Rich Zila

Below: The Newark City Hall dome glistens in the sunshine. Photo by Rich Zila

illegal dumping, and other crimes. A state-of-the-art computer dispatching system also was installed.

* Collection rates for taxes, both current and delinquent, have increased markedly over the last three years, and a crackdown on overdue water and sewer payments is paying off in prompter receipts. A campaign against traffic ticket scofflaws has doubled the payment rate since 1985, and produced $5 million in revenue from outdated summonses in one year alone.

* The city's welfare caseload has been cut by more than 1,000 cases—about 20 percent—through tighter enforcement of regulations and provision of jobs and social services to recipients. Newark's Employment and Training Office has won state praise by exceeding all of its goals, and the city has launched a novel prisoner employment project.

* The Affirmative Action Office has helped arrange more than $30 million in contracts and subcontracts for minority builders, including $3 million for construction of a new City Welfare Center. The city is also buying more than $5 million in supplies and services each year from minority vendors under the aggressive set-aside program. And 87 percent of all new municipal employees are from minority groups and, in the mayor's cabinet, 90 percent of department directors are now black or Hispanic.

In addition, James has initiated an extensive, foundation-funded program of health care for the homeless; plans for the first new firehouses to be built in a quarter-century; cleanup of hundreds of city-owned lots; use of hand-held computers by sanitation enforcement agents for instant retrieval of possible violations; the first cultural programs sponsored directly by the city; installation of colorful banners along main thoroughfares; and many other visible and qualitative improvements.

"Newark is no longer a stationary place," trumpets Richard Roper, head of the Princeton University Council for New Jersey Affairs. "Sharpe James has given the city a sense of forward momentum."

Stephan Kukan, general manager of area development for Public Service Electric & Gas Co., proclaims: "Newark offers the most potential of any city in the United States."

Observes Kevork Hovnanian, one of the nation's foremost builders of low- and moderate-income housing: "Newark is enjoying a resurgence!" Hovnanian is making a $125 million investment in new housing in Newark with the construction of 1,130 townhouses—960 market value and 170 "affordable" houses—plus a major supermarket, retail shops, and a police annex.

Unlike most cities operating a mayor-council form of government, Newark city government functions on a separation-of-powers system with built-in checks and balances that gives each branch limited powers over the other.

In the executive branch, the mayor is responsible for establishing policy, providing efficient and effective municipal services, and representing the city in its dealings with other governments and at public and private ceremonies. The authority to veto ordinances and to appoint directors of operating budgets is vested in the mayor's office.

Above: Additional officers, computer technology, and special squads have been instituted under the James Administration, creating an expanded and up-to-date police force in Newark. The night squad of the city's north district is shown here before starting the evening shift. Photo by Rich Zila

Right: Sergeant T. White of the Newark Police Department stops to converse with a mother and her young children in the city's west district. Photo by Rich Zila

Facing page: Supervising all of Newark's municipal operations is the city's business administrator, Richard A. Monteilh. Photo by Rich Zila

Above: A city employee cheerfully ends his shift. Photo by Rich Zila

Top right: The planned construction of a new fire station, the first to be built in more than 20 years, is just one indication of Newark's pledge to improve the city's conditions and services. Photo by Linda Zila

Through the business administrator, the mayor supervises the city's 10 major administrative agencies with the "advice and consent" of the municipal council.

The council consists of nine members, four at-large and one from each of the city's five wards. The council legislates by ordinance, resolution, or motion. The power to override the mayor's veto is vested in the council.

The council is responsible for reviewing and approving the city's annual budget prepared by the mayor and business administrator. With the exception of national and religious holidays, the public council meetings are held on the first and third Wednesdays of each month at 1 P.M. and 8 P.M. in the council chambers in City Hall on Broad Street.

The city clerk also serves as municipal council clerk. The clerk is parliamentarian and principal aide to the council. The clerk's office is responsible for analyzing proposed municipal legislation, making surveys, preparing reports, and obtaining factual information to aid the council in its decision-making process, as well as issuing periodic reports of council activity and maintaining the necessary checks and balances for the council on all municipal activities.

In addition to the familiar departments of law, police, fire, finance, engineering, development, general services, and health and human services, there is a Land Use Control Department in city government that helps the mayor spruce up Newark's tarnished urban image and improve the quality of life for everyone.

On the vital role of the land-use department, James is emphatic about cleaning up Newark and keeping the city physically healthy for its inhabitants and aesthetically attractive for all, both taxpayers and visitors. "We will continue to enforce, strictly and vigorously, our health and housing codes," James asserts. "We will bring into court landlords who fail to provide tenants with heat and hot water. We will not tolerate 'profitlords' or 'slumlords' in the City of Newark."

James insists that if you own property in Newark—and especially rental property—you have a responsibility to maintain that property, to keep it neat, attractive, safe, and free of health and housing code violations. One's property or apartment should be a mirror image of that person, James feels.

As for debris and litter, James puts the blame squarely where it belongs: "It comes from people who litter and dump illegally."

The mayor's "Keep Newark Clean" campaign is aimed at every resident and property owner, each of whose individual commitment is the only way Newark can be free of litter and graffiti around-the-clock. James has called on parents, teachers, and clergy to instruct the city's children to "respect the rights and property of others."

The mayor also believes that well planned and well managed low-rise, mixed-housing communities are the key to stable neighborhoods.

"During my visits to Paris, France, and Berkeley, California, I witnessed low-, middle-, and upper-income families all living together," James says. "There should be no distinction between public and private housing. We can't create ghettos and then complain about ghettos. We must reaffirm the nation's fundamental commitment to safe, decent, affordable housing."

Toward that end, James is infusing a sense of

City Council President Henry Martinez currently presides over the city's public council meetings, which are held on the first and third Wednesday of each month. Photo by Linda Zila

In an effort to rid the city of litter and graffiti, Mayor James established the "Keep Newark Clean" campaign, pictured here in action along Mt. Pleasant Avenue. Photo by Rich Zila

self-responsibility into the Newark Housing Authority. "My belief is that public housing tenants should be involved in the decision-making process," says James. "The Newark Housing Authority must rehabilitate and maintain every housing unit it can. Turning over public housing units to private developers should happen only after all other alternatives have failed."

James' personal motto is, "Together, we can make a difference." One of his favorite expressions on Newark is the song, "Newark Loves You," with music by Billy Taylor and lyrics by Lou Carter. The song was written in two parts:

Chorus:

Newark loves you and wants you to be
Where people are special and spirits are free
Big city with so much to give
Gateway that leads to the good way we live
Newark loves you, we want you to know
We'll follow our dream and together we'll grow
Your city, that big town with soul
The Gateway to living and reaching your goal.

Interlude:

Largest in New Jersey, an emerald on Newark Bay
And one of the most significant ports in the U.S.A.
Its industry is amazing,
it lights and paints and feeds and cleans
And cans and ships its vans to fill America's needs
And beneath Newark's modern skyline,
great insurance companies thrive
With confidence in a geat city,
so young and so very much alive
Yes, since eighteen thirty-six,
Newark has followed through
To glorify the meaning of the red, white and blue.

A city that cares for the needs and dreams of its people is truly a city of vision and light. Photo by Bob Krist

Economic lifelines from all over the state come together at the transportation hub that is Newark, feeding a steady stream of supply and demand to local businesses. Photo by Michael Spozarsky

XII
The Future

Newark's future is literally riding high—for this historic city by the bay is the only location in New Jersey accessible from any direction by road, rail, air, and water.

Newark is the Garden State's transporation hub. All economic lifelines come together here to form an unparalleled grid compactly comprising a bustling airport, seaport, railport, and interconnecting "roadport" where most of the state's major arteries converge around the 12-lane New Jersey Turnpike—Routes 1 and 9, 21, interstates 78, 80, and 280, and the Garden State Parkway, which lead to other major highways making up the state's ground traveling network.

More than 30 million passengers a year make their way through Newark International Airport, while 75,000 riders a day can be counted at Newark's Penn Station.

Gleaming glass and steel edifices reflect the city's constantly changing skyline. Newark is an eye-catching kaleidoscope of modern office towers, upscale residences with names like Society Hill, Tiffany Park Condos, Forest Hills, and University Heights, new warehouses and manufacturing facilities, attractive shopping malls and supermarkets, excellent hotels and restaurants, leading educational and medical institutions, first-class performing arts centers—and a "great outdoors" of parks, festivals, parades, and the nation's largest cherry blossom display.

On the horizon are Grant U.S.A. Tower, the world's highest skyscraper, New Jersey's Center for the Performing Arts, skyways and "people movers," industrial parks, and stylish marketplaces.

At least 69 projects representing over a billion dollars in investment are in various stages of planning and development throughout Newark's five wards—East, West, North, South, and Central.

The downtown business district is being reshaped into three development districts with their own special identities: Center City, Washington Commons, and Government Center. Center City encompasses the "Market Square" (the businesses surrounding the Macy's department store at Washington and Market streets) and the "Four Corners" (Broad and Market streets). Washington

Above: Newark's glittering skyscrapers reflect an ever-changing array of offices, condominiums, and hotels—a resurgent economy made manifest. Photo by Michael Spozarsky

Facing page: The neighborhood at the intersection of Broad and Market streets is known as "Four Corners," a landmark on the map of Newark business. Photo by Rich Zila

The businesses of Market Street inhabit an area known by local development agencies as Center City. Two other development districts of Newark's business hub are Washington Commons and Government Center; each with its own special identity. Photo by Barry M. Winiker

Commons embraces Washington Park, and Military Park-The Greens—the triangular oasis with its famed war memorial, between Broad Street and Park Place. The Government Center takes in the Riverfront around Penn Station, the Gateway complex, and the Newark Legal and Communications Center.

Renaissance Newark, Inc., the overall development agency for Newark's central business district, envisions that sectioning off the city center provides focus on each district and gives the people in each sector a "meaningful voice" in ensuring a successful future.

Recent building around the downtown district includes Mulberry Street Plaza (47,000 square feet) and Mulberry Market Mall (9,700 square feet), the 18-story One Washington Park edifice, the 33-story office tower and 290-room hotel at One Penn Center, and the peripheral Airport Industrial Center for manufacturing and office space. New hotel/conference centers, including Vista International, are rapidly rising around Newark Airport.

Two key projects on Broad Street—Newark's "main street" —are the $200-million New Jersey Center for the Performing Arts and the billion-dollar tallest tower on earth at 121 stories.

The five-theater centerpiece will put the Garden State on the nation's map with a state-of-the-

art showcase in the heart of downtown Newark. Governor Thomas Kean wants to raise $100 million from private sources and an equal amount from public funds. To be built on the site of the former Hahne's department store at Broad and New streets, the luxurious arts center will house a 3,000-seat concert hall, a 2,000-seat auditorium for the New Jersey Symphony Orchestra and other cultural events, a 1,500-seat auditorium for ballet and opera, a 700-seat theater, a 100-seat children's theater, and galleries and shops. The center will attract many more artists who have been moving into the city during the 1980s in search of studio space and less expensive rents.

A "dream on the drawing boards" is the Grant U.S.A. Tower (3 million square feet of space), the soaring anchor of a billion-dollar project on the two city blocks adjoining the former Central Railroad of New Jersey train station on Broad Street, next to City Hall, and the Federal Complex. Complementing the 1,871-foot-high, marine-blue superstructure—which is a unique series of rising towers embracing the tallest needle—is the Newark Renaissance Mall enclosing more than 250,000 square feet of prime retail space on three levels and featuring national and regional apparel

Above: An increase in construction activity has been prompted by Newark's economic revitalization. Photo by Michael Spozarsky

Facing page: Newark's future is getting off the ground on construction sites all around the city. Photo by Michael Spozarsky

An increasingly popular destination for business and pleasure trips, Newark is meeting an ever-greater demand for hotel accommodations, convention facilities, and nightlife. Photo by Michael Spozarsky

stores, boutiques, jewelry and specialty shops, a full-service restaurant, as well as a third-story "food court."

The visionary Grant U.S.A. Tower and Mall may be connected to Penn Station and Newark Airport by a swift, streamlined monorail. The fast-track service would provide a direct link to the PATH line to the World Trade Center twin towers in downtown Manhattan.

Elaborate plans by Harry Grant, an Englewood, N.J., developer, include, in addition to the main tower and mall, a 30-story office tower on Lafayette Street, two condominium towers, an ice-skating rink, a 650-room hotel and appropriate shops and restaurants, as well as a synagogue at Broad and Green streets.

More than $100 million is being invested in the 108-acre Waverly Yards railroad property lying between Amtrak's main northeast corridor and Newark International Airport. Hartz Mountain Industries, Inc., of Secaucus, has targeted the site for light industrial plants and a hotel and convention center.

A 22-story office tower downtown and a Central Ward shopping mall worth more than $125 million are being developed by the GKC Newark Urban Renewal Corp., a joint venture of the Kramer Group of Morganville, and Goldberger, Moore, Novick & Albanese of Roselle. The $105-million office building has 22 floors of tenant office space cascading from approximately 26,000 square feet at the top three floors to about 32,000 square feet on the first floor. The lobby level provides 6,250 square feet of retail area accessible from the plaza and joining with the Newark Legal and Communications Center to form a pedestrian space. A covered arcade encloses the plaza, providing protected access to train, bus, PATH, and subway, as well as Gateway Center's hotel and retail facilities.

Another shopping center with a first-rate supermarket will further enhance the Central Ward. Located within the University Heights community, the 81,000-square-foot center contains 29 satellite stores and more than 650 parking spaces on a lot bounded by Irvine Turner Boulevard, Avon and Jeliff avenues, and Rose Street.

Other projects in the works are:

- One Penn Plaza, an office tower and hotel

Left: Highly ranked for its business climate, Newark has also been placed higher than New York City among the nation's "most desirable places to live" by **Money Magazine.** *Photo by Michael Spozarsky*

Facing page top: After 400 years of development, Newark finds itself as the state's premiere center of commerce, culture, finance, learning, and transportation. Photo by Rich Zila

Facing page bottom: Historic architecture and modern design stand side by side in the diverse city of Newark. Photo by Rich Zila

featuring a six-story atrium and a two-story rooftop restaurant with a pair of exterior glass elevators and a skywalk between Penn Station and the center, which incorporates the existing 300,000-square-foot Graphic Arts Building.

• The Seton Hall Law School, the most up-to-date academic and library facilities in the country, with an estimated price tag of $30 million. The new law school will have about 200,000 square feet of learning and research space.

• A 20-store mall on Broadway, costing more than $700,000.

• A 50,000-square-foot renovation of the former Salvation Army building at 717 Broadway, for offices, retail stores, and warehouse space, with an adjacent 20,000-square-foot parking lot.

• Elwood Plaza at 609-621 Broadway, a 13-story, 11,000-square-foot retail/commercial center.

Right: While slick reflective surfaces multiply, there still remains much intriguing old architecture to remind Newark residents of their city's past. Photo by Michael Spozarsky

Facing page: Between the city's many inherent advantages and the greater influx of capital in recent years, Newark's local and international businesses are reaching for the sky. Photo by Barry M. Winiker

- The Nevada Mall, a $4 million, 60,000-square-foot shopping center featuring a supermarket with 10 stores (including a pharmacy, laundromat, hair salon, ice cream parlor, and video rentals) and offices, storage areas, and a large parking lot, at Nevada and Court streets.
- Ironbound Transport Park, a 35,000-square-foot terminal.
- Skyport Industrial Park on Astor Street.
- A 500,000-square-foot industrial park in the South Ward, a $65-million joint venture with the Morris Companies, the city, the state and private developers who will build, own or lease a variety of manufacturing facilities, warehouses and related operations.
- A $16-million industrial park on 10 acres in the South Ward, at Frelinghuysen Avenue and McClellan Street. The project consists of two buildings—a 100,000-square-foot site to house Central Paper Company, and a 110,000-square-foot warehouse-distribution center.
- The New Community Corporation's $10-million joint venture with Pathmark to build a 42,000-square-foot supermarket and five adjacent

Society Hill embraces a broad range of housing options, with a selection of townhouses and garden condominiums tailored to various income levels. Photo by Carol Kitman

stores on a 3.3-acre site at South Orange Avenue and Bergen Street.

• The 225,000-square-foot industrial building on Doremus Avenue occupied by New York Bronze, which moved to Newark in 1988.

More than 4,500 housing units worth almost a half-billion dollars are in various stages of completion, and that does not include public housing, such as the 473 dwelling units the Newark Housing Authority is building, the 325 more the authority has commitments to build, and the 840 more awaiting approval of grant applications.

"Recycling" some of Newark's finest buildings into one-of-a-kind housing for all incomes retains much of the city's older charm. Renaissance Towers is a 137-unit luxury condominium ranging from three to 11 stories, originally constructed over a period of 70 years. The home of the *Newark Evening News* until 1972, the old gray fortress was subdivided into condos costing from $60,000 to $400,000 each. The project is next to the Gateway complex and less than a five-minute walk from Penn Station.

There is a special address for anyone seeking convenient urban living in such places as Society Hill (1,130 townhouses, townplexes, and garden condos, including 170 low/medium income units), Tiffany Park (177 condominiums), Forest Hill (138 units), University Heights (70 low- to moderate-income units), Rosa Gardens (18 units), Gate at Roma Commons (18 units), and Villa Rosa (8 units).

The Newark Housing Authority also put up 100 townhouses on land cleared by the demolition of some 800 high-rise apartments.

With the renovation of Newark Symphony Hall, the city will be able to boast of two of the nation's premier performing arts centers along the same avenue—the magnificent "Broadway" of New Jersey.

Within Symphony Hall is The Terrace Room, for many years *the* place for local community events, club meetings, dances, and performances. It was the "living room of the city."

Finally, there is the Black History Collector's Club established by Thomas Frederick Moore, founder of the National Black American Historical Museum in Harlem in 1978.

Moore is looking for a permanent home at 23-25 Elizabeth Avenue, which he plans to transform into a museum where schoolchildren and adults can come and learn about the black experience. Moore's memorabilia include books, documents, dolls, records, and large items such as potbelly stoves and wagons. His first artifact is entitled "Everybody's Mother" —a colored-charcoal portrait of a beautiful middle-aged black woman in turn-of-the-century attire.

As Newark enters the twenty-first century, it will be prepared to meet a future in which seventeenth-Century Puritan values and African-American culture will still be very much alive, harmoniously integrated with contemporary arts and a hi-tech economy flourishing with new ideas and innovations.

After four centuries, Newark has evolved, tumultuously and gracefully, into a microcosm of America, preserving the best and improving upon the rest. Newark is the manifest product of passion, faith and hope, a city whose visionary *ark* is constantly being re-*new*ed.

Just as its economy has closely paralleled the nation's, in many ways America's third oldest major city serves as a microcosm of the country. Photo by Rich Zila

The setting sun highlights the loading facilities at Port Newark. Photo by Rich Zila

PART

II

Greater Newark's Enterprises

XIII

Networks

Newark's energy, communication, and transportation providers and facilities keep products, information, and power circulating inside and outside the area.

Channel 9 WWOR-TV, 234

LS Transit Systems, 235

Continental Airlines, 236-237

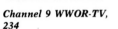

PSE&G, 238-239

New Jersey Bell, 240-241

The Port Authority of New York and New Jersey, 242-243

Ga

NJ Transit, 244-245

Orange, Newark, Elizabeth Bus, Inc., 246

WBGO-FM/88.3, 247

AT&T, 248-249

Gannett Outdoor of New Jersey, 250-251

Maher Terminals, Inc., 252-255

Z100 WHTZ Radio, 256-258

Photo by Michael Spozarsky

CHANNEL 9 WWOR-TV

With a new commitment to live, local programming and shows that build new audiences, super station Channel 9 WWOR-TV has positioned itself as a strong alternative to network programming.

WWOR-TV is strengthening its audience with first-run syndication programming, featuring such shows as "The Cosby Show," "Kate & Allie," "Who's the Boss," and, in coming years, "Head of the Class" and "Amen." With a long-established reputation for some of the best sports programming in the country, the station will continue to feature the Mets and the New Jersey Nets. With its new morning show "9

Pictured here is the multimillion-dollar WWOR-TV state-of-the-art broadcast station, based in Secaucus, New Jersey—one of the newest television facilities on the East Coast. Channel 9 is equipped with high-tech equipment providing live and local programming from its three studios located on the premises. WWOR-TV is an MCA Broadcasting Station. Photo by Richard Marx

Broadcast Plaza," Channel 9 is the only station in the market with a three-hour morning block of live programming that mixes news and talk segments before a live studio audience.

Other shows produced at the station include "Everyday" with Joan Lunden and "Steampipe Alley," a Sunday-morning children's show. One of the longest running shows in television history, "The Joe Franklin Show," has been on the air since 1952.

WWOR prides itself on its first-rate news organization. A strong news team, headed by veteran anchor Rolland Smith, is backed by investigative reporters whose reports, on such topics as lead in drinking water and Jersey City's failing school system, have resulted in legislative and community action taken in New Jersey and New York.

WWOR-TV is known as a station that is concerned with issues facing

the community and with affecting change. The station tries to keep the spotlight on a problem, rather than just pointing to it once and forgetting about it.

One of the outstanding community projects produced by WWOR-TV is "A+ for Kids," a campaign that includes prime-time specials that provide an in-depth look at the problems and promise of education in New Jersey. As part of this proj-ect, the station features vignettes that spotlight outstanding teachers and presents children's comments on important social issues that affect their lives. A WWOR-TV-sponsored A+ For Kids Teacher Network awards grants to teachers who have developed innovative teaching concepts and publishes an annual catalog to disseminate those ideas.

In keeping with the station's interest in education and the professional development of young people, Lawrence P. Fraiberg, president of

MCA Broadcasting, has made a commitment to a strong intern program. Typically, 45 to 50 college interns work at Channel 9 each semester and in the summer. The interns enable station personnel to do more and work more productively while they gain valuable hands-on work experience in the broadcast industry.

The station's tour program encourages schools to bring students interested in communications. Students who think they want a career in television are encouraged to work on their reading, writing, arithmetic, computer literacy, and typing skills.

Other examples of community involvement include seminars conducted by the station about how to use media effectively. On-air personalities fill speaking engagements at fundraisers, and station executives serve on various charitable and civic committees.

Station owner MCA Inc. also owns Universal Studios in California, MCA Records, Motown Records, Putnam Publishers, hotels in Yosemite National Park, and Spencer Gifts. MCA Broadcasting Inc. is the newest and smallest division of the company. When MCA bought the station for $387 million from RKO, it was the second-highest price ever paid for an independent television station.

LS TRANSIT SYSTEMS

LS Transit Systems (LSTS) is a unique firm that combines the freshness and vitality of a new and dedicated company with the experience and focus of a well-established, mature consulting firm. The reason for this dynamic combination stems from the firm's formation in 1985, when the Combustion Engineering and SOFRETU companies recognized the need for a new approach for the transit consulting industry; planning and design based on a strong operations perspective; and the ability to implement new transit systems on a turnkey basis.

The resources and accomplishments of SOFRETU are world renowned. As the commercial engineering arm of the Paris Transit Authority, SOFRETU planned, designed, and implemented many of the most highly acclaimed transit systems in the world—in Montreal, Mexico City, Cairo, Caracas, Santiago, Lille, and 50 other cities. Its permanent staff of more than 300

The proposed new airport connector automated transit system will be able to serve the planned Arts Center.

transit experts is augmented by the 2,000 technicians and 20,000 operators in the Paris network of bus, metro, and commuter-rail systems. Their expertise has been a valuable part of all LSTS projects to date.

Combustion Engineering is a $3.5-billion corporation whose technical and engineering strength encompasses a diversified market of private- and public-sector work, in which LSTS is an integral part. As a Combustion Engineering company, LSTS draws upon the outstanding resources of its sister Combustion Engineering companies to provide multidiscipline project teams.

The LSTS organization that combines the resources of these two technical giants offers tremendous transit and engineering capabilities and the ability to give its clients demand-responsive service.

LSTS and sister CE company, Lummus Crest, Inc., share a Bloomfield, New Jersey, headquarters and its combined staff of more than 300 engineering and technical personnel. Its many local projects have a tremendous impact on the New Jersey-New York metropolitan area.

A $1.3-billion expansion plan for

Construction proceeds, managed by LSTS, for New Jersey Transit's central bus maintenance facility on Doremus Avenue.

---

rail service in New Jersey is based on the findings of LSTS' ongoing Penn Station New York Access Study. LS Transit Systems has also developed revised guidelines and standards for passenger station design throughout the entire New Jersey Transit rail network.

In one of the largest railroad engineering projects in the country, LSTS is leading the team designing $300 million of improvements for the Long Island Rail Road's Jamaica Station Complex, the nation's busiest railroad station.

In Newark, LSTS is managing the construction of New Jersey Transit's central heavy maintenance shops and warehouse for its fleet of more than 2,000 buses, and stands ready to design, build, and operate the proposed automated transit system to connect Newark International Airport with the downtowns of Newark and Elizabeth.

LS Transit is also updating the transportation master plan for the New Jersey Meadowlands on behalf of the Hackensack Meadowlands Development Commission.

With its ability to draw on the expertise of SOFRETU's and Combustion Engineering's staff and specialists, LS Transit Systems provides solutions to every urban mass transit program true to its motto: Improving the Present . . . Preparing for the Future.

CONTINENTAL AIRLINES

On August 4, 1988, Continental Airlines dedicated Terminal C at Newark International Airport, the most modern passenger air terminal in the nation.

Continental chairman Frank Lorenzo was joined at the dedication ceremony by New Jersey Governor Tom Kean, Newark Mayor Sharpe James, Elizabeth Mayor Tom Dunn, port authority chairman Philip Kaltenbacher, and actress/model Brooke Shields, who has been active in promoting New Jersey tourism.

In his dedication remarks, Lorenzo said, "Terminal C has implications for the entire national and international air transportation system. We believe Newark International Airport, led by Terminal C, has the very real potential of becoming the dominant international gateway for Americans traveling east, and for Europeans and others traveling west."

Terminal C, a $255-million facility, is home to Continental's East Coast hub operation. It consolidates all of the airline's operations at Newark: Continental's domestic flights, Washington-Boston shuttles, Continental Express commuter flights, and international flights, including nonstop service to Gatwick Airport in London and Orly Field in Paris, and several nonstop destinations to the Caribbean and Mexico. Continental also has joined with the Scandinavian Airlines System (S.A.S.), in its worldwide alliance with .S.A.S., offering three daily nonstops to Copenhagen, Oslo, and Stockholm.

The terminal features a state-of-the-art baggage-handling system, which includes an automated high-speed optical reader capable of sorting 18,000 bags per hour. In addition, passenger flow is expedited by specially designed Continental Red Coat customer-service counters and automated passenger check-in equipment at ticket counters and gates.

"Terminal C was designed to make the usual hectic airport experience a pleasurable one by providing passengers with state-of-the-art comfort and convenience," according to Lorenzo. "Designed with the passenger in mind, the terminal offers the most sophisticated ground operations services ever invented for air travelers."

The new facility includes 12 curbside check-in stations, 95 ticket counters, 41 aircraft gates, and a separate ticketing and check-in area for passengers with oversize baggage. The terminal also features a variety of national and regional restaurants and shops.

In addition, its Continental Express commuter service has 88 flights per day to 22 cities from Terminal C.

More than 1.8 million passengers have used the new facilities at Terminal C since its operational opening on May 22, 1988. It is estimated that by the end of 1988, nearly 6 million people will have traveled through the terminal.

Continental employs some 2,300 people at Terminal C, with an overall total of approximately 5,300 employees in the Newark area.

Terminal C features the latest in airport operations technology, including the world's largest color flight information system. System One Corporation, the computer reservations and information management systems division of Texas Air Corporation, implemented the new technology at Terminal C and developed its applications to meet Continental's needs. The new technology greatly enhances both customer service and airport operations management.

Double the number of ticket counters compared to most airline's check-in areas make its large size more manageable. These counters have been located to prevent long

lines and congestion within the terminal, as well as for the convenience of the passenger. Baggage is sped with great accuracy from curbside to destination via a computerized system that uses magnetic tags and laser readers.

The terminal provides many amenities that make traveling a truly pleasant experience. In order to bring light into a building of such length, the architects incorporated an 80-foot-wide skylight and three water features within a 50-foot-tall atrium.

Carpeted floors mark concession and waiting areas, while the concourses are terrazzo. The lengthy concourses, dotted with specialty shops and restaurants that are as much a destination as they are a service to passengers, are equipped with a total of 1,540 feet of moving walkways, almost the length of five football fields. The concourses include such amenities as a premi-um restaurant, VIP lounges, conference rooms, private meeting rooms, and a large variety of retail concessions.

Business travelers who are members of Continental's President's Club have access to two private lounges, separate ticketing stations, meeting and conference rooms, secretarial service, a facsimile machine, and other services.

Young children traveling alone can wait in a supervised room with games, toys, and television. Another amenity of the 1980s is diaper-changing tables in the men's restrooms as well as the women's.

Terminal C, with 875,000 square feet, is the largest single terminal in the major New York and New Jersey airports. Continental will fly passengers from 41 gates in Terminal C, compared with only 13 gates operated by the airline in Terminal B. Continental relocated to its new facility from the North Terminal and from Terminal B, where it shared space with Eastern Air Lines, Delta, and USAir.

Terminal C had been designed for operations by People Express Airlines before the discount carrier was absorbed in 1986 by Texas Air Corp., the parent company of Continental.

To further cope with expected growth, the port authority plans, during the next 10 years, to redesign the road network at the airport, build garage parking, and install a people mover system, such as a monorail, between the terminals and the parking areas.

The new terminal will enable Continental Airlines, the airport's largest carrier, to fly 186 flights daily out of Newark. The airport handled 23.5 million passengers in 1987, but volume is expected to reach 45 million by the year 2000.

Continental Airlines dedicated Terminal C at Newark International Airport in 1988. The most modern passenger air terminal in the nation, it is home to Continental's East Coast hub operation.

PSE&G

When the founders of Public Service Electric and Gas Company (PSE&G) knitted the company together from a disparate group of gas, electric, and transit companies at the start of the century, they quite sensibly put the headquarters in Newark. It was then, and is now, the center of the business world of New Jersey.

For more than 50 years PSE&G's corporate offices at the corner of Raymond Boulevard and Park Place were a landmark and a transit hub, when the company was operating bus and trolley routes as well as supplying gas and electric energy.

When PSE&G's management faced the fact in the mid-1970s that its headquarters complex was becoming too scattered in Newark's

central business district, management reaffirmed its initial decision to make Newark its corporate home, electing not to seek a suburban location.

It was just as wise a decision then as it was in 1903. PSE&G has always had a close relationship with the state's urban centers.

PSE&G is the third-largest combined gas and electric utility in the nation and the largest gas and electric utility in the state. It provides electric and gas energy to more than seven in every 10 New Jersey residents. Its service area cuts a swath across the state from below Camden on the Delaware River in the southwest, to the northeast corner of the state, where Bergen County and New York State meet on the Hudson River. In that service area are the state's six major cities, including Newark.

The weather-scarred Wars of America *statue in Military Park, dedicated in 1926, is the largest bronze ever created by Gutzon Borglum, the celebrated sculptor of Mount Rushmore fame. Borglum used himself and his son as models for the faces at left of the statue. Restoration of the statue to prevent its collapse began in 1988.*

Most major firms responsibly meet the challenge of being a good corporate citizen, and PSE&G is not an exception. The wide spectrum of services that a major utility must provide, however, has placed PSE&G in a unique position among other corporate citizens of the city.

Newark's Symphony Hall, for instance, is a grand example of the unique value that older urban centers offer—a structure out of the past that combines cultural history with a potential for service in the present. It became evident in recent years, however, that Symphony Hall was in a dangerous state of disrepair, and that the engineering

The Newark Museum's south face has become the home of massive sculpted bronze doors, an entryway for the former headquarters of PSE&G in Newark. The company donated the doors to the museum when its headquarters was razed, and PSE&G moved into new quarters.

work alone represented significant expense before the necessary restoration work could continue.

PSE&G offered a team of experts from its engineering and construction department to work on the restoration—an architect and technicians who are specialists in electrical and structural work, including an engineer who came out of retirement to contribute to the project. These are experts with more than a half-century of experience in planning and supervising major construction.

Structural buttressing, much in the manner used to strengthen the Statue of Liberty, was done in the fall of 1988, with restoration of the statue's surface following.

As the result of PSE&G's decision to raze its previous corporate headquarters and turn the site into a plaza, both past and present culture are being served. PSE&G's former offices were housed in two adjoining structures. One of them, at 70 Park Place, had originally been the corporate office of the American Insurance Company. Two massive bronze doors served as the entry to 70 Park Place. When the building

Included in the initial rebuilding, which was budgeted at $3.5 million, was the rehabilitation of the Terrace Ballroom, where many prominent musicians played in the era of the big bands.

A new team of the company's engineering and construction de-

Symphony Hall, a Newark landmark, became the subject of study by a team of PSE&G engineers when it needed extensive repair and rehabilitation. They designed and directed a $3.5-million face-lift.

partment is presently at work, helping on a million-dollar project to modernize the Newark Boy's Club.

Nearly every major city has impressive statuary, but Newark is especially fortunate. During the effort of the Downtown Park Association's plan to rehabilitate the city's parks, supported by PSE&G along with the city's business community, it became apparent that the *Wars of America* monument, a massive bronze statue in Military Park, was in danger of collapse.

The thin-shelled work of Gutzon Borglum, best known as the sculptor who carved the faces of four presidents in Mt. Rushmore, was a victim of more than 50 years of

wind and weather. There were cracks and holes in the monument's 42 human figures and two horses. The memorial represented America's sacrifices to preserve its freedom in conflicts beginning with the American Revolution and ending with World War I.

The presence of two major works by Borglum in Newark emphasizes the city's unique cultural value unmatched in the state's suburban areas. In addition to the war memorial, Borglum's *Seated Lincoln* is in front of the federal courthouse in Newark.

The more ambitious war memorial, dedicated in Military Park in 1926, is the largest bronze Borglum ever created. It is unique in that it contains two figures, standing side by side and looking into the distance, for which Borglum used himself and his own son as models.

Restoration experts estimated repair and reconstruction would cost more than $200,000. A senior officer at PSE&G led a specific fund drive, separate from the park improvement planning, to match city funds to do the work.

was razed, PSE&G donated the doors to the Newark Museum, where they now serve as the museum's new south entryway.

The site of PSE&G's former headquarters is now a plaza containing a fountain and reflecting pool. In good weather office workers from surrounding buildings brown-bag it at noon on the plaza steps. Once a week in the summer PSE&G sponsors lunchtime entertainment, and periodically the plaza is the site of fairs and festivals that either originate there or spill over from Military Park.

The company that began life in Newark is reshaping itself. PSE&G is a subsidiary of Public Service Enterprise Group, and the nearly 3,000 employees who staff its Newark facilities are helping change the company to meet a new and challenging energy market. But commitment of the firm and its employees to Newark is unchanged; the company and its employees will continue to respond to the needs of the city.

NEW JERSEY BELL

In 1927, when the Delaware and Atlantic Telegraph and Telephone Company changed its name to New Jersey Bell, headquarters were established at 1060 Broad Street, Newark. Two years later the company's offices at 540 Broad Street were completed, and New Jersey Bell employees filled the art deco building that still serves as its headquarters.

"We at New Jersey Bell believe that to be truly successful, a company must be a good corporate citizen," says president James G. Cullen. "We have an obligation to make life better for the people who live and work in our state. And it is a commitment that we do not take lightly."

Both the company and its individual employees have continued to work hard for Newark. Evidence can be seen at Dayton Street School, where a garden is named for Brud Davis, a New Jersey Bell external affairs manager. Davis, who initiated and organized the project, was honored in 1986, the 10th anniversary of the garden.

Other Newark schools are being helped by about 20 New Jersey Bell employees who conducted the company's Choices program for nearly 800 public school freshmen during the 1988-1989 school year. Begun in 1986, the program stresses the importance of staying in school

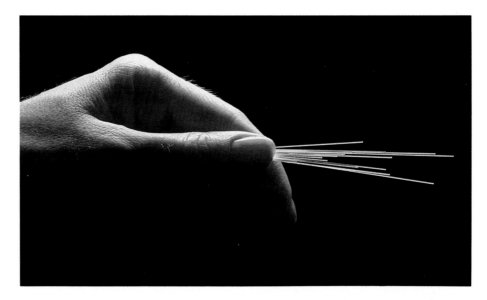

Fiber-optic cable being installed by New Jersey Bell is paving the way for the introduction of innovative new services. At the close of 1988, 88,642 miles of fiber-optic cable had been installed statewide.

and is designed to discourage students from dropping out before graduation.

Love Newark, a joint committee of the Greater Newark Chamber of Commerce and the City of Newark, is headed by Art Guida, another New Jersey Bell external affairs manager. Originally established to clean up litter around the city, the six-year-old project has expanded its scope to inject more pride in the people who live and work in Newark. These projects are just three examples of New Jersey Bell's continuing commitment.

During its first year, when 600,000 telephones were connected to the firm's network, New Jersey Bell adopted certain principles about quality and service to which

New Jersey Bell's Network Management Center, housed at One Washington Park in Newark, allows the company to keep an eye on the network that provides service to its 3.3 million customers. With approximately 4.3 million access lines, New Jersey Bell watches the network day and night to ensure customers continue to receive top-quality service.

it has adhered throughout the past 62 years. And the company is proud that its telecommunications services are part of the reason people and businesses choose New Jersey for their homes.

Providing high-quality service at a low price comes from skillful deployment of technology, product innovation, a commitment to service, and sound management. As part of Bell Atlantic, New Jersey Bell uses the expertise and product offerings of its sister Bell Atlantic companies, responding fully to customer needs with an expanded package of communications offerings.

Through joint marketing with Bell Atlanticom Systems, Inc., New Jersey Bell offers business customers the ability to buy telecommunications services and equipment from one source. This allows New Jersey Bell the chance to offer customers a more integrated approach to meeting their communications needs.

With the lowest basic residential and short-distance toll rates offered by any Bell operating company in the country, New Jersey Bell helps customers keep expenses low. Residence and business customers in Newark and other parts of northern New Jersey also enjoy discounts available through New Jersey Bell's New York Link Service. In addition to long-distance carriers, New Jersey Bell offers service between portions of northern New Jersey and the five boroughs of New York City. The firm's discounted service options can save customers from 10 to 40 percent.

New Jersey Bell's 2.8 million residence and 432,000 business customers can look forward to continued low prices. Under a plan approved in 1987 by state regulators, basic local service and New Jersey Bell toll rates, which went into effect in May 1985, will not increase for the next four years. The plan means that customers will be getting service in 1993 at 1985 prices.

New Jersey Bell is able to keep costs low by actively managing technology and putting it to work in its statewide network. More than $600 million went into capital improvements in 1988, with plans to invest a similar amount in 1989. At the close of 1988, 88,642 miles of fiber-optic cable had been installed statewide, and 201 of the company's 213 switches were electronic or digital electronic, paving the way for the introduction of innovative new services.

For example, New Jersey Bell is offering seven advanced calling features called CLASS Calling Service. One CLASS feature, Caller ID, lets customers know the number of the caller before they answer the phone. Another feature, Return Call, automatically dials the number of the last incoming caller, even if the call was not answered. The company will offer CLASS statewide by 1993.

Trials in Holmdel and Red Bank tested ISDN, the Integrated Services Digital Network. ISDN is an all-digital network that will allow customers to send and receive voice,

New Jersey Bell's commitment to excellence in both quality and service has remained steadfast for the past 62 years. Today, as part of Bell Atlantic, New Jersey Bell's 20,000 employees continue to build on that commitment to quality.

data, and image signals simultaneously over existing telephone lines. When fully implemented in the 1990s, ISDN technologies will make it possible for customers to have access to those various signals as easily as they make a telephone call today.

St. Joseph's Hospital in Paterson is reaping the benefits of a Local Area Network (LAN). Through a new application of existing network technology, New Jersey Bell is using existing wiring to provide simultaneous voice and data transmission among a number of hospitals.

With some regulatory restraints recently lifted, New Jersey Bell is looking at new information services, including message answering, voice mail, and a coin-phone message system.

Aimed at residential customers, message answering service works like an answering machine, but requires no equipment in the

home. The subscriber records a personal greeting, which is played for callers when the subscriber's line is busy or is not answered within a certain number of rings. Callers then may leave a message, and a special dial tone or other signal will notify the customer that a message is waiting.

Voice mail, a similar but more advanced service, will allow businesses to have their phones answered 24 hours per day without the need for any equipment except a standard telephone. Another service being tested in 1989 allows a coin phone customer to leave a message for someone who cannot be reached. The message will be delivered later when the person is available.

These are just a few examples of how New Jersey Bell is working with business and residence customers to provide the quality service and products that meet customers' ever-growing telecommunications needs.

New Jersey Bell's headquarters at 540 Broad Street, Newark, was built in 1929, just two years after the company opened its doors for business. Today the art deco-style building still serves as the firm's headquarters.

THE PORT AUTHORITY OF NEW YORK AND NEW JERSEY

On April 30, 1921, as the first of its kind in the Western Hemisphere, the Port Authority of New York and New Jersey came into being. The new agency's area of jurisdiction was called the Port District, a 17-county bistate region within a 25-mile radius of the Statue of Liberty.

The Port Authority's commitment to economic health has made Greater Newark a major hub for land, sea, and air commerce.

The mandate of the agency was to promote and protect the commerce of the bistate port and to undertake port and regional improvements not likely to be invested in by private enterprise nor to be attempted by either state alone—a modern wharfage for the harbor the two states share, tunnel and bridge connections between the states, and, in general, trade and transportation projects to promote the region.

The Port Authority has, with the encouragement of the two states, broadened its mission and has committed hundreds of millions of dollars in its active role of stimulating regional renewal and redevelopment.

The Port Authority's long-standing commitment to the metro area's economic health includes substantial efforts in Newark. Greater Newark area-based projects under way include the new $300-million Essex County Resource Recovery facility and PATH's new 54-acre $205-million PATH-Harrison Maintenance Facility to service its modernized and expanded fleet. Further, the new $74-million Newark Legal Center, which is now being built, is located in downtown Newark and is slated to house the city's major law firms.

Under the auspices of the Port Authority, Newark International Airport, the PATH transit system, extensive port facilities, and a broad-reaching complex of highways make the greater Newark area a major hub for land, sea, and air commerce.

A 25-year lease was signed with Continental Airlines for Newark International Airport's Terminal C. Terminal C completed in 1988, is one of the largest and most modern air terminals in the nation. It handles all the airport's international passenger arrivals as well as some departures.

The agency is as committed to community well-being as it is to economic development. A major portion of service and commodity contracts are awarded to businesses owned and controlled by minorities and women. Its Local Assistance Program provides technical and professional support to community projects. Working with the Private Industry Councils and other community groups, the agency expanded its own job training program, and it provides tax credits to businesses hiring disadvantaged area residents.

As the bistate agency sustains its

singular commit-
ment of agency
resources to meet
today's and tomor-
row's regional
needs, it must also
continue to fulfill its
commitment to
regional economic
development. At
the same time, the
Port Authority is
focusing new ener-
gies and resources
on expanding and
upgrading its essen-
tial trade and trans-
portation facilities—
the bistate vehicular
and passenger cross-
ings, marine facili-
ties, and its three
regional airports.

The fulfillment of these needs is
the basis for the governors'
approval of the Port Authority's
multibillion-dollar, five-year capital
investment program covering both
the agency's outstanding commitments and programs and the major
new capital and service
improvements it will make to its
core trade and transportation facilities over the next decade.

The Port Authority's three major
objectives are to modernize and
expand the capacity of vital transportation services without disrupting their daily operation; to sustain
and improve the level of service of
surface transportation, aviation, and
port complexes; and to induce further economic growth through targeted investments in urban
commercial development, telecommunications, and international
trade services.

The past decade has marked an
impressive economic turnaround
for the New York-New Jersey
metropolitan area, with population,
employment growth, and new public and private sector development
still gaining momentum. Through
this pivotal era, the region has
relied heavily on the efficient per-

formance of the Port Authority's
vital transportation systems and its
ability to finance their renewal and
improvement as state and local governments have moved from fiscal
crisis to fiscal health.

To sustain and expand the benefits of regional growth, The Port
Authority of New York and New
Jersey has proposed to both states a
comprehensive capital investment
strategy to rehabilitate and expand
its core transportation facilities, and
to fulfill the economic development
commitments proposed in 1978,
when the agency responded to the
need for new investment to help
rekindle commercial development
and infrastructure renewal in the
Port District.

Unlike some other government
entities, the Port Authority's system
of facilities must be self-supporting,
since the agency does not have the
power to tax, to pledge the states'
credit, or draw on most federal capital grant programs. While commercial tenants share in the costs of
some facility improvements under
lease arrangements, implementation
of the program depends on the
availability for adequate revenues
from tolls, fares, other user charges,

*Newark International Airport is under the juris-
diction of The Port Authority of New York and
New Jersey, which covers a 17-county bistate
region within a 25-mile radius of the Statue of
Liberty.*

and rents to support both operating
costs and debt service on Port
Authority bonds—both those currently outstanding and those issued
to support the capital program.

Port Authority executive director
Stephen Berger noted that, "This is a
bistate effort—not simply because
we have by statute certain obliga-
tions on each side of the Hudson,
but because the area we serve is
truly one economic region. The
facilities we operate and the services
we provide help knit the region
together. Our program is thus, in
many ways, a reaffirmation of the
commitment made when this
authority was created in 1921—to
benefit the New York and New
Jersey economy by providing the
'terminal, transportation, and other
facilities of commerce' needed by
residents and businesses in the
region, and by transcending the
political boundaries that artificially
divide the two states."

NJ TRANSIT

More than 60,000 riders pass through Newark Penn Station every day.

Newark is clearly "on the move." One of the main reasons is the city's extensive public transportation network—making Newark the Gateway to New Jersey.

Quality public transit services that are convenient and reliable are central to the economic growth of any city. As New Jersey's statewide public transportation corporation, NJ Transit has recognized the importance of public transit to the economic well-being of Newark and the state, and has worked to ensure that public transportation plays an integral role in the city's renaissance.

Just as Newark is the Gateway to New Jersey, then Newark Penn Station is certainly the hub of the state's transportation network. In total, more than 300,000 daily passengers ride NJ Transit buses and trains within New Jersey and to New York and Philadelphia. NJ Transit operates approximately 175 bus routes in 20 out of 21 counties and has more than 500 scheduled trains that run on 10 rail lines serv-

NJ Transit runs bus service to and from Newark International Airport. The No. 300 runs between the Port Authority Bus Terminal in Manhattan and the airport. Photo by Katherine Spina

ing 155 communities. More than 75,000 people use Penn Station daily, making it the state's busiest commuter facility.

In 1984 NJ Transit assumed management control and operation of the station from Amtrak. A two-phased project totaling more than $34 million in renovations has transformed this art deco station, built in 1935, and returned it to its past glory. Today it is one of the most modern, efficient, and convenient-to-use facilities in the nation, and has helped spur a variety of commercial and office development in the surrounding area.

At Newark Penn Station residents have many transit options to choose from. There are three NJ Transit rail lines (the Raritan Valley Line, the Northeast Corridor, and the North Jersey Coast Line) that serve residents from central New Jersey to Monmouth and Ocean counties.

More than 25 NJ Transit local and commuter bus lines serve Newark and go to points statewide and to New York. In addition, the terminal

serves passengers who use PATH, Amtrak, Greyhound, and local private bus carriers.

Often called Newark's best kept secret is the Newark City Subway, which carries almost 15,000 resi-

NJ Transit's articulated buses run on several heavily patronized bus routes in the city, including the No. 39, which runs through the heart of the city on Broad Street. Photo by Katherine Spina

dents and runs to and from Newark Penn Station through the city's central business district along Branch Brook Park to the Newark/Belleville border. NJ Transit completely renovated the 4.3-mile City Subway in 1984, as it marked its 50th anniversary of service.

Another popular bus service is Airlink, which links Newark with Newark Airport. Airlink serves Broad Street Station, the Quality Inn in Newark, and Newark Penn Station and runs frequently from early morning to late at night.

At the other end of the city's central business district is the Broad Street Rail Station, which serves commuters on the Morris & Essex lines. Adjacent to the station is Broad Street Transfer, which was constructed by NJ Transit in 1987 and provides a comfortable and convenient site for bus and rail service.

In 1988 NJ Transit and the City of Newark implemented bus-only lanes on Broad and Market streets in the central business district during

Newark Penn Station is the largest commuter facility in New Jersey. It serves NJ Transit, Amtrak, and PATH trains; NJ Transit, Greyhound, and other private buses; and the Newark City Subway. Photo by Katherine Spina

morning and evening rush hours. The dedicated bus lanes are a significant initiative, making bus commuting more reliable for the almost 80,000 bus riders daily in Newark.

Since the early days, when it was created by the state legislature in 1979, NJ Transit and its employees have called Newark "home." NJ Transit's corporate and rail operations headquarters are located in the

city along with NJ Transit's major bus maintenance facility.

Striving to be a good neighbor, NJ Transit management and staff are involved in a number of projects and programs that make Newark a good place to live and work. The works of local artists are often displayed at Newark Penn Station, and local musicians are spotlighted during holiday and special concerts. NJ Transit employees actively participate in the United Way's Charitable Campaign Drive and the city's Adopt-A-School Program. NJ Transit sponsors tours of Newark Penn Station, poster contests for students, and helps organize the Newark Festival of People.

To ensure that New Jersey and Newark continue the economic renaissance, NJ Transit is hard at work on a number of projects to meet the state's current and future transportation needs. These projects will enable New Jersey residents to travel much easier within the state, as well as to New York and Philadelphia. One such initiative will, for the

NJ Transit's commuter trains link the state's largest city with cities and other communities statewide.

first time, enable residents from Bergen County to travel directly to Newark via a new rail connection that will be in Secaucus.

NJ Transit is committed to continuing to work to ensure that public transportation keeps New Jersey and Newark "on the move."

The City Subway is known as "Newark's Best Kept Secret," but it is no secret to the 12,000 daily commuters who use the line between Newark Penn Station and Branch Brook Park on the Newark/Belleville border. Photo by Katherine Spina

ORANGE, NEWARK, ELIZABETH BUS, INC.

When its 30,000 daily riders see the big ONE logo of the Orange Newark Elizabeth Bus Company painted on the front of their bus, they know it stands for number one in service and dedication to the public's needs.

Founded in November 1986, the ONE Bus Company is a merger of three Newark-area family-owned independent bus lines. Prior to the merger, these three companies competed with one another and New Jersey Transit. After ONE Bus was formed, the organization worked cooperatively with New Jersey Transit to achieve "route rationalization" that eliminated duplication of service and subsequently made more efficient use of both companies' resources to provide more consistent service for local passengers.

ONE Bus provides the bulk of the bus service on Central Avenue, Broad Street, and to the Freylingunsen Corridor into Elizabeth and Elizabeth Seaport. Its lines also include Central Avenue to Penn Station on the 44 Tremont Avenue line.

As a result of the route rationalization, shuttle lines were eliminated in favor of through buses, and night service was extended. The increase in business due to route rationalization enabled the bus line to increase route frequency from sites such as the VA Hospital and East Orange General. The company was also able to add buses to provide more service in the Frelingunsen Avenue corridor. In response to the needs of the many Newark residents who work in Elizabeth, the firm increased its former 30-minute

This old Packard bus belonged to the White Bus Company, one of the three private companies that merged to form the Orange Newark Elizabeth Bus Company.

service in Elizabeth to every 7.5 minutes.

The ONE Bus fleet is considered to be one of the best maintained in the state, with each bus featuring four-season climate control that includes air conditioning. Buses are radio equipped for the safety of the driver and passengers. Although buses are leased from the State of New Jersey, the ONE Bus Company is an independent, unsubsidized enterprise.

The firm's facility is considered state of the art. Every one of its drivers undergoes a defensive driving course conducted by an in-house staff that includes two certified safety instructors. As a public service, ONE Bus provides senior citizens and students with reduced fares.

ONE Bus also includes an affiliate company that provides tour

Although its buses are leased from the State of New Jersey, the ONE Bus Company is an independent, unsubsidized enterprise. The ONE Bus fleet is one of the best maintained in the state and provides consistent service to its passengers.

buses. In addition, the firm provides factory transportation to enable large groups of workers to commute to New Jersey from urban areas. For example, a group of temporary workers recruited from the Bronx for a company's busy season may require short-term daily service from the Bronx to a New Jersey work site.

The Gallagher, White, and Revere families have been in the local bus service business since the mid-1920s. Today the organization includes three generations of the Revere and White families and two generations of the Gallagher family.

Robert White serves as corporate secretary and Frank Gallagher as president. Gallagher is also the president of New Jersey Motor Bus Association and both serve on the Private Carrier Advisory Committee to New Jersey Transit.

"With the development of the downtown Gateway area, Newark is growing into a communications hub. Law firms and other professionals are moving back into the city. Elizabeth is also expanding. Residents and commuters appreciate the easy access to New York, Newark Airport, and the the trains to South Jersey," says Frank Gallagher. "Good public transportation systems help attract and retain business."

WBGO-FM/88.3

Newark's WBGO-FM/88.3 has become one of the most listened-to nonprofit radio stations by offering around-the-clock jazz programming. Further, WBGO has become a jazz institution by combining the full spectrum of the music with jazz events, featuring jazz greats of yesterday and today.

The premier jazz station celebrating its 10th year of distinctive programming offers mainstream, blues, swing, big bands, vocals, instrumentals, contemporary, bebop, salsa, fusion, ragtime, hard bop, traditional, progressive, boogie-woogie, Harlem stride, and live performances—in short, the whole spectrum of jazz, with a special focus on young jazz players on the rise.

This National Public Radio station offers jazz and a solid lineup of news and public-affairs shows largely through the support of about 15,000 members. That support, which accounts for more than half of the station's $1.8 million annual budget, is further evidenced by the attendance at the station's ambitious series of outside events and benefit concerts.

WBGO/Jazz 88 has a policy of

Wylie Rollins, deputy general manager/program director.

producing concerts with every attempt to secure co-sponsors in order to avoid the risk to "public money." Among those it has forged co-sponsorship with is Lincoln Center, a first for Lincoln Center to be involved with as a jazz production entity. The station promotes the events on air, plays the featured artists' records as another form of promotion, tries to arrange tie-ins that help the sales of tickets (if the event is not free), and supervises the availability of talent.

A partial list of organizations that have supplied direct support for the station include Philip Morris International, Dodge Foundations, AT&T, Broad National Bank, Coopers & Lybrand, Bill Cosby, GRP Records, Hoffman-LaRoche, Howard Savings Bank, Metropolitan Life Foundation, Mutual Benefit Life, Public Service Electric & Gas, Prudential Foundation, Courvoisier, New Jersey Bell, New Jersey Transit, National Westminster Bank NJ, the Coca-Cola Bottling Company of New York, Inc., Gilbey's Gin, and Cognac Hennessy.

WBGO-FM has a basic audience of 250,000 with a footprint that reaches from Princeton, New Jersey, to New York's Westchester County—basically impacting most of the New York metropolitan market.

In addition to being a jazz station, WBGO hosts record fairs, jazz cruises, in-studio concerts, art gallery openings, members' parties, and trips with a jazz focus: New Orleans Jazz & Heritage Festival,

Anna Kosof, general manager.

Brazil carnival, Africa, and the South of France. It produces concerts in the metropolitan area and also co-produces concerts with corporate funding.

The station management believes the events away from the station help to stimulate corporate involvement, and that more corporate involvement in events (with definite results) continues to perpetuate the ever-widening awareness of the station and what it stands for—to promote jazz, "America's classical music."

Says WBGO's general manager, Anna Kosof, "All of us are proud to be part of such an overwhelming success, especially in this, our 10th anniversary year. This is the first time a jazz public radio station has been able to attract such an enormous audience. We are grateful for the support of our listeners in Newark and throughout the metropolitan area."

AT&T

With 52,000 New Jersey employees, AT&T is by far the state's largest private employer. Working at more than 200 facilities in 20 of 21 New Jersey counties, AT&T people live in more than 500 communities throughout the state. Some 1,200 employees work in Newark.

AT&T's large physical presence in New Jersey stimulates an equally impressive economic presence, with annual salaries, taxes, rents, purchases, dividend payments, philanthropy, and other expenditures injecting more than $5.4 billion into the state economy each year. Some 15,000 New Jersey businesses, including many in Newark, provide goods and services to AT&T each year.

Backed by a highly skilled sales and service force, AT&T provides a full range of computer and communications products and services. It also supplies sophisticated networking applications that tie disparate voice and data systems together into integrated networks.

AT&T's Worldwide Intelligent Network is widely regarded as the central nervous system of world communications. But what is less widely known, yet no less important, is that the core of that system is

---

AT&T is New Jersey's largest private employer, with 52,000 employees statewide. Pictured here is the employee lounge in Gateway II.

in the Garden State. Nestled in the foothills of Bedminster, the AT&T network control center is unlike any other telecommunications facility. Completing more than 75 million calls each weekday, it manages virtually every component of the most sophisticated information-handling system on earth.

That system—an intricate web of computers, lasers, lightwave and copper cables, satellites, microwave stations, and more—spans the nation and connects with more than 250 countries. With a total of more than 98,000 route miles, its advanced digital transmission systems ensure that 999 out of every 1,000 calls are completed on the first

AT&T is widely regarded as the central nervous system of world communications, and the core of this telecommunications system is in New Jersey.

---

attempt.

AT&T Bell Laboratories, a New Jersey fixture for more than 60 years, is a world leader in scientific research and development. Averaging a patent a day since the 1920s, AT&T Bell Laboratories has produced some of the world's most profound inventions, including the transistor, the laser, sound motion pictures, satellite technology, lightwave communications, the digital computer, and much more.

Today AT&T Bell Laboratories' scientists—who have earned seven Nobel Prizes and four National Medals of Science—are leading the way in such areas as superconductivity, microelectronics, and advanced computing. UNIX®, an AT&T-developed computer operating system, is fast becoming an

Completing more than 75 million calls each weekday, the AT&T network control center manages virtually every component of the most sophisticated information-handling system on earth.

industry standard, and technological developments in a host of other areas are helping to ensure New Jersey's place in an increasingly competitive world.

AT&T's heritage is rich with community involvement. Today that tradition lives through financial and personal contributions to a wide range of cultural, educational, and human services organizations throughout the Garden State.

More graduates of New Jersey colleges and universities are employed by AT&T than any other corporation, so the firm takes an active role in supporting education. Contributions range from grants to math and science programs for younger students to computer donations and financial support for New Jersey colleges and universities.

AT&T also supports a host of health care and social service agencies, ranging from hospitals and fire and rescue squads to community-

AT&T system of computers, lasers, lightwave and copper cables, satellites, and microwave stations allows for the transfer of information and provides a communication network that crosses the nation and connects more than 250 countries.

based rehabilitation groups and the United Way. AT&T encourages its employees to volunteer in community and statewide activities, and thousands have answered the call.

The Telephone Pioneers of America, the world's largest industrial service organization, is one of the proudest elements of AT&T. Composed of more than 720,000 current or retired members of the communications industry, the Telephone Pioneers are dedicated to serving the lonely, the disadvantaged, and the disabled. In New Jersey, more than 29,000 members regularly contribute their time and talent to community service products.

GANNETT OUTDOOR OF NEW JERSEY

The Garden State is the most densely populated state in the nation, with 70 percent of the state's population in the 12 New Jersey metro-area northern counties, which are covered by Gannett Outdoor of New Jersey, owner of more than half the billboards in the state.

Gannett Outdoor is a part of the Gannett Corporation, a nationwide organization that has built a leadership position in communications that includes television stations, radio stations, more than 90 daily newspapers, and America's most widely read daily newspaper, *USA Today.*

Gannett Outdoor advertising provides locational flexibility that lets advertisers hit any geographic region—from a multistate area to a single local street. Advertisers can adapt their messages to target specific ethnic or demographic groups where they live. Outdoor advertising is considered a highly efficient medium because advertisers can buy market by market. Industry statistics show that it has the capacity to reach more people per dollar than television, radio, or print advertising.

Gannett Outdoor advertising is especially powerful in finding and reaching hard-to-reach groups, including working women, high-income families, and today's active seniors. While evening television tends to concentrate toward older, less affluent, stay-at-homes, Gannett Outdoor advertising is ideally suited to upscale, mobile consumers whether the advertising format is rotary bulletins, permanent bulletins, posters, or backlights.

Measuring 14 feet high by 48 feet long, rotary bulletins are Gannett Outdoor's largest standard format. They locate the client's message on commuter arteries and high-circulation streets and are moved to different locations every two months. Superflex bulletins, painted by computer, give clients superior color rendition, durability, portability, and production efficiency.

Headquarters for Gannett Outdoor is located at Route 46 West in Fairfield.

Gannett Outdoor's permanent bulletins can either take the standard bulletin format or be designed uniquely to fit building sides or other special sites. It offers the advantages of desirable, high-traffic location and long-term duration.

With dimensions of 12 feet by 24 feet, the poster carries its design area to the edge of the display frame. Posters are especially appropriate for covering defined areas and can also focus on special retail zones or target groups. They give the client immediate reach and frequency exactly where wanted.

Gannett Outdoor's most dramatic medium is backlights, the medium that utilizes internal illumination—not unlike a giant television in the sky—for a literally glowing effect that intensifies color vibrancy. The highly popular backlights are

available at selected sites statewide.

These billboards are produced in a building the size of an airplane hangar. The posters are printed separately and pasted to each sign. The larger bulletins are painted by hand by Gannett's highly experienced artists. Each bulletin begins as a small layout, then an enlarger projects the image on a 14-foot by 48-foot wall of paper. A pattern designer traces the outline, and the paper is perforated and affixed to the billboard. The surface is then rubbed with charcoal cloth so the outline is left on the plywood and the paper can be reused for additional signs.

Many advertisers use Gannett

other popular heavily trafficked locations."

Gannett Outdoor clients represent a full spectrum of industries—financial services, telecommunications, auto dealers, health insurance, education, banks, and many more.

Gannett Outdoor prides itself on its commitment to quality and customer service that goes from the top down. Outdoor advertising locations are selected strategically for results. Structures are well maintained and updated periodically. The company's painting and posting standards are at the top of the industry. And its technical innovations, including Superflex and the modern trim poster panel, are creating the future of Gannett Outdoor today.

Gannett Outdoor's marketing and creative expertise can help clients make the most of this advertising medium. Gannett marketing experts help clients enhance their display's impact, develop location and placement strategies, and determine how to best combine outdoor advertising with other media in the client's marketing plan.

Gannett Outdoor Group is the founder and manager of Outdoor Network, USA, the only nationwide marketing and service network of outdoor advertising. The sophisticated marketing resources of the network offices can make a big difference when a client's outdoor

advertising strategy reaches beyond its local area.

Gannett acquired the former United Advertising Corporation in 1979. Founded in Newark during 1891 by Samuel Pratt as the Newark Billposting Company, the firm was taken over and renamed United Advertising in 1914. Through a series of acquisitions, Leonard Dreyfus, its new president, spearheaded the company's growth to the third-largest outdoor advertising firm in the United States. Today Gannett Outdoor sales are $25 million annually, garnered from the 3,200 nine-foot by 21-foot printed posters and 500 hand-painted bulletins it operates.

Responsive to community needs, Gannett donates space to civic and charitable organizations each year. In 1988 the Gannett Foundation made a substantial contribution to the Newark Collaboration, an organization dedicated to economic rebirth of the city.

According to Collins, "We feel Newark is turning around, and we see the continual growth of all types of business, including national and international companies in areas where we operate. Our advertisers benefit from the economic vitality of Newark and the greater Newark areas."

Pictured here is one of Gannett's new modern-trim poster panels.

Outdoor advertising because it reaches consumers at the point of purchase. Some are located close to retail outlets to give advertisers' products top-of-mind awareness among consumers on their way to buy. Other advertisers focus coverage in the specific geographic areas where their target groups are concentrated.

Gannett Outdoor's buying flexibility lets clients target specific interest groups selectively: for example, frequent travelers near airports or executives near office parks and central business districts.

According to marketing vice-president Bob Collins, "For pure circulation it's difficult to beat the New Jersey Turnpike, especially in the Newark International Airport area. Route 80 in Bergen County and the Lincoln Tunnel area are

MAHER TERMINALS, INC.

It is not coincidental that the growth of the greater Newark area in world trade, especially in the maritime transportation industry, dovetails with the great growth of Maher Terminals, Inc.

When one gazes at the 500-acre expanse that constitutes the Maher terminal complex and notes the great modern facilities and equipment that serve the world's commercial fleets, one cannot imagine the humble beginnings of this company that now contributes so greatly to the economic well-being of greater Newark.

Today the Maher name towers hundreds of feet above Newark Bay, where it is painted atop 14 gantry cranes that effortlessly carry thousands of cargo containers to and from the mammoth ships that berth at the company's Port Elizabeth terminal.

Every day the terminal's employees handle ocean cargo that touches virtually every segment of life in the metropolitan area. Maher Terminals directly employs more than 2,500 people to handle the numerous vessels that generate more than 3,000 truck moves daily and have an economic impact on the Newark community of $250 million annually, yet this company still retains the independence and moral awareness that it had in its humblest beginnings, when it was established in 1946.

Major Michael E. Maher, the

firm's founder, served with the Army Transportation Corp. during World War II. Fortified with a legal education from St. John's University and a familiarity with the waterfront inherited from his father, who had a modest but honored career in the maritime industry, young Maher flashed his independent spirit and struck out on his own. A small nest egg allowed him to acquire four 5,000-pound forklift trucks. Thus was Maher Terminals established.

Today it is an independently owned corporation, and management is in the hands of its stock-

Michael E. Maher, chairman. Courtesy, The Star Ledger.

holders, who are actively engaged in the daily operations of the company. Michael E. Maher, the firm's chairman, works with his sons M. Brian, the president since 1981, and Basil, senior vice-president/operations. Customers deal directly with people who can reach decisions quickly and decisively.

For the 10-year period following

World War II, the Port of New York consisted of hundreds of small finger piers stretching out over New York City's vast waterfront. Ship sailings were numerous, and the average stay in port was three days. Cargo was loaded and discharged from vessels in sling loads of one ton, and 25,000 longshoremen were busy 10 hours per day, discharging a mean of 1,200 tons and loading about 900 tons for foreign ports.

Each of the more than 200 liner services that called at the Port of New York had its own terminal that it leased directly from the City of New York or one of the private terminal owners, such as Bush, New York Dry Dock, American Dock, Pouch, or Harborside. In 1946 Port Newark had just two active vessel berths, which handled only lumber and domestic specialty cargoes. Elizabeth marine terminal did not yet exist.

More than 20 stevedoring companies performed the actual work as invitees of the steamship lines. Competition among the stevedores was fierce, but the business of stevedoring involved little or no investment. It was in this atmosphere that Maher launched his business on the New York City waterfront with his four pieces of

From left: Michael E. Maher, founder and chairman, with sons Basil Maher, senior vice-president/operations, and M. Brian Maher, president since 1981.

cargo-handling equipment.

In 1948 Maher Terminals, Inc., made its first appearance in Port Newark, handling the stevedoring of a shipload of sugar into a local Port Newark warehouse. For the next 10 years the stevedoring business grew at Port Newark with the handling of such specialized cargoes as sugar, frozen meat, drummed cargo (tallow, vegetable oils), cork, wood pulp, canned pineapples, and many others.

This decade corresponded with the acquisition of Port Newark by the Port Authority of New York and New Jersey and their programs of wharf, general cargo, and specialized facility development.

In 1958, after 10 years of gradual growth, Maher Terminals, Inc., took a major step. The firm bid successfully to become the agent for the port authority of all the public lumber movements handled at the port that involved back loading from vessels, storage, and distribution.

Maher's great aplomb in handling this commodity greatly increased the lumber activity in the region and was the springboard for the metamorphosis of Maher Terminals, Inc., from a stevedore to an independent terminal operator.

Shortly thereafter, in 1960, Maher became the lessee of Shed 141 at Port Newark, and that launched Maher's activity into world trade as a general cargo, independent terminal operator of a multiuser terminal.

As the Maher operation grew in this area, its efficiency in handling

overseas cargoes not only encouraged new liner services within the Newark area and the growth and development of new terminals, but also attracted entire new activities, such as the handling of import automobiles in shipload lots; the importation of steel from Japan, Holland, and Italy; and the importation of motorcycles from Japan.

During the decade from 1958 to 1968 containerization was developed and spread. It began with coastal, intercoastal, and offshore domestic movements, and it reached the European trade routes by 1968. Maher had already entered this activity by loading containers on general cargo vessels of Zim, Hellenic, Orient Overseas, Marchessini, and other major carriers.

Analyzing the growth in container operation, the port authority had acquired and developed a site in neighboring Elizabeth, and the first container terminal was opened in 1967. The Port Elizabeth expansion swelled Port Newark-Elizabeth to 2,200 acres just across the New Jersey Turnpike from Newark International Airport.

In 1970 Maher Terminals, Inc., was launched into the container terminal business with the opening of

loaders, and others. A good deal of the cargo is carried in tractor-trailer-size containers that are swung from deck to truck chassis and vice versa by cranes that ride steel rails on wheels larger than pickup trucks.

Keeping track of all the goods is done by a large computer network. In fact, many of the longshoremen who once used hooks to grapple with cargo now wield keyboards just as deftly. An on-line data-processing system that can record each transaction and inventory all the equipment and containers by category line, type, and size is the back-

the Tripoli Street Terminal in Elizabeth on the Newark Bay channel. Since that date Maher has devoted all its efforts and investments toward improving and developing its container and specialized facilities to attract new business into the greater Newark area.

According to Michael Maher, "The principal gateway for ocean-borne cargo in and out of the East Coast of the United States is the port of New York-Newark. As a result of our ongoing growth in New Jersey, we have expanded our operations to serve this port."

Maher operates the largest and most advanced public container facility in New York-Newark—the biggest port in the United States.

Presently the Maher Terminal handles the major carriers from every one of the world's trade routes—Japan, China, Southeast Asia, Europe, the Mediterranean, Africa, Australia, and several domestic operations, such as Puerto Rico and the northeast coast of the United States.

The overriding principle at Maher Terminals is to provide improved and more efficient service to its customers by continually upgrading the facilities and systems

upon which the services are based. Maher spares no expense in obtaining the best container cranes, the most reliable transtainers and other container equipment, and the most sophisticated computers and software.

A totally equipped modern container terminal is required in order to service today's containerships in a multiuser facility. Specialized equipment includes container cranes, yard hustlers, chassis, top-

bone of an efficient terminal.

Moreover, it takes tremendous know-how in order to meld all the functions of a terminal into a smooth, efficient flow of boxes to and from vessels and in and out of the terminal gate complex without error or damage, while also providing such ancillary services for the user steamship lines as container and chassis repair.

Obtaining the data-processing equipment and the cargo-handling facilities required to run the most efficient terminal in the United States necessitated that the Maher organization raise a great amount of capital, which was amassed through constant and total reinvestment of income and the resultant increases in

The know-how of Maher's staff is supplied by a talent-searching and training program that provides not only experienced and dedicated top management but also an able, broad-based pyramid of middle management and supervisory personnel to run the system and keep it vibrant.

Maher Terminals brings to its customers a staff of thoroughly trained, experienced professionals who are completely knowledgeable

borrowing position from local banks.

Maher's willingness to take extra steps means that its customers gain extra benefits. Maher works with each line to develop services tailored to its specific needs. Such vessels as containerships, Ro/Ro vessels, or conventional break-bulk ships can be accommodated at Maher Terminals. A carrier's special-purpose containers, its distinct chassis, its unusual mix of cargo, or its particular requirement for information reports are handled with dispatch.

Small lines and infrequent callers at ports served by Maher also gain through the company's extra efforts. Their vessels are welcomed at Maher terminals, and the lines are encouraged to take advantage of existing facilities, systems, and services.

Chassis are stored upended to conserve space.

in container terminal operations. Maher managers communicate with customers on all levels to define and meet their needs. They reflect the customer service attitude and philosophy of the company's top management.

The firm's customer service program is designed to satisfy its direct steamship line customers and to be responsive to the needs of shippers, consignors, truckers, and freight forwarders as well.

The growth of Maher, and its resulting contribution to the region, can be attributed to independence, customer service, dedication, ingenuity, and flexibility. These elements are provided by a dedicated staff with tremendous experience in the terminal operations, finance, data processing, and marketing in the maritime industry.

For the past 20 years Michael E.

Maher served as a director of the New York Shipping Association, which represents 90 steamship and terminal employers in labor relations with the International Longshoremen's Association. He is a member of the board of managers of the Seamen's Church Institute of NY/NJ, a trustee of St. Peter's College, and has held important positions on the boards of many similar organizations.

According to Maher, "Our combination of facilities, advanced technology, and services places our steamship customers in a highly advanced position in terms of costs and services they need. Efficient operations and effective terminal management techniques, combined with the ability to grow with the greater Newark region, have enabled us to be a successful business."

Vax 870 computer clusters.

Z100 WHTZ RADIO

Though commercial radio broadcasting was already in its seventh decade of operation by the early 1980s, there are millions of metropolitan area residents who will say that the medium was reborn on August 2, 1983.

Just after 6 a.m. on that day, listeners accustomed to the sounds of The 101 Strings and Montovanni heard a soon-to-be familiar voice announce: "At this time radio station WHTZ signs on the air; it's time to wake up!" As "Eye of the Tiger," the theme that brought Rocky to victory, began to spin on the turntable, Z100 was born. Seventy-four days later the station that had been virtually last in the all important ratings race had become the most-listened-to station in America.

That "worst to first" performance instantly established "The Hot Rockin' Flame Throwin' Z100" as the most talked about—and imitated—radio station in the country. The exciting brand of personality Top 40/contemporary hit radio ushered in by Z100 hadn't been heard in the area since the demise of legendary MusicRadio WABC.

While the speed of Z100's growth was truly amazing, the station's phenomenal success doesn't seem quite as surprising given the background of the company and individuals responsible for putting WHTZ on the air.

The story began when local beautiful music station, WVNJ-FM, was purchased by the Malrite Communications Group of Cleveland, Ohio. Malrite was formed in 1956, when founder Milton Maltz purchased a small radio station in Plymouth, Wisconsin. By 1983 the pioneering Maltz had built his company into one of the largest, fastest growing, and most respected broadcasting organizations in the nation. Malrite's numerous radio and television properties included the famous "Buzzard" of Cleveland, WMMS, one of America's premier

The Z100 Team competes each year in the annual Great Bed Race, helping to raise funds for the Muscular Dystrophy Association.

rock and roll radio stations.

Based on instinct and experience backed by extensive market research, Milton Maltz had determined that without a single Top 40 station serving the New York/ Northern New Jersey region there was a sizable void waiting to be filled. In his boldest move yet, the chairman and chief executive officer of Malrite decided to fill that void by turning the small station at 100.3 on the FM dial into WHTZ/Z100, the new home for the hottest hits in radio. That effort got a considerable boost when Malrite received permission from the FCC to move WHTZ' antenna from Livingston, New Jersey, to the top of the Empire State Building. Since FM radio can only be heard along a line of sight to the horizon, the new location allowed Z100 to cover the entire region with its high-energy music format. The rest, as they say, is history.

The small team that first put Z100 on the air has since grown to include more than 50 full-time employees and a nearly equal number of part timers and interns. What has remained consistent and simple, however, is Z100's winning formula that combines the most hit music with the best personalities, heavy

promotion, and extensive community involvement. The station has dominated the number-one position in the ratings race by staying plugged in to the pulse of the listening public.

Each morning it is "The Z100 Morning Zoo" that kicks things off and sets the tone for the rest of the day. While the Zoo is filled with music and up-to-the-minute information, the program's slashing wit and frenzied, unpredictable humor are what really make it stand out on the radio dial. Though the morning antics can reach truly zany dimensions (such as the time Z100 shook up listeners and the local media with the story that Michael and LaToya Jackson were really one and the same person), the Zoo always remains the type of program that the whole family can listen to while sitting around the breakfast table. In fact, "The Best of The Z100 Morning Zoo" has been immortalized in a series of albums produced by Arista Records. In its very first release, the Zoo album became one of the area's top 10 sellers, with all of the proceeds going to The Z100 Children's Charities.

Community involvement is what makes Z100 much more than just the place to turn to for music and entertainment. The station has joined together with scores of charities, schools, civic organizations, hospitals, and corporations to work on everything from raising funds to building awareness about key issues. Crucial to this involvement has been the work of Z100's much-honored public affairs director, John Bell. Both on air and off Bell has been a well-known figure in the region for many years through his ongoing community involvement. Bell's voice has been heard at 100.3 on the dial since the days of WVNJ. Now, when he's not contributing his information about public affairs or sports to "The Morning Zoo," or working on his weekly community-oriented broadcast, "New Jersey and You," John Bell may be found hosting a telethon, participating in the Muscular Dystrophy Association's Great Bed Race, or playing in a charity softball game.

A good deal of Z100's commitment, concern, and enthusiasm is directed toward the youngest members of the community through the Z100 Children's Charities. This special arm of the station has channelled many thousands of dollars to such organizations as the Make A Wish Foundation, the Multiple Sclerosis Center, and the Fresh Air Fund. A number of organizations have recognized Z100's contributions to their caus-

es with commemorative plaques, some of which fill a wall of honor off the main corridor of the station. In addition to those mentioned above, a wide range of organizations are represented, including Special Olympics, the American Heart Association, the American Cancer Society, the Cystic Fibrosis Association, Children's Miracle Network, the March of Dimes—Walk America, the Spina Bifida Association, the Juvenile Diabetes Foundation, and more. Z100 is also closely involved with M.A.D.D.—Mothers Against Drunk Driving, spearheading the Don't Drink and Drive campaign.

Looking at Z100's track record both on the air and in the community, it's not surprising that the station has attracted a lot of attention from other segments of the media. In fact, while WHTZ now runs an extensive schedule of television and outside advertising, things were quite a bit different back at the beginning in 1983. During that worst to first period, virtually all of the station's publicity was by word of mouth or through press coverage

of this new radio phenomenon.

To date Z100's press clippings fill several large volumes. In addition to features on network and local television (including "Good Morning America," "CBS Morning News," "Today," "20/20," "West 57th," "Oprah Winfrey," "Regis Philbin," Channels 2, 4, 5, 7, 9, and 11), and both MTV and VH-1, the WHTZ call letters regularly appear in national, local, and industry publications. There have been stories in *Newsweek*, *The Wall Street Journal*, the *New York Times*, *The Sunday Daily News*, *Forbes*, *Business Week*, *Venture Magazine*, *Cosmopolitan*, *USA Today*, and the *London Times*. *Billboard* magazine devoted an unprecedented 10-page special layout to the Z100 story.

Not a station to rest on its laurels, Z100 continuously strives to produce fresh ideas and unique promotions as its personalities provide the audience with the hottest hit music.

Z100's "King Kong Master Blaster" is a state-of-the-art mobile studio that brings Z100 to listeners all over the metropolitan area.

With the kind of aggressiveness that has come to be expected from this company, WHTZ's multimillion-dollar marketing and promotional efforts have created a high level of excitement in the listening community. With one phone call, the fabulous Free Money Birthday Contest has given listeners the chance to win up to $30,000 just for knowing which day they were born. Z100 has supported its unique position as the 10-Songs-in-a-Row radio station by giving away 10 Cars in a Row to listeners who could provide the titles to go with a list of brief song clips.

Z100 has also thanked its audience with prizes that range from homes, cars, and vacations, to $100 bills, gift certificates, and concert tickets. Whenever the station's Party Patrol or Beach Patrol vans spot a car sporting one of the millions of Z100 Superstickers now in circulation, the driver of that vehicle becomes eligible for some very special prizes, such as entry into a drawing to win a classic Corvette convertible. Of course, that's in addition to the tens of thousands of Z-shirts, jerseys, caps, gloves, hit radios, mugs, key chains, shoelaces, and buttons that have been handed out to lucky listeners.

Whether it's featuring concerts with the hottest bands and artists such as homegrown New Jersey heroes Bon Jovi and Bruce Springsteen, screening hit movies, bringing listeners together for the hippest parties in town, or hosting the world premier and press conference for Madonna's latest film, Z100 can always be counted on to be first on the scene at the most talked-about events.

Obviously, its status as the Most Listened to Radio Station in America hasn't stopped Z100 from striving to achieve the highest possible quality in everything the station undertakes. Members of the Z100 staff are especially proud that this excellence has been recognized by their broadcasting peers on a number of occasions. From individual recognition for Program Director of the Year, General Manager of the Year, Operations Manager of the Year, Music Director of the Year, and Air Personality of the Year, to collective acknowledgement in the prestigious *Billboard* magazine Station of the Year Award, Z100 has won praise as a leader and innovator in the radio industry.

All in all, WHTZ/Z100 is a success story that works: as entertainment for the listeners, as a leader in the community, and as a vehicle for advertisers. A mention on the station has been known to attract record-breaking crowds as well as to overload incoming phone lines.

Defining Z100 seems easy enough. The station is exciting, original, and fun, featuring top personalities combining the best hit music with humor, information, and fantastic promotions. Those elements, however, don't tell the entire story.

What really makes Z100 stand out is its soul. Contained in its electrical components is something akin to a heartbeat. The station's success is based on a relationship with its audience and involvement in their lives and community. People feel like they know the members of the Morning Zoo. You see the emotional link in the faces of the children who come for the frequent tours of the studios. There is more communication between WHTZ and the more than 2.5 million listeners who share its day than the printed word could ever begin to show. The ratings companies may show that WHTZ is the number-one radio station in the country, but for the listeners Z100 is special because it's *their* radio station.

Ross Brittain (left) and Brian Wilson (right) took The Z100 Morning Zoo on the road to celebrate St. Patrick's Day.

Photo by Rich Zila

XIV

Business and Professions

Greater Newark's professional community brings a wealth of service, ability, and insight to the area.

Midlantic Corporation, 262-263

The Greater Newark Chamber of Commerce, 264

City Federal Savings Bank, 265

McCarter & English, 266-267

Carpenter, Bennett & Morrissey, 268

The CTS Group, 269

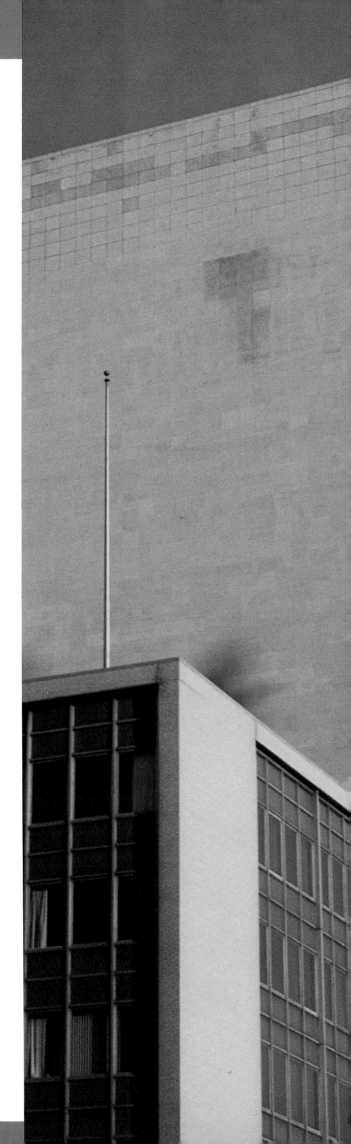

The Mutual Benefit Companies, 270-271

Clapp & Eisenberg, 272-273

The Prudential Insurance Company of America, 274-275

Apruzzese, McDermott, Mastro & Murphy, 276-277

Howard Savings Bank, 278

Wharton/Lyon & Lyon, 279

Stryker, Tams & Dill, 280-281

Crummy, Del Deo, Dolan, Griffinger & Vecchione, 282-283

National Westminster Bank NJ, 284

Lewis Advertising Agency, 285

First Fidelity Bank, 286-287

Lowenstein, Sandler, Kohl, Fisher & Boylan, 288-289

Penn Federal Savings Bank, 290-291

Blue Cross and Blue Shield of New Jersey, 292-293

Samuel Klein and Company Certified Public Accountants, 294-295

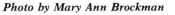

City National Bank of New Jersey, 296

Photo by Mary Ann Brockman

MIDLANTIC CORPORATION

Midlantic Corporation, headquartered in Edison, New Jersey, is a premier banking organization in the mid-Atlantic region, that operates a network of 510 offices, with domestic facilities located throughout New Jersey, eastern Pennsylvania, and New York, and in Delaware, Florida, Maryland, and Texas.

These operations, combined with the capabilities of Midlantic's overseas offices in London, Hong Kong, and Grand Cayman, provide individual, corporate, institutional, and governmental clients with a complete array of financial programs that include corporate, international, investment, mortgage, brokerage, trust, and personal banking services.

Midlantic's aggressive operating philosophy and record of strong financial performance have established it in the forefront of the financial services industry. It is an

organization characterized by a highly attractive banking franchise and superior levels of service. Midlantic has continued to enhance its leadership position within the banking industry through a long-term program of corporate growth and expansion.

Through a combination of acquisitions, de novo market penetration, and the reorganization and consolidation of its bank network, Midlantic has built a leading banking franchise in the vibrant markets of New Jersey, eastern Pennsylvania, and New York.

Midlantic's expansion has been particularly rapid in recent years. In 1970 the firm was first to take advantage of the New Jersey law permitting the formation of multibank holding companies within the state. Midlantic launched a program of expansion through acquisition that served as the catalyst for its growth during the 1970s. Since 1978 Midlantic has acquired and successfully integrated into the corporation 14 organizations ranging

Today Midlantic Corporation is a $23-billion interstate bank holding company headquartered in Edison, New Jersey.

in asset size from $45 million to $5.3 billion.

In 1987 Midlantic created the framework for continued growth through the establishment of Midlantic Corporation. This interstate bank holding company was formed through the affiliation of Midlantic Banks Inc. with Continental Bancorp Inc. of Philadelphia. The acquisition marked the first entry by a New Jersey bank holding company into the vibrant Philadelphia and eastern Pennsylvania markets.

A significant share of Midlantic's marketing effort as a major super-regional bank is directed to medium-size companies. Midlantic staff members have earned their reputation as the "hungry bankers" by developing innovative banking services that are tailored to the requirements of these companies.

Midlantic also aggressively seeks to serve the nation's largest corporations, placing emphasis on firms headquartered in New Jersey and Pennsylvania and on national companies that maintain facilities in these states. Midlantic's success in this highly competitive sector

Midlantic's original banking office was established in 1804 as New Jersey's first bank.

results from the expertise of bank account officers, their specialized product knowledge, and the quality of the company's lending and non-credit services.

With its superior port facilities and excellent transportation systems, New Jersey is an ideal location for companies active in international trade. Capitalizing on these strengths, Midlantic facilitates and finances international trade and investment activities for regional corporations with operations overseas, local domestic affiliates of foreign companies, and area businesses engaged in international trade.

While the continuing evolution of the financial services industry has had a strong impact on all banking activities, it is in the consumer market that dereg- ulation has caused the most sweeping changes.

Midlantic's diverse banking programs serve personal financial needs as basic as a home mortgage or as sophisticated as an investment planning program. These activities are supported by Midlantic's direct banking systems and by an extensive network of automated teller machines that provide customers with 24-hour access to their accounts.

Midlantic has long recognized the importance of serving the growing number of individuals and families whose financial planning benefits from highly personalized banking services. Increasing levels of personal income in New Jersey are coincident with the influx of corporate executives, professionals, and entrepreneurs. Midlantic draws upon the expertise of lending professionals, backed by a strong foundation of trust and investment management services,

Midlantic National Bank president Desmond P. McDonald, at Sacred Heart Cathedral in Newark, exemplifies Midlantic's involvement and support of community activities.

to meet the complex needs of these individuals.

A bank is regarded as one of the most essential elements of the community, and Midlantic is committed to serving as a responsible corporate citizen within the many communities it serves. For almost 200 years the corporation has supported the growth of New Jersey and its institutions. Midlantic provides specialized banking services and financial support to hospitals, schools, and

Chairman Robert Van Buren, in Tokyo with key corporate leaders, demonstrates Midlantic's commitment to industry needs and international banking.

cultural organizations.

The company has a long-standing history as a major force in the greater Newark area. Its lead bank, Midlantic National Bank, has been headquartered in Newark since its establishment in 1804 as the first banking organization in the State of New Jersey. As Midlantic continues to expand, it retains strong ties to the city, its residents, and businesses by maintaining corporate offices in Newark.

The bank's first branch office was opened in the Ironbound section of Newark in 1928 and still remains a keystone of the community, as do its branches in the Haynes Avenue industrial area, in the central business district, and in University Hill.

Close ties to various organizations reflect the firm's commitment to improving the community. Midlantic fosters the continuing growth and development of the region by encouraging staff members' involvement in cultural, community, and educational organizations that benefit from their volunteer services and management expertise.

As a leading super-regional bank, Midlantic has the resources, staff, and sophisticated services to meet the needs of New Jersey's expanding markets. These important capabilities are reinforced by Midlantic Corporation's commitment to providing an extra measure of service to its customers in the mid-Atlantic region, including the greater Newark market.

THE GREATER NEWARK CHAMBER OF COMMERCE

An overview of downtown Newark.

The Greater Newark Chamber of Commerce is the region's leading advocate for business. The Chamber traces its origin back to the Patriotic Society of Newark, organized in 1793 to promote trade and commerce and to improve the area. This association took its modern form in February 1868 as the Newark Board of Trade and was officially incorporated as the Chamber of Commerce in 1920.

The Chamber has undergone a dramatic expansion in the past eight years as Newark has experienced a renaissance. In 1980 the Chamber represented 500, mostly cityand Essex County-based, firms. Today it represents 2,500 independent businesses located in 18 of New Jersey's 21 counties and with a large concentration in neighboring New York City. The year 1988 saw the Chamber's most successful membership drive ever—520 new members.

Although the organization represents several *Fortune* 500 companies, more than 80 percent of its membership consists of small businesses that rely on the many benefits of Chamber membership to improve their bottom line.

The Chamber offers numerous programs and services to its members, including strategic seminars, networking sessions, discounts on publications and advertising, low-cost financing, business referrals, research data and statistics, cost-effective and comprehensive insurance programs, and small business assistance programs. In addition to these many direct benefits, the Chamber offers a number of programs that benefit the Metro New Jersey business community indirectly, such as monitoring legislation and supporting pro-business issues and promoting economic development in the region.

The Chamber works closely with city hall, county government, community-based groups, and a number of independent agencies, such as the Port Authority of New York and New Jersey, to meet its mission.

The role of the Chamber is to represent area businesses in dealings with government, working to improve the general business climate of the Metro New Jersey region, improving the overall quality of life in order to support broader economic activity, and advancing human progress through the free enterprise market system.

The Chamber has played a leading role in creating several independent organizations, such as Renaissance Newark Inc., the Newark Economic Development Corporation, the Economic Development Corporation of Essex County, and the Convention & Visitors Bureau of Metro New Jersey/Meadowlands, to facilitate the promotion and economic growth of the area.

Through its 20 committees the Chamber is involved with every aspect of Newark's development. These committees work to promote the port and the airport; improve transportation; support the retention, expansion, and attraction of business; promote cleanup and safety efforts; assist small businesses overcome paperwork and regulatory obstacles; and promote new high-technology and minority entrepreneurship.

Through such projects as the Love Newark Committee, the Leadership Institute, the Municipal Government Committee, the Black Churchmen Job Training Program, and the School Partnership Program, the Chamber is strongly committed to community involvement and improvement.

The Greater Newark Chamber of Commerce's 40-person board of directors, made up of most of the largest and some of the most successful small companies in the area, is a strong advocate for the overall improvement of the City of Newark. Their faith, hard work, and commitment has been essential in helping to strengthen the city and secure its destiny as an unsurpassed center of commerce.

CITY FEDERAL SAVINGS BANK

City Federal Savings Bank is New Jersey's largest savings institution. It is also one of the state's oldest banks, building on more than 100 years of tradition.

The bank began as the Citizens Building and Loan Association of Elizabeth, New Jersey, in 1887. From a neighborhood mutual savings association, City Federal has grown to become a major regional savings bank.

City Federal's Retail Banking Group now serves more than 500,000 households in the major population centers of New Jersey and South Florida. The system has more than 100 retail banking branches and a proprietary network of more than 130 automated teller machines (ATMs). Through City Federal's participation in shared ATM networks, its customers have access to more than 20,000 ATMs nationwide.

City Federal offers its customers a full line of retail banking services. These include a variety of money market, checking, and savings accounts; certificates of deposit; consumer and mortgage loans; and investment and insurance products. City Federal also provides important financial services to corporations, municipalities, and other public entities.

Continuous product development, marketing, and attention to customer service are critical for City Federal as the bank seeks to reinforce its competitive position in its prime markets. Product development aims to take advantage of new technological possibilities to enhance service levels. The introduction of electronic phone banking and point-of-sale (POS) payments capabilities for City Federal cus-

tomers and the expansion of City Federal's access to national and international ATM networks illustrate the benefits of this approach.

Similarly, the development of City Federal's cross-sell capability has enhanced service levels for customers while improving the bank's product delivery. For example, the integration of mortgage and consumer lending into Retail Banking has enabled City Federal to provide the full line of consumer financial services through its branch network, thus reducing costs while improving market penetration.

At a time when the continuing

John W. Atherton, Jr., chairman and chief executive officer of City Federal, is focusing the bank on its core businesses in its prime markets.

consolidation of the financial services industry will be the order of the day, City Federal is concentrating on its basic businesses and its primary markets, of which New Jersey remains the most important by far.

According to John W. Atherton, Jr., City Federal Savings Bank's president and deputy chief executive officer, "There are no magic formulas in our business. We have more than 100 years' experience as a real estate-oriented leader and as a provider of retail financial services. Times change, and the manner in which we conduct those businesses does so accordingly. But our priorities for today and for our planning horizon are to stick to our main lines of business, to continue what we do best. We feel confident that this is the best way to make City Federal stronger and to take advantage of the opportunities that will certainly arise in a dynamic future."

City Federal's retail banking branches, like this one in Larchmont, offer customers a full range of consumer financial services, including money market accounts; savings accounts; mortgage, home equity, and personal loans; as well as insurance, securities, and other investment products.

McCARTER & ENGLISH

McCarter & English recently moved into its new corporate headquarters at Gateway IV, conveniently located next to Newark's Penn Station. Gateway IV is a joint project of the firm and the Prudential Insurance Company.

Very much a part of Newark's proud history and current renaissance, McCarter & English is New Jersey's oldest and largest law firm. A full-service firm with specialists across the range of modern commercial practice, McCarter & English meets the increasingly varied and complex legal needs of corporations and partnerships as well as individuals.

The firm traces its origins back to 1844, when Thomas N. McCarter and Martin Ryerson established a joint practice of law in Newton. McCarter, the son of a judge of New Jersey's highest court, moved his practice to Newark in 1865 to be at the heart of the state's burgeoning industrial economy. From that time to the present, the firm has maintained a continuous presence in Newark.

McCarter & English recently reinforced its commitment to Newark by moving into new corporate headquarters at Gateway IV, a joint project of the firm and the Prudential Insurance Company. Conveniently located next to Penn Station, the firm's offices at Gateway IV include the largest and most complete private law library in the state as well as state-of-the-art computerized and technological support systems.

The 1980s have been a period of

explosive growth for McCarter & English. In the past five years the firm has added more than 100 attorneys and has experienced growth in all areas of practice. This growth in size and scope has been matched by geographic expansion. McCarter & English maintains regional offices in New York City; Cherry Hill, New Jersey; Wilmington, Delaware; and Boca Raton, Florida. This strong regional presence enhances the firm's ability to serve clients whose needs transcend state jurisdictions.

Today, with more than 170 attorneys, McCarter & English continues to build on the strength of its traditions, while anticipating changes in the law and the needs of its clients. Long known for its litigation, corporate, tax, trusts and estates, and real estate practice, the firm has added talent and expertise in the fields of

McCarter & English is a full-service law firm with specialists to meet the diverse legal needs of corporations and partnerships as well as individuals.

bankruptcy, securities, mergers and acquisitions, intellectual property, and environmental law. It has also developed a national public finance practice.

McCarter & English has grown rapidly by maintaining its traditional commitment to delivering high-quality, cost-effective legal services while remaining at the forefront of new legal developments. The firm is able to meet stringent deadlines by calling upon large manpower and support staff capabilities, often at a lower cost than available elsewhere in the New York metropolitan area.

McCarter & English is meeting the evolving needs of its clients in a wide variety of areas. In the area of litigation, for example, the firm manages major products liability cases and also acts as national coordinating counsel in cases pending nationwide. McCarter & English serves as counsel in significant commercial and trade regulation cases, corporate control disputes, toxic tort regulation cases, and insurance coverage disputes.

The firm has responded to the sharply increased need for legal services to the financial services industry. In the corporate law and securities area, the firm serves as general counsel to clients engaged in extraordinary corporate transactions, including public offerings, financings, reorganizations, recapitalizations, mergers, and acquisitions.

McCarter & English's ability to provide innovative legal services has also been evident in the public finance area. The firm developed, in conjunction with a major New York investment banking firm, one of the first innovative "low floating demand bonds," and represented the investment bank in successfully marketing the program in Louisiana, Wisconsin, Texas, and Kansas. In New Jersey, McCarter & English led the way in structuring financial alternatives for resource recovery and responses to the state's garbage disposal crisis.

McCarter & English engages in a true general practice, distinguished by the depth of its services as well as the specialized expertise that it brings to bear on a diverse range of matters. The firm maintains the highest professional standards through the recruitment of exceptional law school graduates. All attorneys are encouraged to con-

sult with their colleagues in different specialties, and frequently attorneys with diverse backgrounds establish teams to serve client needs better. The firm encourages an atmosphere of collegiality, believing it establishes the best environment for providing creative, dedicated service.

Leadership in New Jersey's civic and business affairs is a tradition at

McCarter & English's new offices at Gateway IV combine old-world charm with state-of-the-art computerized and technological support systems.

McCarter & English. The firm's attorneys contribute to their communities through a broad range of civic and charitable organizations. Many of the firm's attorneys are actively engaged in teaching in area law schools as well as in writing and speaking nationally on their respective areas of specialization.

McCarter & English's reputation as one of New Jersey's leading law firms has been earned over a period spanning nearly a century and a half. Without compromising the firm's professional, personalized service, McCarter & English has developed the specialized, diversified, cost-effective legal capabilities required by today's client. A standard of excellence and an approach that draws on the talents of a diverse group of highly dedicated attorneys continue to set McCarter & English apart.

CARPENTER, BENNETT & MORRISSEY

The firm of Carpenter, Bennett & Morrissey, with more than 80 lawyers, conducts a diverse law practice in almost every field of state and federal civil law. These include business litigation, labor and employment, corporate, product liability, environmental, tax, employee benefits, international, estate planning, workers' compensation, real estate, antitrust, securities regulation, and bankruptcy and creditors' rights.

Carpenter, Bennett & Morrissey represents

many multinational and national corporations. Although many of its clients are situated in New Jersey, a substantial number are located throughout the United States, Europe, and the Far East. These clients are in a broad range of businesses, including automotive, petrochemical, transportation, communications, publishing, banking, manufacturing, insurance, real estate development, scientific research, and health care. The firm also represents major universities, institutions, and business and trade associations.

A number of the firm's lawyers have distinguished themselves in

Carpenter, Bennett & Morrissey conducts a diverse law practice, with more than 80 lawyers, in almost every field of state and federal civil law.

the public sector. The firm was founded by Lindley Miller Garrison, who formed a partnership with Frances T. McManus in 1898 and later became Secretary of War under President Woodrow Wilson.

The firm's name was changed to Carpenter, Bennett & Morrissey in 1958. Headed by James D. Carpenter, Jr., who had achieved a national reputation after serving as a special prosecutor for the State of New Jersey and enjoyed a long and noteworthy career, the firm grew to become one of the principal law firms in New Jersey by the 1970s. Its senior partner is now Thomas L. Morrissey.

Today, maintaining the firm's tradition of serving the public, many of its lawyers are actively involved in local community affairs in Newark and in their own residential areas. The firm helps sponsor the Mentor Program,

conducted by the Newark Board of Education and Seton Hall University, which introduces high school students in Newark to the legal profession.

The firm's lawyers also play an active role in local, state, national, and international bar associations, and serve on committees concerned with improving professional practice and advocating legislative reform.

Carpenter, Bennett & Morrissey, now completing three decades in Newark, moved to its present offices in Three Gateway Center in 1985.

Carpenter, Bennett & Morrissey, now completing three decades in Newark, moved to its present offices in Three Gateway Center in 1985.

THE CTS GROUP

The CTS Group architectural offices have been located in Newark's Military Park Building since the firm's inception in 1952. According to the company's current president, Olaf Stechow, "We have always had an optimistic outlook about Newark's potential. We are seeing a dramatic increase in the revitalization of the city."

With a wide range of experience in building construction projects as well as facilities planning and interior design, the firm's guiding principle in the execution of its work is attention to detail. The diversification in assignments enables CTS Group to bring fresh insight to each project. According to Stechow, ". . . the goal always is to create practical, economical solutions for a project as a whole, and to complete the work on schedule and within budget."

CTS has received recognition for outstanding design for several projects over the years. The most notable facility is the Jos. L. Muscarelle Center for Building Construction Studies at Fairleigh Dickinson University, Teaneck, New Jersey. The three-story structure, which houses a four-year Bachelor of Science program has become a landmark on the university campus.

One area of expertise is transportation. Studies for introduction of small automated transit systems into existing urban areas have been done for several American cities. CTS designed the prototype stations and structures for the first automated downtown people-mover system in Morgantown, West Virginia.

Olaf Stechow received his architectural degree from Pratt Institute in 1963 and was licensed six years later. His dedication to the field of design and construction began during his apprenticeship in cabinetmaking and architectural woodworking. "We think of ourselves as a young firm that has been around for a long time. We are well established, and we continually seek to improve our practice with technical innovations, such as computer-aided design and drafting," says Stechow.

"The transformation of Newark has been ongoing, although it has really only become visible in the past few years. We consider ourselves very fortunate to be a part of it," says Karin Stechow, AIA, who has been with the firm since 1981.

Much of the firm's work in Newark has been focused on rehabilitation and adaptive use of existing buildings. Projects of this type require a great deal of ingenuity to maintain the assets of the existing structure and yet fulfill new program requirements.

As a result of increasing local waterfront development, CTS Group was commissioned to design an addition to the Seamen's Church Institute facilities in Port Newark to better serve the seafarers from all parts of the world. Firm members are also active in the Hudson Waterfront Museum, an organization involved in the preservation of local maritime heritage and sensitive long-term waterfront development.

"Many of Newark's first-time developers are unique in that they have a real commitment to their projects, beyond just dollars and cents," says Karin Stechow. "American cities are young in relation to other urban areas around the world. . . with careful planning, every cycle adds to the complexity and interest of the urban environment. It is gratifying for us to make contributions, however small, in this process."

The window replacement on New Jersey Bell's historic corporate headquarters on Broad Street in Newark was done by CTS Group in association with Hyun +Siri.

Designed by the CTS Group, the Jos. L. Muscarelle Center for Building Construction Studies at Fairleigh Dickinson University has become a landmark on the Teaneck campus.

THE MUTUAL BENEFIT COMPANIES

From its beginnings in New Jersey in 1845, Mutual Benefit Life has evolved into a full financial service organization, headquartered in Newark, New Jersey; Kansas City, Missouri; and Providence, Rhode Island, with offices nationwide.

Much of the firm's managed growth, especially in recent years, has been in response to social, economic, and regulatory change. For all its size and sophistication, however, the Mutual Benefit family of employees, associates, and affiliated brokers continues to be engaged in the very personal business of helping clients achieve financial security. The company's mission is "to be recognized by our customers and our prospective customers as a major provider of quality financial products and services to individuals, affiliated groups, and businesses."

In just a few years Mutual Benefit has made a remarkable transition from a traditional life insurance carrier to a responsive and responsible full financial services company. Individual life insurance, Mutual Benefit's primary focus for more than 100 years, has evolved from traditional whole life to a variety of forms specifically designed for today's—and tomorrow's—lifestyles and family needs. The firm's expanding insurance lines include increasing premium insurance; adjustable life,

which provides the policyholder with unparalleled flexibility; and interest-sensitive whole life. Through its wholly owned subsidiary, The MBL Life Assurance Corporation, the company also offers term insurance and single-premium deferred annuities.

Operating out of Newark's corporate headquarters and regional sales and service offices, Mutual Benefit's group pension divisions design, market, and administer a wide variety of funding and investment arrangements for pension plans, thrift, profit sharing, and tax-sheltered annuity programs of small to medium-size businesses and *Fortune* 500 companies, as well as public employee systems, state lottery systems, hospitals, educators' groups, and the military.

Headquartered in Kansas City, Missouri, Mutual Benefit's group life and health division provides disability income protection and rehabilitation benefits in addition to group life and health insurance products. Its clients range from small businesses and trade associations with five or six members to national corporations employing thousands.

At the Providence, Rhode Island, headquarters of the Mutual Benefit Financial Service Company, financial professionals research and carefully develop outstanding investment opportunities. Proprietary products reflecting timely market demand have been developed in the areas of public and private real estate, natural resources, equipment leasing, and fine arts and entertainment. In addition, a full complement of mutual funds, bond funds, and unit trusts are offered.

Operating out of Newark's corporate headquarters and regional sales and service offices, Mutual Benefit's group pension divisions design, market, and administer a wide variety of funding and investment arrangements.

Investments in real estate joint ventures are made by Muben Realty, a rapidly growing company affiliate. Projects range from office buildings and shopping centers to rental apartments and luxury condominium projects.

High-rise office buildings, shopping centers, and industrial properties are among investments chosen and managed by the firm's real estate investment division.

A majority-owned subsidiary of MBL Holding Company, Markston International, Inc., manages marketable equity securities portfolios for Mutual Benefit, its separate accounts and related companies, as well as for outside institutional investors. Markston's average equity accounts have outperformed Standard & Poor's 500.

Farm mortgages are administered through the farm loan office headquartered in Ames, Iowa. Mutual Benefit's farm loan operations have a long-standing tradition of support for America's farmers dating back to the Depression.

In pursuit of the highest overall yield consistent with the safety of principal, Mutual Benefit's Investment Division stresses soundness, flexibility, and diversity. Experienced professionals utilize their extensive knowledge and industry background in making portfolio selections that best serve Mutual Benefit's investment strategies and goals.

The Capital Markets Division is responsible for all Mutual Benefit investments in fixed-income securities, publicly and privately issued bonds and notes, and privately placed equity securities. Capital Markets also manages Mutual Benefit's investments in venture capital, providing funds for fledgling companies through limited partnerships and the purchase of private placement equity securities. Returns on these investments have been among the highest in the company.

Mutual Benefit takes great pride

in the people who make up its family, including more than 1,500 representatives in agency offices nationwide and more than 3,000 employees. By encouraging performance and fostering self-esteem, the company is continually developing its greatest asset—its people.

As a major employer in its home office cities, Mutual Benefit recognizes and welcomes responsibilities within the communities it serves. Accordingly, the company shares its resources with many organizations involved in education, social services, and community improvement.

Mutual Benefit's corporate commitment is complemented by its many employees who serve in Newark-area community groups by giving generously of their time and talents. The volunteer spirit demonstrated by Mutual Benefit employees represents more than just a commitment of time and energy. The caring attitude they bring to the Newark area and other communities is a reflection of the concern and involvement Mutual Benefit has made part of its mission to provide insurance, financial services, and security nationwide.

By joint efforts with area public school systems as well as with colleges and technical schools, Mutual Benefit helps students acquire the education and skills needed to become productive members of their communities. By establishing and supporting private-sector programs to train and employ community residents, Mutual Benefit helps insure a vibrant future for cities such as Newark. Through summer internships, promising students acquire skills and industry-specific knowledge that will prepare them for careers with Mutual Benefit or other employers. Mutual Benefit employees have also assumed leadership roles on private business councils.

Changing, growing, anticipating a better and brighter tomorrow—that is Mutual Benefit.

CLAPP & EISENBERG

Clapp & Eisenberg, a major New Jersey law firm, was founded in Newark 30 years ago and has chosen to remain there. The firm believes that Newark is regaining its commercial vigor. It believes Newark is a good place to practice law. It is here to stay.

The firm has specialists in all the main fields of law—in complex commercial and governmental litigation; in business counseling, negotiation, and drafting; in banking and bankruptcy; in real estate and municipal bonds; in casino law and public utilities; and in trusts and estates. There are specialists and, depending upon the problem, interdisciplinary teamwork. There is a conscientious effort to keep client costs down. The firm's objective is first-rate service and concern for client needs.

Although statewide (and

Above: Alfred C. Clapp, founder; left: Jerome C. Eisenberg, founder.

beyond) in professional focus, Clapp & Eisenberg maintains a strong interest in Newark-related clients and issues. The firm represented Amtrack in the sale and lease back of Penn Station. It was special counsel to the City of Newark in a case involving Newark's watershed lands and advocated Newark's position before the New Jersey Supreme Court in Mount Laurel II. The firm has represented the Prudential Insurance Company, Mutual Benefit, First Fidelity, United Hospitals, and many other Newark-based clients, large and small.

The scope of Clapp & Eisenberg's interest in Newark-related matters extends beyond the practice of law. One of the partners was a founding trustee of the Newark Legal Services Project (New Jersey's first legal services project), and the firm has continued its strong commitment of time and money to that project's successor, the Essex-Newark Legal Services Project. Partners have served as members and chairman of the supreme court's Ethics Committee for the Newark district. Partners have taught at Newark's law

The law firm of Clapp & Eisenberg, although statewide and beyond in professional focus, maintains a strong interest in Newark-related clients and issues. Photo by A.J. Sundstrom, 1988

schools—Rutgers and Seton Hall. The firm has consistently supported chamber of commerce and United Way activities.

Beyond Newark, the firm's professional, governmental, and charitable activities have been quite diverse. For example, it is representing a *Fortune* 100 company in an international commercial arbitration pending in Switzerland, The Chase-Manhattan Bank as a creditor in bankruptcy proceedings, the Englewood Board of Education in a major constitutional and school law case, and Donald Trump and Trump Casinos in a host of counseling and litigation activities. The firm's partners have helped draft New Jersey's corporation laws; have lectured and

published scholarly legal articles; have chaired major state bar association sections and committees; have served as mayor, as chairman of a state college's board of trustees, and in other governmental and political party positions; and have participated in a wide range of community activities.

Clapp & Eisenberg was founded by the late Alfred C. Clapp, a former Essex County senator, Rutgers Law School dean, and appellate division judge, and Jerome C. Eisenberg, one of New Jersey's most respected litigators. The firm has grown to more than 50 lawyers, but still maintains the ideals of its founders—professional excellence, responsiveness to clients, and community service.

THE PRUDENTIAL INSURANCE COMPANY OF AMERICA

Prudential's Plaza Building on Broad Street in Newark.

The Prudential Insurance Company of America is the manifestation of a working man's dream of providing basic life insurance for the working classes.

The dreamer was John F. Dryden, and the dream was to bring industrial life insurance—small policies with weekly premiums—to Americans of modest means. It was the fundamental product that would catapult his firm from a small company into the nation's largest insurer.

Founded in 1875 as The Prudential Friendly Society, the name was changed to the Prudential Insurance Company of America in 1877. At that time the firm opened a sales office in Paterson, and branches in Jersey City, Elizabeth, and Camden followed within the next two years.

The Prudential established offices in New York and Philadelphia in 1879. By 1885 assets exceeded one million dollars, with a field force comprised of about 1,500 people. In 1892 The Prudential built an opulent, 11-story building at Broad and Bank streets in Newark. In 1900 four more buildings were being added in Newark, and by 1909 Prudential agencies were in every state and territory. Two years later Prudential's assets exceeded a quarter-billion dollars, the result of Dryden's dream and a few thousand dollars from early investors.

During the 1950s The Prudential developed its first group major medical contract and its individual sickness and accident insurance plans. Its first family policy came in 1956; within four months a quarter-million families had purchased $1.5 billion worth of this new insurance, making it The Prudential's best-selling policy.

In 1960 Prudential moved into its new, 24-story Plaza Building in Newark, which serves as its corporate headquarters today.

In 1965 The Prudential opened its northeastern home office, a 52-story building that became Boston's major modern landmark. That year The Prudential also created the eastern home office in Newark, separate from the corporate home office. At that point Prudential home offices were located in Chicago, Illinois; Houston, Texas; Los Angeles, California; Minneapolis, Minnesota; Toronto, Ontario, Canada; Fort Washington, Pennsylvania; and Jacksonville, Florida.

Through the 1960s the Group Pension Department became an industry leader, and Prudential's Real Estate Investment Department was a top player in its field, adding the Empire State Building to its impressive portfolio of properties in 1961.

At the same time The Prudential was strengthening its Group Insurance Department, which in 1974 boasted the best sales year in the industry's history. By that time Prudential's common stock portfolios were the largest in the life insurance industry, valued at more than $4 billion.

In 1981 the company acquired the Bache Group, Inc., parent company of Bache, Halsey, Stuart Shields Inc.—one of the nation's largest investment brokerage firms—and renamed it Prudential-Bache Securities.

The Prudential restructured its individual insurance operations into four regional home offices in 1983. At that time group operations were reorganized into five regional group offices.

The Prudential today has assets of $153 billion, and the face value of all life insurance policies issued by The Prudential still in effect stands at $756 billion. With some 98,000 employees, The Prudential continues to be an industry leader, with 65 million people owning or benefiting from its products and services.

An anchor in city development,

The Prudential is responsible for the construction of four outstanding commercial buildings—Gateway Center One, Two, Three, and Four—one of the largest mixed-use complexes in the New York metropolitan area. In addition to Gateway Center's modern design and high-tech amenities, tenants benefit from the convenient access the location affords to international airports and New Jersey's ports, railroads, and major highways. The center boasts 2.5 million square feet of space and a 250-room hotel, which includes conference and meeting rooms and four restaurants.

Prudential's involvement in Gateway Center goes back to 1970, when it provided $47 million to develop the Hilton Gateway Hotel and the first two office buildings in the complex. In 1976 The Prudential became the center's owner and sought to expand it. The

Prudential itself remains the major tenant of Three Gateway, which was completed in 1985.

Prudential's newest development in downtown Newark, Four Gateway Center, a $40-million, 15-story office tower, celebrated its grand opening in 1988 as home to an impressive list of companies. The Prudential is the general partner of Four Gateway, in which the tenants act as limited partners or part owners.

Says Robert C. Winters, Prudential's chairman and chief executive officer, "Gateway is a physical expression of the spirit of partnership that has developed in Newark between the public and private sectors."

Prudential's Gateway Center, Gateway Three and Four, is located in Newark.

APRUZZESE, McDERMOTT, MASTRO & MURPHY

The name partners of Apruzzese, McDermott, Mastro & Murphy are (seated) Vincent J. Apruzzese, (standing, from left) Francis A. Mastro, James F. Murphy, and Frank McDermott.

The law firm of Apruzzese, McDermott, Mastro & Murphy represents management in all phases of employer-employee relations, including union-related problems. It also represents clients in commercial matters.

The firm's concentration in the labor-management field covers a wide spectrum of activity, including collective bargaining, arbitrations, and state and federal actions before both administrative agencies and the courts. Many of the firm's clients are not unionized but are occasionally subjected to union organizing attempts or other union pressures. It also has a strong department that specializes in discrimination cases of all types—age, race, sex, etc.—and wrongful termination suits. It also serves as general counsel for various companies.

In 1965 Vincent J. Apruzzese, then a private practitioner, joined forces with Frank X. McDermott to form Apruzzese & McDermott. Based in Newark from 1965 to 1970, the firm moved to its current location in Springfield while still maintaining many business contacts in Newark. In 1984, with the addition of new principals, Francis A. Mastro and James F. Murphy, the firm's name changed to Apruzzese, McDermott, Mastro & Murphy.

Early in his career and for some 25 years Vincent J. Apruzzese represented the Building Contractors Association of New Jersey, the largest organization of commercial, institutional, and industrial builders in New Jersey. This activity led to the representation of many major construction companies, owners and various associations in the construction industry, and work on many major multibil-

lion-dollar projects. He has done much work in the utility industry and for nuclear plants, including the negotiation and implementation of the Three Mile Island Recovery Project Agreement.

Frank X. McDermott's background is also in the labor-management field. He had worked for American Cyanamid Company and was on the staff of the New Jersey Manufacturers' Association, handling legislative and labor problems. When the partnership was formed, he was a New Jersey assemblyman and was executive director of the New Jersey Organization for a Better State (NEW JOBS), which promoted legislation that would make New Jersey a better state in which to do business. He subsequently became a state senator, serving in the highest leadership positions, including president of the senate.

As the practice has evolved, the firm has continued its concentration in the labor-management field, attracting talented associates and developing a solid client base of

substantial private companies and organizations nationwide. The firm has also worked in the public sector—for the cities of Bayonne, Rumson, Chatham, and Eatontown, as well as Essex County, Union County, the Garden State Parkway, and Garden State Arts Center.

Some of its private clients are First Fidelity Bank, N.A., New Jersey; Public Service Electric & Gas; General Public Utilities; Prudential Insurance Company; Jersey Central Power & Light; Atlantic Electric Company; Butler Aviation International; the New Jersey Savings League; Colgate-Palmolive Co.; Johnson & Johnson; Warner Lambert; Revlon; Schering-Plough; Forbes; Foster Wheeler Corporation; Stone & Webster Engineering; and Combustion Engineering. It also represents Newport, a $10-billion apartment and office project in Jersey City at the mouth of the Holland Tunnel. This project is the largest of its kind in the nation.

The firm has represented national organizations in many important cases before the United States

Supreme Court. In a number of these cases, the firm has appeared as "amicus curiae," or "friend of the court." In this capacity the firm advances the cause of a particular industry or area of the law of great interest to the business community.

Commenting on this type of work, Apruzzese observes, "These cases allow us to be on the cutting edge of labor law. Moreover, an organization or industry can select any firm in the country to represent it. Accordingly, we are proud of the fact that we have been selected to represent many major national organizations and corporations in this work."

The firm represented the American Metal Stamping Association and the United States Chamber of Commerce to uphold a change in OSHA standards of great significance to the industry vigorously opposed by the AFL-CIO. The matter was successfully concluded before the United States Supreme Court.

Another example of this type of case involved a strike at the Elizabeth *Daily Journal* which was owned by a national newspaper chain. During the strike, the parent company sent out-of-state employees to New Jersey to fill positions held by striking employees. The

Pictured here are Barry Marell (left) and Frederick T. Danser III, two of the principals of Apruzzese, McDermott, Mastro & Murphy.

union contended this was illegal strikebreaking in violation of a New Jersey criminal statute, and the editor of the paper was threatened with a jail sentence. The firm, representing the newspaper as well as the United States and New Jersey chambers of commerce, had the law set aside and declared unconstitutional.

Other cases involving participation before the United States Supreme Court have concerned antitrust labor law issues, striker benefits, secondary boycotts, and reverse discrimination. Frank Mastro played a major role in all of these efforts.

The firm works closely with in-house counsel of its corporate and institutional clients. The clients' other law firms welcome the participation of Apruzzese, McDermott, Mastro & Murphy because of its specialized expertise and broad range of experience.

Its complement of lawyers includes attorneys who formerly worked for Ingersoll-Rand, Mobil Oil, Allied Signal, American Home Products, Carter Wallace, Hertz Corporation, and others. In addition, many firm members have worked for the National Labor Relations Board, both in the regional and Washington, D.C., offices, as well as other organizations and governmental agencies.

The firm takes an active role in bar activities. Apruzzese and Frank Mastro have both served as chairman of the New Jersey State Bar Association Labor and Employment Law Section. Currently Apruzzese serves on the governing council of the American Bar Association Labor and Employment Law Section.

Apruzzese is a past president of the New Jersey State Bar Association and past chairman of the New

Jersey State Bar Foundation. He was recently elected to the 33-member board of governors of the American Bar Association. He has also served as an officer of the International Labor Law Society, a group that focuses on international labor law developments of importance to multinational corporations, and served on the government's task force to review the National Labor Relations Act on the occasion of its 40th anniversary.

Frederick T. Danser III heads the public-sector department of the firm. Richard C. Mariani, a special-

The firm concentrates on all aspects of employer-employee relations, including collective bargaining, arbitrations, and state and federal actions before both administrative agencies and the courts. Pictured here are attorneys Richard C. Mariani (seated), Sharon Margello (left), Rosemary Laura (center), and Jerrold Wohlgemuth.

ist in discrimination and wrongful termination cases, heads this burgeoning area of the practice. Barry Marell, another of the firm's younger principals, leads the group dealing with the commercial areas of the practice.

All of the other members of Apruzzese, McDermott, Mastro & Murphy bring a rich background of experience and talent to bear on their tasks as the firm positions itself for its continuing growth and challenges of the 1990s.

HOWARD SAVINGS BANK

The Howard Savings Bank is a vital part of New Jersey's past, present, and future. With almost $5 billion in assets, a network of some 74 branch offices statewide, and seven subsidiaries in real estate and financial service areas, today's Howard has come a long way from its modest beginnings more than 130 years ago.

The bank opened for business in Newark on May 5, 1857, as the Howard Savings Institution. Among the 27 community civic leaders who established the Howard were Moses Bigelow, a varnish manufacturer and mayor of Newark, and Beach Vanderpool, a former mayor, who became the bank's first president.

The bank was named for John Howard, a noted eighteenth-century social reformer, because the incorporators saw Howard as an "inspiration and the embodiment of the thrift ideal—helping people help themselves."

By 1882 the Howard had made two moves to larger quarters, the latter to 768 Broad Street. Outgrowing this facility, the company erected a new building on the site in 1899. A dignified granite structure, its pediment supported by graceful Ionic columns, it presented an appearance that, except for subsequent additions, is substantially the same today as when it was built.

The Howard began expanding to branch offices in 1927, opening the first savings bank branch in New Jersey, on Newark's Bloomfield Avenue. In 1929 the Howard became the first mutual savings bank in the nation to establish a trust department.

The First Howard Savings Institution office was opened on May 5, 1857, on the northwest corner of Broad and Bank streets in Newark.

Following World War II mortgage lending became a primary Howard service, as FHA and VA-insured mortgages became popular.

The Howard became a leader in the banking industry's technological revolution in 1956, contracting with the Teleregister Corporation to engineer and design what, in 1961, would become the world's first on-line electronic data-processing system linked to teller stations. The bank moved further into automation in the early 1980s, joining a major automated teller machine network, the Money Access Center (MAC). In 1985 the Howard established a toll-free customer-service phone center that permits customers to accomplish many banking transactions by phone.

During the 1970s the Howard entered into other financial service areas, such as residential real estate development, that started in 1979 through 768 Broad Corporation. Howco Investment Corporation was formed in 1980 and has become a

major factor in commercial and residential real estate development today. The Howard has also acquired a mortgage banking company, a federal savings and loan association, a casualty insurance agency, and an actuarial firm. In addition, the bank has established life insurance agency and discount brokerage subsidiaries.

In the early 1980s the most significant banking legislation since the 1930s paved the way for the Howard's July 1983 conversion from a mutual to stock institution, and for entry into commercial banking and lending services.

Today Howard Savings Bank has some $4.9 billion in assets and continues to be a major presence in Newark and the surrounding Essex County area, with a network of 74 branch offices, 24 of which are located in Essex County.

WHARTON/LYON & LYON

The insurance firm of Wharton/ Lyon & Lyon specializes in industrial, wholesale, retail, and real estate insurance. As in its beginnings in 1912, the firm concentrates its business as an insurance agent for business clients.

The firm serves a broad spectrum of clients in manufacturing, wholesaling, retailing, and service businesses. Although most of its accounts are closely held businesses, some of its major accounts have facilities nationwide with executive offices in New Jersey. First Fidelity Bank is among the many public corporations included on the client roster for Wharton/Lyon & Lyon.

Richard T. Hebert, president, is in charge of overall administration of the office and handles several major accounts. In the insurance business since 1961, he is a member of the Circle Agents Council of the Continental Insurance Company.

According to Hebert, "We offer a full package of insurance services. When we see a new account we evaluate existing programs, analyze them, and prepare a client proposal showing what the client has, relative costs, and what their program may be lacking. We offer options and solutions regarding what coverage they should consider so they can make a decision based on need and cost. Our principal responsibility is to ensure the client has the proper coverage."

The firm is ranked in the top 100 U.S. insurance brokers by *Business Insurance* magazine. It is also among the top 25 insurance brokers

The Livingston, New Jersey, office of Wharton/Lyon & Lyon.

in the New York metropolitan area.

The firm's structure is the result of a merger in July 1976 of the firm Lyon & Lyon, founded in 1912, and Wharton Inc. Associates, founded in 1926 as Joseph A Klein & Son, both originally based in Newark. The majority of the company's business remains commercial property and casualty insurance.

Albert L. Klein, the firm's chairman and chief executive officer, began working for the family agency while still in high school. He led General American Life Insurance as top producer nationwide four times. He also is a 30-year life and qualifying member of the Million Dollar Round Table Club.

Dedicated to his Jewish heritage, Klein was honored in 1988 with the Fortieth Anniversary Medal of the State of Israel to commemorate his leadership in the sale of Israel bonds.

In his role as chairman and chief executive officer Klein has been a major force in the firm's expansion, and spearheaded the acquisition of more than 24 agencies that have greatly expanded the customer base of Wharton/Lyon & Lyon. Klein's son, Dennis F. Klein, CPCU, ARM, and Bruce Gilson, vice-president, are the family's third generation in the agency.

Bruce joined the firm in 1981. He handles major accounts and is responsible for overseeing the data-processing systems.

Dennis also joined the firm in 1981. Handling major accounts and large-line new business sales, he is responsible for the development of risk management services.

Pictured here is Albert Klein, chairman and chief executive officer, and Claire Fridkis, administrative assistant.

According to Andrew F. Stillo, senior vice-president and a senior marketing executive with the Home Insurance Company before joining the firm in 1983, "The tendency in the insurance business is to sell price. Although we are competitive on price, we come in and analyze our clients' insurance needs to give them comprehensive coverage. We make sure our clients' coverage is written correctly. As it should be, our clients are primarily concerned with making their businesses profitable. They need someone to rely on to give them good advice and to let them know where their exposures are."

The firm maintains offices in Livingston and Ocean Township. Its staff of support and sales people numbers more than 100. The company's operation is fully computerized for accounting and all customer information, including such information as policy limits and types of policies.

According to Klein, "Our philosophy from a management standpoint is to help our employees grow. From a customer's standpoint it is to do the best job we can and to encourage loyalty."

STRYKER, TAMS & DILL

The firm of Stryker, Tams & Dill was founded on May 2, 1898, in the city of Newark by three prominent attorneys who set high standards for themselves and for their successors. By the turn of the century, Newark had become the center of legal activity in New Jersey. As the city grew and prospered, the firm's reputation for the highest professional standards, ethics, and integrity fostered strong and steady growth.

Founding member Richard V. Lindabury was one of the foremost corporate attorneys in the country. He incorporated United States Steel Corporation, was its first general counsel, and served on its finance committee. Lindabury represented many other major corporations, including American Tobacco Company and Standard Oil.

Having recently commemorated its 90th year of practice, Stryker, Tams & Dill continues to set the legal standard, embodying the same uncompromising principles on which its enduring reputation is based. The firm's primary goal is to serve the needs of its clients to the fullest possible extent, utilizing cur-

rent technology and the most cost-effective methods.

Stryker, Tams & Dill takes pride in the fact that its partners are hands-on lawyers and always available to the firm's clients. William L. Dill, an outstanding leader of the bar who has been with the firm since 1928 emphasizes that, "We have long distinguished ourselves as a firm with the personal touch, providing a positive environment in which to work."

The firm is organized in several practice area groups. Its clients include a broad spectrum of major corporations, financial institutions, and medium and small-size businesses.

The corporate/commercial practice group handles bank regulatory work; forms corporations, partnerships, and other business entities; oversees acquisitions and mergers; and handles financial and other business transactions. Serving both corporate and municipal clients, the firm gives antitrust advice, does bankruptcy work, employment law, securities work, and helps businesses in their day-to-day legal matters. This group also represents not-for-

The law firm of Stryker, Tams & Dill was founded on May 2, 1898, with the highest professional standards and ethics. Today the firm continues to set the legal standard, serving the needs of its clients to the fullest possible extent. Photo by A.J. Sundstrom.

profit foundations and entities. The firm has served as U.S. and New Jersey counsel for subsidiaries of foreign corporations for the past several years. Its full-service capability combined with its specialized expertise in corporate and commercial matters enables it to serve its corporate and other business clients well.

The litigation department handles a full range of sophisticated commercial litigation, including antitrust, toxic tort, insurance coverage, employment law, white-collar criminal litigation, as well as the defense of product liability claims. The firm defends clients in legal, accounting, and medical malpractice suits as well.

The environmental department handles regulatory and litigation matters before state and federal environmental bodies and courts. It provides clients with opinions on environmental questions and assists with environmental compliance.

The tax team assists with federal and state corporate and partnership taxation and provides individual tax planning. It represents clients in specific tax matters involved in federal and state litigation. The firm also handles criminal tax work and employee benefit matters, including benefit plans, ERISA compliance, and employee compensation.

The trust and estate group helps its clients in planning and administration. This includes federal and state tax advice and handling trust and estate litigation such as contested wills.

The insurance group concentrates on insurance regulatory work and insurance defense work. The firm represents the New Jersey Property/Liability Insurance Guaranty Association. It also represents insurance companies before legislative bodies and commissions, handles insurance company insolvency work, and assists in mergers and acquisitions.

The firm has recently acquired an

Keeping pace with new technologies, Stryker, Tams & Dill utilizes computers as a more efficient and comprehensive means of serving its clients. It also has one of the largest private law libraries in the state of New Jersey. Photo by A.J. Sundstrom.

expertise in the legal aspects of the standardbred horse business. Its representation in this area includes syndication, as well as the usual issues concerning buying, selling, owning, and racing standardbred horses.

The public utilities department provides a full spectrum of legal services to many of the state's utilities and handles all phases of regulatory and rate-making proceedings before the New Jersey Board of Public Utilities. Its work includes the development and financing of cogeneration and resource recovery facilities. The firm also acts as counsel to the New Jersey Utilities Association, the trade association to which all of New Jersey's major utilities belong.

Stryker, Tams & Dill's real estate department concentrates on the development of commercial real estate such as office buildings and industrial properties. The firm works with developers from the beginning to the end of the development process, from acquisition to formation of ventures, to municipal zoning approval, state and county approvals, construction financing, construction contracts, and leasing.

The firm is able to attract and retain highly experienced and qualified lawyers drawn to its congenial yet diligent and thoroughly professional atmosphere. The firm also does substantial pro bono work. It encourages its members' support of local charitable and cultural institutions by serving on such boards as the Kessler Institute of Rehabilitation, Newark Boys Chorus School, the Center for the Analysis of Public Issues, and the New Jersey Shakespeare Festival.

The firm's attorneys are also active in county and state bar associations and the American Bar Association. One of

its partners served as chairman of the Taxation Section, while another served as chairman of the Corporate and Business Law Section, both of the New Jersey State Bar Association. Two of the firm's former partners serve as U.S. District Court judges; another former partner is a superior court judge in New Jersey. A current partner is a former state court judge who also served as a commissioner of New Jersey's Board of Public Utilities.

Stryker, Tams & Dill is committed to continued growth consistent with its standard of excellence. The firm's headquarters remains in Newark, still the state's legal hub, with satellite offices in Morristown and Princeton.

Keeping pace with new technologies, office automation continues to expand. Numerous partners utilize the capabilities of Macintosh computers, while office administration, word processing, casework, and legal research are performed on IBM-compatible equipment. Its 18,000-volume library is one of the largest private law libraries in the state of New Jersey.

To foster expansion into new areas, the firm has begun a middle-market practice that provides the same expertise to small to medium-size businesses that the firm brings to its large corporate clients.

The firm has been involved in a number of high-profile cases and substantial matters in its many years of practice. It has taken an active role in restructuring New Jersey corporate laws over the years. Partners in the public interest have been involved in various legislative initiatives related to updating and revising state policies and approving state laws to keep New Jersey at the forefront of the nation.

Stryker, Tams & Dill is a vital part of New Jersey's and Newark's past, present, and future. From traditional roots to high-tech expertise, the firm will continue to provide professional services with individual attention to its clients.

CRUMMY, DEL DEO, DOLAN, GRIFFINGER & VECCHIONE

Crummy, Del Deo, Dolan, Griffinger & Vecchione is a highly diversified law firm engaged in a domestic and international general practice. As one of New Jersey's largest and most rapidly growing firms, it represents a sophisticated array of clients that includes businesses, individuals, and nonprofit organizations. Crummy, Del Deo, Dolan, Griffinger & Vecchione is committed to Newark and has been since its founding.

The firm's roots can be traced back to the 1950s, yet the present leadership of Crummy, Del Deo, Dolan, Griffinger & Vecchione is young. From its beginnings, under the name of Crummy, Gibbons & O'Neill, the firm has grown to become highly visible in all aspects of its practice. During the 1970s and 1980s Andrew Crummy passed on, John Gibbons became a judge on the Third Circuit Court of Appeals, and Tim O'Neill pursued other career alternatives. The leadership mantle of the firm fell upon the current senior partners, and the name of the firm evolved to reflect its present-day leadership.

With this leadership has come a reaffirmation of the firm's desire to continue its strong presence in Newark. Formerly a tenant of Gateway in Newark, the firm is now in the Legal Center at Riverfront Plaza, built by the Port Authority of New York and New Jersey, where it occupies the top floors of the building in a facility designed to accommodate the firm's continuing growth and development. The firm also maintains satellite offices in Europe and in New York's Wall Street area. According to Ralph Del Deo, "We feel our 90,000-square-foot facility is the premier legal center in the business and commercial hub of the state of New Jersey. We have assured ourselves a permanent location, which will enable us to grow and expand as the city continues its now-thriving economic revitalization."

The firm's practice has diversified as the organization has grown. There are seven departments in the firm, including litigation, corporate, real estate, banking, land use and municipal finance, tax, and insolvency. Although the firm is large in size, it is organized into smaller specialized working groups within these large departments.

Indeed, the development of the firm and the growth of its various practice areas has to a large extent paralleled the economic prosperity of the state of New Jersey and, more important, the revitalization of the City of Newark as the commercial center of the state. Whether one looks to the land use department, which handles a wide variety of commercial and residential developments, or to the ever-expanding environmental department, which tends to the environmental concerns of the firm's clients and of the public at large, it is readily apparent that the expansion of the firm in these areas underscores the fact that the City of Newark has retained its leadership role in the business development of the state and that the surrounding communities are participating in that development as well.

The real estate department is actively involved in these expanding opportunities and works on a wide variety of real estate matters, from the simple to the sophisticated. Of course, the firm's banking group is intrinsically involved on behalf of not only the borrower but often one of the major banking institutions in the state by way of its commercial and mortgage lending activities, as well as its corporate trust work.

The vibrant industrial and commercial growth in Newark and its surrounding communities has also had an impact upon the growth and maturity of the corporate department of Crummy, Del Deo. From the simple steps of incorporating a client to the complexity of a corporate acquisition or subsidiary divestiture, the world of

Crummy, Del Deo, Dolan, Griffinger & Vecchione occupies the top floors of the Legal Center at Riverfront Plaza. This modern office facility is located in the heart of Newark's business district, adjacent to Penn Station and within walking distance to courthouses, shops, and restaurants.

corporate law is one that is thoroughly familiar to the attorneys of Crummy, Del Deo. Over the years the firm has represented both private and public corporations and has tended to their various corporate needs.

As a complement to this corporate counseling, there is also a tax department that provides assistance not only on the state and federal fronts, but in the international arena as well. As the economic growth of the community spurs the corporate and tax needs of the firm's clients, so do the concerns of its clients for their employees, and, as a result, the firm provides a full range of services concerning employee compensation and benefit programs.

When Crummy, Del Deo's clients look beyond the transactional services of the firm and seek the assistance of the litigation department, they find a mature and fully developed department capable of handling any complex commercial matter that may be presented to it. Over the years the firm has handled sophisticated antitrust cases involving international clients in the electronics industry, trademark and copyright cases, patent litigation, and intellectual property disputes between corporate adversaries of such a wide variety of description that they defy enumeration here. Hard work, a dedication to professionalism, and client loyalty have earned the firm an excellent reputation not only in the state and federal courts of New Jersey, but throughout the nation.

The same can be said of the firm's insolvency department, which has handled such interesting and complex matters as the reorganization of a privately owned institution of higher education as well as the reorganization of a financially troubled Atlantic City casino. In addition to advising debtor companies with regard to pre-bankruptcy planning as well as counseling throughout the course of the reorganization proceeding, the insolvency department also provides advice to secured creditors and other general creditors of debtor companies involved in insolvency proceedings. In this regard, the firm has worked closely with a number of major financial institutions in advising them in their participation in various bankruptcy proceedings.

Just as Newark maintains a dynamic posture in the regional development of the greater metropolitan area located in New York, New Jersey, and Connecticut, so Crummy, Del Deo, Dolan, Griffinger & Vecchione has maintained its place in the forefront of a legal community dedicated to that city. As the firm grows and the city continues to prosper, Crummy, Del Deo looks forward to continuing its intrinsic involvement in the future of this great city.

NATIONAL WESTMINSTER BANK NJ

National Westminster Bank NJ, formerly First Jersey National Bank, is a member of the NatWest Bank Group, one of the world's largest and most profitable banking institutions. In existence for 125 years, the bank operates more than 145 offices in 17 New Jersey counties.

NatWest NJ's presence in the Newark area dates to 1969, a year in which several important events took place. The bank was reorganized into a one-bank holding company, and it acquired the six-branch Bank of Commerce of Newark. This was the bank's first expansion outside of its home base in Hudson County.

As an institution that historically had been, and still is, responsive to the needs of the communities it serves, the bank set about not only to increase its business in the greater Newark area, but to identify areas where its resources could be used to create positive effects.

The bank has provided construction and mortgage financing for numerous low- and moderate-income housing projects in Newark, including the Forest Hills town house condominiums and La Casa de Don Pedro.

NatWest NJ is a long-standing supporter of the Small and Minority Business Council of Newark Collaboration, Neighborhood Housing Services, New Communities Cor-

La Casa de Don Pedro, an affordable housing project, was financed by NatWest NJ. The former bakery is neighbor to Newark's Sacred Heart Cathedral.

poration, the Newark Economic Development Corporation, and Renaissance Newark. The bank also has been a major force in supporting Project Pride's renowned debating team, and its chairman, Thomas J. Stanton, Jr., was the catalyst in establishing a foundation for the team.

Playing an important role in representing the bank is the Economic Development Department. Established in 1969, the department works with community groups and municipalities in Newark and many other areas in the state to revitalize older business districts and support affordable housing programs.

NatWest NJ's Newark offices are in diverse locations of the city, from the Ironbound, where the Adams Street office provides a full range of banking products and services to the large number of Hispanic and Portuguese businesses and residents in the area, to the city's commercial hub at Gateway Center. Gateway serves as a focal point for the bank to assist the city's corporations and individuals in fulfilling their credit and financial management requirements.

NatWest NJ's Commercial Banking Group plays a vital part in supporting the many small and medium-size businesses in the Newark area. Business officers, trained to work with the decision makers of these companies, provide construction and commercial real estate lending, asset-based loans, and a comprehensive selection of international trade and cash-management services. Specialized lending sectors, such as the bank's medical and dental banking team, forge partnerships with clients by

One of NatWest NJ's busiest offices is located at Gateway One, a focal point for business and industry.

understanding their particular needs and developing tailored credit packages.

The bank's statewide Trust Division is headquartered in Newark, where trust officers provide financial management of estates and investment portfolios for individuals, manage assets in pension and profit-sharing plans, and supervise trustee relationships for issuers of public and municipal debt securities.

According to W. Richard Hazen, president and chief administrative officer of NatWest NJ, the role of good corporate citizen is integral to the bank's continued progress. "In particular," he says, "the prosperity of the greater Newark area is vital to the state as a whole. We have always looked at Newark as an urban center brimming with possibilities, and we are very excited about being part of its bright future."

LEWIS ADVERTISING AGENCY

Lewis Advertising Agency was formed in 1943 by Milton Lewis after a five-year stint with Grey Advertising in New York, the growing giant of the industry. With a major national cigar company, a fragrance manufacturer, and a local carpet chain leading its client roster, Lewis was on its way by 1948 to becoming a major factor in the Newark and New Jersey advertising scene.

In 1945 Lewis became a true pioneer of television, the medium that was to change the world. Lewis clients were among the first to sponsor such Dumont Broadcasting (WNDT-TV) shows as "Howdy Doody," "Uncle Fred Sayles," and "Weekly Boxing from Laurel Garden."

During Lewis Advertising's growth through the 1950s and 1960s, it established a strong base of longtime clients, many of whom have stayed with the agency for as long as 20 years. Under the management of Milton Lewis the agency gained retail, industrial, and consumer clients.

During that time Lewis acquired the Gottesman Agency, Town Advertising, and the Weinstein Agency

The lighting and design of the reception area is a focal point for the agency.

in order to increase the staff, the account billing, and the geographical mix of the agency.

In 1965 the Gottesman Agency brought in automotive, auction, and classified business. Buying Town Advertising in Hackensack in 1971 resulted in additional strengths in real estate advertising and financial marketing. The Weinstein Agency brought expertise and businesses in architectural suppliers, pool manufacturers, financial, and promotional activities.

With the passing of Milton Lewis in 1979, the agency kept a firm stance on its past standards of excellent customer service by expanding its staff and in-house capabilities to accommodate substantial increases of both accounts and billing.

Today recognized as one of New Jersey's leading full-service agencies, Lewis holds the same belief in customer service. "Professionalism in account service has been, and always will be, the key to continued growth. Experienced account executives and their assistants are always in touch and in control of their accounts. They work directly

Lewis Advertising account service and creative teams meet in the Art Department.

with them, one on one, to get any vital advertising and marketing tasks done right and on budget. Customer service has truly remained as the hallmark of our agency," says Fred Lewis, the second-generation president.

New in-house photostat and typography systems and multiple fax machines have increased the ability of the agency to handle volume; but responsive account people are still the key to stability and growth in the future.

As Lewis Advertising moves toward its 50th anniversary in 1998, its place in the growing rebirth of Newark and the dramatic strength of New Jersey will be a focal point.

Being near its client base is an agency essential. It is becoming easier to effectively serve agency accounts in the south, to Princeton and Cherry Hill; in the north, to Ramsey and Mahwah; and in the renaissance centers of Jersey City, Elizabeth, and Union, due to excellent new highways near its Newark base as well as the electronic capabilities for communicating with both clients and media.

According to Lewis, "Professionally and personally, doing great ads that work has always been our business, and the source for creativity always has begun with knowing our customers. From our standpoint, that means providing total service like no other agency can."

FIRST FIDELITY BANK

First Fidelity Bank, NA, New Jersey, has been headquartered in Newark since 1812, and its role today is in many ways the same as it was then—operating in the thick of the business and economic life of the city and the state.

New Jersey in the 1980s has seen one of the most remarkable surges of economic growth and prosperity in its more than 300 years of history. During these same years First Fidelity, through mergers, acquisitions, and internal growth, has vaulted in size at the parent company level by more than tenfold, to become a $29-billion banking organization and among the nation's 20 largest. First Fidelity has achieved this transformation by doing what it has done for 175 years—staying close to, and deeply involved in, the nuts and bolts of business and commercial activity in its home market area, and in the day-to-day financial needs of its individual customers.

Nothing characterized First Fidelity's involvement and commitment to the future health of Newark more than its participation in 1969 in the construction financing for the start of Gateway, now a spectacular, multiple high-rise building complex stretching west from Penn-Central Station. Today more than $150 million has been invested in that complex, with its network of pedestrian bridges linking the office and hotel structures. When work started in 1969, Newark was still reeling from the impact of the riots of 1967. With the help of First Fidelity's financing, however, Gateway went forward, as did a number of other developments in Newark that were supported by financing from the state's largest bank.

A more dramatic example of First Fidelity's commitment to the business of Newark and New Jersey arose in 1973, when the anticipated start of construction

on what came to be New Jersey's Meadowlands Sports Complex, was threatened by a serious financial snag. New York financial interests sought to kill the $300-million bond sale for the project, and with it the entire stadium-racetrack complex.

At that point First Fidelity Bank, in the person of its president, Robert R. Ferguson, Jr., stepped into the breach, aggressively pulling together a consortium of major New Jersey financial institutions to underwrite enough of the $300-million issue to ensure its successful sale.

More of the same occurred in connection with the financing needed to get casino-hotel development started in Atlantic City in 1976-1977, after the public had overwhelmingly approved a referendum clearing the way for casinos in that city.

For First Fidelity the issue was not one of support for, or opposition to, the idea of casino gaming. Bank officials, in public statements at the time, made clear their view: The public had spoken. Whether New Jersey should have casinos was a settled question. Now it was the obligation of major New Jersey banking institutions to implement this public policy and make it succeed.

Accordingly, First Fidelity took the lead in providing bank financing for the construction of Atlantic City casino-hotels and in encouraging other banks to do the same.

These are three examples that stand out among the countless instances where First Fidelity Bank and First Fidelity Bancorporation took a leadership position in matters of great importance to the life of the region. This position culminated in two mergers, each of which was, when completed, the largest in the history of American banking.

The first, effected in 1984, was the acquisition by then First National State Bancorporation of

the banks of the former Fidelity Union Bancorporation, creating an organization of about $10 billion in assets.

The second, completed on February 29, 1988, brought together First Fidelity with Fidelcor, Inc., of Pennsylvania. The newly-resulting First Fidelity Bancorporation grew in size from more than $15 billion to interstate, or super-regional, status at nearly $30 billion. The parent corporation's actual headquarters base remains in New Jersey. In mid-1989 the firm moved to its new headquarters office in Lawrence Township. In the meantime, its Newark base remains firm, with First Fidelity Bank, NA, New Jersey, the lead New Jersey bank and the largest in the system, headquartered there, at 550 Broad Street.

The long First Fidelity involvement in the mainstream of New Jersey events was characterized by the leadership roles played by those who founded the bank in 1812 as the State Bank of Newark.

The institution's first president was William S. Pennington, a Revolutionary War captain who resigned only eight months after the founding of the bank to campaign for governor of New Jersey. He succeeded in his quest for the office. A son, William Pennington, followed in his famous father's footsteps, first serving as the bank's attorney (1822-1835) and later winning election as governor.

The bank obtained a national charter in 1865, becoming the National State Bank of Newark.

The years between the Civil War and World War I saw Newark emerge as a major diversified center of manufacturing, and the

Headquartered in New Jersey since 1812, First Fidelity Bank leads a $29-billion banking organization, among the nation's 20 largest.

bank responded by developing its own expertise in the service of the business and industry that thrived in and near the city.

The bank rode out the storm of the Great Depression in excellent form, and those years also saw the accession to First Fidelity's leadership of W. Paul Stillman. In 1931 he succeeded William I. Cooper, who had served for 55 years.

In 1949 there began a series of post-World War II mergers that greatly increased the bank's size and strength. In 1965 the institution's name was changed to First National State Bank of New Jersey.

In 1966 Ferguson was elected president, thus beginning his own long era of leadership in the organization's growth and expansion.

Today the affiliates of First Fidelity occupy a stronger position than ever in the life of the region and in the banking industry. The affiliates include seven full-service banking companies, whose combined facilities are arrayed throughout New Jersey and eastern Pennsylvania, and also a New Jersey state-chartered savings bank, Morris Savings Bank. First Fidelity is well prepared to meet the challenges of the new and highly competitive interstate banking era.

LOWENSTEIN, SANDLER, KOHL, FISHER & BOYLAN

"Lawyers serving the business community." That was the goal set when Lowenstein, Sandler, Kohl, Fisher & Boylan was founded in 1961 in Newark. Dramatic growth and success have given the firm a preeminent role in New Jersey's business-industrial community.

Lowenstein, Sandler has become one of the largest banking and corporate law firms in New Jersey, with 110 lawyers, 25 paralegals, and a total staff of 250. The firm's impressive and diversified list of clients includes a number of New Jersey corporate and financial giants, but also many mid-size and smaller businesses, both publicly owned and closely held. The number of out-of-state clients continues to expand as awareness of the firm's capabilities increases.

The philosophy of the firm and its commitment to clients are clearly stated by chairman and founder Alan V. Lowenstein, "Our clients expect—and receive—quality and creativity equivalent to the best offered anywhere. We believe they are entitled to nothing less. Whether the client is a major corporation or a small enterprise struggling with problems, we seek, as professional advisers, to provide the understanding, dedication, objectivity, and personal involvement that are the hallmarks of every dedicated professional person or organization."

Lowenstein, Sandler has been a catalyst in shattering the long-held belief that New Jersey businesses need to turn to New York or Philadelphia for high-powered corporate legal services. A striking example has been Lowenstein Sandler's representation of First Fidelity Bancorporation over a period of 20 years. During that time, First Fidelity grew internally and through multiple acquisitions and mergers from a small Newark based banking institution to a $30-billion multistate bank holding company ranking in size among the 25 largest banking companies in the United States. This effort was carried out by a team of lawyers, led by John Schupper.

The firm has the specialists to meet the most current client needs in mergers and acquisitions, state and federal taxes, corporate and public finance, securities law, environmental law counseling and litigation, and in the growing area of corporate employee ownership.

The firm's Environmental Law Department, chaired by Michael L. Rodburg and comprised of 15 attorneys, is widely recognized in New Jersey and also enjoys a nationwide practice.

The versatility of Lowenstein, Sandler is demonstrated by the fact that this prominent banking and corporate law firm is also recognized for the quality of its white-collar criminal defense. Ted Wells was lead defense counsel in the celebrated criminal trial in which former U.S. Secretary of Labor Raymond Donovan was acquitted in 1987. Matt Boylan, former director of the New Jersey State Division of Criminal Justice, was the recipient of the 1987 award of the Trial Attorneys of New Jersey for distinguished service in the cause of justice.

The firm offers a wide range of specialized services. The Business Law department provides a broad range of services to companies operating in manufacturing, distribution, retailing, and service businesses. The chairman, Richard M. Sandler, has more than 30 years of experience in complex corporate and financial transactions.

John R. MacKay II, who heads the Banking Law group, serves as chairman of the New Jersey Corporation Law Revision Commission. In 1988 the commission spearheaded the first comprehensive overhaul of New

Alan V. Lowenstein, chairman and founder.

Jersey's Business Corporation Act in 15 years.

Health Care Law advice to proprietary and nonprofit clients, including community and private hospitals, charitable and proprietary nursing homes, medical practices and other health care providers is offered by Bruce D. Shoulson, who has more than 20 years of experience in business and real estate law and litigation, with emphasis on health care law.

The Litigation Department provides assistance to the firm's business clients and to other clients referred by lawyers who seek Lowenstein, Sandler's skills in litigating both criminal and civil matters. The chairman, Gregory B. Reilly, has extensive experience in state and federal courts.

Real Estate Law assists clients in contracting, financing, zoning, site plan, subdivision, environmental, and tax aspects of real estate transactions. It is headed by Joseph LeVow

Steinberg, who brings more than 25 years of experience in all phases of real estate law.

Securities Law expertise is offered in all phases—from representing issuers of public offerings to going-private transactions, including leveraged buyouts. Peter H. Ehrenberg, who heads the group, is former chairman of the Securities Law Committee of the New Jersey State Bar Association.

Tax Law provides the kind of highly specialized services for which New Jersey corporations once had to depend on a few New York tax attorneys. Benedict M. Kohl, the chairman, has more than 30 years of experience as a tax and corporate specialist.

Employee Benefits assist clients in designing and implementing employee compensation programs, including stock option, stock bonus, deferred compensation, pensions, and profit-sharing plans. It is head-

ed by Howard S. Denburg, with more than 15 years of experience in employee benefits and executive compensation planning.

Estate Planning and Administration provides sophisticated estate and income tax planning for individuals and closely held corporations. Arnold Fisher, chairman, has more than 30 years of experience in complex tax analysis and estate planning.

The firm was founded in Newark, where Lowenstein was a leading figure in community and charitable organizations, including the chairmanship of the city's governmental charter reform movement in the 1950s and service as president of the United Way. Although the firm's rapid growth prompted a move in 1980 to spacious offices in Roseland, the tradition of community

service to the city and the greater Newark area continues as strong as ever. Lowenstein, Sandler partners and associates are leaders in providing pro bono legal services, and serve on the boards of many community-service organizations. And the firm's clients still include many of Newark's largest and most venerable employers and major institutions.

To expand into the growth areas of central New Jersey, Lowenstein,

Lowenstein, Sandler's 20,000-volume law library—with on-line access to computerized law libraries and data bases—provides all the research capacity to analyze the most complex legal problems.

Sandler opened a full-service office in Somerville in 1985. The managing director is Steven B. Fuerst, former president of the Somerset County Bar Assocation.

Lowenstein, Sandler offers its specialized expertise to the business community in other ways. The firm develops bulletins on significant and current business legal issues. It presents seminars on new business topics. Its newsletter, *Enviro-Notes*, addresses the fast-changing field of environmental law and regulation.

They are all part of the lawyers of Lowenstein, Sandler, Kohl, Fisher & Boylan's commitment to, indeed, be "lawyers serving the business community."

The Lowenstein, Sandler offices in Roseland.

PENN FEDERAL SAVINGS BANK

"Penn Federal Savings Bank began with a commitment to service the financial needs of the community of Newark," recalls president Joseph L. LaMonica, who grew up in the Ironbound area of Newark. "Over the years, through innovation and responsiveness, we have been able to prosper with the communities we serve."

Today, with assets of more than $417 million, Penn Federal boasts 14 strategically located branches across the state of New Jersey. The institution offers a full range of banking products for both consumers and businesses.

The recent opening of the new Operations Center in West Orange symbolized the culmination of a dream—one that has survived the turmoil of the Great Depression, World War II, and revolutionary changes in the banking industry.

The new Operations Center, a modern white concrete and smoked glass building, houses the bank's accounting, marketing, mortgage, personnel, consumer loan, and other various back-office operations. Since the opening of the Center, Penn Federal has been able to increase the range of its products and services, to deliver them all more efficiently, and to expand into new financial arenas, such as discount brokerage services, as the banking laws continue to evolve.

While the custom-designed center provides a glimpse of Penn Federal's future, the bank's headquarters remains where it first began—at 36 Ferry Street in Newark. Says LaMonica: "We were born in the shadow of Penn Station, named our bank after it, and just as it has endured, so have we. To maintain your strength and perspective, you have to draw upon your roots."

Those roots go back to 1941, when a consortium of building and loan associations pooled assets to qualify for federal insurance and incorporated as Penn Savings and

Loan. In 1981 the institution became the first in New Jersey to receive a federal savings bank charter and was renamed Penn Federal Savings Bank.

The charter was the initial step on a long road to developing first-class banking products that have reflected the needs of the community for more than four decades. In the post-Depression early 1940s, when Newark citizens went back to work and began to contribute extensively to the war effort, Penn Federal made sure their hard-earned savings were protected. In the late 1940s, as thousands of servicemen and -women returned from overseas, the bank offered government-secured loans to help them buy new homes. As new businesses began to blossom in the 1950s, the bank offered small commercial loans to help get them started. In the turbulent 1960s, when the financial future of Newark and many other larger cities in the nation was shaken, Penn Federal was there

Penn Federal is committed to its branch locations and to the neighborhoods it serves. Banking will be beautiful at the Wilson Avenue office, which is currently undergoing renovations to enlarge and redecorate the office. Pictured here (from left) are Joseph L. LaMonica, president and chief executive officer of Penn Federal; Andrew Zalewski, president, A. Zalewski Contracting, Inc.; and William C. Anderson, chairman of the board, Penn Federal, president John Young Co., Realtors.

with financial assistance and advice to help the community renovate and rebuild.

Today Penn Federal offers a full range of banking services to complement Newark's economic renaissance. In 1988 Penn Federal exceeded $312 million in outstanding residential mortgage loans, including ARM and fixed-rate mortgage loans, jumbo mortgage loans, and special lower-interest 10-year mortgage loans. To accommodate the wide diversity of the area's consumer needs, the bank provides automobile loans, home equity loans, IRAs, certificates of deposit, savings accounts, NOW checking accounts, and a variety of personal and business loans and services.

A comprehensive network of Penn Federal branches blankets the state, with offices located in Brick, East Newark, Farmingdale, Harrison, Marlboro, and Mt. Laurel. There are three offices in Newark, including the main office; two branches in Parlin; two in Sayreville; and the bank's newest branch at the Operations Center in West Orange.

To help manage all of these branches and programs, the bank recently installed a state-of-the-art computer system. The computer,

which links every branch in the Penn network, offers tellers and officers instant communication with headquarters. In addition, the bank's representatives are able to access a customer's entire banking history or complete any banking procedure from any branch office.

Paralleling Penn Federal's growth as a financial institution is its growth as a force in the community. From sponsoring a float in a parade in the Ironbound, to supporting Little League baseball teams, to joining with the United Way in a Holiday Season Toy Drive, or joining in the School Partnership Program of Newark, Penn Federal has become an active community leader.

LaMonica sums it all up best,

The Operations Center located in West Orange houses many of the bank's back-office functions. It stands solidly against a quiet winter backdrop to let all know that the bank is growing, safe, strong, and here to stay.

Penn Federal's commitment to the communities it serves includes offices designed to service customers in a comfortable, inviting, and efficient environment.

"No matter how fast we grow or how busy we get, we will always have time for our customers and the people living in our communities."

BLUE CROSS AND BLUE SHIELD OF NEW JERSEY

Blue Cross and Blue Shield of New Jersey and the City of Newark share a long and productive history of growing together and working for a healthier city and life-style for its people.

Blue Cross of New Jersey, the first of what became the nationwide network of Blue Cross and Blue Shield Plans, was founded 56 years ago in the City of Newark to serve area hospitals. Since then Blue Cross has thrived. It merged with Blue Shield of New Jersey. And it has grown into the largest health insurer in the state, and one of the largest Blue Cross and Blue Shield Plans in the nation.

The special relationship between the city and Blue Cross and Blue Shield has matured with the health insurer's deep interest and involvement in community activities, civic affairs, parks development, and special events. The relationship extends beyond good citizenship, as well, with Blue Cross and Blue Shield providing health coverage for Newark's 4,800 municipal workers and their families.

Retracing the history, Blue Cross of New Jersey was founded in 1932 and became operational the following year during the depths of the

The Newark Corporate Run, which begins and ends in front of the Blue Cross and Blue Shield building on Washington Street in Newark, is one of many events sponsored by the health insurer to promote healthy life-styles.

Depression, when health care was almost a luxury and health insurance was virtually unknown.

At that time a council of Newark-area hospitals was formed to coordinate health care "in ways which would be beneficial to patients and hospitals alike." Basing its concept on a prepayment plan used for teachers in Dallas, Texas, the council founded the Associated Hospitals of Essex County, forerunner of New Jersey Blue Cross.

The group offered prepayment coverage at the subscription rate of $10 per year, about three cents per day, and began taking subscribers in January 1933. More than 5,000 people enrolled that first year.

The prepaid approach to health care had been used before at single hospitals, but the New Jersey Plan was the first to try it on a multi-hospital basis. The Plan offered subscribers a choice among the 17 participating hospitals in Essex County. The program came at a time when many hospitals were near bankruptcy. People were postponing needed care, going without it, or receiving it without being able to pay.

The Associated Hospitals of Essex County was reorganized into the Hospital Service Plan— Blue Cross of New Jersey—in 1933. The first office of Blue Cross was in Newark, in the National Newark & Essex Bank Building.

The Blue Cross Plan was the first to offer assured payment for services. In addition to giving financial stability to

Blue Cross and Blue Shield of New Jersey is a mainstay of the Newark business community. The operations of the statewide Plan are directed from this modern, 18-story executive office building on Washington Park. Photo by Craig Hammel

the voluntary hospital system, it provided a form of financial security for patients.

During the 1940s Blue Cross of New Jersey membership more than quadrupled from its initial levels. In 1947 the Plan reached a milestone with the enrollment of its one-millionth subscriber.

The Medical-Surgical Plan of New Jersey—the Blue Shield Plan—was founded by The Medical Society of New Jersey in 1942 to offer quality health care to everyone at the lowest possible cost. The Blue Cross and Blue Shield Plans merged in 1986.

In order to centralize operations and improve service, the New Jersey Blue Cross and Blue Shield headquarters building was erected in Newark in 1970. Many Plan employees and operations are housed in this modern 18-story structure, in the heart of Newark's business district and the historic James Street Commons restoration area.

The Blue Cross and Blue Shield corporate tower in Newark—a striking white granite and glass office building—is also one of the most distinctive and recognizable buildings in the city's skyline, topped on all four sides by the Blue Cross and Blue Shield insignia. The corporate logo is lit at night, serving as an around-the-clock reminder of Blue Cross and Blue Shield's place in the city.

Blue Cross and Blue Shield of New Jersey has been developing innovative systems of health care delivery and financing for many years. In 1973 it introduced the first Health Maintenance Organization (HMO) in New Jersey. The Medigroup HMO program made its debut at Mercer Regional Medical Group in Trenton, offering a system of health care aimed at the prevention as well as the treatment of illness and disease.

Today "I have Blue Cross" has become a household phrase nationwide, and the Blue Cross and Blue Shield ID card is accepted in many foreign hospitals as well.

The New Jersey Blue Cross and Blue Shield Plan is a recognized leader in the health insurance field, providing health care service protection to nearly 4 million New Jerseyans. It is the second-largest Plan in the national Blue Cross and Blue Shield network, which insures more than 85 million Americans.

Today the Plan's hospital claims processing system is considered the best of its kind in the nation. Claims are processed within 24 hours by direct computer link-up with hospitals. Cost savings and cash flow realized by hospitals through this automated system are two reasons that, under New Jersey's hospital rate-setting law, Blue Cross and Blue Shield receives a price advantage on the amount it

pays to hospitals. This helps hold down premium costs for both individual and group subscribers.

New Jersey Blue Cross and Blue Shield provides health care protection to individuals regardless of their health. Group programs are

An individual is never too young to have the security of health care coverage from Blue Cross and Blue Shield.

available to as few as two employees. Medicare recipients and students can enroll in special coverage programs. Individual subscribers and groups can choose a plan to fit their needs: one covering expenses

Don Daniels, president and chief executive officer of Blue Cross and Blue Shield of New Jersey (center), chats with a group of participating physicians staffing the medical team for one of the many running events sponsored by the Plan. From left: Ed Bravick, M.D.; Joe Hayes, M.D.; Daniels; Dan Roche, D.P.M.; and Ken Indahl, D.P.M.

incurred from the first dollar or one with copayment and deductible features.

Blue Cross and Blue Shield also offers coverage for alternative health care delivery systems such as HMOs—both group practice and individual practice association (IPA) HMOs. Some innovative services offered by Blue Cross and Blue Shield include Student plans, Major Medical, Dental, Prescription, Comprehensive, and Wraparound, as well as major coverage for new technology services such as CT scans, dialysis, and bypass.

In 1984 Blue Cross and Blue Shield began a corporate restructuring designed to make it more customer-oriented. Now each customer segment (national accounts, large groups, small groups, and individual subscribers) has its own division. The reorganization is helping the Plan better meet the specific needs of its different groups and individual subscribers.

SAMUEL KLEIN AND COMPANY
CERTIFIED PUBLIC ACCOUNTANTS

Samuel Klein, a certified public accountant and attorney at law, founded Samuel Klein and Company in 1921. Today the public accounting and consulting firm that bears his name consists of 10 partners, 2 principals, and more than 75 professional and clerical staff members.

The company has wide-ranging and diversified experience in auditing of commercial enterprises, financial institutions, municipalities, schools, colleges, not-for-profit organizations, and hospitals. Its expertise has also been developed in the areas of taxation, management consulting, computer installations, mergers, acquisitions, and SEC reporting.

Samuel Klein and Company provides the highest-quality services for its clients to help them achieve greater growth and profitability.

For most of its clients, a Client Service Team composed of representatives from each practice area (audit, management advisory services, and tax) is designated. The specialized disciplines of these personnel help assure that all client problems can be addressed by a staff familiar with the unique circumstances of each client. The team operates continuously on a coordinated basis under the overall super-

Samuel Klein and Company serves the City of Newark as its independent auditor and counts the Episcopal Diocese of Newark among its many clients located in the city.

vision of the engagement partner. Samuel Klein and Company's Audit and Management Advisory Services (MAS) personnel work together in evaluating data-processing controls and applying audit techniques to computer records.

Throughout the conduct of any engagement in a computer environment, MAS and audit personnel are utilized so that the special knowledge of each discipline can most effectively be brought to bear in resolving problems on a timely

basis. The special expertise of the firm's tax personnel is utilized in planning and reviewing the tax position of each client in connection with the engagement.

Auditing is a function of the certified public accountant and is one of the principal services performed for the firm's clients. The accountant's opinion letter, which must accompany financial statements, is of fundamental importance to investors, stockholders, credit grantors, banks, underwriters, regulatory authorities, and others. As part of its annual examinations, Samuel Klein and Company audit clients are given an independent professional opinion on financial statements and recommendations to

The professionals in the firm explore all appropriate opportunities to help clients with tax matters.

offer the widest range of services, both traditional and innovative, provided by experts in their respective fields.

The partners and several staff members are certified public accountants and are members of the American Institute of Certified Public Accountants. Several are members of other state-certified public accounting societies as well. Those registered municipal accountants in the firm are also members of the Registered Municipal Accountants Association. Partners and staff members hold important offices and committee positions in local and national professional, community, and social organizations.

The firm continuously expands its staff training program and requires all members of its professional staff to attend classes in technical and professional development matters.

Samuel Klein and Company has conducted its business since its inception from Newark offices—without interruption. The firm is happy and proud to be part of the newfound vitality and overall renaissance of the city.

improve internal controls and many other aspects of their operations. These reports often point the way to significant economies for the client and provide meaningful information to guide management in its decisions.

Other areas of the practice include business planning, specialized accounting, management reporting, and development systems that control the productivity of labor and other resources. Samuel Klein and Company can monitor and evaluate the efficiency of systems and clerical procedures, act as a consultant regarding the selection and utilization of data-processing equipment, and apply

quantitative analysis techniques.

The firm's tax personnel include certified public accountants and attorneys who are able to evaluate each alternative course of action from a tax viewpoint and define available options and probable consequences for its clients.

The firm also provides litigation support, assisting clients in technical, analytical, financial, auditing, and accounting matters.

Another growing area of business for Samuel Klein and Company is its assistance to clients in mergers and acquisitions.

The firm believes in developing and maintaining long-term relationships, not in simply having clients; more than 65 years of reliability and integrity demonstrate this philosophy. Company leadership believes that a professional business must

Utilization of computer technology is an integral part of the accounting, auditing, tax, and management information services offered by the firm.

CITY NATIONAL BANK OF NEW JERSEY

Steady growth, consistent leadership, persistence, and commitment are behind the success story of City National Bank, New Jersey's only minority-controlled and -operated bank.

Under the strong leadership of Charles L. Whigham, its president and chief executive officer, and a dedicated board of directors, the bank has grown to become a highly regarded financial institution both locally and nationally.

The inspiration to create the bank began in the aftermath of the riots that shook Newark during the 1960s. Whigham, a Newark funeral director, discussed the need for a financial institution responsive to the needs of the minority community with other professionals, led by R. Dudley Bennet, who continues as a strong force on the board of directors today. The group's goal was to help rebuild the city by fostering local entrepreneurs and beginning businessmen.

They embarked on a three-year journey of paperwork, meetings, and discussions with the U.S. Comptroller of the Currency, which led to incorporation and the eventual sale of shares to raise the $1.5 million needed to fund the venture.

The $1.5 million had to be raised through the sale of capital stock with no one person owning more than 5 percent of the shares. The group decided the bank would be community supported in both ownership and operation to increase local employment and create a positive image of minority leadership.

The institution obtained a charter in 1972, and City National opened its doors after local church groups, businesses, and individuals made an investment in purchasing bank stock. The wisdom of their investment became evident quickly because the institution was profitable from the beginning. Its first dividends were declared in 1977.

City National has continued to turn an annual profit, due in large part to its prudent approach and strong management. Today the bulk of the bank's customers include small-to medium-size businesses, a segment of community people who make up a sizable part of the deposit base, and a large number of *Fortune* 500 companies that support the bank through minority investment programs designed to encourage the growth of minority business. A significant portion of the institution's deposits also come from federal and state government agencies.

Investing capital back into the community, City National has also participated in funding for local development projects such as converting the Newark News building into condominiums and constructing the Legal Communications building on Raymond Boulevard, the Newark Symphony Hall, the Vogue Housing, and La Casa De Don Pedro.

One of the keys to the bank's success has been employing people with substantial banking backgrounds, as well as encouraging growth from within by providing opportunities for employees to gain management experience and further training. The bank has also made it a practice to have an officer and employee staff that is a reflection of the community and its services.

Charles L. Whigham has played an active role in Newark by serving on the boards of the Newark Economic Development Commission, Private Industry Council, New Jersey Council of Churches, Boy's Club of Newark, and several other community organizations. One of his proudest accomplishments is the bank's record of profitability and the numerous financial contributions it has made to develop business in the black and hispanic communities.

According to Whigham, "Every city should have a bank to help the community and develop programs to improve the urban city's capital base. City National has managed to do that, consistently, for more than 15 years, and we look forward to continuing for many years to come."

Photo by Carol Kitman

XV

Building Greater Newark

From concept to completion, Newark's building industry and real estate professionals shape tomorrow's skyline.

Photo by Rich Zila

298

DAMON G. DOUGLAS COMPANY
CONSTRUCTION MANAGERS/GENERAL CONTRACTORS

The diversity and skills of the Damon G. Douglas Company is reflected in the broad spectrum of services it provides its clients.

Damon G. Douglas has served such widely ranging industries as health care, automotive, chemical, brewery, food, electronics, electric generation and distribution, telecommunications, steel fabrication, pharmaceutical, printing, transportation, materials handling and distribution, and financial services.

Commercial facilities the company has constructed include shopping malls, banks, office buildings, conference centers, fitness centers, computer centers, and department stores as well as real estate developments throughout New Jersey, southern New York State, and eastern Pennsylvania.

Damon G. Douglas Company is able to function as a construction manager, general contractor, or design builder for clients. Highly trained managers and executive staff are supported by professional engineers, architects, and specialists in carpentry, concrete, demolition, and masonry.

The firm is led by professional engineers Tullio "Ted" J. Borri, PE, president and chief executive officer, and John Sheehan, PE, executive vice-president. The engineering background of the organization's principals and associates enables it to play an important role on the design team by assisting in the planning process for alterations and new structures.

The firm does "hard-dollar bidding" and is able to do so because of its vast experience in other projects. This means clients are given a price and are guaranteed that the project will be completed within that agreed-upon budget.

The company's effectiveness is greatest when it's able to become involved early in the design of a client's project. Early involvement leads to lower costs, better constructability, quality, and on-time scheduling. The design process begins with conceptual drawings that enable engineers to draw up preliminary budgets and establish project feasibility parameters. To

ensure on-time construction the company uses a sophisticated computer system that identifies and monitors approval, long-lead items, and design and construction milestones as the project progresses.

According to John Sheehan, "Clients know they can build around and plan around our schedules. We provide responsive service and give owners confidence in our work. With each project, we build, plan, budget, and design as economically and as efficiently as possible."

The firm's commitment to provide quality construction and full-value construction for all clients was established by Damon G. Douglas, who founded the company in 1931. Today Damon G. Douglas employees not only work for the corporation but also are shareholding co-owners who have a vested interest in producing construction services that satisfy their clients.

The firm's 93 percent rate of return business attests to the ability of its people to respond to clients' needs and to establish good ongoing working relationships with them.

The firm's highly motivated employees pride themselves on taking on the challenge of managing complicated jobs that require extra

Damon G. Douglas Company consolidated two suburban facilities into a 200,000-square-foot, three-story office building for the corporate headquarters of Thomas & Betts Corporation.

Damon G. Douglas' own craftsmen perform tenant fit-out work and interior finishes on many projects similar to the Thomas & Betts Corporation project shown above.

care and planning. Some of the most challenging projects include building an ocean wave simulator for pressure testing of Bell Labs underwater cables, adding new floors above existing hospitals while maintaining all the hospitals' critical care services, and removing asbestos from a building and then reconstructing it while parts of the facility remained in operation.

According to company president Tullio Borri, "We believe that in the process of being a self-performing company, we can control quality, cost, performance, and distinguish ourselves from our competitors."

Damon G. Douglas is one of New Jersey's most experienced health care construction specialists. The firm's many projects include major new additions, highly technical installations, and complex renovations for hospitals, rehabilitation centers, and nursing homes.

The company's expertise in critical path method scheduling enables it to coordinate renovation and new work without disrupting daily operations and, keeping the project on schedule.

According to Borri, "Health care facilities are the most complicated and sophisticated build-

Damon G. Douglas Company was the general contractor on the major expansion program of St. Michael's Medical Center, the flagship hospital of the Archdiocese of Newark.

ings to build. Intimate knowledge of HVAC, operating suites, and patient areas are required. It's also essential to understand equipment being used by the facility in order to provide special services to accommodate it."

Among the firm's special services, Damon G. Douglas Company offers clients Construction Facility Service programs that handle immediate construction requirements under an annual contract. The firm provides manpower to perform miscellaneous carpentry, masonry, and other construction tasks on an as-needed and low-cost basis. This service gives clients the flexibility of a large maintenance staff without the problems of directly employing these individuals.

The firm's Construction Facility Service clients include many of New Jersey's leading *Fortune* 500 corporations. According to client William W. Wilson of the American Cyanamid Company, "Through the Damon G. Douglas construction maintenance program, we have been able to realize efficiencies and improved services. Damon G. Douglas' people are quick to respond, energetic, and effective."

The firm also does a great deal of work that involves the rehabilitation of old facilities to meet new tenants' needs. This includes alterations and renovations known as "tenant fix-up work." The company renovated the First Fidelity Bank facility in Newark by gutting the building and adding new HVAC and electrical cabling as well as new floors, walls, and ceilings.

The firm also provides turnkey design-build services, from architectural service to construction, where its knowledge of cost and design enables it to give clients a reliable estimate and fast-track construction.

According to Borri, "As a company, we have responded to changes in the economy. We had a heavier industrial emphasis when we first started, but now we are focusing more of our efforts on service industries to reflect the shift in the economy away from manufacturing. Our growth as a company exceeds the growth of the state itself."

The key to the Damon G. Douglas Company's success is reflected in the words of the firm's founder, "We shall build good buildings at a profit if we can, at a loss if we must, but always good buildings."

Damon G. Douglas Company received a special New Good Neighbor Award for the construction of the Public Service Electric & Gas Park Plaza in Newark. Park Plaza features a 100-foot-diameter amphitheater surrounded by seating for 1,000 people. The amphitheater is bordered by a 220-foot-long crescent-shape waterfall that is seven feet high.

K. HOVNANIAN ENTERPRISES INC.

On October 30, 1986, Newark's recently elected mayor, Sharpe James, stood alongside one of many empty lots bordering the city's downtown business district, gazed toward one of several burned-out buildings, and, seemingly ignoring the scene before him, said that the city was in the midst of a renaissance. At the same time, he lamented the lack of affordable housing in the city and uttered a prediction that some observers found hard to reckon with.

Scooping up a shovelful of dirt in breaking ground for the first section of K. Hovnanian Enterprises Inc.'s ambitious Society Hill housing development, he stated, "People who have been looking for home ownership will stay in Newark, and I think there are going to be many people that left the city who are going to be looking to move back."

Skeptics had had plenty of time to reflect on the mayor's forward-sounding words by June 18, 1988, when Society Hill at University Heights opened to the general home-buying public. And if there were still any doubts that those positive phrases, sounded by him nearly two years before, could come about, they were shattered on that

With downtown Newark in the background, this aerial photo shows the first several dozen homes in the Society Hill complex and their relationship to the city's business district.

Saturday morning.

For on that brutally hot June day, a line of 350 people, the vast majority of whom were present or former Newark residents, stretched along an entire city block as sales in the condominium community opened. Some of those waiting on line had camped out at the foot of the sales office for more than three days prior, but each person was waiting for the opportunity to buy into the renaissance the mayor had spoken about months before—to become home owners of Society Hill at University Heights. All 143 homes made available to the general public sold out that day, an accomplish-

On grand-opening day for Society Hill at University Heights, K. Hovnanian executives congratulate one another on providing affordable housing in the heart of the city, as hundreds line up to purchase the new condominium homes.

ment few would have ever suspected possible back in October 1986.

K. Hovnanian saw the potential that affordably priced homes would have in Newark and was excited about taking part in the rebirth of this once-important residential address. "The question is not why the development is taking place in Newark, but rather why not," says Steven Goldin, director of marketing and sales for Hovnanian's Inner City Division, which is developing the project. "This site in the Central Ward was the city's biggest wound. Its redevelopment will show that no matter how deep a wound is, it can be healed."

The Society Hill community, just off South Orange Avenue in the University Heights section of the city, will eventually contain approximately 1,250 homes, and integrated into the community will be a wide variety of retail establishments and commercial enterprises totaling

115,000 square feet, a bank branch, and a police annex.

While the firm is known for its affordably priced Society Hill developments statewide, Society Hill at University Heights in Newark contrasts sharply with its suburban counterparts.

The homes at Society Hill at University Heights, such as those in the three-story Townplex building, were designed for an urban setting. And their starting prices of $69,000 for a one-bedroom condominium, $82,000 for a two-bedroom town house, and $97,000 for a three-bedroom town house were in keeping with the firm's long-standing reputation for affordable housing. Prices included off-street parking and centrally monitored security systems.

Quality homes maintained with pride.

Like other private builders who have undertaken developments in the city, Hovnanian believes its projects will appeal to young professionals who want to live near their jobs, and longtime Newark residents, either renters or home owners, looking for alternative housing that before now was not available.

"Newark is just at the start of its residential revival," said Mayor James. "Private money is coming into the city, but it has a long way to go to complete its journey back."

An influx of people with a wider range of incomes, Newark officials believe, will strengthen the city's economic base and result in the eventual improvement of an array of services—from education and safety to sanitation.

The principles upon which the company was founded are borne out today in Newark and for many years by the thousands of Hovnanian home owners throughout New Jersey. When Kevork S. Hovnanian, chairman of the board of Hovnanian Enterprises Inc., started the firm in 1966, he targeted the lower-priced end of the market, building affordable condominium complexes and communities of attached homes.

"In the beginning I decided to produce housing that the majority of the public could afford. First we made a conscious decision that affordable attached homes and condos were the kind of product we wanted to develop, and then we designed a product around it. Our many successful projects show it turned out to be the right move," says Hovnanian.

The company prides itself on state-of-the-art design with cost efficiency in mind. Standardized units without expensive add-ons reduce

An artist's rendering of the entry drive to Society Hill at University Heights.

subcontractor costs and subsequently reduce the cost to the home buyer. Due to its large size, the firm can take advantage of economies of scale in buying building materials, in marketing, and in overhead. Typically, Hovnanian housing is sold at 10 to 20 percent below market value, keeping demand high among buyers who benefit from the appreciation of their property.

Growth has been steady for Hovnanian. The company has grown from $15 million in revenue in 1977 to $350 million in 1988. The firm has 800 full-time employees and provides jobs for almost 3,000 workers, including subcontractors.

K. Hovnanian Enterprises Inc.'s roots go back to the late 1950s, when Kevork Hovnanian and his three brothers fled their homeland of Iraq during the revolution. Kevork, who had owned a road-building company in Iraq, used his expertise in construction to start his new home-building firm in America.

"The market is and has been growing tremendously," says Hovnanian. "There's a big need for this type of housing, not only in Newark but throughout New Jersey, and the need will continue. We are proud to add an important aspect to the resurgence of Newark. As we say in our advertisements, 'K. Hovnanian put the New back in Newark.'"

NEW COMMUNITY CORPORATION

New Community Corporation, a totally grass-roots venture, was created in 1968 by a dedicated group of residents from Newark's Central Ward.

Spurred into action by the pressing crises of urban poverty, these residents sought to create a new community that would allow them to determine their own destiny by making the housing, educational, economic, and political decisions that would govern their lives.

Today New Community acts as an umbrella corporation for a group involved in real estate planning and development, construction, finance and asset management, and public relations. It oversees housing ventures, day care, an employment center, commercial real estate, health care, and business development.

New Community Corporation is the largest nonprofit housing corporation in New Jersey and one of the largest in the nation. The organization and its affiliated corporations employ more than 700 people, who work in all areas of real estate and health care.

New Community Corporation is

NCC provides its services to the community through a cooperative network that includes, among other projects, Babyland Nursery, pictured here with the children receiving a visit from Santa.

proud of its part in Newark's renaissance. It has a real estate investment in the city of more than $100 million, and every year it pays more than $1.8 million in real estate taxes to the City of Newark.

NCC provides its services to the community through a cooperative network that includes the housing corporation and its components, Babyland

Nursery, and St. Rose of Lima Parish.

Network involvements also include a federal community credit union, a health care center with medical group practice, an extended health care facility, protective services for children, a family violence center, nutrition and food services for young and old, a computer system, and a monthly newspaper, the *Clarion.*

Since its founding in 1968, New Community Corporation has been a major contributor to the revitalization of the city of Newark. New Community Corporation owns 10 housing developments in Newark, which provide attractive, safe, sound, and affordable housing for more than 6,000 peo-

New Community Corporation is the largest nonprofit housing corporation in New Jersey and one of the largest in the nation. Pictured here are two NCC projects: At left, NCC Homes, the first development constructed by NCC, on Morris Avenue, and above, NCC Commons family town houses with surrounding courtyard area, on Morris Avenue.

ple. Its 2,400 apartments, built at a total cost of $88 million, created 4,000 construction jobs and produced $30 million in construction wages. New Community Corporation also provides a full range of services for each development it completes, including property management, maintenance, security, and social services.

In addition to new construction, New Community Corporation acquired the Convent of the Little Sisters of the Poor and the Douglas Hotel and transformed them into individual apartment units for senior citizens.

New Community Corporation also acquired, from Prudential Insurance Company, the apartment complex known as Douglass-Harrison Homes, which was built in 1935. The company now operates and maintains these buildings as part of its network. NCC has also acquired five individual properties that have been rehabilitated for use as private family homes and special services.

New Community Corporation's Harmony House will provide transitional housing for 102 homeless families and is considered a model for the state.

In April 1985 New Community Corporation completed the renovation of St. Joseph Church, which is listed on both the national and state Registers of Historic Places. This $2.5-million undertaking has created 24,000 square feet of commercial space. This fully occupied facility created 75 new jobs and pays $40,000 annually in real estate taxes.

New Community Corporation headquarters is located on the third level of the Atrium, which includes the Priory Restaurant, a spa, medical offices, a lounge, a sandwich shop, a credit union, and a conference center.

The design of this historic landmark preserves as much of the character of the original structure as is practical, including the height and spaciousness of its interior and the beauty of its exterior design.

In January 1986 New Community Corporation completed construction of an extended care facility that contains 168 nursing beds and 60 medical day-care spaces. This $10.9-million facility is now fully occupied and employs 168 people.

In March 1985 the New Community Federal Credit Union

lion. The project created 80 construction jobs and produced $630,000 in construction wages. The finest day-care space in the nation is provided for 320 children at Babyland's four day-care centers. A new day-care center for HIV-infected babies and toddlers is the latest addition to the Babyland network. In addition, a program for training, education, and day care for single parents was established in September 1988.

New Community Corporation's commitment to the citizens of Newark continues with plans for a Pathmark neighborhood shopping center, affordable housing, and a neighborhood recreation center.

A spotlight cast on Newark today would show a proudly revitalized city, steadfastly emerging from long

NCC oversees housing ventures, day care, an employment center, commercial real estate, health care, and business development. Pictured here are three NCC ventures; below, NCC Manor, a senior citizen high-rise, on Orange Street, right, an extended day care facility with medical day care, on South Orange Avenue, and above, a renovated day-care facility for babies with AIDS, on Orange Street.

(NCFCU) began operation. NCFCU has 750 members and has more than one million dollars in assets.

In 1981 New Community Corporation also built the new Babyland III day-care center/office at 755 South Orange Avenue. This facility was built at a total cost of $1.9 mil-

years of neglect. The ideas that were only part of a dream in 1968 are today a reality, standing as proud symbols of the vision of its founders: decent affordable housing; a safe, secure neighborhood; responsible day care; vital human support services; quality, dignified health care; increased employment created by its economic-development process; and creation and control of income-producing businesses.

THE HENKIND-ENGEL ORGANIZATION

The Henkind-Engel Organization is a partnership of Sol Henkind, Lewis Henkind, and Sydney Engel. These partners have worked together for more than 25 years in the development, financing, design, construction, and management of major real estate projects throughout the United States and particularly in the New York-New Jersey metropolitan area.

A major focus of its business is the total rehabilitation of buildings ranging in size from 150,000 to 300,000 square feet and the recycling of those buildings for new uses. A great deal of its renovation work has been in New Jersey, including many buildings in Newark that are significant both in size and in historical importance. The company's forte is acquiring buildings at a reasonable price, recycling them, and making them functional again.

The Henkind-Engel Organization's commitment to Newark is long-standing and significant. Including its rental housing, health care facilities for senior citizens, office buildings, and other commercial projects, the aggregate value of The Henkind-Engel Organization's developments in Newark exceed $80 million.

The Henkind-Engel Organization's management arm is headquartered in Newark. Among the firm's subsidiaries is the Essex Plaza Management Company, which manages 3,500 housing units in Newark, East Orange, Trenton, Brooklyn, Queens, and the Bronx that are owned or syndicated by Henkind-Engel.

Essex Plaza is a 702-unit apartment complex of several buildings, the center of which is 1060 Broad Street. It is considered a premier

senior citizen housing development and has been recognized by the U.S. Secretary of Housing and Urban Development as well as local, state, and federal politicians as one of the "best developed and managed Section Eight senior citizen housing projects in the country."

An imposing building, 1060 Broad Street was formerly used by many important businessmen and politicians whose offices were located there. Today The Henkind-Engel Organization provides free space for a nondenominational chapel, a food program, and a medical clinic for the 800 residents of the building. A beautifully maintained architectural masterpiece, Essex Plaza is a source of great pride for The Henkind-Engel Organization.

Henkind-Engel's Renaissance Towers, the first significant nonsub-

sidized housing built in Newark in two decades, was the impetus for the newly emerging residential market in Newark. The former Newark Evening News building complex, Renaissance Towers has been renovated into a widely acclaimed multipurpose condominium complex containing residential, office, and commercial space as well as a 450-car garage. It offers the most luxurious condominums in Newark, and the success of the project has encouraged other developers to pursue residential projects throughout the city.

Adjacent to Renaissance Towers

Two views of Renaissance Towers—the first significant nonsubsidized housing built in Newark in two decades. Formerly the Newark Evening News building complex, it was renovated by Henkind-Engel into a widely acclaimed multipurpose condominium complex. Above photo by Michael Spozarsky

is the 150,000-square-foot 31 Clinton Street building, which is being rehabilitated by The Henkind-Engel Organization as a first-class office building with occupancy scheduled for spring of 1990. The top 11 floors will be leased to the State of New Jersey, and its lower level will include restaurants and retail stores.

According to Sydney Engel, "These buildings are still important to Newark, and it makes good aesthetic and economic sense to save them rather than destroy them and build something new."

The Hospitality Care Center at 300 Broadway was originally built in 1927 as the main headquarters for the Mutual Benefit Life Insurance Company. After Mutual Benefit relocated in 1954, the building was taken over by the Archdiocese of

Newark as the site for Essex Catholic High School. A magnificent six-story structure with imposing granite columns, it currently serves as a 420-bed health and extended care facility for the elderly.

"As developers, we believe there is a heritage in Newark. Our facility at 300 Broadway is a beautiful building that is important to the history of Newark. Many thousands of boys went to Essex Catholic High School, and before that thousands worked there when it was the Mutual Benefit office," says Lewis Henkind.

The firm has contributed to improving the quality of life for Newark residents not only through its efforts to revitalize the city and provide reasonably priced housing for the elderly and economically disadvantaged, but also as a source of employment.

"We feel that what we have done in Newark has significantly

A beautifully maintained architectural masterpiece and a premier senior citizen housing development, Essex Plaza is a source of great pride for the Henkind-Engel Organization.

improved the lives of those with low to moderate means. To serve the needs of 840 patients, our nursing homes employ more than 500 people, many of whom are in entry-level positions. The 822 subsidized housing units we developed enable more than 2,000 people to have a significantly higher quality of life," says Lewis Henkind.

The Henkind-Engel Organization is also proud of its record for employing minority subcontractors and providing on-the-job training programs to meet all applicable affirmative action and equal opportunity requirements on its projects.

The firm's relationships with financial institutions are strong, and it is well versed in the special requirements of federal, state, and municipal agencies. Contributing to The Henkind-Engel Organization's ability to act as a successful developer in Newark has been the continuing support the firm has had from the mayor's office under both the Gibson and James administrations as well as the understanding and help of the city council. The principals of Henkind-Engel appreciate the active interest on the part of the city in encouraging local development, including rehabilitation projects.

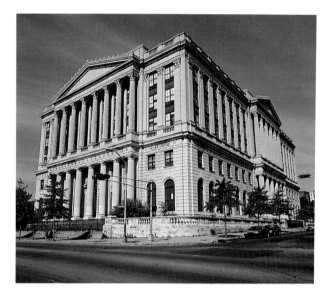

As part of Newark's heritage, 300 Broadway was originally built in 1927 as the main headquarters for the Mutual Benefit Life Insurance Company. The building was later taken over by the Archdiocese of Newark as the site for Essex Catholic High School. Today, due to Henkind-Engel's renovation work, it serves as a 420-bed health and extended care facility for the elderly.

"Most of our work has involved renovation. We prefer to do large projects that have a significant impact. Newark offers the advantage of offering large properties and buildings we can acquire at a reasonable cost that can be renovated," says firm partner Sol Henkind.

"We are optimistic about Newark," says Lewis Henkind. "We've developed projects in four different parts of the city. The projects have been profitable, and the surrounding neighborhoods have benefited from our having improved the areas. Projects such as Renaissance Towers have been the key to the revitalization of the housing market in Newark. We plan to keep focusing our efforts on providing affordable low-cost housing and projects to attract middle-income residents to Newark. We have led the way by encouraging others by our example to build housing and do business in Newark."

BELLEMEAD DEVELOPMENT CORPORATION

An artist's rendering of One Newark Center in Newark—a Bellemead-Seton Hall redevelopment project.

Since its incorporation in 1923, Bellemead Development Corporation of Roseland, New Jersey, has consistently balanced the needs of business and industry with responsibility to the environment and the community.

The company has earned a host of awards for environmental sensitivity, aesthetic achievement, and contributions to the economic well-being of the community. Bellemead is dedicated to continued growth through the development of new office parks, urban complexes, and residential communities wherever the market warrants.

This full-service real estate organization has, in more than a half-century of activity, based its growth on an ability to assess accurately new areas and to enter these markets with development marked by intelligent planning and sensitive execution. In this regard, Bellemead is likely best known as the pioneer of commercial development in the New Jersey Meadowlands, an area once regarded as a wasteland and now considered one of the nation's leading multinational business centers.

As a planner of total environments, Bellemead attributes much of its unique strength to its maintenance of tight control throughout the course of the construction process. From concept to completion, whether developing single buildings or corporate parks, Bellemead operates as the expert overseer in all stages of planning, construction, marketing, and management.

With a working philosophy that a corporate center will only be successful if it enhances the environment of the community, Bellemead acquires development sites and goes on to secure the zoning, subdivision, and planning approvals necessary to create projects that are in harmony with their communities. Acting as general contractor, Bellemead also ensures high quality and on-time completion of its projects.

A wholly owned subsidiary of The Chubb Corporation, an insurance holding company with assets exceeding $9 billion, Bellemead enjoys a solid financial footing that provides the company with enormous purchasing power. This fact alone adds cost effectiveness to its buildings, resulting in bottom-line savings for its clients.

In developing corporate and residential communities, Bellemead has gained a wide reputation for not losing sight of the human needs within the environment, as well as the quality construction the firm has been providing for more than 65 years.

"In Newark, as elsewhere, we will continue to be guided by a commitment to both economic value and ecological awareness," says Bellemead president, Donn Norton. "We heartily believe that it is by these standards that we continue to be successful." Despite geographical diversification, New Jersey still accounts for 70 percent of the firm's activity.

Bellemead's New Jersey corporate centers, each with its own commercial success story, include The Princeton Corporate Center, Somerset Hills Corporate Center, 78 Corporate Center at Lebanon, Branchburg Corporate Center, Meadowlands Corporate Center, Waterview Corporate Centre in Parsippany, 280 Corporate Center, and Parsippany Corporate Center.

Although Bellemead's eight New Jersey complexes bring an average of 50,000 square feet of new space on line annually, the firm is not content to be a leading developer of corporate parks in its home state. Continually stepping up its search for new markets to conquer, Bellemead also has established centers in suburban areas of Michigan, Illinois, Maryland, and Florida.

As New Jersey's leading developer of corporate centers, Bellemead also has the capability to market financial services to the advantage of both tenants and investors. With a portfolio of financial services that includes build-to-suit, sale, lease, and joint-venture arrangements, the firm designs innovative financial structures that can capitalize on the current fiscal and economic environment, thus enabling clients to maximize the value of their custom-designed facilities.

Bellemead Development Corporation will continue to be guided by the corporate motto that has been responsible for its success throughout many decades—to create environments of excellence.

As a wholly owned subsidiary of The Chubb Corporation, Bellemead Development Corporation enjoys a solid financial footing that provides the company with enormous purchasing power. Pictured here is the Chubb Corporation world headquarters in Warren, New Jersey.

TORCON, INC.

In slightly more than 20 years Torcon, Inc., has established itself as a major player in New Jersey's physical and economic development. Starting with just seven employees, the construction firm currently has a work force of more than 150 and an annual business volume in excess of $300 million.

Since its inception in 1965, Torcon has grown to become New Jersey's largest building construction firm and one of the top 100 in the nation, according to *Engineering News Record*, an authoritative industry voice.

Based in Westfield, Torcon was founded by Benedict Torcivia on the principle of building quality relationships with clients and working partners. That philosophy has earned Torcon such loyal clients as Prudential, AT&T, Dow Jones, Merck & Co., Ciba Geigy, IBM, Travelers Insurance, Mercedes-Benz, First Boston, and ADP.

Torcon has completed some of New Jersey's most impressive office, commercial, research and development, retail, and institution-

Prudential's Three and Four Gateway Center, an 800,000-square-foot office complex, were completed by Torcon in Newark's central business district.

The Newark Airport Marriott Hotel was built by Torcon in two phases—the 10-story, 414-room original structure in 1984, and a 10-story, 100-room addition in 1988.

al facilities, including the American Re-Insurance headquarters in Plainsboro, Merck Research Lab in Rahway, Hilton Hotel in Short Hills, AT&T Technologies headquarters in Berkeley Heights, various facilities for Seton Hall University in South Orange, and many more.

Torcon has been an active force in the recent rebirth of Newark as a commercial business center. The firm's first major project in the city was Prudential Insurance Company's Three Gateway Center, an 18-story office tower begun in 1982. In addition to providing top-quality rentable office space for Newark, Three Gateway Center also resulted in landmark Equal Employment Opportunity and Minority Business Enterprise participation programs during construction. Subsequently, Torcon has acted as Prudential's construction manager for Four

Gateway Center and the comprehensive modernization of the Hilton Gateway Hotel.

Torcon's other activities in Newark have included the Newark Airport Marriott Hotel and interior office construction for prestigious law firms such as McCarter & English and Carpenter, Bennett & Morrissey. Torcon has also completed major building programs at several of the city's outstanding medical centers.

Torcon sees Newark as a solid market in the years to come, according to company president Ben Torcivia. "Newark is just beginning to reclaim its place as the commercial and cultural center of New Jersey. We are fully committed to the city and confident of its economic future."

Torcivia has been the recipient of numerous industry accolades. He was named Construction Man of the Year in 1981 by the New Jersey Ready-Mixed Concrete Association and the New Jersey Chapter of the American Concrete Institute. He also served as president of the Building Contractors Association of New Jersey and the Construction Congress of New Jersey. Torcon itself was recently named Construction Manager of the Year and has twice been named General Contractor of the Year by the New Jersey Chapter of the American Subcontractors Association, and the firm's projects have won many New Good Neighbor awards.

Torcivia has a tradition of personally standing behind every Torcon, Inc., project. This tradition of personal involvement continues at the family-owned corporation as his sons, Benedict Jr. and Joseph, manage the firm's operations.

Photo by Rich Zila

XVI

Quality of Life

Medical and educational institutions contribute to the quality of life of Newark area residents.

Seton Hall University School of Law, 314

Kean College, 315

United Hospitals Medical Center, 316

Cathedral Healthcare System, 317

The University of Medicine and Dentistry of New Jersey, 318-319

UMDNJ-University Hospital, 320-321

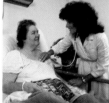

Clara Maass Medical
Center, 322-323

The Essex Substance
Abuse Treatment Cen-
ter, Inc., 324

Rutgers, The State Uni-
versity of New Jersey,
325

Newark Beth Israel
Medical Center,
326-327

New Jersey Institute of
Technology, 328

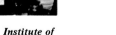

Photo by Mary Ann Brockman

SETON HALL UNIVERSITY SCHOOL OF LAW

Seton Hall University School of Law was established in 1951 with Miriam Rooney as dean, the first female dean of law in the country. At that time, Seton Hall merged with John Marshall School of Law in Jersey City. The School of Law is constructing a new building that will provide increased space and facilities.

Between100 and 110 employers, which include law firms, government agencies, and public accounting firms from both New Jersey and New York, visit the law school each year to interview for summer positions and permanent positions after graduation. Approximately one-third of the graduating class is named to judicial clerkships at the state and federal level.

Seton Hall's law students have always accepted the responsibility of involvement with the community through the many clinics at the law school.

The Legal Services Clinic is a joint operation of the law school and Essex-Newark Legal Services. Full-time staff attorneys supervise students in assisting indigent clients.

At the Family Law Clinic, students serve as counsel, under supervision, to clients in divorce and adoption cases. The Hispanic Clinic provides legal assistance in civil matters to members of the Hispanic community.

Students in the Juvenile Justice Clinic litigate criminal trial cases before the Juvenile and Domestic Relations Court while working with the County Prosecutor's or Public Defender's Office.

Juvenile Counseling aims to prevent delinquency and future crime by providing young people in trouble with one-to-one counseling with concerned legal professionals. The clients are selected by the Essex

County Probation Department.

The Legislative Bureau provides the New JerseyAssembly with research, report writing, and drafting services and also publishes the *Seton Hall Legislative Journal*. An active MENTOR program, conducted by law students, prepares area high school students for possible law careers.

The law school also has Moot Court programs, faculty assistantships, and such student organizations as the Student Bar Association, *Res Ipsa Loquitor* (the law school newspaper), Black Law Students Association, Christian Legal Society, Spanish-American Law Students Association, Women's Law Forum, International Law Society, Environmental Law Forum, the Law Review, the Legislative Bureau, the Peter W. Rodino Law Society, Phi Alpha Delta and Delta Theta Phi fraternities, Computer Law Society, and the Jewish Law Students' Society.

In a new pro bono program, final-year students volunteer their legal services to the poor and needy

This architect's rendering shows Newark Center for Commerce and Education, a 1.2-million-square-foot complex being built in Newark, which includes the 200,000-square-foot Seton Hall University School of Law. The new law school includes a 65,000-square-foot law library and a 300-seat auditorium.

for no renumeration or academic credit.

In addition to the traditional careers in law firms and government, the school's graduates are excelling in business, university administration, public interest law, legal services, mental-health organizations, foundations, unions, social services, and research consulting organizations.

According to Monsignor John T. Petillo, chancellor of Seton Hall University, "We are very proud of those who, by their actions and achievements, reflect our belief in the vast importance of a truly ethical education. Our law graduates are committed to better their communities and to serve their clients with dedication and conscientiousness."

KEAN COLLEGE

A small college with the advantages of a large university, Kean College offers a friendly atmosphere where each of its students can develop both professionally and as a person.

The first-rate faculty at Kean College comprises more than 350 full-time professors and more than 360 part-time instructors, adjuncts, and experts from surrounding metro-area corporations. While monitoring students' progress, Kean College professors continue to engage in ongoing research, releasing new published material and serving as consultants in their fields.

Personal, individualized attention is the key at Kean College. With fewer than 30 in a class, students receive personal attention from their professors.

Whether students choose to live off campus or in residence halls or commute by car or public transportation, they find activities that fulfill the social aspects of college life. Clubs and organizations hold regular parties, and there are fraternities and sororities to join. Kean also offers some 15 sports for intercollegiate competition for men and women.

Students begin their academic careers by taking a series of liberal arts courses designed to give them a strong background in English, the arts, mathematics, and science.

The variety of academic majors gives students many choices, all offering solid career preparation. The largest number of students choose business or computer science, including computer-assisted design and manufacturing. Technology offers electronics and manufacturing. The health professions draw men and women interested in science; communications, theater, and the arts attract those talented in such areas.

Internships and cooperative work opportunities are widespread in New Jersey, New York, and Washington, D.C. Theater and communication students, for example,

intern at ABC and WPIX Television News and with community cable television networks. Many students work on campus in order to pay for their education.

Kean College is well respected for its excellent health professions curriculum. Students receive an exceptional education in the areas of nursing, medical technology, occupational and physical therapy, and medical record administration.

Not only does Kean College offer the ability to acquire a computer savvy in any discipline, but computer science majors can take advantage of cooperative-education programs and earn credit for paid employment positions in programming and other related data-processing jobs. Many firms contact the college, seeking students for these programs, and sometimes hire them full time after graduation. Students who select the natural sciences have the opportunity to work on a variety of special projects, including chemistry and chemistry/physics projects for the National Science Foundation.

Kean has long had a commitment to quality education and responsiveness to changes in society and the work place. Launched in 1985, Kean's Excellence and Equity program is the result of The Governor's Challenge Grant program, a concerted effort to achieve excellence.

The program consists of four key elements:

Students' academic progress and their satisfaction with campus life is assessed on an ongoing basis to improve programming. Kean is one of the few colleges in the nation to implement an assessment system to improve undergraduate education by measuring progress over the course of the students' college experience.

A new general education program gives students the fundamental tools they need to succeed: writing, speaking, calculating, and critical thinking. The program establishes objectives for each major.

With a solid liberal arts core, Kean College offers a variety of academic majors to its students.

Kean is recognized as a national leader in integrating computers across the curriculum in all academic programs. To achieve this ambitious goal, Kean has conducted workshops to improve faculty computer literacy so the skills can be passed on to the students.

The college has installed a campus-area network that will use fiber optics as the backbone transport technology. The system will link all academic buildings and has the capacity to accommodate future plans for voice and image transfer.

Kean has long had a significant impact on the business community. It has established close, cooperative ties with local businesses, industry, and governmental agencies. Further proof of Kean's impact on business came via the recent study showing that it generated $76.4 million of income and 3,249 jobs in 1987.

The goal of Kean College is to help students develop a solid base of knowledge, self-confidence, and tangible skills to meet the challenges of today and the twenty-first century.

UNITED HOSPITALS MEDICAL CENTER

United Hospitals Medical Center is a unique teaching hospital that was established in 1959, when four Newark hospitals merged to achieve greater levels of excellence and efficiency. Today United Hospitals comprises four units that provide family health care services to the local community and highly specialized services to patients statewide.

Presbyterian Hospital, founded in 1909, forms the cornerstone of today's United Hospitals Medical Center. This unit has grown into a highly sophisticated health care system dedicated to providing quality medical care to the residents of Newark. Because there are fewer physicians in private practice, more city residents are seeking primary care at the hospital than ever before. Presbyterian Hospital has become the community's family doctor and the provider of essential medical services. Presbyterian Hospital is noted for always offering a helping hand to those who are suffering from illness or injury.

Children's Hospital of New Jersey is essentially a "hospital within a hospital." Founded as Babies Hospital in 1894, Children's Hospital is now a complete diagnostic and treatment center for infants, children, and adolescents. This 135-bed unit offers subspecialty programs in all major pediatric disciplines, including cardiovascu-

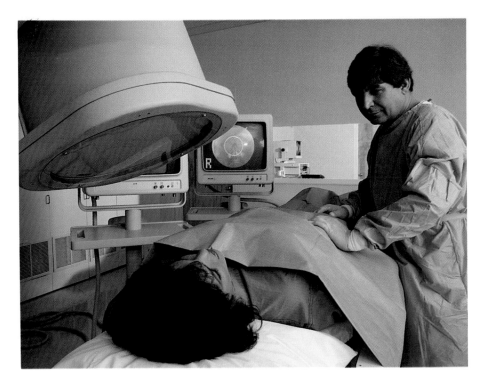

Digital Subtraction Angiography is a state-of-the-art diagnostic technique utilized by Dr. M. Khademi of United Hospitals Medical Center.

lar surgery, newborn intensive care, and hematology/oncology. Children's Hospital serves as the major teaching site for the department of pediatrics of the University of Medicine and Dentistry of New Jersey/New Jersey Medical School. Together these institutions provide New Jersey with superior programs in teaching, service, and research.

United Hospitals Orthopedic Center was founded in 1892 as Crippled Children's Hospital. Today this unit provides comprehensive orthopedic care to adults and children throughout New Jersey. The Orthopedic Center provides a unique environment for diagnosing and treating a wide range of musculoskeletal problems, including joint reconstruction and replacement. This unit serves as the major orthopedic teaching facility for the University of Medicine and Dentistry of New Jersey/New Jersey Medical School, and offers highly specialized services for arthritis, scoliosis, muscular dystrophy, and sports medicine.

The Newark Eye and Ear Infirmary, founded in 1880, and the Eye Institute of New Jersey, established in 1970, are dedicated to the

preservation and restoration of sight, hearing, and speech. As the only such specialty facilities in the state, the Newark Eye and Ear Infirmary and the Eye Institute of New Jersey serve as the major teaching sites for the University of Medicine and Dentistry of New Jersey/New Jersey Medical School departments of ophthalmology and otolaryngology. These units of United Hospitals utilize the latest technology to diagnose and treat disorders of the eyes, ears, nose, and throat, making their state-of-the-art resources available to patients throughout New Jersey who require specialized care.

Satellite facilities operated by the United Hospitals Medical Center provide access to primary health care throughout the city of Newark. These include United Hospitals Community Health Center, United Family Health Center, New Community Health Center, and the Adolescent Health Care Center at Barringer High School.

Highly specialized services in ophthalmology are available at the Newark Eye and Ear Infirmary, a unit of United Hospitals Medical Center.

CATHEDRAL HEALTHCARE SYSTEM

"What distinguishes Cathedral Healthcare System is our commitment to Catholic health care ministry, and to the values of love, compassion, justice, and reverence for life," states Sister Margaret J. Straney, president and chief executive officer.

Sponsored by the Archdiocese of Newark, Cathedral Healthcare System includes Saint Michael's Medical Center and Saint James Hospital in Newark, and Saint Mary's Hospital in Orange. With 800 beds, 750 physicians, and 2,500 employees, it is one of the largest multihospital systems in New Jersey and one of the largest employers in the city of Newark.

Cathedral Healthcare System is committed to making sure that all the health care needs of its community are served in the most appropriate and cost-effective manner.

At Cathedral Healthcare System, state-of-the-art technology is offered within the context of the Catholic health care mission, where humanism in medicine is stressed at all times and where patients' physical, psychological, social, and spiritual needs are addressed through professional and expert care.

Saint Michael's Medical Center, a 411-bed regional referral and teach-

Saint James Hospital's busy maternity service is an integral part of Newark's Ironbound community. Courtesy, O'Brien & Mayor Photography

ing hospital, is on the leading edge of cardiac care, and it has earned a national and international reputation in the diagnosis and treatment of a variety of infectious diseases. Affiliated with the University of Medicine and Dentistry of New Jersey and with Seton Hall University Graduate School of Medical Education, Saint Michael's offers advanced training to more than 100 resident physicians.

A $90-million rebuilding program, scheduled for completion in 1992, includes plans for a six-story structure that will centralize outpatient services and include new emergency and operating rooms, an innovative single-room maternity care program, and a new lobby.

Saint James Hospital has been an integral part of Newark's Ironbound community since its founding in 1900. Over the years the hospital has continued to respond to the ethnic diversity of its community. Today Saint James offers an active obstetrics program, including a high-quality maternity clinic, a busy emergency department, a same-day surgery program, and many other health care services.

Saint Mary's Hospital, located in nearby Orange, offers the latest technology, including a new Pain Management Center dedicated to the treatment of chronic and cancer-related pain. Saint Mary's Laser Center offers the most comprehensive laser treatment in New Jersey. Saint Mary's also has the state's only laser lithotripter, the

Saint Michael's Medical Center was the first hospital in New Jersey to perform open-heart surgery, and it remains a leader in providing cardiac care. Courtesy, O'Brien & Mayor Photography

newest technology for removing kidney stones.

In addition to the services offered at the three hospitals, Cathedral Healthcare System provides other programs to the community. Cathedral Home Care is a home health agency that provides nurses, therapists, and home health aides to help ensure a smooth transition for patients between hospital and home.

Cathedral Health & Fitness Center, in Newark's Gateway One, is dedicated to promoting the health and well-being of the community.

HealthNet is a physician referral service that helps match new residents and other individuals to the physician who best meets their needs.

The Cathedral Health Foundation was established to support the many services and programs of Cathedral Healthcare System by soliciting financial contributions from the community.

THE UNIVERSITY OF MEDICINE AND DENTISTRY OF NEW JERSEY

From High Point in the north to Cape May in the south, the University of Medicine and Dentistry of New Jersey (UMDNJ) proudly serves the health needs of all New Jerseyans.

The largest health sciences university in the nation, UMDNJ's growth as a biomedical health sciences system has been unprecedented. Created in 1970 by the New Jersey State Legislature to consolidate existing public educational programs in medicine and dentistry, UMDNJ today spans the state with six health sciences schools, including three medical schools, at major campuses in Newark, Piscataway-New Brunswick, and Camden-Stratford.

The institution enrolls some 3,000 medical, dental, graduate, and allied health students, and annually awards degrees and certificates to more than 700 individuals. It also trains an additional 1,100 postgraduate physicians and dentists in more than 50 residency programs at four core teaching hospitals and a network of more than 125 affiliated hospitals and other health care facilities located in 19 of the state's 21 counties.

"The fact is, New Jersey got a late start in health professions education and had a lot of catching up to do," says Dr. Stanley S. Bergen, Jr., UMDNJ's first and only president.

When the university was founded, it was given a broad-based mandate to develop into a first-class health sciences system that would serve all New Jerseyans. Indeed, through its educational programs, health care services, and career opportunities, the university does touch the lives of most citizens statewide.

The university's first and largest campus was developed on a 60-acre tract in Newark's Central Ward. In 1970 Newark faced not only staggering economic and social problems, but also inadequate health services to deal with some of the

nation's highest rates of infant mortality, venereal disease, tuberculosis, lead poisoning, and heart disease.

In terms of health care, the university, through its UMDNJ-University Hospital, serves as both "family physician" to the community and as a major state referral center for specialized care. The hospital offers a unique array of 40 outpatient services in addition to its specialized centers for trauma care, high-risk pediatrics, cancer, reproductive medicine, adolescent medicine, and neurosurgery.

The hospital also operates the Emergency Medical Services (EMS) unit, which responds to 5,000 calls for help each month. Recently the hospital's Trauma Center and EMS launched NorthStar, a regional aeromedical rescue program featuring the most advanced medically equipped helicopter available.

Mental health services, ranging from individual, group, and family counseling to day-hospital and inpatient care, are provided by UMDNJ's two Community Mental Health Centers, located in Newark and Piscataway. The Newark campus center provides services to some 4,000 clients making 40,000 visits annually.

UMDNJ also has emerged as a national leader in recruiting and retaining minority students and recruiting minority faculty. In Newark, minority groups—blacks, Hispanics, and women—account for 25 percent of the enrollment at UMDNJ-New Jersey Medical School, nearly 5 percent above the national average. Further, blacks make up 6.6 percent of the medical school faculty, compared with the national average of 1.8 percent.

Research is another focal point at

The University of Medicine and Dentistry of New Jersey was created in 1970 by the New Jersey State Legislature to consolidate existing public education programs in medicine and dentistry. Today it is the largest health sciences university in the nation.

UMDNJ. In 1988 the university held some $37 million in grants supporting biomedical and clinical research into AIDS, heart disease, cancer, liver disease, genetic diseases, Parkinson's, epilepsy, eye diseases, dental and oral conditions, and environmental threats.

The university is a leading center in the AIDS battle. In Newark, the pediatric program—one of the nation's largest—is led by Dr. James Oleske, who first identified AIDS in

children. An adult AIDS center is based at the New Brunswick campus. Both are part of the research program of the National Institutes of Health.

With regard to the economy of the area, the university's $250-million Newark campus complex employs more than 5,800; of those, more than 1,300 are Newarkers who account for an annual payroll of nearly $27 million. Surrounding communities in Essex County

account for another 1,900 employees and $53 million in salaries.

The economy also has been enhanced by UMDNJ's Special Vendor Program, created to ensure UMDNJ's compliance with the state's Minority and Women Business Set Aside law, passed in 1986. In 1988 the program awarded $21.8 million in business contracts to minority- and female-owned firms and small businesses, more than doubling its 1987 total, which

then set a state precedent.

In 1986, New Jersey Governor Thomas Kean challenged UMDNJ to become a national "top 25" health science center by the year 2000. The challenge has inspired the university to set a course for progress that would take it through the 1990s.

At the Newark campus, this is reflected in the more than $100 million in construction projects in various states of planning and develop-

ment. These include a new Children's Hospital, a facility for the Sammy Davis, Jr., National Liver Institute, a building for the joint New Jersey Cancer Center/Center for Molecular Medicine and Immunology, and a medical office complex. Parking garages are being built to provide the surface space for these projects.

"A spirit of vitality and determination has been evident here from the start," says UMDNJ's president Bergen. "This is an institution on the move, growing in intensity and resolve with each advancement. We have been most fortunate to have the unflagging support of the state. We intend to respond in kind by delivering on the governor's challenge and giving New Jersey one of the nation's premier centers of health sciences education, health care, and research."

UMDNJ-UNIVERSITY HOSPITAL

For almost two decades the phrase "City of Newark" conjured up images of a riot-torn city, crumbling into complete devastation. Residents and observers alike wrote off the city as a lost cause, never believing that Newark could rebuild itself.

That is the Newark that most people remember, but the new word about Newark has been quietly spreading, and the secret is finally out—Newark is alive and well and prospering. And one of the driving forces of the emerging renaissance is another of New Jersey's best-kept secrets, UMDNJ-University Hospital.

As an owned and operated unit of the University of Medicine and Dentistry of New Jersey (UMDNJ), the state's health sciences education system, the hospital is an integral part of New Jersey's commitment to the training of its future health professionals and to the health and well-being of its citizens.

MATCHING A 200-YEAR HEAD START IN LESS THAN 20. Some of the country's finest and oldest teaching hospitals surround New Jersey, and for more than two centuries New Jersey's residents have turned to them for their specialized care. UMDNJ-University Hospital is changing all of that with its own growing list of centers of excellence, concentrating on developing first-rate resources in services currently unavailable in New Jersey.

One such resource is the Sammy Davis, Jr., National Liver Institute. Incorporated as an independent, nonprofit organization in 1984, this institute is the first medical resource center in the world devoted solely to the research and treatment of liver disorders.

As a testimony to his personal commitment to fighting liver disease, Davis personally chose the hospital as the site of the institute because of the consistent level of educational expertise and research capabilities available there. This level of expertise is perhaps best demonstrated in the state's first and only liver transplant program, based at UMDNJ-University

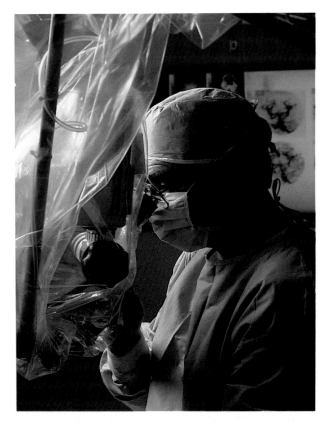

Dr. Abbott Krieger performs a delicate neurosurgical procedure with the aid of an operating microscope. Photo by Peter Byron

Hospital. Starting with the first transplant in February 1989, the program has given New Jersey's residents a chance to receive the life-saving treatment they need and deserve in their home state.

University Hospital's array of other surgical super-specialties rivals those of the most celebrated medical centers in the country. The intricacies of the human brain are confronted daily in complex neurosurgical procedures rarely conducted elsewhere. Aided by the latest technology, such as Magnetic Resonance Imaging, and supported by the state's only neurosurgical intensive care unit, surgeons have turned miracles into the routine.

UMDNJ-University Hospital has many other areas of regionally and nationally recognized expertise. Its

Sammy Davis, Jr., is joined by Frank Sinatra and Liza Minelli at a recent benefit performance for the Liver Institute. Photo by Bill Kostroun

Center for Fertility and Reproductive Medicine, for example, provides the most advanced evaluation and treatment available today in the areas of infertility, reproductive endocrinology, prenatal diagnosis, and high-risk obstetrics. The center has received referrals from all over the world for its highly successful in vitro fertilization program. Physicians at the center have taken this delicate procedure one step further with the introduction of a donor egg program that offers previously unavailable help for women who cannot produce their own eggs. The program's first success also marked the first known birth in the Northeast utilizing this technique.

The hospital has also received the highest level designation for its high-risk obstetrical and neonatal services. Its Perinatal Center brings together the hospital's multidisciplinary efforts, including obstetrics, pediatrics, and anesthesiology, as well as a host of clinical and social support services, to improve the outcome of high-risk pregnancies and to give struggling newborns the chance to have healthy lives.

CLOSING THE GAP BETWEEN TRAGEDY AND RECOVERY. The Golden Hour is a period of approximately one to two hours in which the lives of a majority of critically injured trauma patients can be saved if definitive surgical intervention is provided. The New Jersey Department of Health decided that UMDNJ-University Hospital was the best facility in the northern part of the state to make the most of those precious minutes when it designated the hospital as a Level I Trauma Center.

The countdown begins in the field, where the hospital's Emergency Medical Services program is the sole source of advanced life support for the cities of Newark, East Orange, Orange, Newark/Elizabeth Seaport, and Newark International Airport.

More distant areas in the northern portion of the state are served by NorthStar, an aeromedical transport program provided in conjunction with the State Police and Department of Health. Specially equipped aircraft flown by State Police pilots and staffed by UMDNJ-University Hospital nurses and paramedics airlift trauma victims and speed them back to the Trauma Center for the care they so desperately need.

The countdown continues at the Trauma Center, where the designated in-house Trauma Team always includes a board-certified trauma surgeon and specially trained nurses. Specially equipped and supported by a multidisciplinary array of human expertise, UMDNJ-University Hospital's Trauma Team is prepared to treat the most critical of injuries before time runs out.

FAMILY DOCTOR, FAMILY FRIEND TO NEWARK'S GENERATIONS. From its beginning UMDNJ-University Hospital forged a tight bond with the people it serves. More than 40 outpatient services, from the most general to the most specialized, accommodate more than 100,000 patient visits each year. The hospital has become the family physician and the super-specialist for the Newark community, including the thousands of men, women, and children who have no other means of medical treatment.

But it has become more. It has become a family friend, surrogate parent, personal mentor, role model, teacher, and employer. It has reached out not just to treat medical conditions but also to deal with the social conditions that cause or complicate them.

UMDNJ-University Hospital's Adolescent Health Care Services are perhaps the most dramatic and comprehensive example. More than 5,000 teenagers each year visit the hospital's adolescent clinics, presenting everything from AIDS to acne. About 1,000 of them come because they're pregnant, and these young patients (up to age 19) enter the hospital's Maternal and Infant Care Program. Through it, they receive the most advanced prenatal, perinatal, and postpartum care in America, including counseling, nutritional guidance, health education, as well as pediatric follow-up care until the baby is two years old.

The program is designed to address the medical and social complications faced by pregnant girls at risk because of their own poor nutrition, addictions, medical conditions, or youth. In a highly unique program, the hospital provides teenage fathers with the counseling and support they need to become involved with the care of their own infant. Parenting skills such as feeding, diapering, and bathing are taught along with the values needed to complete an education and seek out employment opportunities.

In the shadow of Newark's turbulent past, UMDNJ-University Hospital has developed its unique approach to medicine and health care with little fanfare. But the existence of a world-class academic medical center in what used to be a ghost town of a city is a secret that shouts to be shared. There's a new spirit of vitality, growth, and determination in Newark—in the city and in University Hospital. And that's the sort of news that everyone in New Jersey should know.

NorthStar transports a critically injured patient to the Trauma Center at UMDNJ-University Hospital. Photo by A.J. Sundstrom

CLARA MAASS MEDICAL CENTER

Since Clara Maass Medical Center opened its doors in 1870, its medical staff, trustees, administrators, and employees have been committed to a threefold mission: to deliver the highest-quality medical care, to be responsive to the changing needs of the communities they serve, and to maintain financial stability while financing continued growth.

In 1987, in order to maintain its leading role as a regional provider of health care services, Clara Maass Medical Center formed the Jerseycare health care network. The goal of the corporate restructuring is to expand existing services while creating new operational frameworks to meet future challenges and opportunities.

Jerseycare is now the parent of Clara Maass Medical Center, of the reorganized Clara Maass Foundation, and of three newly formed affiliates: Clara Maass Community Services, Clara Maass Continuing Care Center, and Premium Health Systems.

The medical center enjoys shareholder status in Voluntary Hospitals of America, Inc., a nationwide network of nonprofit health care organizations. Under a state-approved certificate of need, a $24-million renovation program of the medical center's buildings and departments was begun in 1988. New technology is continually added in the medical departments, with outpatient laser eye therapy and vascular laser surgery among the new capabilities.

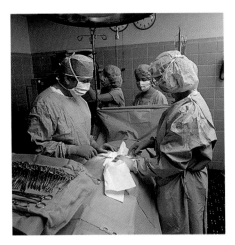

The entrance to Clara Maass Medical Center, in Belleville at Branch Brook Park.

The development of the first effective treatment for a serious form of multiple sclerosis was among the medical center's recent breakthroughs in research. The Medical/Oncology Unit, with its special approach to cancer care and

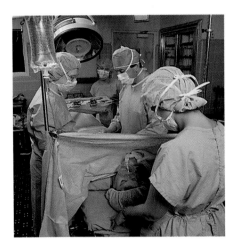

Skill and technology combine in the Clara Maass surgical suite.

treatment, is one of the largest in New Jersey.

The medical center's Maternal/ Child Department, home of The BirthDay Suite, has attained a position at the forefront of the field. An expectant mother can choose from a wide range of options. Using an innovative approach to reduce the stress on mother and child during

labor and delivery, the first underwater birth in a hospital in the eastern United States took place at Clara Maass in 1988.

Under the Jerseycare corporate umbrella, several health service programs were developed to meet the special needs of families, the elderly, busy working people requiring minor surgery, and local employers. Clara Maass Community Services is the Jerseycare affiliate devoted to direct delivery of health-maintenance and informational services. Its educational programs and diagnostic screenings are available to all members of the community, regardless of where they receive their medical care.

The Clara Maass Continuing Care Center is a nursing home, located on the medical center campus, committed to enhancing the quality of life of its adult residents. It provides a carefully planned program of services and activities in an atmosphere of warmth and understanding, stressing mobility as a means toward lifelong well-being.

Clara Maass operates three Same Day Services programs for patients who require minor procedures or

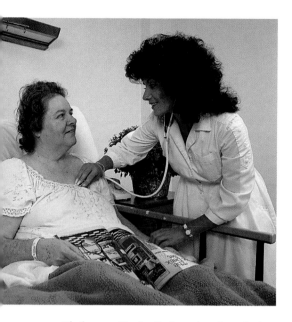

The human side of patient care is an important part of the Clara Maass tradition.

diagnostic tests: Same Day Surgery, Outpatient Surgery, and Non-Surgical Day Services. Same Day Surgery allows patients to leave the medical center, after postoperative observation, to recuperate at home.

To help local employers reduce workers' compensation costs while providing employees with quality treatment for work-related injury and illness, Clara Maass Medical Center offers the Med Plus program. This plan provides participating businesses with emergency medical care 24 hours per day, using the total health care resources of the medical center.

Since its inception in 1976, the Clara Maass Foundation has provided financial support for Clara Maass Medical Center. The foundation is devoted to fund raising and grant making on behalf of the Jerseycare network.

Premium Health Systems was created in 1987 to conduct business activities related to the interests of the other Jerseycare affiliates. The first major project of Premium Health Systems was building and managing a three-story medical office building, which houses an important new Imaging Center and

provides offices for Clara Maass physicians.

The Clara Maass School of Nursing offers preparation in as few as 22 months for a career as a registered nurse. Day, evening, and weekend programs, with both full-time and part-time registration options, provide opportunities for men and women to begin or change careers.

"Generation after generation, our employees, medical staff, volunteers, and trustees have given of themselves. This generosity, beautifully epitomized in the brief life of Clara Louise Maass, has perpetuated the traditions envisioned in our 1868 charter," says Robert S. Curtis, president and chief executive officer.

The medical center is named for nurse Clara Louise Maass. An 1895 graduate of the School of Nursing, she eventually became head nurse at the original hospital in Newark. Later she volunteered for service in the Philippines and, in 1900, in Cuba. There she heroically volun-

teered for an experiment to determine whether the stegomyia mosquito was responsible for transmitting yellow fever—a crucial first step in conquering the malady. It was this young nurse's sacrifice—her death—that demonstrated, beyond a doubt, the mosquito's culpability.

A young woman of great spirit and courage, Clara Maass exemplified the traditions of commitment to life and caring for others that the hospital has proudly continued through the decades.

"From our modest beginnings in Newark," Curtis says, "we have become one of the largest medical centers in the state of New Jersey. Our goal is to provide the diverse health care programs and services that our community needs today and well into the future."

The newest generation of linear accelerator provides precisely targeted X rays of up to 18 million electron volts.

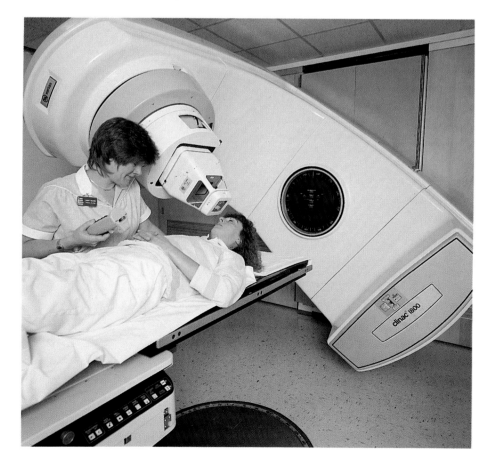

THE ESSEX SUBSTANCE ABUSE TREATMENT CENTER, INC.

The Essex Substance Abuse Treatment Center, Inc., is dedicated to providing a specialized program of treatment to opiate abusers, including the use of methadone. The program enables clients to turn their energies toward having productive lives. The Essex Substance Abuse Treatment Center staff works together to pull people toward life and away from drugs and possible death.

The center's medical staff consists of four highly qualified medical doctors, a nurse supervisor, a head nurse, two full-time nurses, and six part-time nurses. Clients receive comprehensive medical examinations prior to acceptance in the program, including AIDS testing. Whenever appropriate, the center provides drug-free counseling for clients rather than methadone treatment.

The center's 15 substance abuse counselors are qualified to do one-to-one counseling and run groups. Counseling is done on an individual basis and sometimes includes other family members. To ensure clients are seen with the proper frequency, counselors have a production quota to see clients in various phases of treatment.

Unlike many other facilities, the center provides adult day care for many clients, and has a van service

The Essex Substance Abuse Treatment Center, Inc., is dedicated to providing a specialized program of treatment to opiate abusers, enabling them to work toward productive, drug-free lives.

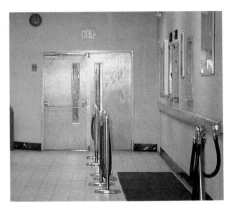

In addition to a staff of medical doctors, nurses, and counselors, the center provides adult day care for many clients and has van service to transport clients.

to transport clients.

Frequently counselors utilize the services of other mental health professionals on staff and community agencies in order to afford the client the best-possible treatment. The center is also affiliated with a network of similar organizations nationwide.

Detoxification treatment is composed of programs ranging from 21 days up to 180 days, during which an individual is physically withdrawn from heroin by systematic use of methadone. The client is administered diminishing doses of methadone until completion. At the end of the scheduled period the individual is free from physical addiction to narcotics.

Methadone Maintenance is a program designed to aid opiate-addicted clients who have failed to become drug free after going through various other forms of treatment. Eligibility for treatment is dictated by strict federal guidelines. This program is designed for individuals who are mature enough to be able to maintain productive and socially acceptable lives with the assistance of the social service staff. Individuals with serious emotional problems and/or non-opiate drug addiction are not acceptable for treatment and are often referred

elsewhere.

The Essex Substance Abuse Treatment Center functions as a liaison service between the client and area employers to enhance the employment possibilities of its clients through a comprehensive vocational testing, assessment, and referral program. Clients are urged to seek job training, obtain a G.E.D., and, if indicated, a college education.

The chief executive officer, Dr. Lennard, has more than 30 years of experience in drug treatment, including 20 years in the U.S. Air Force and several years in management of New Jersey State drug abuse facilities. Lennard credits much of his success to key staff members, including Frederick Stiff, director of security and transportation; Lewis Ware, director of clinical services; and George Worsley, director of the Detoxification Intake Unit.

According to Lennard, "Our existence is here for our clients. My staff and I are dedicated to establishing the best methadone treatment center possible."

RUTGERS, THE STATE UNIVERSITY OF NEW JERSEY

As Rutgers, The State University of New Jersey, stands on the threshold of becoming one of America's premier public research institutions, its Campus at Newark is a full participant in that ambition.

Offering academic excellence with equal access to all, Rutgers-Newark is a thriving center for undergraduate, graduate, professional, and continuing education—while assuring its students Rutgers' quality and stature and providing convenient daytime and evening classes for residents of the metropolitan North Jersey area.

The campus has been a key player in Newark's history and revitalization. It traces its roots to schools founded in the nineteenth century—schools that were consolidated as the University of Newark in the 1930s and became the Newark Campus of New Jersey's State University in 1946.

Today's modern complex, constructed largely during the past 20 years, is home to seven degree-granting units. The Newark College of Arts and Sciences and the evening division of University

Academic excellence with equal access to all, Rutgers-Newark is a thriving center for undergraduate, graduate, professional, and continuing education. Photo by A.J. Sundstrom

College-Newark both offer bachelor's degrees. On the graduate level, advanced degrees are offered by the Graduate School-Newark, the Graduate School of Management, the School of Law-Newark, and the School of Criminal Justice.

Research-oriented units are the Center for Molecular and Behavioral Neuroscience, the Institute of Animal Behavior, and the Center for Negotiation and Conflict Resolution. Resources also include the Institute of Jazz Studies, the John Cotton Dana Library, the Ackerson Law Library, the Criminal Justice Collection, the Robeson Center Art Gallery, and the landmark Golden Dome Gymnasium.

Most of Rutgers-Newark's 10,000 students commute from within the state, and many are older working people. In addition, graduate scholars from all over the United States

Above: A city skyscape with Rutgers' Golden Dome Gymnasium in the foreground. Photo by A.J. Sundstrom

and a number of foreign countries are attracted by the campus' academic reputation, its cosmopolitan flavor, and its easy access to Manhattan.

On-campus housing is available in a 350-bed apartment complex for graduate and professional students. Another 350-bed dormitory and dining facility for undergraduates is scheduled to open in 1990.

Some 500 distinguished faculty members not only teach the tradi-

Rutgers stands on the threshold of becoming one of America's premier public research institutions. Here a graduate student and professor work with an electron microscope. Photo by A.J. Sundstrom

tional humanities and inspire future scientists, they also focus on issues central to the city's, and the state's, prosperity. Five law clinics directly assist the public; nurses are trained to staff area hospitals; criminal justice graduates range from probation officers to judges; county and municipal leaders earn master's degrees in public administration; graduate management students gain hands-on experience through a cluster of centers as they serve small and minority businesses; and pre-college programs prepare Newark high school students for higher education.

Rutgers-Newark hosts a variety of public conferences, seminars, and workshops, and its educational options are complemented by programs in cooperation with the University of Medicine and Dentistry of New Jersey and joint degree programs with the New Jersey Institute of Technology. With nearby Essex Community College, the four institutions form the Council on Higher Education in Newark (CHEN); all four are active partners in Newark's revitalization.

NEWARK BETH ISRAEL MEDICAL CENTER

In 1901 the Daughters of Israel Hospital Association and the Hebrew Hospital and Dispensary Association joined forces to form the Newark Beth Israel Hospital. The nonsectarian hospital was located in a frame house on the corners of High and West Kinney streets in the city of Newark. Five years later an 84-bed modern brick hospital was built on the same site.

Always an institution dedicated to medical education, Newark Beth Israel acquired another Victorian mansion in 1920 for a school of nursing. In 1922 the hospital added a children's wing and expanded to 100 beds. The medical staff and board, interested in future growth, set their sights on a piece of farmland located in the southernmost area of the city. By 1923 ground had been broken on the present Lyons Avenue site for the most modern hospital in New Jersey at that time.

In 1928 a 350-bed, fireproof hospital was dedicated with a five-story school of nursing and a complete, four-story outpatient clinic building attached. The entire complex cost $3.3 million, of which one million dollars was pledged by a single donor, Felix Fuld. The hos-

With 545 beds and more than 2,800 employees, The Beth provides all of New Jersey with the finest health care services available and has built a reputation for excellence in health care.

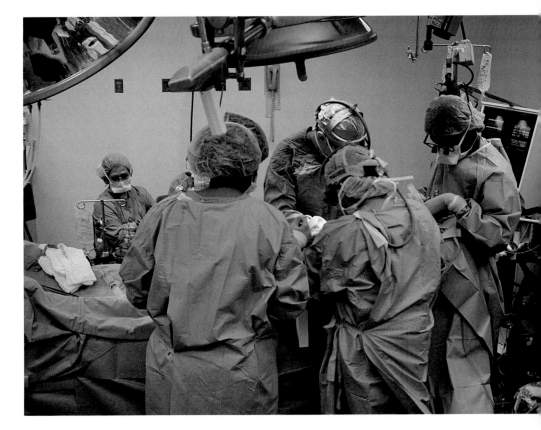

Newark Beth Israel Medical Center has the 10th-largest Cardiovascular Surgical Center in the United States, where more than 1,100 open-heart surgeries are performed annually. In this photo doctors are performing bypass surgery.

pital had barely become operational before the Great Depression hit, forcing the staff to handle only emergency patients.

During the late 1930s and 1940s physicians at NBIH concentrated on research. The first hospital-based blood bank was established; work was begun on the Rh factor, sulpha drugs, and blood derivatives. There were advances reported in the treatment of hemophilia, and the state's first hemophilia center opened. Pioneering work began in the fields of cardiac catheterization, cardiac pacemaker, biomedical engineering, hemodialysis, pulmonary function, and the treatment of vascular disorders.

The exodus of Jewish families from the Weequahic section of the city caused many to pressure the board of trustees to relocate the hospital to a more suburban area. However, in 1965 the commitment was made by the board to remain in Newark and to render the ultimate in patient care to the community immediately surrounding the hospital complex, as well as to all of New Jersey.

In 1969 the hospital officially became Newark Beth Israel Medical Center (NBIMC or The Beth), and an affiliation was effected with the University of Medicine and Dentistry of New Jersey. The medical center's historic master plan to replace and rejuvenate the facility began a six-phase renovation and construction program that lasted well into the 1980s. During those years the medical center grew, especially in its reputation for excellence in patient care, research, and medical education.

Pacemaker patients were introduced to a telephone monitoring system that made travel abroad possible, and the world's first American-made nuclear-powered pacemaker was implanted in patients at NBIMC. The state's first children's dialysis center opened, as did the organ preservation laboratory. A high-risk-infant transport system was developed to transport newborns from referral hospitals in support of NBIMC's designation as a Level III Perinatal Center. In 1983 The Beth received designation as the New Jersey Poison Information and Education System site.

The early 1980s also marked the opening of the Adult Day Care Center, the Cystic Fibrosis Chronic Lung Disease Pediatric Center, the Beth Prime Care Family Health Center, the Diabetes Treatment Center, and the Flo Okin Oncology Center.

In 1985 The Beth received approval for a heart transplant program and on January 1, 1986, performed New Jersey's first heart transplant operation. That same year the medical center's corporate restructuring created the parent company, Beth Health Care Services Corporation.

The guidance of the new parent corporation helped point the medical center toward the next century, while overseeing the activities of affiliated health care entities such as the freestanding Parkside Dialysis Center in Newark and Doctors on Duty, the immediate care center in Union, New Jersey.

In 1986 Newark Beth Israel joined Premier Hospitals Alliance, Inc. Premier is a voluntary alliance of 40 leading teaching hospitals and systems located nationwide. The alliance develops programs to help its owner hospitals generate cost savings, improve operating efficiency, and increase their revenue base and market share.

Today, with its 545 beds and more than 2,800 employees, The

Beth provides all of New Jersey with the finest health care services available and has built a reputation for excellence in health care. NBIMC is noted for an ultramodern, multimillion-dollar patient care pavilion with 12 surgical suites, 14 diagnostic radiology rooms, an active emergency department, and model patient care rooms.

Some of the medical center's many outstanding specialty services include a Sleep Disorders Center, a Pacemaker Center, a Community Mental Health Center, a Children's Center, a Women's Health Center, and the 10th-largest Cardiovascular Surgical Center in the United States, where more than 1,100 open-heart procedures are performed annually.

The Beth's most recent additions have included the Center for Geriatric Health Care, focusing on specialized care for the elderly; the development of Beth First, a private

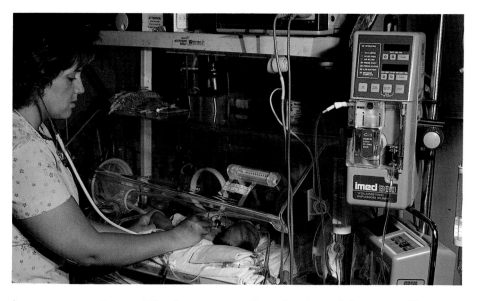

home-care service; and the formation of the Beth Health Care Foundation, a separate, nonprofit organization responsible for the medical center's fund-raising activities.

Physician training programs and fellowships reflect an important community service and a measure of the hospital's excellence. Leading physicians continue to be drawn to The Beth to teach, to

share, and be stimulated by contact with the best and brightest of upcoming generations of physicians. The affiliation with the University of Medicine and Dentistry of New Jersey has allied NBIMC with a nationally recognized leader in teaching and research.

In 1987 The Beth held true to its commitment of excellence with the start of the Phase VII construction program in an effort to meet the growing health care needs of residents from all over New Jersey. The $15-million program will include the construction of a new cardiac catheterization suite and modernization of the existing one; construc-

---

A high-risk-infant transport system was developed to transport newborns from referral hospitals in support of NBIMC's designation as a Level III Perinatal Center.

tion of a state-of-the-art cardiac surgery suite; the addition of a new critical care unit for cardiac surgical patients; and the complete reconstruction and relocation of the neonatal intensive care unit.

The fundamental mission and creed of the Newark Beth Israel Medical Center to treat "patients as people, not cases" remains as alive today as it did in 1901 when it was written.

NEW JERSEY INSTITUTE OF TECHNOLOGY

New Jersey Institute of Technology was founded in 1881 at the urging of the Newark Board of Trade. Since then it has maintained close ties with industry, preparing successive generations of students to assume leadership roles in an increasingly technological society.

The university offers programs in engineering, technology, architecture, computer science, actuarial science, management, mathematics, the sciences, and the humanities.

Enrollment exceeds 7,700 students, with one-third of the student body pursuing graduate degrees. Bachelor's, master's, doctoral, and professional degrees are offered through Newark College of Engineering, the School of Architecture, the College of Science and Liberal Arts, and the School of Industrial Management.

Graduate and undergraduate courses and programs are also offered at numerous off-campus sites. The Division of Continuing Education offers noncredit programs, at various locations,

designed to help working professionals keep up with advances in their fields. Extension programs in manufacturing and information sciences, and various services for small businesses are offered in cooperation with state and federal agencies.

The university is recognized nationwide for developing and offering enriching pre-college programs to educationally and economically disadvantaged young people.

Industry-university partnerships help researchers find solutions to major questions through the application of advanced technologies. Efforts are focused especially on protecting the environment, improving health through biotechnology, and strengthening the nation's competitive position through computer-integrated manufacturing and the skillful management of technology.

NJIT receives funding for research from corporations and state and federal agencies totaling approximately $10 million annually. The university is the location for two Advanced Technology Centers of the New Jersey Commission on Science and Technology, one in hazardous substance manage-

Sima Baghari, assistant professor of civil and environmental engineering at the New Jersey Institute of Technology, answers questions about aerial geographic survey photos of New Jersey.

New Jersey Institute of Technology offers programs in engineering, technology, architecture, computer science, actuarial science, management, mathematics, the sciences, and the humanities. Here Philip Goode, chairman of the Department of Physics, tests the graphics capabilities of newly installed computer equipment.

ment and the other in manufacturing systems research.

Approximately a quarter-million square feet of new facilities to house these and other research centers and laboratories are being constructed on NJIT's 40-acre campus. These buildings are part of a $125-million expansion program that includes increased student housing and physical education facilities, as well as classrooms, laboratories, and offices.

Says NJIT president Saul K. Fenster, "For more than a century New Jersey Institute of Technology (NJIT) has been tied closely to the economic development of the state and region. NJIT, the state, and the corporate community have been good partners from the post-Civil War industrial revolution to the revolution now taking place—the emergence of the information society."

Photo by Allan Reider

XVII

The Marketplace

Newark's retail establishments, service industries, and products are enjoyed by residents and visitors to the area.

Brantley Brothers Moving & Storage Inc., 332

A Nossa Terra, 333

Avitex, 334

New Jersey Wire Forming Co. Inc., 335

Olsten Services, 336-337

Brenner Business Interiors, 338-339

Hudson Blue Print Company, 340

City Fire Equipment Co., Inc., 341

Hilton Gateway and Towers Gateway Hotel Management Company, 342-343

Parsippany Hilton, 344-347

Photo by Rich Zila

BRANTLEY BROTHERS MOVING & STORAGE INC.

Brantley Brothers Moving and Storage Inc. serves corporate and residential clients nationwide.

Brantley Brothers provides a full range of services for its corporate and industrial clients from shipping merchandise worldwide to moving clients so efficiently they can resume operations almost immediately upon move in.

To meet the needs of corporate clients, the firm not only installs open-plan office furniture systems but also specializes in electronic and computer equipment moving. Trained crews use special equipment to move computers, communications equipment, broadcasting apparatus, and other electronic devices, and the company moves and stores trade show exhibits for corporate marketing departments.

Brantley Brothers extends the same care it gives corporate clients to its residential customers. To provide personalized service, an account executive is assigned to each move. The company's attention to detail includes packaging possessions and helping new residents notify the post office, utility companies, and other relevant concerns.

Brantley Brothers is able to select the right equipment for each job and pass on savings to customers because it operates a variety of vehicles, including air-ride trailers, trucks, and vans. With interstate rights for 29 states issued to Brantley Brothers by the Interstate Commerce Commission, the firm is able to deliver to all contiguous states.

The Brantley Brothers Moving and Storage Company was founded in 1966 by Malachia and Thomas Brantley. In 1971 the firm acquired its first storage facility, a 17,000-square-foot warehouse it still maintains. In 1986 the company purchased the former Sears' building, a landmark in Newark for years, and converted it into a storage facility.

In contrast to its beginnings as a home-based business, the firm maintains a high-tech computer system to track shipments and maintain control of stored goods. In addition to its capability as a mover, the company maintains 120,000 square feet of commercial storage.

The firm's major clients include AT&T, Merck, New Jersey Transit, New York City Transit, IBM, and several *Fortune* 500 companies. The organization is noted for finishing jobs in advance of the contracted time. It is "8A certified" under a federal program to encourage minority business. The certification has led to doing work for Fort Monmouth, the U.S. Army, Naval Air, the Small Business Administration, and the SBA's subsidiary divisions.

Brantley Brothers acquired its first storage facility in 1971—a 17,000-square-foot warehouse it still maintains. In 1986 the company purchased the former Sears' building, a landmark in Newark for years, and converted it into a storage facility.

In 1986 Brantley Brothers was recognized as one of the outstanding minority businesses in the United States and received a citation as the Minority Business of the Year from President Ronald Reagan, the Small Business Administration, and the New York/New Jersey Purchasing Council.

It is still a family business, and Isaac, the eldest son of Malachia, serves as vice-president/sales. The founder's son, Malachia Brantley, Jr., worked summers during high school and college and joined the firm on a full-time basis in 1982 as office manager. Katheryn Brantley, Malachia's wife, has been the company's bookkeeper from the beginning, and his other sons—Melvin and Tim—also take an active role in the business.

A NOSSA TERRA

A Nossa Terra, a retail clothing store started in 1969 on Ferry Street, is a family business that exemplifies the values of hard work, close family ties, and the spirit of entrepreneurship. The thriving enterprise is located in the heart of the Ironbound section of Newark, a fast-growing area known for its friendly neighborhood atmosphere and its many Spanish-Portuguese restaurants.

However, the true story of A Nossa Terra started with the arrival of 16-year-old Manuel Yglesias from Spain in 1926. His father, Tomas, was then working as a coal miner in Springfield, West Virginia. He became homesick and brought his wife and children—Manuel, Gerardo, and Mary—to the United States. In search of better wages,

Manuel Yglesias arrived from Spain in 1926. After World War II he opened a grocery store, Tropical Food Market, which became the largest restaurant supplier in the greater Newark area. Manuel Yglesias died in 1988 and is survived by his wife, children, brother, and sister.

the family soon moved to Philadelphia. There Manuel and his brother and sister attended school, and his father applied his trade as a stone cutter. Within a year the family moved again in search of work, this time to Brooklyn.

One of Manuel's first jobs was as a busboy in the Forest Hotel, New York. He and his brother also worked as waiters in the Waldorf-Astoria Hotel. During World War II Manuel served in the U.S. Army. Upon being discharged, he and his father went to Spain, where he met his wife, Herminia. When they returned to the United States, they bought a small grocery on Bruen Street, Newark; on their best day they made $40.00. They invested their savings and purchased a building and grocery store, Tropical Food Market, located around the corner on Elm Street.

Tropical Food turned out to be a sound but tough business that required working more than six days per week. Featuring products

that catered to local businesses and residents, the firm was one of the first European and Latin groceries in the area. Because of Manuel's dedication the operation became the largest restaurant supplier in the greater Newark area. This business, which he sold to his partner, is still serving most of the restaurants in Newark.

After many years in business, being a full-time housewife was not fulfilling to Herminia; she opened A Nossa Terra to make her day more complete. Soon, with his usual eagerness, Manuel was drawn back into business and convinced his sons to join him. Today the Yglesias family owns three businesses on Ferry Street.

Manuel and his wife were known by friends and family as hardworking individuals that made an effective business team, and their business successes became an inspiration to residents in the area. Manuel Yglesias died in 1988; he is survived by his wife, children, brother, and sister. His wife and children dedicate this profile to his memory.

Manuel Yglesias and his wife, Herminia, worked together to make A Nossa Terra a successful retail clothing store in the city's Ironbound section of New Jersey.

AVITEX

Style and quality are knitted into every yard of trimmings and specialty fabrics Avitex produces for its sports/activewear apparel clients.

The manufacturing process starts with the careful purchase of yarns compatible with today's fashions. Knitting, steaming, finishing, and cutting machines spin and whir throughout the Avitex factory until the fabrics are packaged and shipped to domestic and international apparel manufacturers.

Avitex knits flat and circular piece goods in solid, stripes, and jacquard patterns and in matching colors in piece-dyed or yarn-dyed fashion to coordinate trimmings for shorts and jacket waistbands, cuffs, and collars. Also produced is a full line of knitted fabrics and trimmings for military uniforms that meet government specifications.

Born in Israel, Avi N. Lazarovits earned an engineering degree and a Masters of Business Administration. He published a marketing article in *Harvard Review* that set the tone for his career in business. Considering himself "born for marketing," Lazarovits believes that creativity is at the heart of establishing a strong, marketing-driven manufacturing process.

"Diversity and the ability to respond to designers' and manufacturers' needs have made Avitex an expanding company," states Avi Lazarovits, founder of Avitex, seen here viewing a new product line set up.

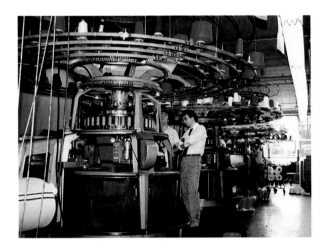

Using his creativity to give the firm that employed him an edge against foreign competition, he set up knitting mills to handle short-run specialty orders that overseas operations could not turn around quickly enough. The demand for this special service led to Lazarovits starting his own company in 1985.

Frequent participation in trade shows enables Lazarovits to further develop working relationships with garment manufacturers. Avitex enables customers to "dress" their clothing design lines in a variety of colors and fabrics that will attract more shoppers by offering a variety of styles.

According to Lazarovits, "Diversity and the ability to respond to designers' and manufacturers' needs have made Avitex an expanding company. Our national sales force extends the company's reach into many segments of the apparel industry. Our specialized equipment enables us to quickly provide knitted material to our clients' exact specifications."

By serving in an advisory capacity during the design process, Avitex can suggest alternatives for product construction that reduce cost without sacrificing style.

Lazarovits investigated several options before basing his operation in Newark. High New York rents and active support from New Jersey state and local government agencies convinced him. The site's proximity to New York's garment district and easy access from Newark Airport, Penn Station, the PATH, and

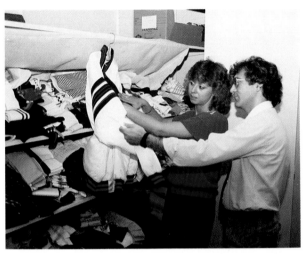

By serving in an advisory capacity during the design process, Avitex can suggest alternatives for product construction that reduce cost without sacrificing style.

to major highways provided further incentive.

Financial help from the Department of Commerce and Economic Development and the New Jersey Economic Development Authority enabled Lazarovits to buy equipment and transform a former sewing factory into a productive knitting operation. The building houses Avitex' 50,000-square-foot operation, with the remaining 25,000 square feet leased to a state agency.

The company attracts top-notch apparel operation workers by offering better working conditions and a positive work environment. Proud of the friendly, cooperative work atmosphere throughout the company, Lazarovits credits much of the firm's success to having outstanding people in management, sales, and production.

"We have succeeded by structuring our business to serve many types of clients and adapting to fit the economic conditions in our industry. We are seeking additional growth in specialized markets. As we expand our business, we will continue to improve our production capability. We are growing with the city of Newark."

NEW JERSEY WIRE FORMING CO. INC.

New Jersey Wire Forming Co. Inc., noted for its wire artistry, produces displays that reach out to the consumer and present products in the most attractive way possible.

Its displays are used for merchandising, advertising, graphic specialties, point of purchase, dispenser brackets, and pegboard hangers for marketing and merchandising of goods and products. Other applications include household bath and kitchen devices, industrial fixtures, medical products, architectural products, and communications hardware such as antennas.

New Jersey Wire Forming translates and designs its clients' technical requirements into visually pleasing effects. The aesthetic appeal of its products increases the market attraction and sales appeal of clients' products and merchandising aids.

Each display is designed and engineered to meet clients' product specifications. New Jersey Wire Forming has extensive design and production support to ensure customers' satisfaction from concept to the delivered product. With 50

Here Dan Iannascolio sets up a four slide. Photo by A.J. Sundstrom

These operators are doing gang welding on a multiwelder. Photo by A.J. Sundstrom

years' experience in wire forming, New Jersey Wire Forming Company has developed many techniques for cost effectiveness in both short- and long-run welding production.

New Jersey Wire Forming provides fast action and service on information, engineering, and quotes. Because of its depth in machine sizes, technical capability, and efficiency, New Jersey Wire offers production flexibility and versatility.

According to president and owner Daniel Iannascolio, "We are a very service-oriented company. Unlike many other domestic or foreign companies in our business, we do short-run projects and can provide quick turnaround to meet clients' needs."

Each New Jersey Wire Forming engineering/production project includes a quality checklist, with the process continuing throughout setup, trial, and full production to assure quality control at every step.

"Wire forming is, for the most part, what is known as four-slide work. We pride ourselves on making an art of it and use the four-slide wire-forming process in its most imaginative context. We produce

displays that are amazingly versatile in size and scope with a variety of finishes," says Iannascolio.

Iannascolio prides himself on the work of his nearly 25 employees—all from the Ironbound section of Newark. His plant foreman Daniel Pierre, who started as an apprentice while going to school at night, has worked closely with Iannascolio for two decades.

As a result of his and his employees' efforts, the firm has more than 200 accounts from Florida to California to its home in New Jersey. Clients such as General Electric, Troll Books, Revlon, Hubbell Lighting, and Grand Union are why New Jersey Wire Forming Co. Inc. has grown each year.

According to Iannascolio, "I believe in Newark. I'm proud that I grew up here and make my living here. People see our company in a more positive light because Newark's image has improved, and I expect the city to continue to improve even more."

OLSTEN SERVICES

Since its founding in 1950 Olsten has emerged as an industry leader, providing more than a half-billion hours of temporary work to business and industry throughout North America.

Olsten Services and Olsten Health Care Services are divisions of the Olsten Corporation, a leading provider of temporary help to business, government, industry, and health care. In 1988 the Olsten Corporation placed nearly 300,000 workers on assignments in the United States and Canada from its network of more than 520 owned, licensed, and franchised offices.

Olsten works with clients, large and small, who rely on its personal management expertise and professional service for temporary help in the areas of office services, office automation, legal support, professional accounting, records management, technical support, light industrial, and marketing services.

Olsten provides a cost-effective way for businesses to cut their personnel expenses by using flexible staffing when work flow varies. Temporaries handle special projects, work during seasonal peaks, and help companies meet urgent deadlines.

Olsten also helps employers control overhead costs such as health benefits and other fringe benefits including workers' compensation. Unemployment insurance as well as training and record keeping for taxes are all handled by Olsten Temporary Services. Companies using Olsten Services only have to pay employees the hourly rate, and Olsten handles the administrative details.

Responding to the growing needs of business and industry, Olsten has developed an exacting procedure for accessing temporary skills and abilities, which allows the firm to provide clients with temporary help that is precisely suited to their needs. The process begins with thorough interviewing, skill evaluation, and reference checking of every Olsten applicant to ensure that clients receive competent temporaries who can be immediately productive.

Olsten account representatives train in personnel planning, in the effective utilization of temporary help, and analyze work place needs for clients, which enables them to custom match a temporary worker's skills to a client's specifications, thus assuring quick and accurate placement.

Olsten prides itself on attracting and retaining motivated individuals who take satisfaction in a job well done. To recruit and retain the best-possible temporary work force, Olsten offers its temporaries a comprehensive benefits package. This

Frank N. Liguori, president of Olsten Corporation.

includes weekly pay, vacation with pay, skill improvement in word processing, and cross training on PCs that includes all major software programs and dedicated systems. Referral bonuses, a cash and hospital plan, and medical and dental insurance plans are among its other incentives.

According to Bill Olsten, chairman of the board and chief executive officer of the Olsten Corporation and a pioneer in the temporary help concept, "Our caring attitude makes

William Olsten, chairman of the board and chief executive officer of Olsten Corporation.

every temporary feel part of the Olsten family. This attitude has helped us retain loyal employees who value the respect and personal attention we pay them, and it has motivated our employees to perform to the very best of their abilities."

One of the fastest-growing temporary help agencies in the country, the company has grown by continuing to provide temporary personnel with more specialized and diversified skills. To keep pace with high technology, office personnel are trained to an extensive array of learning materials, including hands-on training, software programs, video training packages, and Olsten reference guides used as desk references.

In recent years Olsten has added specialized departments to meet corporate needs. These include professional accounting to answer the need for accountants, MBAs, CPAs, and auditors. The company also provides professional help to assist businesses with such projects as systems conversions, audit preparation, and fiscal closings. The firm's technical support service meets the demand for higher level skills, particularly in the areas of drafting and design.

Health Care Services is one of the

Olsten is a major employer in the city of Newark and throughout New Jersey, and is the only national temporary service that maintains offices in the city of Newark. Above photo by Michael Spozarsky

corporation's fastest-growing areas. Shortages in registered nurses precipitated heavy demand from hospitals for Olsten licensed professionals. Through a series of innovative recruitment activities, Olsten has been able to meet the demand, particularly in the highly specialized areas of intensive care, coronary critical care, and emergency room nursing.

Olsten is a major employer in Newark and throughout New Jersey. Its Newark office was the seventh to be opened by Bill Olsten in 1962. With 29 offices in New Jersey, Olsten is the only national temporary service that maintains offices in the city of Newark. Olsten's presence reflects its commitment to Newark as the state's largest city and to New Jersey as a leader in high-tech industries.

The company serves major *Fortune* 500 accounts statewide as well as small- and medium-size businesses. Its accounts include

firms such as Prudential, AT&T, PSE&G, Schering-Plough, Merck, ADP, and Hoffmann-LaRoche.

The company maintains an aggressive and innovative recruiting program in New Jersey that goes beyond classified ads. Local offices are supported with advertising in national magazines and newspapers and with direct-mail and radio promotions.

Olsten professional staffers participate in job fairs and actively recruit a wide variety of applicants from colleges, business schools, and service organizations. The firm also offers prizes to motivate recommendations so new temporaries will join the work force.

The company's growth in New Jersey has reflected the economic growth of the state, particularly the influx of large corporations and

high-tech business, which has created a demand for Olsten Services.

The company takes an active role in community affairs, including the Greater Newark Chamber of Commerce, the Black Churchmen's Association, and the United Way. In 1988 the firm provided the United Way with free temporary help during a fund-raising drive.

The company is proud of helping women in many single-parent families make the transition back into the work force. And it helps many college students who work during vacations to gain business experience.

According to New Jersey regional director, Joseph T. Palestina, "If you have the skills, attitude, and desire, Olsten will find the job for you. Our temps are our assets. We are deeply committed to them."

BRENNER BUSINESS INTERIORS

Brenner Business Interiors (BBI), a Newark-based interior office planning service, is one of the top 50 suppliers of open-area office systems and furniture in the country. Corporate management personnel use BBI as the "one source" for the overall coordination and continuity of projects, from prelease space planning straight through to the specification, selection, and procurement of furniture.

BBI has created finely tuned customized office environments for many corporations of varied sizes relocating to and within New Jersey. The major portion of the firm's projects range from 10,000 to 30,000 square feet. BBI's prelease space planning services ensure clients that their facility and furnishing investment is a sound one.

"The two are very closely related," states company president Robert Brenner, who roughly 15 years ago recognized the need for a professional service that could incorporate space planning services with furniture recommendations, procurement, and installation. As a result, Brenner assembled a unique group of experts comprised of space planning professionals, many of whom have architectural degrees and backgrounds. Brenner says,

Creating finely tuned customized office environments for many corporations of various sizes relocating to and within New Jersey defines the aim and occupation of Brenner Business Interiors.

"The group's primary focus is to provide services to the corporate user—prior to signing a new lease for space—that will save both time and money. Professional interior space evaluation at the prelease stage is most effective in comparing the variables of available facilities as well as the costs of functionalizing the space. Every aspect of the relocation is examined prior to the lease signing."

Brokers and developers also take advantage of prelease space planning services, which enables them to quickly deliver facility recommendations that meet or exceed the prospective tenant's space needs, along with substantial support of those recommendations on paper, in order to close the deal.

Quality in the production of plans is equally important. Creatively designing the use of space is only one aspect of the planning process. Producing working drawings that spell out to the potential user the least expensive

way to build a space is just as critical. In 30 years of experience and involvement in architectural design, Brenner has come to know the standards and procedures that allow clients to save both time and money.

Following space programming, Brenner Business Interiors develops interior decorative concepts with respect to the coordination of floor and wall finishes, appropriate lighting, and functional furniture.

BBI's Contract Furnishings Group handles all the logistics for a well-planned and -coordinated systems furniture project. By utilizing both divisions of BBI, corporate management can rely on one firm to do everything from creating the initial plan to installing the furniture, all accomplished within critical time and budgetary guidelines.

According to Brenner, "We accept total responsibility for the end result, and that means we support design concepts, meet commitments, stand by the products we represent, make certain that deliveries are on time, supervise the installation, and expedite any required

Encompassing the individual space and furniture needs of each corporation it serves, Brenner Business Interiors gives many relocating corporations a viable means of creating highly functional office surroundings.

follow-up service. These combined services represent one point of control, which is something very few other dealerships in the country can offer."

With 65 years in the business, BBI has built relationships with a broad range of manufacturers that represent a large variety of products that can be incorporated into most projects and designs. "We offer to our clients the knowledge and experience necessary to obtain the best values across the board. We buy directly from manufacturers and mills, bypassing all middlemen. Millions of dollars in purchases annually gives us the ability to favorably negotiate corporate purchasing agreements on behalf of our clients.

"The project management process begins with a series of interviews designed to establish budgetary guidelines and the critical dates necessary to establish a realistic time frame for furniture ordering, manufacturing, shipping, and installation. Facts uncovered from these interviews also contribute to the basis of our recommendations for furnishing and environmental systems," Brenner adds.

Another aspect of the project management effort includes the preparation of detailed purchase orders, along with special tagging instructions to facilitate delivery of products in the proper sequence and to designated areas.

A detailed list of furnishings by item, quantity, description, price, and tagging instruction is entered into a data base for future orders and service information.

All plans, orders, and deliveries are checked and rechecked to ensure a smooth project with complete coverage. Recounting thousands of parts and reverifying every

Brenner Business Interiors, the Newark-based interior office planning service, is one of the top 50 suppliers of open-area office systems and furniture in the country, providing professional service that incorporates space planning services with furniture recommendations, procurement, and installation.

order number are all part of standard procedure. Coded installation plans and workstation diagrams are created to convey assembly requirements to a knowledgeable team of installers who see to it that every component is placed properly, adjusted, leveled, and cleaned. Each job is concluded by a thorough inspection.

In addition to brisk furniture sales on a strictly purchase basis, Brenner Business Interiors has become strongly involved in contract furniture leasing arrangements as well. "We offer one of the most competitive leasing arrangement capabilities in the New Jersey market. Our relationships with some of the largest financial institutions enable us to be highly creative with this purchasing alternative. Our leasing group takes an aggressive approach in providing our clients with the best, most suitable arrangements to meet their needs, while a wide variety of product line availabilities also give us a tremendous amount of flexibility," Brenner states.

The services of the Interior Planning Group, the Contract Furnishings Group, and the Project Management Group of Brenner Business Interiors have been responsible for providing many relocating corporations with a viable means of creating highly functional office surroundings that have ultimately increased worker productivity as well as corporate profitability.

HUDSON BLUE PRINT COMPANY

Hudson Blue Print Company was founded in 1927 by William G. Gerhard, an engineer familiar with the specialized needs of architects, engineers, designers, and manufacturers.

Starting with just one blueprint machine and one photostat machine in Jersey City, the company moved to Newark in 1940 and grew by adding Diazo blueline services, photo offset, xerography, photo reproduction services, and drafting supply sales. The company derived its name from its original headquarters in Hudson County.

Hudson's successes have been based on maintaining quality control and giving prompt service. Computerized cameras, high-speed Xerox copiers, oversize electrostatic copiers (up to 36 inches wide), automated Diazo white printers, and the latest additions—laser color copiers and a high-speed, modem-based, plotter service—have all played major parts in Hudson's reprographic service developments.

Hudson's duplicating equipment, the most modern and versatile in the industry, can duplicate

In 1969 Hudson Blue Print Company moved to its corporate headquarters in Irvington, where it currently occupies a 15,000-square-foot facility at 883 Clinton Avenue.

from nearly any type of original, including typed pages, paste-ups, printed pages, colored forms, ball-point pen, pencil, and crayon. The company can duplicate any quantity by using high-tech equipment and its personnel, who boast years of experience. The advantages Hudson Blue Print offers the busy professional result in both time and cost savings.

Because of its growth, additional space was required. Consequently, Hudson moved to Irvington in 1969, where it now has its 15,000-square-foot headquarters at 883 Clinton Avenue. With its proximity to Newark and the Garden State Parkway, Hudson can serve nearly all of New Jersey with its prompt pick-up and delivery and while-you-wait service.

"We constantly try to improve and to add to our services. Today we offer the most complete and modern reproduction service in New Jersey. Our main objective, through a continued growth program, is to offer a complete service to our customers with the highest quality for the lowest price and fastest turnaround. The key to our business has and always will be customer service. We at Hudson Blue Print are the 'problem solvers,' consultants to serve every customer's needs," says Michael F. Bartow,

Michael F. Bartow, chief executive officer of Hudson Blue Print Company.

chief executive officer.

The firm maintains a service staff on premises for its Diazo and drafting machines, as well as any other equipment it sells. For quick service, the company stocks a host of parts and supplies. Its experts test and guarantee all equipment, including furniture. Everything is carefully examined by the critical eye of an expert at Hudson.

In June 1985 Hudson returned to Newark with a satellite store in the Gateway III Concourse to service the needs for office supplies and furniture as well as oversize, high-speed, and color copying services.

States Hudson Blue Print Company president Bartow, "Because of our in-depth knowledge of reproduction, we can tell you exactly what is needed and how long it takes to bring any reproduction job to completion. Any piece of equipment bought from Hudson has already been tested by our experts. We stand behind everything we sell, plus guarantee and service all our machinery and furniture."

CITY FIRE EQUIPMENT CO., INC.

A Newark-born fire fighter, who sought additional means of income to support his family, proved that you can run a successful business if you stick to what you know.

In 1954 William Bretzger, Sr., opened the doors of City Fire Extinguisher and began refilling fire extinguishers out of a small garage in Newark. In 1962 a corporation was born, and City Fire Extinguisher became City Fire Equipment Co., Inc. And, in 1983, in an effort to offer a more complete fire protection package, City Fire opened a new systems division. Capable of installing, serving, and maintaining fire alarm systems, specialized fire suppression systems, and automatic

City Fire Equipment Co. is the choice of commercial, industrial, construction, and specialized firms for all of their fire safety requirements.

fire sprinkler systems, this new division is run by William Bretzger IV. After three moves Bretzger purchased a building on Ferry Street in the Ironbound section of Newark, and has operated the business from that address since then.

Today City Fire Equipment Co. is the choice of commercial, industrial, construction, and specialized firms for all their fire and safety requirements. Its customers are as diverse as the business world itself: office and apartment complexes, restaurants and kitchens, airports and terminals, computer rooms and

City Fire Equipment Co. provides complete hydrostatic servicing of both liquid and powder extinguishers.

warehouses, factories and shopping malls, to name just a few.

Every City Fire Equipment Co. representative conducts surveys and consults with each client to determine fire safety needs for individual businesses and locations. Then the representative recommends the best possible plan, system, and equipment to meet those requirements. After the fire safety plan is implemented, the firm conducts fire safety seminars at the customer's location.

All service is performed to manufacturers' standards and meets all guidelines listed in the *National Fire Protection Association Pamphlet.* City Fire Equipment Co. is also a Department of Transportation-certified facility with technicians and supervisors qualified to perform critical hydrostatic testing of carbon dioxide equipment.

City Fire provides complete hydrostatic servicing of both liquid and powder extinguishers. The firm also recharges all types of extinguishers using state-of-the-art recharging apparatus to assure accuracy. City Fire repairs self-contained breathing apparatus and airline respirators and recharges all S.C.B.A. tanks. For its customers' convenience, the firm also offers fire hose testing.

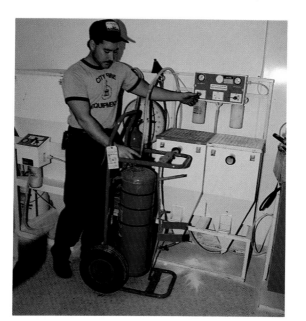

City Fire Equipment Co., Inc., has operated out of a building in the Ironbound section of Newark since 1962.

City Fire Equipment Co. maintains a fleet of self-contained repair shops ready to bring full service to its clients' locations, and the organization's mobile unit technicians charge and refill all types of fire extinguishers. City Fire's large mobile parts supply is ready for on-the-spot repairs of all types of fire extinguishers and fire protection systems.

Presently, Bill Sr. and Bill III share ownership in City Fire Equipment Co., Inc., and Paul McGrath is vice-president and general manager. The cumulative years of the three men exceed 75 in the fire equipment business.

According to Bill Bretzger, Sr., "Our goal is to be the best fire equipment sales and service company in the fire protection industry. Our experience in fire safety and understanding business needs speaks for itself."

HILTON GATEWAY AND TOWERS
GATEWAY HOTEL MANAGEMENT COMPANY

The Hilton Gateway and Towers, in the largest and most prestigious office hotel and retail complex in New Jersey, is closer to more corporate offices than any other hotel in the state. According to general manager Michael J. Hobbs, "The Hilton Gateway and Towers enjoys an excellent location inside the Gateway Center with direct indoor access to New Jersey Transit, PATH, and Amtrak trains, which provide inexpensive travel to Madison Square Garden or the World Trade Center in 15 or 20 minutes. The hotel is also just 15 minutes from Newark International Airport and the Meadowlands Sports Complex, making the location ideal for the business or leisure traveler."

The hotel's 254 luxury guest rooms and suites are designed with the customer's comfort in mind. In addition to each room's exceptional

The Hilton Gateway and Towers' excellent location inside the Gateway Center makes it the ideal choice for the business or leisure traveler.

amenities, full health club facilities are right in Gateway Center, and guests can enjoy its rooftop swimming pool in season.

For guests' special needs, a separate Towers Level offers the attentive service of a professional concierge and the executive environment of a private club. The Towers Club Lounge is the perfect setting for conducting business, planning the day's activities, or simply relaxing.

Known for its "home away from home" atmosphere, the Hilton

Gateway and Towers offers elegant dining, casual "fun fare," or quiet cocktails in three restaurants and lounges. Newly remodeled meeting and banquet facilities—11 in all—are managed by an experienced staff, and a talented chef and professional kitchen cater to individual needs with enthusiasm and creativity.

The hotel is managed by the Gateway Hotel Management Company, whose creative approach offers comprehensive professional management and productive systems of operations.

John Connolly, president of Gateway Hotel Management Company, and his staff have been highly successful in turning hotels into profitable ventures through specialized management, marketing, and operational programs. These include its successful management of two properties for the Prudential Insurance Company of America, the Hilton Gateway and Towers in

Newark since 1976, and the Midland Hilton in Midland, Texas, since 1982. Connolly has more than 20 years of proven experience in the hotel management field.

According to Connolly, "Our success in Newark is attributable to the dedication of our management team, many of whom have been with us in excess of 10 years. We are firmly committed to the principle that people make the difference in service and profitability."

Gateway Hotel Management Company offers a full range of services, from feasibility studies to opening planning, in addition to responsible management of hotel investors' assets. The personal touch that Connolly and his staff pride themselves on ensures that investors will have a comprehensive staff-training program with emphasis on rooms management, food and beverage management, personnel recruiting, and technical assistance. Further, Gateway has instituted a streamlined and standardized system of accounting and controls for maximum results, ensuring solid protection of the owner's investment.

Exemplifying the Hilton Gateway's personal touch is its role as a leader in community service in Newark. When Connolly began in 1976 to revitalize what had been a poorly managed hotel facility, he realized his efforts would be rewarded because he could foresee the coming revitalization of Newark. His staff, who have helped bring the hotel to its current prominence, include Lou Dell'Ermo, (a retired Newark police officer), director of life safety; Katherine Mosberg, front office manager, specialist in guest relations training; Maria Perez, reservations manager noted for her excellent work with corporate clients; and Michael J. Hobbs, general manager.

According to Hobbs, "Based on its current rate of development, we see a bright future for Newark. Our location in a vital business community with easy access to New York has enabled the Hilton Gateway and Towers to become a great asset to the local business community."

Connolly and his team at the Hilton Gateway and Towers have played a leading role in the economic development of the Gateway area. In addition to his work with the chamber of commerce and his being a founder of the Convention Business Bureau, Connolly has worked closely with Monsignor Hourihan of St. John's Roman Catholic Church on Mulberry Street.

Both St. John's and the Hilton have grown together over the years. Connolly and Hourihan became close friends and have worked

The Hilton Gateway and Towers offers elegant dining, casual "fun fare," or quiet cocktails in three restaurants and lounges.

together to make the hotel and St. John's successful. As the hotel prospered, St. John's prospered. In fact, Connolly and his family were the first family in the St. John's parish when they lived at the hotel during the first seven years of his tenure at Gateway. Hourihan's efforts have enabled St. John's to develop an extraordinary program to feed Newark's hungry and homeless. In 1987 the parish served more than 675,000 meals. Connolly and his staff members have assisted with fund raising and have provided substantial support for this effort.

Reflecting the close relationship between St. John's and the Hilton Gateway and Towers, Prudential Insurance built an interfaith chapel at the Gateway Center where the monsignor conducts Mass and hosts other interfaith services. According to Lou Dell'Ermo, "The chapel has added greatly to the feeling of community that's present throughout the Gateway complex."

Echoing this sentiment, Hourihan believes, "The business community is interested not only in business but in people. The business community has played an active role in civic and community affairs. We are a city that has a sense of neighborhood. One example of this is the 300 volunteers from the business community and from local residents who assist us in the food program."

"As the city has changed, the business community has changed by tak-

The rooftop pool is just one of the extra amenities offered at the Hilton Gateway.

ing an active role in the community. What is good for Newark is good for New Jersey," Connolly continues. "We need business, government, and a spiritual force so that the community works together."

According to Caroll Gerathy, a retired Prudential senior vice-president who currently works as a consultant for Prudential and was instrumental in the development of Gateway and the upgrading of the Penn Station area in Newark, "We are very optimistic about the future of Newark. Our operation has developed a response to the demands from the business community. We are proud to play a continuing role in Newark's revitalization."

PARSIPPANY HILTON

Northern New Jersey's largest new hotel is nestled in 15.7 landscaped acres of Garden State countryside. Located on Route 10 between Routes 287 and 202, with easy access to Routes 80, 280, and 46, the Parsippany Hilton features 508 superbly furnished guest rooms and 27 public meeting rooms for virtually any kind of business gathering or social function.

Attention to detail defines the true essence of the Parsippany Hilton, and that attention to detail makes the difference between arranging a meeting and creating an event. Detailed interiors and elegant, understated service set the Parsippany Hilton apart and make a world of difference in the quality of a guest's stay.

The Parsippany Hilton earned national recognition when the American Automobile Association selected the hotel to receive its Four Diamond Award, an honor achieved by only 7 percent of the 18,000 approved accommodations reviewed by AAA.

The only Four Diamond hotel property in the three-county area of Morris, Essex, and Union, the Parsippany Hilton was awarded this rating for possessing exceptional accommodations, amenities, and personnel. The hotel and its rating are featured in AAA tour books.

According to Rafael Juan, general manager of the Parsippany Hilton and a 20-year veteran of the Hilton Corporation, "We are proud of our entire staff. We've put a great deal of care and imagination into the Parsippany Hilton to create a truly unusual hotel—one that is sophisticated and elegant, yet warm and friendly. We strive for perfection, and we provide a meticulously run yet comfortable and relaxed place for the business and leisure traveler."

Possessing exceptional accommodations, amenities, and personnel, the Parsippany Hotel is the newest four-diamond hotel in the three-county area of Morris, Essex, and Union, New Jersey.

The staff members of the Parsippany Hilton are creative people who care about their guests' needs. From the concierge to the waiters to the bellmen to the wine steward, the hotel's personnel are trained to give guests the comfort, luxury, and service that reflect the high standards set by Hilton Hotels worldwide.

According to Ken Simmons, hotel director of sales, "Every one on our staff feels personally responsible for the quality of our guests' stay. This effort to please, to satisfy our guests, pervades throughout. We pride ourselves on the fact that our people are more than courteous; they are gracious and genuinely concerned

With skylights, lush greenery, flowers, black lac-quered screens, and Oriental decor, the Atrium Court creates an exotic and relaxing locale within a hotel lounge setting.

with the guests' comfort."

Efficient service begins with making check in as smooth and effortless as possible via a comput-erized system. In the timeless tradi-tion of European hotels, the concierge desk is near the registra-tion area for guests' convenience. Information is available on taxis, airport shuttle service, tours (including Atlantic City), theater tickets, sports and recreational events, and points of local interest. Whatever the guests' concerns, the concierge is always attentive to their requests.

One of the most dramatic focal points is the hotel's luxurious Atrium Court. Not only does it pro-vide an entrance into a portrait of aesthetic beauty, but it's also pre-cisely arranged for convenient access to suites, meeting rooms, recreation facilities, and restaurants.

The Atrium is the ideal place to meet business associates or friends for a quiet drink. The airy ambience of classical open-seating areas makes it a wonderful place to con-duct informal business meetings.

Skylights, lush greenery, and flowers are a perfect backdrop for a melody from the hotel's baby grand piano. Black-lacquered screens and

Oriental decor comple-ment the leafy beauty of ficus trees, an indoor waterfall, and huge sus-pended hanging plants. A few steps away is the Piano Bar, open seven days per week, providing an intimate setting for lis-tening and relaxing.

The Parsippany Hilton offers an Executive Business Service for busi-ness travelers' secretarial needs, valet service, safe-deposit boxes, car rental referral, airport limousines, foreign exchange, medical and dental refer-ral, floral services, and a gift shop. These courtesies are provided to make the traveler's stay as pleasant as possible.

The Parsippany Hilton is noted for offering diners something unique for every palate. In 1988 and 1989 the hotel received *New Jersey Monthly*'s Fifth Annual Readers' Choice Award for having the best brunch in northern New Jersey.

The Atrium is the stage for this award-winning brunch. A dazzling selection of international foods is offered every Sunday to eager diners. The bountiful feast, creat-ed by chef Victor Ingrid and his staff, features homemade Belgian waffles, fresh-baked breads, made-to-order omelets, traditional and unusual salads, and an extensive dessert selection.

Comments food and beverage direc-tor Phillip Deblinger, "I am proud of our entire staff. We are honored to receive this prestigious award and will con-

tinue to maintain the high standards of the Parsippany Hilton."

Livingston's offers lavish conti-nental cuisine. Changing its menu four times per year, it provides din-ers with the best of each season in a tantalizing array of dishes. Livingston's has one of the most extensive wine selections in north-ern New Jersey. Each day three wine selections are featured, and a myriad of domestic and foreign wines are also available. Discreet service and understated elegance are an integral part of Livingston's success.

Like a flowered clearing in the woods, The Meadows provides an open-air atmosphere and an infor-mal approach to dining. It is a spe-cial place for any meal, offering such dishes as Salad Nicoise from the Light Fare menu or Lamb Chops

Livingston's is part of the hotel's fine dining experience. Specializing in continental cuisine, Livingston's understated elegance and excellent service, including its extensive wine list, provides the basis for the restaurant's local renown.

The 10,000-square-foot Grand Ballroom serves as a conference room or as a commercial show exhibit space as well as providing the more traditional space for parties, banquets, and other occasions.

Marechale, one of the many Meadows specialties.

The Parsippany Hilton entertains guests with music and dancing at Shadows, which is open six nights per week and offers upbeat music with a sophisticated disc jockey. The unusual greenhouse windows and glassed decor are designed to offer a view of both the inside and the outside of the hotel.

The Parsippany Hilton Hotel has 508 newly furnished rooms and 27 public meeting rooms with complete conference facilities. An exceptional staff of more than 400 is available to handle conference or function needs. All conference facilities are centrally located on the first level to maximize the success of any business agenda.

The impeccably decorated facilities are well lit, soundproof, and equipped with audiovisual systems and closed-circuit television. Most meeting rooms have a built-in screen, a blackboard, and sliding glass doors or windows. Rooms are climate controlled, so a long or short meeting is always comfortable.

The 12 Algonquin rooms are fitted with wet bars, small refrigerators, bathrooms, and house phones. Reflecting the hotel's attention to detail, tables are

freshly laid out with clean pads, sharpened pencils, and a sparkling beverage tray.

The epitome of refined good taste, the polished natural wood table and thickly padded upholstered armchairs of the board room provide the atmosphere needed for high-level decision making.

The 10,000-square-foot Grand Ballroom is another outstanding conference feature. It can adapt to exhibit use for any kind of commer-

cial show and can also be divided into four separate rooms for meeting use. To accommodate conference needs, the ballroom can be set up theater style, holding up to 1,250 people.

The Parsippany Hilton's fine catering service brings rich distinction to each affair. The Grand Ballroom holds more than 1,000 people. Recently renovated, the Grand Ballroom creates a warm country feeling that softens the immensity of the ballroom while enhancing its sophisticated elegance with Oriental overtones.

The majestic Grand Ballroom is handsomely appointed with a 16-foot mirrored ceiling and is dressed in rose and maroon. A separate ballroom entrance provides the privacy and exclusive background for a banquet, wedding, or bar mitzvah. There is also an assembly area outside the ballroom, creating a perfect location for predinner cocktails.

Small and large affairs are equally welcome at the Parsippany Hilton. Luscious hors d'oeuvres include everything from shrimp tempura to baby lamb chops. Canapes range from fresh Nova Scotia salmon and caviar to ham-and-cheese ribbons.

The hotel's gourmet chefs are devoted to the fine art of presentation. Each dish is prepared carefully with fresh ingredients and served with a flourish. Many dishes are prepared before the diners' eyes—dishes that run the gamut in international flavor.

Coffee breaks take on artistic proportions with monthly theme decorations—a refreshing change of pace, that is designed to stimulate conversation.

Theme parties and tailored menus are the norm at the Parsippany Hilton. Flexible, personal service is the cornerstone of the hotel's catering. The expertly trained catering staff can provide anything from the formal pageantry of white-glove service to the natural beauty of dining under tents outdoors.

All the hotel's rooms are generous in size and amenities. Spacious guest accommodations are tastefully decorated in a Queen Anne decor of blue and rose. Chippendale accent pieces, live plants, and Oriental art give the rooms warmth and color.

House phones, alarm clocks, and climate control are standard in all rooms. For the guests' relaxation, color televisions, in-room movies, HBO, ESPN, and CNN are also standard. Wake-up calls are cheerful and accurate, and room service is responsive to every guest's needs.

Details, such as an additional vanity in most rooms and a bridge desk with an extra phone, show that nothing has been overlooked for the traveler's comfort. An advanced electronic fire-detection and automatic sprinkler system ensures safety.

The Hilton Family Plan allows children to stay free with their parents. Single rates apply to each additional room for the family.

The Parsippany Hilton offers two outstanding options for the traveler—a variety of multipurpose parlors, and large, elegant rooms with concealed bedding. A guest scheduled to entertain can use the penthouse, and deluxe suites feature gleaming wet bars, living rooms, and spiral staircases. The penthouse suite is dramatically appointed with an eye-catching loft bedroom. Both offer charming alternatives for informal business gatherings.

A wide range of recreational facilities offers pleasure and relaxation. The indoor and outdoor pools are adjacent to one another off the Atrium Lounge. At the outdoor pool, cocktails and light snacks are available in season. The indoor pool includes a Jacuzzi.

A fully equipped exercise room, featuring a Universal Gym and a tanning bed, is ideally located near both pools. A basketball court, two well-lit tennis courts, and a volleyball court are also available. For young children, the hotel's play area is complete with jungle gym and slides. Other unique features for the fitness-minded include jogging routes, bicycle rental, and prearranged golfing at an exclusive country club golf course.

According to Rafael Juan, "The Parsippany Hilton is a first-class Hilton Hotel, and we are committed to continue to strengthen our position as the business and leisure traveler's first choice in Northern New Jersey."

The hotel's recreational facilities include an indoor and outdoor pool and a Jacuzzi.

PATRONS

The following individuals, companies, and organizations have made a valuable commitment to the quality of this publication. Windsor Publications and The Greater Newark Chamber of Commerce gratefully acknowledge their participation in *Greater Newark: A Microcosm of America.*

Apruzzese, McDermott, Mastro & Murphy*
AT&T*
Avitex*
Bellemead Development Corporation*
Blue Cross and Blue Shield of New Jersey*
Brantley Brothers Moving & Storage Inc.*
Brenner Business Interiors*
Carpenter, Bennett & Morrissey*
Cathedral Healthcare System*
Channel 9 WWOR-TV*
City Federal Savings Bank*
City Fire Equipment Co., Inc.*
City National Bank of New Jersey*
Clapp & Eisenberg*
Continental Airlines*
Crummy, Del Deo, Dolan, Griffinger & Vecchione*
The CTS Group*
Damon G. Douglas Company Construction Managers/General Contractors*
The Essex Substance Abuse Treatment Center, Inc.*
First Fidelity Bank*
Gannett Outdoor of New Jersey*
The Henkind-Engel Organization*
Hilton Gateway and Towers Gateway Hotel Management Company*
K. Hovnanian Enterprises Inc.*
Howard Savings Bank*
Hudson Blue Print Company*
Kean College*
Samuel Klein and Company Certified Public Accountants*

Lewis Advertising Agency*
Lowenstein, Sandler, Kohl, Fisher & Boylan*
LS Transit Systems*
Clara Maass Medical Center*
McCarter & English*
Maher Terminals, Inc.*
Midlantic Corporation*
The Mutual Benefit Companies*
National Westminster Bank NJ*
Newark Beth Israel Medical Center*
New Community Corporation*
New Jersey Bell*
New Jersey Institute of Technology*
New Jersey Wire Forming Co. Inc.*
NJ Transit*
A Nossa Terra*
Olsten Services*
Orange, Newark, Elizabeth Bus, Inc.*
Parsippany Hilton*
Penn Federal Savings Bank*
The Port Authority of New York and New Jersey*
The Prudential Insurance Company of America*
PSE&G*
Rutgers, The State University of New Jersey*
Seton Hall University School of Law*
Stryker, Tams & Dill*
Torcon, Inc.*
UMDNJ-University Hospital*
United Hospitals Medical Center*
The University of Medicine and Dentistry of New Jersey*
WBGO-FM/88.3*
Wharton/Lyon & Lyon*
Z100 WHTZ Radio*

*Participants in Part II, Greater Newark's Enterprises. The profiles of these companies and organizations appear in chapters 13 through 17, beginning on page 230.

BIBLIOGRAPHY

Chapter 1
A HISTORICAL PERSPECTIVE
Newark's rich cultural heritage and cosmopolitan flavor are rooted in a diverse ethnic background and colorful local history.

Asbury Park Press. Asbury Park, N.J.

Atkinson. *History of Newark, New Jersey.* 1878.

Becker, Donald W. *Indian Place Names in New Jersey.* Cedar Grove, N.J.: Phillips-Campbell Publishing Co., 1964

Cummings, Charles. *Newark: An American City.* Newark: Newark Bicentennial Commission/Newark Public Library, 1976.

The International Association of Newarks. Muriel L. Wiesen, co-founder, 1968.

McSharry, John T., ed. *Historical Newark in Bronze.* Newark: The Schoolmen's Club of Newark, 1966.

Newark: Genesis of a City. New Jersey Humanities Project sponsored by the Rutgers NCAS-Newark Museum Training Program, the Newark Public Library, and Robeson Campus Center, 1981.

The New Columbia Encyclopedia. New York: Columbia University Press, 1975.

Rice, Arnold S. *Newark: A Chronological & Documentary History, 1666-1970.* New Jersey: Oceana Publications, Inc., 1977.

Star-Ledger. Newark, N.J.

Studley, Miriam V. *When Newark Was Younger.* From a series of articles in the *Newark News.* April 10, 1949-May 28, 1950.

Chapter 2
GEOGRAPHY AND TRANSPORTATION
Newark's strategic location astride the most important transportation corridor in the East, serving more than 50 million people, has richly enhanced its diversity and vitality over the last three centuries.

Arend, Geoffrey. *Air World's Great Airports,* New York: Air Cargo News, Inc., 1978.

Commemorating the Opening of Pennsylvania Station. Pennsylvania Railroad, March 23, 1935.

The Draft Preliminary State Development and Redevelopment Plan. Trenton, N.J.: State Planning Office, January 1988.

Johnson, Frank E. *Eight Minutes to New York.* Gettysburg, Pa.: The National Historical Society, August 1974.

New Jersey Transit, Public Affairs Office, Newark.

The Port Authority of New York and New Jersey, Public Affairs Office, New York.

Schwab, David, and Baehr, Guy. *Star-Ledger.* Newark, 1985, 1986, 1987, 1988.

Special Report 10: Preliminary Report on the Geology and Ground-Water Supply of the Newark, New Jersey, Area. New Jersey: State of New Jersey Department of Conservation and Economic Development, Division of Water Policy and Supply, 1951.

Urquhart, Frank J. *A Short History of Newark.* Newark: Baker Printing Company, 1916.

Wolfe, Peter E. *The Geology and Landscapes of New Jersey.* New York: Crane, Russak & Company, Inc., 1977.

Chapter 3
PARKS AND RECREATION
No city in America of comparable size can match the number of Newark's resplendent green acres and historic sites utilized as parks and public recreation areas.

Moore, Terence D. and Barry, Mildred E. *A Revised Policy Concerning Newark's Pequannock Watershed.* Newark: Rutgers University, Office of Newark Studies, Bureau of Community Services, University Extension Division, May 1971-August 1972.

Newark Evening News. Newark, July 11, 1929.

Newark Sunday News. July 26, 1970, Newark.

The Realtor. Official publication of the Real Estate Board of Newark, Irvington, and Hillside, April 1957.

Star-Ledger. Newark, February 22-25, 1976.

Sunday Call. Newark, March 29, 1936.

The True Story of the Passaic River, (Leaflet No. 30). Newark: Board of Education, 1914.

Your County Parks. Newark: Essex County Park Commission, June 1964.

Chapter 4
LANDMARKS AND HISTORIC SITES
As the third-oldest major city in America, Newark today stands as a unique living testament to more than three centuries of American history.

Byrd, Frederick W. "Newark This Week." *Star-Ledger,* Newark.

Del Tufo, Liz and Dust, Don. The Newark Preservation & Landmarks Committee, 1983-1987.

Dust, Don. "Let's Tour Our Town." *Metro Newark Magazine,* 1983.

The Herald-News. Passaic-Clifton, N.J., April 7, 1975.

Karschner, Terry, ed. *Industrial Newark.* 14th Annual Conference of the Society for Industrial Archeology, 1985.

Newark News. Newark, April 24, 1932; January 22, 1938; August 22, 1948; May 27, 1951; October 23, 1966; March 1, 1969.

New York Times. October 28, 1973.

Smith, James A. *The Advocate.* Clifton, N.J., April 1, 1976.

Star-Ledger. Newark, August 12, 1956; March 29, 1976; June 15, 1981

Sunday Call. Newark, August 1, 1946, April 28, 1958.

Chapter 5
HEALTH CARE
The residents of Greater Newark are served by several of the nation's finest medical and health care facilities.

The 1987 *Annual Reports* of each medical institution and special reports provided by the public affairs office of each facility. The Archdiocese of Newark on the Archdiocese's medical health care activities in the city, including St. Mary's Hospital in Orange, prepared by Kevin Moriarty, Director of Community Relations. Robin Preisler, associate director of marketing for UMDNJ, edited the section on New Jersey's medical university and University Hospital.

Chapter 6
EDUCATION
Numerous and varied demands on Newark's educational system are answered by a broad spectrum of opportunities and alternatives.

The material for University High School was extracted from Gloria Sheldon's March 1972 thesis on "School Within A School." Walter Genuario, math/science department chairperson, also submitted background information. The history of the Newark School of Fine and Industrial Art was gleaned from the school's "Fact Sheet" and a feature article by Eileen Walsh in *Metro NEWARK!,* the magazine of the Greater Newark Chamber of Commerce. Other materials were furnished by the respective schools and institutions public affairs and academic offices.

Chapter 7
ETHNIC NEWARK
Greater Newark is entering the twenty-first century as a modern "melting pot" embracing some 50 nationalities from all over the world.

Borondy, Kinga. "Portuguese fest," *Star-Ledger,* June 13, 1988.

Byrd, Frederick W. "Activist urges more involvement for Hispanics in business, government." *Star-Ledger,* October 23, 1987.

Lucas, Caryl R. "Black pride, heritage on parade." *Star-Ledger,* May 30, 1988.

North Ward, Vol. 1, No. 1. North Ward Center, March 1986.

The Peopling of Essex County. Tercentennial Writing Project, Essex County Division of Employment Training (SYEIP), 1982.

Program Overview. La Case De Don Pedro, Inc., March 1, 1987.

Quick Facts About the Urban League Movement. National Urban League, Communications Department.

Stewart, Angela and Thomas, Jerry. "Playground of pride." *Star-Ledger*, June 4, 1988.

Stewart, Angela and Thomas, Jerry. "Black Heritage Parade hails Newark revival." *Star-Ledger*, June 6, 1988.

Unified Vailsburg Services Organization. *Program Report.* December 1987.

Urban League of Essex County. *Fact Sheet.*

Chapter 8
CULTURE

Newark ranks tenth among American cities in the quality of its cultural and performing arts institutions.

About New Jersey Network. New Jersey: New Jersey Network.

Campbell, Bob. "Now you see it." *Star-Ledger*, June 7, 1988.

Gallman's Newark Dance Theatre. *Fact sheet.* 1988.

The Garden State Ballet, A History. 1988.

"Jazz 88—WBGO FM 88.3 on your dial." *Portfolio*, 1988.

Kanzler, George. "WBGO marking milestones." *The Star-Ledger*, March 16, 1988.

Krupnik, Jerry. "The man that put Channel 13 on top." *The Star-Ledger*, April 19, 1988.

Robinson, Lauren. "Eventful summer." *Star-Ledger*, June 20, 1988.

Skoov, Ed. "A Look Back." *Only the Best-Thirteen 25th*, special magazine edition, 1987.

Sterling, Guy. "Festival reigns supreme." *Star-Ledger*, September 14, 1987.

Stewart, Angela. "Newark festival celebrates a diverse union." *Star-Ledger*, September 14, 1988.

Thomas, Greg, Ed. *Prologue* (Ironbound Theatre's quarterly newsletter). May 1987.

Viapree, Donald. *Gateway Cable.* 1988.

WNET/THIRTEEN. *1986-87 Annual Report.*

Chapter 9
ORGANIZATIONS

A feeling of community spirit is fostered by several organizations that strive to keep the 'family of Newark' together.

Branche, J. Elizabeth. *The YMWCA: An Integral Part of Newark, New Jersey.* 1988.

Catholic Community Services, Archdiocese of Newark. *Annual Report.* 1987.

"City Life." *Star-Ledger*, special edition, October 12, 1988.

Finley, Charles Q. "United Way Helps FOCUS Help Hispanics." *Star-Ledger*, October 12, 1975.

The Leaguers. *Opportunity Through Education.*

New Community *Clarion*, March 1988.

Protestant Community Centers, Inc. *1987 Annual Report.*

The Salvation Army of Greater Newark. *The Salvation Army & Youth—A Future With A Purpose.*

Stewart, Angela. "4 Years of Collaboration." *Star-Ledger*, May 22-23, 1988.

Chapter 10
BUSINESS

Newark's new-found popularity can be attributed to the fact that it is New Jersey's premier center of commerce, finance, and trade.

Around The Clock, Bamberger's, July 1980.

The Greater Newark Chamber of Commerce. *1988 Metro New Jersey Economic Overview.*

Jett, Jason "Largest law firm lauded." *Star-Ledger*, April 27, 1988.

Krementz, Richard Jr. "The Early Years," "The Middle Years," "1950 to Present." *The Karat Patch*, Krementz & Company, February, March, April 1982

Chapter 11
GOVERNMENT

Local government in Newark meets the challenges of the future with a unified vision and progressive spirit.

"A Message from Mayor Sharpe James." Second State of the City Address, January 14, 1988.

City of Newark. "NEWARK Puts People First!" 1988.

NFBPA Forum. January 11, 1988.

Office of the City Clerk. "Know Your City Government." December 1986.

Chapter 12
THE FUTURE

Newark's future is literally riding high—for this historic city by the bay is the only location in New Jersey accessible from any direction by road, rail, air and water.

Byrd, Frederick W. "Grand plans." *Star-Ledger*, March 25, 1987.

Byrd, Frederick W. "Leaders bullish as Newark turns corner." *Star-Ledger*, February 7, 1988.

Byrd, Frederick W. "Plans unveiled for Newark tower." *Star-Ledger*, March 9, 1988.

Byrd, Frederick W. "30 story office tower." *Star-Ledger*, April 9, 1988.

Byrd, Frederick W. "Building will start on downtown mall." *Star-Ledger*, April 24, 1988.

Byrd, Frederick W. "Mall delay in Newark." *Star-Ledger*, July 17, 1988.

Byrd, Frederick W. "Newark unveils plan for industrial park." *Star-Ledger*, September 4, 1987.

Bryant, Gloria. "Newark's Renaissance: Cooperation Replaces Confrontation." *New Jersey Success*, February 1988.

Frank, Al. "Study for developer weighs arts center." *Star-Ledger*, June 26, 1988.

The Greater Newark Chamber of Commerce. "1988 Metro New Jersey Economic Overview." (special edition).

"Housing plan unveiled for University Heights," *Star-Ledger*, November 15, 1987.

Jett, Jason. "Newark to erect 100 townhouses." *Star-Ledger*, March 22, 1988.

"Newark is . . ." Renaissance Newark, Inc., 1988.

Redmond, Michael. "Artists boost a cultural complex." *Star-Ledger*, June 26, 1988.

Renaissance Reporter, Vol.1, No.3., January/February 1988.

Stewart, Angela. "Ground broken." *Star-Ledger*, June 17, 1988.

Stewart, Angela. "Historian hopes to open museum in Newark." *Star-Ledger*, July 5, 1988.

Van Fossan, Robert V. "Why Newark Is Making A Comeback." Mutual Benefit Life Insurance Company, 1988.

Wattkis, Michael A. "Newark will split downtown into 4 business districts." *Star-Ledger*, June 1, 1988.

PROFILES INDEX